Asian America

P.D.: For my children, a part of Asian America I continually learn from.

R.R.: For my son, Amado. It is because of you that books like these are important.

Asian America

Sociological and Interdisciplinary
Perspectives

PAWAN DHINGRA AND
ROBYN MAGALIT RODRIGUEZ

polity

First published in 2014 by Polity Press
Reprinted 2014, 2015, 2016 (twice), 2018 (twice), 2019, 2020

Polity Press
65 Bridge Street
Cambridge CB2 1UR, UK

Polity Press
350 Main Street
Malden, MA 02148, USA

ISBN-13: 978-0-7456-4703-6
ISBN-13: 978-0-7456-4704-3(pb)

A catalogue record for this book is available from the British Library.

Typeset in 9.5 on 12 pt Utopia by
Servis Filmsetting Ltd, Stockport, Cheshire
Printed and bound in the United States by LSC Communications

For further information on Polity, visit our website: www.politybooks.com

Contents

Foreword and Acknowledgments

This book is a labor of love. Labor in the sense that trying to represent social science perspectives on Asian American Studies is a daunting task, given the flourishing of quality scholarship over the past several years and the number of topics to represent. But it quickly became work in which we found great pleasure. Being able to take a bird's eye view of the field impressed upon us the important scholarship and debates within it.

Our goal has not been to summarize social science or even just sociological perspectives on Asian Americans. Instead, we put forth our view of how sociology and other social sciences connect to and rub against Asian American Studies and related work in critical race and ethnic studies. We do this along a number of theoretical and substantive topics. We seek to move forward the scholarship in this area by identifying what are the key debates and how to progress towards resolutions on them.

In some sense, this book has been a decade-long project for us. Each of us has been trained within sociology PhD programs and has been employed in sociology departments, even training future sociologists. Yet we also have studied within and been employed within American or Asian American Studies programs/departments in the West Coast, Midwest, and East Coast. This dual upbringing has made us acutely aware of the benefits but also gaps within any one particular school of thought. We see Asian Americans as not simply a fundamental population of the United States but as a necessary site, alongside other minority and immigrant groups, for elucidating social science questions on the nation, globalization, intersectional approaches to race and class, media, interpersonal solidarity and conflict, identity, and much more. As the neoliberal academy moves towards greater collaboration across departments/ programs and demands more measurable "output" from scholars and teachers, we believe that recognizing the history and contributions of the study of Asian Americans across a variety of fields is all the more urgent.

This project came to be because of the foresight of Polity Press. We would like to thank Emma Longstaff for initiating this book and advancing this project. Special thanks also to Jonathan Skerrett for guiding us with a gentle but measured hand. Working with them both has been a pleasure. Co-authoring a book is a unique and special process. Pawan Dhingra was approached by Polity Press to propose a book and started drafting some of the chapters. Robyn Rodriguez joined to offer insights and draft other chapters. Together we have accomplished a piece neither of us could have done on our own.

This book is only possible because of a number of colleagues. With a book such as this, there are too many individual scholars to list for special acknowledgment, so we will not even try. In some respects, this entire book is an acknowledgment of the work they have done. We would like to give special recognition to our past and present colleagues at Oberlin College, the Smithsonian Institution, Tufts University, Rutgers University, and the University of California, Davis. We would like to thank our families and close friends for putting up with yet another book project. Their support and enthusiasm around this project have made this all the more worthwhile.

Pawan Dhingra
Robyn Rodriguez

1 Introduction

Asian Americans are overrepresented among college graduates, with 50 percent of Asian Americans age 25 and older having earned at least a bachelor's degree, compared to a quarter of the US population as a whole.[1] They are accomplished professionals in fields ranging from the sciences to the arts. They have a high rate of small-business ownership. They are seen as model workers. At the same time, a greater percentage of Asian Americans than non-Hispanic whites live in poverty, and Asian Americans are more likely than the US population overall to be uninsured.[2] A range of Asian Americans rely on public welfare programs, work in low-wage and segregated jobs (often owned by co-ethnics), encounter racial stereotypes as foreigners, suffer from untreated mental health diseases, and are victims of hate crimes.[3]

Yet, even with all of this variation and contradictions, it is not the multifaceted lives of Asian Americans alone that make them necessary subjects of study. The experiences of Asian Americans speak to more than just this group alone. Their lives provide insight into a host of broader topics that have been key topics of study. These topics include how race shapes people's lives; how immigrants gradually assimilate – or do not – to their surroundings; how transnationalism influences people's social and economic opportunities; how small groups come together or engage in conflict; how people self-identify; what leads to academic success and failure; and more. The goal of the book is to shed light on such general sociological questions through the experiences of Asian Americans.

Learning how Asian Americans experience these and other issues, moreover, tells us about the United States as a nation, for the nation is often understood based on how it treats its newcomers. According to the United States' self-proclaimed national creed as a nation of immigrants, all persons are welcome to make a new life here. But is there true equality in schools, the workplace, media, and elsewhere for all persons, regardless of country of origin, religion, gender, or other social categories? Can the nation become truly multicultural, or will the cultural definition of the United States remain Anglo-Saxon and Christian? How does the United States' pursuit of global capitalist ascendancy impact immigrants and minorities? Do immigration laws give immigrants control over their lives upon entering the United States, or do they privilege the interests of others? Does growing economic globalization create more transnational lives? How have racism and empire been key aspects of American history and contemporary life? In other words, the challenges and opportunities that Asian Americans face inform the true nature of the nation, and these are central issues that this book grapples with.

And of course, the study of Asian Americans matters for Asian Americans themselves and those who are interested in their well-being. A text that centers on the lives of Asian Americans affirms their experiences while also informing the human social condition more broadly.

Table 1.1 *Population size*

Group	Population, 2010
United States	311,591,919
Asian	15,020,419
Cambodian	253,830
Chinese	3,361,879
Filipino	2,538,325
Hmong	241,308
Indian	2,908,204
Japanese	756,898
Korean	1,449,876
Laotian	186,013
Vietnamese	1,669,447
Other Asian	1,079,820

Source: United States Census Bureau; American Community Survey, 2010 American Community Survey 1-Year Estimates, Table S0201[4]

Who are Asian Americans?

The number of Asian Americans has been increasing at a quick pace, due to both continued immigration and children born in the United States. According to the 2010 US Census, "The Asian alone population and the Asian alone-or-in-combination population both grew substantially between 2000 and 2010, increasing in size by 43 percent and 46 percent, respectively. These populations grew more than any other race group in 2010."[5] There were more than 15 million Asian Americans (not even including multiracial Asian Americans) as of 2010, comprising about 5 percent of the US population. As Table 1.1 indicates, Asian American groups range widely in their numbers, with five groups (Chinese, Indian, Filipino, Vietnamese, and Korean) comprising well over a million or even two million individuals each.

"Asian Americans" refers to individuals living in the United States who immigrated from (e.g. first-generation immigrants) or whose ancestors immigrated from (e.g. second-generation immigrants and beyond) Asian countries and Asian diasporas (i.e. settlements in other countries). Asian Americans consist of Bangladeshi, Burmese, Chinese, Cambodian, Filipino, Hmong, Indian, Indonesian, Japanese, Korean, Nepalese, Pakistani, Sri Lankan, Taiwanese, Thai, and Vietnamese Americans, among others originating from Asia. As will be discussed in chapter 3, Asians have lived in the United States in large numbers since the 1800s. Historically, scholarship on Asian Americans focused on the largest groups to first immigrate, namely Chinese and Japanese Americans. Chinese, Japanese, and Filipino Americans drove the Asian-American Movement of the 1960s, which gave rise to Asian American Studies and increased research and writing about the Asian American experience. The Immigration and Naturalization Act of 1965 altered the demographics of the United States and precipitated a much larger immigration of Asians. Asian-American demographics have continued to change since then with continued voluntary immigration and also due to war and imperialism. Southeast Asians have arrived mostly since the 1970s as refugees and as family members sponsored by those refugees.

Defining terms

The term "Asian American" is often extended to be "Asian American and Pacific Islanders" in order to indicate their connections to each other. However, it is important not to conflate these groups. In this book, we use the term "Asian American" and mean it in an expansive way. Pacific Islanders receive attention in this book, although not to the same degree as other Asian Americans. Arab Americans also receive attention, even though they are not traditionally considered to be Asian American. The definitions of racial groups change over time, with some groups included and other groups excluded, depending on social and political contexts. For instance, South Asian Americans were classified as nonwhite in the US Census over the decades until 1970 when they were classified as white, and then in 1980 they were newly classified as Asian American after political lobbying by the community.

When one says "Asian American," it has little resonance for most people beyond some standard stereotypes: Asian Americans are considered hard-working, strong in math and sciences, exotic (for women), asexual (for men), possibly threatening (economically), and foreign. Yet, when one speaks of Chinese Americans, Filipino Americans, Vietnamese Americans, and so on, more nuanced images come to mind. In this text, we will attend to both pan-ethnic (i.e. referring to trends across Asian American ethnic groups) and ethnic-specific trends. While the differences between groups receive recognition, their similarities are emphasized because they too shape individuals' lives and illustrate how Asian Americans experience key social phenomena (e.g. migration, culture, race, employment, media, etc.) in comparable (not necessarily identical) ways, which in turn illustrates how Asian Americans and other groups are impacted by and in turn influence the nation and global trends.

Sociological and interdisciplinary approaches

To attend to the range of issues that Asian Americans inspire, we need to take a heterogeneous research approach. The book privileges the social sciences, in particular sociology, but also draws from other fields. In particular, it is informed by the interdisciplinary field of Asian American Studies.

Sociology as a discipline refers to the study of the social causes of why and how humans think and behave. Why do we do what we do? Our biological instincts may guide us. Philosophical arguments about ethics perhaps suggest to us certain options over others as morally appropriate. Monetary constraints can often dictate our choices. But sociologists, more so than other social scientists and humanities scholars, focus primarily on social causes of our actions and attitudes. Social causes refer to how individuals, groups, and social institutions – such as one's family, the labor market, groups, the media, the nation, etc. – impact individuals and are impacted by us. Sociologists place us, everyday individuals, within a social context in order to understand how we interact with our environments as well as how our environments came to be in the first place.

As we consider the social dimensions to people's behavior, we build up what noted sociologist C. Wright Mills (1959) called the "sociological imagination." According to Mills, the "sociological imagination" challenges us to see ourselves not simply as unique individuals with particular life histories. Instead, we should recognize that we are part of social groups and spaces and embody certain roles. We experience our families, for instance, through our roles as daughters, siblings, fathers, and so on, rather than as individuals. Once we recognize this, we better appreciate the social environment that is outside of us but which influences our lives, and which we act back on.

A sociological imagination is one that recognizes that individuals' lives are crucially shaped by social institutions (defined below) like media, the government, the family, and the economy. These institutions place individuals in positions of relative privilege and/or disadvantage based on social class, race and ethnicity, and gender. Even though we have distinctive biographies and unique identities, institutions shape our lives and we participate in their transformation. Asian American Studies analyzes how Asian Americans experience institutions and even how the formation of institutions has been shaped by Asian Americans.

Inequalities, institutions, and identities

As we develop our sociological imagination, sociologists concern themselves with three key, interconnected dimensions of social life central to this book: inequalities, institutions, and identities. Social inequality occurs when resources are not distributed equally but instead tend to favor one group over another due in part to historical and/or contemporary unfair treatment or opportunities. Sociologists attend to national, racial, gender, class, sexual, age, (dis)ability, and other bases of inequalities. Asian Americans, like African Americans, Latinos, and Native Americans, can experience inequalities relative to whites. This can take place in the labor market, such as when Asian Americans encounter limited opportunities for upper management despite ample experience and education (i.e. they face the "glass ceiling"). This can take place in the media, such as with limited and often stereotypical portrayals. This can take place in politics, such as when Asian Americans must defend themselves from being attacked as being un-American by virtue of having Asian roots. And so on. Sociologists and scholars of Asian American Studies are committed to advancing social justice, which requires unearthing the causes and consequences of social inequality.

The ways that Asian Americans experience inequalities depend on their gender, sexuality, ethnicity, class, and other social statuses. Asian-American women encounter different stereotypes than men, for instance. To date, same-sex marriage is not recognized at the federal level, which impacts Asian-American gays and lesbians. Post-9/11, South Asian and Arab Americans have faced greater scrutiny than have other ethnic groups within Asian America. Economic status, such as differences in the labor market and school system, is fundamental to a group's well-being. Asian Americans with different education levels and skill sets will have varying advantages and disadvantages.

The primary way that sociologists analyze inequalities is within social institutions, as noted above. Social institutions refer to a society's publicly agreed-upon ways to take care of its members' needs. One can think of social institutions this way: as an individual, all one needs to survive is food, clothing, and shelter. Yet, for a society to survive and prosper, there must be a set of established means for individuals to pursue their interests and get along together. For example, there must be a means to raise children in the main norms and expectations of the society. This takes place within the institution of the family. There must be a means to train people for the occupations that the society will need. This takes place within the institutions of education. There must be a means to organize the contrasting needs of large numbers of individuals. This takes place within the institution of politics.

Sociologists analyze how social institutions are constructed, what functions they intend to serve, who wins, and who loses in how they are run, and how individuals engage in them and possibly change them. Because institutions are so central to how individuals relate to their environment, much of sociology is dedicated to understanding them. This book attends to the main institutions relevant to the study of Asian Americans. We attend to possible inequalities but, especially, to how Asian Americans experience institutions generally. We consider how Asian Americans experience family life, how they take part in politics, how they practice religion, how they fare at school, how they are framed by the media, and more. Asian Americans inform how these institutions work from the vantage point of an ethnic/racial minority position. For example, given how Asian Americans practice their religion and are treated as religious people, what do we learn about how culturally tolerant the nation is? From there, we can consider how well institutions are serving society's needs and what changes should be made to address possible problems.

Within institutions, we come to learn about ourselves and develop our self-identities. How one sees oneself as an Asian American is one's identity (or more accurately, one identity). Identity is a significant issue for all persons because everyone is a member of multiple sets of social groups (e.g. a family, school, workplace, political party, church, etc.) but has special relevance for racial minorities because of the ways US society has long categorized people. Asian Americans can identify with their ethnic group (i.e. Filipino, Indian, Japanese, Vietnamese), their pan-ethnic group (i.e. Asian American), their religious group, and more. We develop our identities based on influences from our families, the media, schools, and other social institutions. So, it is necessary to know how these institutions refer to Asian Americans. Other social categories, such as sexuality or gender, also shape our identities. Queer, lesbian, gay, bisexual, and transgender Asian Americans understand what it means to be Asian American differently than do straight Asian Americans. Our self-identities are central to our major lifestyle decisions, such as whom to befriend, where to live, how to raise our children, what rituals we perform, and so on.

Various complications arise in the identity development of racial minorities. How much choice do visible minorities have in their identity selections? For instance, can a Chinese American choose not to identify with his Chinese background if others keep referring to it? How do people of multiracial background choose to identify and form relations with others? Similarly, how do adopted Asian Americans make sense of their race if it differs from their adoptive parents? Can people (people who are non-Asian as well as those who are) bring together conflicting identities, such as "ethnic" and "American," or are these kept apart? Do Asian Americans identify with only their ethnicity or also pan-ethnically? Answers to these questions inform what motivates individuals and how racial dynamics are shifting. While one chapter in this book concentrates on identity, the issues surrounding identity permeate multiple chapters.

Race, culture, and power

The three key elements of social life – inequalities, institutions, and identity – comprise the major parameters of the sociological study of Asian America. This book will examine how Asian Americans negotiate with and make sense of institutions (like the media, schools, global markets, the government, the family, etc.) while positioned as an immigrant minority group in American society. As the book explores these elements, two main dimensions of Asian America will receive priority: race and culture. Race and culture shape the context through which Asian Americans (and others) experience inequalities, institutions, and identities. Such an examination shows how race works beyond the black–white binary that currently defines race in the United States. That is, though racial power inequalities as typically discussed are only between blacks and whites, in reality race is more complex. This book aims to broaden our understanding to illustrate how race implicates people who are and who are not black or white. This is not to suggest that race more than other factors (e.g. class, gender, etc.) shapes the lives of individual Asian Americans. But across Asian America, common racial background leads to some degree of shared experiences. Elucidating those experiences informs the power of race as it intersects with other social categories.

Tied to race is colonialism and empire. The United States historically and currently has been a colonial or neocolonial state. This is seen in a series of historical acts, including the genocide of Native Americans, slavery of Africans, wars with Latin Americans, recruitment and mistreatment of Asian labor, internment of Japanese Americans, and wars and active colonization abroad (e.g. Philippines, Puerto Rico, Hawai'i). While US laws and institutions have become more equal and facilitated the great achievements of many minorities, including of course Asian Americans, this current state-driven inequality remains relevant.

Also, cultural differences matter greatly within the three topics of inequality, institutions, and identity. Asian immigrants make up the majority of contemporary Asian Americans. They and their descendants often have distinct cultural sensibilities and practices. Culture also matters because the nation is a cultural, not just legal, entity. As such not all groups find equal acceptance of their cultural backgrounds, especially as they stress transnational cultural ties (e.g. in terms of religion or rituals). Culture also informs the extent to which "Asian American" exists as a meaningful entity. While the term "Asian America" suggests a single entity, it is important to keep in mind the significant differences within the population. There are not only ethnic cultural differences but also differences of generation, income, citizenship status, and more. To what extent does "Asian America" really exist, or is it more appropriate to speak of a variety of groups with only a little in common? This book examines this question rather than takes for granted a cohesive population.

Perspectives on Asian America

In studying how Asian Americans and others experience these topics, scholars have devised certain theories to piece together observed trends. The theories explain how the three major topics of inequality, institutions, and identity relate to one another. Reviewing these theories elucidates what kinds of information scholars look for and what assumptions they bring to the study of Asian Americans. This book draws extensively from these theoretical approaches in order to explain the causes and consequences of the experiences of Asian Americans.

Assimilation theory

Within sociology, the most prominent perspective on immigrants' adaptation to a new environment is assimilation theory. Assimilation occurs when an immigrant group's differences with the mainstream dissipate. This can happen as ethnic items become popular in the nation (e.g. "Chinese food"), so that consuming them does not appear foreign to most residents. More often, assimilation occurs as immigrant communities lose their distinctiveness and become more like the majority as they adopt dominant culture and social structure, akin to Anglo-conformity (Gordon 1964). They become socialized (or re-socialized as adults) within mainstream institutions, such as schools, popular media, civil society, and religion. As immigrant groups learn English, shop at popular clothing and grocery stores, befriend people outside their group, and so on, they gradually assimilate. Descendants of immigrants start to see mainstream culture as "normal" and may conceive of their ethnic background as strange or inferior. This assimilation need not be intentional. Instead, it occurs as immigrant groups seek better opportunities for themselves and their children, which are believed to be outside of one's ethnic group and within the mainstream (Alba and Nee 2003; Salins 1997).

According to assimilation theorists, this integration is possible because race matters less today than in the past, as evidenced by the numerous legal protections against discrimination and the general improvement in racial attitudes (Alba and Nee 2003). So according to assimilation theory, the labor market, schools, restaurants, and other spaces do not treat immigrants differently because of their ethnic origin, which enables Asian Americans to become a full part of the nation. Under these conditions, the main (not only) obstacle preventing assimilation, according to those who adopt the assimilation framework, is groups' own lack of effort to culturally and structurally assimilate.

Assimilation into the host society originally was framed as not only inevitable but also prescriptive (Kivisto 2005). In other words, those who adopted an assimilation standpoint believed that immigrants *should* gradually abandon parochial interests, like their ethnicity, and embrace the modern, American lifestyle in which people supposedly are judged, based on their accomplished categories, such as education level, occupational status, marital status, and so on. Assimilation theory assumes a mostly meritocratic United States. Such an adaptation was seen as in the best interests of the immigrant group in the nation. Today, assimilation theorists have dropped the moralistic tone. Still, there is an implied belief in the benefits of assimilation for immigrants.

Diverse modes of incorporation

Other scholars, however, disagree with both the likelihood and benefits of straight cultural and structural assimilation for ethnic minorities. Instead, immigrants can follow different trajectories based on their "mode of incorporation" into the country

(Portes and Rumbaut 2006). According to this approach, immigrant groups encounter a *segmented* assimilation, that is, they can assimilate into different segments of society beyond simply into the white middle class assumed within assimilation theory (Portes and Zhou 1993). For instance, they may live in inner cities with poorer African Americans or Latinos as neighbors than middle-class whites. Assimilation can look different in this context than normally imagined. According to these theorists, it may be to an immigrant group's advantage not to assimilate if the local group they would assimilate into does not often advance within school or in the labor market. Instead, groups often benefit from maintaining their ethnicity. Ethnic groups can achieve mobility by relying on members' assistance, values, and employment opportunities. Strong ethnic ties also can facilitate children's success within institutions like education, the labor market, and more (Gibson 1988; Waters 1999; Zhou and Bankston 1998). Maintaining transnational ties to one's homeland can help groups adjust to their local surroundings (Smith 2006). Otherwise, groups could be at risk of a "downward" trajectory (Gans 1992).

Despite its differences from standard assimilation theory, this emphasis on groups' diverse outcomes is similar to it in that it expects ethnic groups' gradual "incorporation" into the host society. As Portes and his co-authors write about the second generation, "the central question is not whether the second generation will assimilate to American society, but to what segment of that society it will assimilate" (Portes, Fernandez-Kelly, and Haller 2005: 1000). There are few, if any, entrenched barriers, such as racism, that cannot be overcome with the right resources (e.g. community oversight, educational support).

In addition to downplaying race as a pervasive constraint on minorities, these various assimilation paradigms stress the significance of culture in determining economic and social outcomes. Over time, immigrants who culturally assimilate akin to previous European immigrants are expected to become economically stable. They may hold onto certain cultural elements, such as traditional foods on special occasions, but these become mostly "symbolic" and ceremonial, rather than influential on people's lives (Alba 1990; Waters 1990).

According to these first two theoretical perspectives, groups gradually become more like their host society along key dimensions, including educational attainment, residential location, language preference, self-identity, marital partner, and so on. If poor immigrants have access to supportive co-ethnics (i.e. people who share their ethnic background) and do not encounter too many obstacles (e.g. discrimination), they too can achieve mobility. The major difference between the theories is that segmented assimilation stresses that the road to economic stability often drives through strong ties to one's ethnic group, whereas standard assimilation stresses the benefits of letting go of these ties. And as stressed within segmented assimilation theory, without sufficient support from co-ethnics, the second generation may assimilate in a downward fashion, marked by limited mobility (Portes and Rumbaut 2001).

Racial formation theory

In contrast to these assimilationist perspectives, other sociologists and those in Ethnic Studies highlight the significance of race and inequality facing ethnic minorities. The racial formation perspective argues that race is fundamental to how society is organized and so continues to matter for minorities, even if they are economically secure (Delgado and Stefancic 2001; Omi and Winant 1994). Whites gain materially and psychologically in all sorts of ways, such as when attaining a mortgage or paying for a car, at the expense of minorities (Lipsitz 1998). Racial formation theory draws attention to how minorities are racialized, that is, how they are socially defined and treated as racial groups rather than as individuals. This racialization changes with historical and contextual circumstances based on political and social circumstances. The way groups are framed suits the white dominant establishment (e.g. government, the military, corporations). For instance, Chinese Americans went from "good" minorities during World War II to "bad" minorities post-World War II as China became increasingly communist and seemed a threat to the government. Japanese Americans switched from "bad" to "good" during this same time period. Our everyday interactions also reflect the power of race. We may talk to someone or even shake the person's hands differently, based on her/his race.

Racism is allowed to continue because racial ideologies make it socially permissible. For instance, even an ideology of "color-blindness," which seems to downplay the relevance of race, limits minorities (Bonilla-Silva 2003; Omi and Winant 1994). It suggests that we should be "blind" to race, should ignore it, and that the real problem is those who keep talking about it, as well as programs like affirmative action. So, minorities who complain about racism become blamed for perpetuating racial differences. Indeed, some might suggest that, since the United States has elected the first African-American president, it has truly achieved a post-racial, color-blind society. However, sociologists and other scholarly critics point out that, even with his election, race continues to organize American life and cannot be ignored (Okamura 2011).

The racial formation perspective helps explain trends that assimilation theory either cannot or that it overlooks. For instance, even as more minorities appear on television, they remain in often stereotypical depictions (Davé, Nishime, and Oren 2005). People's attitudes to race might have become more benevolent, therefore supporting assimilation theory assumptions about a merit-based United States, but that does not mean that minorities have ample opportunities. The US prison population has become overwhelmingly black and brown compared to the general population, for example, and not because those populations started committing more and more crime (Alexander 2010). Meanwhile, even as Asian Americans and Latinos have become more welcome within urban development, welfare laws discriminate against immigrants (Fujiwara 2008). Nor is this mistreatment relegated to poor immigrants. Wealthy Asian Americans experience barriers to full inclusion, due to racist and/or culturally prejudiced attitudes from the majority. According to this perspective, middle-class Asian Americans are "a part" of the mainstream but "apart" from it (Kibria 2002).

The "model minority" stereotype exemplifies this dynamic. It argues that Asian Americans succeed due to their Asian values of hard work and family support. In fact, Asian Americans' success in schools and workplaces may be due in part to such racial stereotypes rather than a sign that stereotypes are fading (Dhingra 2007). But, within this stereotype Asian-American men and women are characterized as sexually deviant (i.e. Asian-American men are figured as effeminate; Asian-American women, as hyper-sexualized), overly passive, and apolitical. White elites within the capitalist structure benefit the most from this institutionalized discrimination. According to the racial formation perspective, a lack of equality for immigrants is not their problem but that of the state and institutions, which promote inequality.

The broader theme within the racial formation perspective is a lack of trust in the nation-state and its institutions to promote full equality among racial groups. The United States, like other western, hyper-capitalist nations, is neither the "land of opportunity" nor even a benign force relative to ethnic minorities. Instead, according to critics, it is an imperial force that wages wars mostly in Third World nations and also engages in business practices that suit established interests more than minorities at home (Melamed 2006). Moreover, the racial formation perspective recognizes that, from its inception, the United States has been a country that was founded on white supremacist rationale. The fact that naturalization, for example, was restricted to only whites, or that slavery was actually permitted in the US Constitution is evidence that race has organized American society. Even when these laws have changed, it is because of struggles by minorities and/or in response to US foreign and economic interests. Legal reforms do not fully eradicate the racializing logics. Immigrant minorities may do well economically, but they must suffer through greater hurdles and indignities en route. For instance, Filipino-American men have attained a moderate middle-class status through working for the US navy. But, they can be relegated to subservient, emasculating positions in the process (Espiritu 2003).

A racial formation perspective also helps explain how immigrant minorities respond to racist interactions. Asian Americans, even those raised in the United States, accentuate their cultural and social commonalties with one another rather than their ties to the mainstream (Dhingra 2007; Purkayastha 2005; Tuan 1998). Even if ethnic minorities live in mostly white neighborhoods, they often seek out one another for solidarity. People identify with their ethnicity rather than as simply "American." These trends contradict predictions based on an assimilation perspective.

Pan-ethnicity

The growing pan-ethnicity among Asian Americans serves as another challenge to assimilation theory. Pan-ethnicity refers to Asian Americans' increasing collaboration and identification along racial, rather than only along ethnic, lines. As pan-ethnicity occurs, group boundaries start to change, with a new group (i.e. "Asian American") forming. Pan-ethnicity can result from a shared racial formation among ethnic groups but also from a sense of cultural connections, and so is not reducible to racial formation. Asian Americans identify pan-ethnically due to a shared culture (e.g. Confucian heritage), shared categorization by others (e.g. stereotypes of "Asians" as all foreigners), shared institutions (e.g. pan-ethnic student organizations that promote this identification), and shared interests (e.g. to eradicate racism). Understanding why pan-ethnicity happens, when it takes place or does not, and how strong it is informs the process of group identity formation more broadly.

Global political economy

The increasing interdependency between countries also complicates immigrants' adaptation. Globalization refers to the connections between nations economically, culturally, politically, and socially. For example, the fact that we learn about what is happening on the other side of the planet instantaneously through the internet, or the fact that most of the products we buy are made in another country is evidence that our lives are being shaped by forces beyond our country. A global political economy perspective draws attention to the relations between nations that spurs migration (Baldoz 2011). Because developing countries do not have enough employment opportunities for their population, or the jobs pay too little or options for upward mobility are limited, individuals seek fortunes elsewhere. But individuals rarely just migrate anywhere. One's country's relationship with other nations influences where one migrates to. For instance, colonial histories between countries create lasting pathways of immigration. Also, to develop their economies, countries will train citizens for jobs in other countries. Migrants are then expected to send back money or expertise to their homeland (Rodriguez 2010). Would-be migrants hear of jobs in a particular country through state- or corporate-sponsored advertisements or through their personal networks. In other words, to understand immigration, one must understand the relationships between nations.

A global political economy perspective downplays the assimilationist model of immigration and adaptation. Assimilation theory frames migrants as independent actors who seek out a new country to make their living and settle their families. In contrast, a global political economy perspective highlights the sustained ties between migrants and their homeland. Immigration is not so much an act of pure volition as a consequence of global economic and political factors within which immigrants make calculated decisions. Within this perspective, it makes sense that immigrants maintain transnational ties to their homeland. Transnationalism originated as a topic of study as a critique of assimilation theory's assumption that one's adopted nation defined immigrants' subjective and material experiences. Instead, immigrants can live across borders. For instance, they may both receive and send money from and to a homeland, follow the political and cultural changes of the nation, visit home often, and more. Rather than consider immigrants' adaptation relative to the United States, as is the case within assimilation theory, it may be more relevant to consider it within a broader diaspora or widely dispersed community.

A global political economy perspective is often combined with other ones. For instance, global dynamics connect to racial formation processes. In such cases, analysts frame international relations within a context of global power inequality, with developed nations utilizing immigrants from developing nations to their advantage (Parreñas 2001). Yet more recently, scholars have come to analyze immigrants' transnational lives within an overall assimilation paradigm. Immigrants' commitments abroad need not detract from their general integration within the United States (Levitt and Waters 2002). Transnational individuals can follow both homeland and US politics, for instance. Experiences in the homeland can give individuals the cultural tools, such as pride in their background, to help them feel supported when in the United States (Smith 2006). So, while transnationalism and globalization are receiving increasing attention, what they mean for immigrant groups is not settled.

A case study of theoretical convergence

A single case illuminates how different theories lead to distinct conclusions. Asian-American women are closely associated with garment manufacturing in New York

City and Los Angeles. Perspectives emphasizing assimilation explain that the large number of immigrant minority women working on the production line is due to their typically low human capital (i.e. lack of advanced education or English-language skills). They do not have the capacity to perform many other jobs in that geographic area. Also, their network ties lead them to the industry. From an assimilationist perspective, consideration is given to how people feel about their jobs and whether they gradually move out of them or not, as dependent on their education, skills, family needs, co-ethnic resources, and so on. For instance, many garment workers learn about work through relatives and friends, and they prefer these jobs because the work schedules suit their needs as mothers (Chin 2005). For such persons, the industry works relatively well, even if it does not pay much. Unfair exploitation of the women may take place, but they can leave these jobs as they accrue more education or skills. They face no inherent marginalization.

More critical scholars, such as those who adopt a racial formation and/or global economic perspective, differ in their thinking about this trend. Their questions are: Why are Asian American women seen as "natural" fits for such manufacturing jobs? How does this impression shape how they are treated on the job? Why is migration structured around women's supposedly nimble fingers? In what way do manufacturing firms and general consumers depend on these women to produce cheap goods? People's gender and nationality sharply define their job prospects, which means that people are not treated equally, based on skills, but instead face unequal options. Moving out of a gendered job sector is unlikely. From such a critical perspective, attention is paid to the injustices workers must resist and to the effect of work on power relations within their families (Su and Martorell 2002). In other words, one comes to different conclusions on these immigrant women's adaptation depending on one's perspective and which information one therefore prioritizes. In reality, garment workers experience aspects from both types of perspectives, and their lives are more fully understood as such. We attend to multiple perspectives in this book as we discuss social trends.

Studying Asian America

Social scientists utilize two major ways of studying a population: quantitative and qualitative methods. Quantitative methods refer to data-collection procedures that capture respondents' opinions, as well as demographic and socioeconomic conditions through numerical measurement. Surveys are the most common type of instrument for quantitative methods. The most popular national surveys are the US Census (including its American Community Survey). This method provides a wide range of information on large numbers of people. Questions are descriptive in nature. For instance, if one was interested in what enabled poor refugees to become middle class after settling in the United States, one could survey hundreds of refugees, both poor and middle class. Included in the survey could be questions on respondents' education level, English abilities, career background, number of siblings, and other variables that might influence mobility. From there, researchers using statistical procedures could determine which variable, such as English-language ability, most impacted mobility.

Yet, still unresolved by this survey would be why or how these variables influenced mobility. Surveys and quantitative methods generally cannot probe respondents' reasons for their actions to learn why individuals act as they do. What is it about one's career background, for instance, that leads to different mobility patterns? Qualitative methods are best suited for this latter kind of question.

Qualitative methods refer to a mode of investigation meant to assess people's reasoning and motivation for action, that is, how they feel and think about their lives. Common techniques include in-depth interviews and observations of human behavior (i.e. ethnography). Qualitative methods can answer "why" and "how" people behave, whereas quantitative methods address "what" people do, "how much" they do it, and "with what consequence."

Like quantitative methods, the qualitative approach also has its drawbacks. Interviewing or observing others in depth is very time consuming. For instance, some ethnographers spend years in "the field," that is, within a single community, learning about its members' way of life. Such an approach prevents learning about a large number of people, as surveys allow. Instead, qualitative methods enable a "case study." A case study refers to the study of a single group or individual who is thought to be representative of a broader phenomenon or population. For instance, for the study of mobility among refugees, one could find a group of middle-class refugees and poor refugees of the same ethnicity and living in the same city. Interviews and observations with fifty individuals from each class group would provide detailed information, such as how they perceive the job market, how their lives abroad influence their job aspirations, and the like. Even as this method targets a small number of refugees, it would offer insight into how socioeconomic class affects the refugee experience and vice versa. Such a study, combined with the quantitative approach, would create a robust set of findings. Given the pros and cons of quantitative and qualitative methods, the best research strategy incorporates both types.

The theoretical perspectives frequently – not always – map onto particular methodologies. The various assimilation/incorporation paradigms often use quantitative methods. Because the theories concern how much a group is like or unlike the majority or other minorities, statistical evidence is most useful. In order to ascertain how individuals understand their background and what meaning race and other social categories have for people, it is best to utilize qualitative methods. This is most typical of the racialized minority approach. Having said that, scholarship increasingly uses a heterogeneity of methods and perspectives.

Chapter outlines

The goal of this book is to demonstrate how Asian Americans inform broader topics that impact them, other Americans, and diasporic communities generally. It brings together the various theoretical perspectives when possible. In the process, the book advances the conversation on the direction of studying Asian Americans, rather than just summarizing it. Throughout the book, we are especially concerned with the ways Asian Americans negotiate with institutions, given the kinds of inequalities they experience and the sorts of identities they possess.

Chapter 2: Race, Ethnicity, Gender, and Sexuality

This chapter explains how Asian Americans experience race in particular, along with gender and sexuality, which future chapters then elaborate upon. The chapter first defines key terms and reviews the dominant Asian-American stereotypes: the "model minority" and "yellow peril" (including the post-9/11 "terrorist"); the geisha and dragon lady; and the effeminate gay and the nonexistent lesbian. Beyond reviewing the stereotypes, the chapter explains how race, gender, and sexuality operate within the larger constructs of nation, patriarchy, capitalism, and imperialism. Substantive issues that demonstrate these hierarchies include hate crimes (most notably the murder of Vincent Chin), the exotification of gay Asian men, the treatment of other minorities relative to Asian Americans, and more.

Chapter 3: Arrival and History

Any discussion of the contemporary experiences of Asian Americans must include a review of major historical episodes. The chapter explains the arrival and major changes in each ethnic group, including gender differences between them. In particular, why did Asians come to the United States in the 1800s and later construct bachelor societies? How were Asian Americans treated legally and how did they contest that, including Japanese-American internment? How did Asian Americans move discursively from a despised to an admired minority post World War II? Why did the United States invade the Philippines, and with what impact on Filipino emigration? What were the social protests of the late 1960s? Why did Asians arrive after 1965 and as refugees, tied to US imperialism? And what occurred during the 1992 Los Angeles riots involving Korean Americans? In explaining this progression of topics, the chapter argues that Asian Americans have been brought in as labor, as seen within immigration laws, and often constructed as threats. This is not to say that Asian Americans have not benefited from the process. But this colonial dynamic disrupts the immigrant narrative of the United States having fairly incorporated immigrants.

Chapter 4: Class and Work Lives

Most broadly, this chapter asks how race – along with other hierarchies – matters in the workplace for the economic security of individuals. Employed Asian Americans are professionals, low-wage laborers, and entrepreneurs. How do people end up in certain occupations; how do men and women experience their racial and ethnic differences at work? The chapter explains that professionals and laborers are read as the hard-working "model minority," which helps them at work but contributes to a glass ceiling and worker exploitation (especially of low-wage women). Regarding entrepreneurs, the chapter reviews the causes and types of small-business ownership, along with associated challenges and opportunities. The chapter recognizes that many Asian Americans have achieved considerable success in the labor market and small business while many others have not, and explains how these findings inform broader social trends. A disproportionate number of Asian Americans live in poverty, even while working. Rather than frame the economically secure and the poor as opposite poles on an economic binary, we connect them to see how race, culture, gender, and other forms of social differentiation have impacted both groups.

Chapter 5: Education

This chapter reviews reasons for Asian American successes and difficulties in school within the broader conversation on race and education. Asian Americans have played a major discursive role in the politics of education, whether in the recently popular "Tiger Mom" fascination or when used to argue for the dismantling of affirmative action programs. Yet, in the process, the true story of educational attainment and challenges facing Asian Americans remain overlooked. These measures include college acceptance rates, ESL (English as a Second Language) programs, and more. The chapter argues that many Asian Americans are immigrants and refugees who need educational assistance, but that their incorporation into the racial politics of education limits attention to their needs. The rise of Asian American Studies has addressed this in part but not fully.

Chapter 6: Family and Personal Relations

The concern in this chapter is whether (and how) the systems of stratification (as explained in the previous chapters) affect people's formation of personal relationships. The private sphere links to the public sphere rather than exists separately, which the experiences of Asian Americans illuminate. The chapter reviews the causes and consequences of co-ethnic marriage, intermarriage, gay/lesbian relationships, work–home tensions for women, domestic violence, transnational adoption, and transnational families. The chapter also asks what these family patterns suggest for Asian Americans' adaptation. For example, does interracial marriage or transnational adoption by white families signal Asian American assimilation, or does it indicate the prevalence of racial and gendered stereotypes, or some combination? The chapter argues that Asian Americans' family formations often reproduce, but at times critique, various social hierarchies surrounding them.

Chapter 7: Citizenship

This chapter asks how Asian Americans become full citizens of the United States along legal, social, and cultural dimensions, while recognizing the limitations of citizenship as a means to advance equality. Citizenship pertains first and foremost to its legal definition. More Asian Americans than typically recognized live without full legal status. The United States as a restrictive, neoliberal state becomes more apparent through the lens of legal citizenship. Social and cultural citizenship are also elusive concepts for many Asian Americans, even citizens. How do Asian Americans claim a social and cultural belonging when they are depicted as foreigners, associate primarily with co-ethnics, and join social and cultural associations, most notably religious ones? In the process of elucidating these trends, the broader meaning of citizenship within a global system is explained. The chapter gives significant attention to the institution of religion and to the cultural practices of the second and later generations. It is argued that most Asian Americans become full citizens by performing "American" practices and by embracing their background in a multicultural manner, that is, by showing a respect for those cultural differences that support a dominant (mostly Anglo) culture and neoliberal status in the public sphere.

Chapter 8: Media and Popular Culture

Media, broadly defined, is a tool both for promoting discourses on minority groups and for contesting those discourses. This chapter explains both ends of this issue. The media, for this purpose, consist of film, television, print (i.e. magazines and newspapers), theater, and the internet. These are key institutions for the production, dissemination, and consumption of popular culture. The chapter starts with a socio-logical discussion of the media as social institutions to appreciate how they function. It then examines key questions within this topic: how have Asian Americans been depicted in the media over time? What have their reactions been to those depictions (e.g. protests or appreciation)? What do Asian-American performers think of their performances? What images are presented within Asian Americans' own artistic creations? These questions inform the relationship of minorities to the media more broadly. The chapter argues that fuller images of Asian Americans today are due to the increased presence of Asian Americans as a consuming market, but that Asian Americans' productions offer more nuanced portrayals.

Chapter 9: Identity

Self-identity is a major topic for all people but in particular for college-age students. Why do people choose one identity(ies) over another (e.g. an ethnic over an American identity); how do they express identities; and how do they deal with multiple identities? These are central issues within the social science literature on identity, which research on Asian America can speak to. The chapter reviews these theoretical topics for the 1.5 and second generation of many ethnic groups. While the chapter is grounded in sociology, it brings in both psychology and cultural studies. Considerable space is given to whether Asian Americans construct pan-ethnic and transnational identities as well. In reviewing the literature, the chapter moves past the notion of a "cultural conflict" or a "marginal man" in describing those with dual identities, and instead argues that individuals bring together their identities in crea-tive ways. The implications of identity styles for adaptation are broadly discussed.

Chapter 10: Inter-Minority Relations

The guiding questions for this chapter are when do people-of-color come together across group lines and when do they engage in conflict? Whereas most of the book focuses on relations between Asian Americans and the majority, this chapter concen-trates on pan-ethnic and inter-minority relations. The chapter first studies popular explanations of why ethnic groups do or do not come together, drawing off of sociol-ogy and anthropology. Among other examples used to elaborate on these theories, significant attention is given to reviewing the contested relations between Korean Americans and African Americans. In addition, why certain Asian Americans come together more often than others is discussed. The chapter concludes by asking in what contexts groups cross ethnic or racial lines. Blanket statements of solidarity or conflict among Asian Americans and between them and other races should not be made.

Chapter 11: Social Movements and Politics

Social movements and politics share a common cause: to create social change. Regarding social movements, whereas the previous chapter explained when people join groups, this chapter explains when people pursue a cause which may or may not join them together with other groups. Why do people start and join social movements and why do some movements succeed while others fail? This is not only a major sociological question but one of direct relevance to Asian American Studies, given its emphasis on social change. This chapter also asks what major movements Asian Americans have been part of, and what their effect has been. Attention is given to labor movements, the late 1960s, and current episodes. Electoral politics similarly serves as a means of change. How involved are Asian Americans in politics as voters, candidates, and elected officials, and what are the main issues they care about? How are Asia and Asian Americans framed discursively within politics, such as issues like campaign contributions? Finally, how effective will politics be as a means to address social inequalities, given the sometimes conflicted relationship of Asian Americans to the state?

Discussion questions

- Use your "sociological imagination" about some of the social institutions that have influenced your life and some of your group identities. What are some of the inequalities and/or privileges you encountered? On a sheet of paper, write a personal reflection and/or draw an image that represents these institutions, group identities, and inequalities and privileges. Make connections between them and be creative!
- Either in a group or individually, pinpoint a type of inequality, institution, or identity and then suggest how quantitative and/or qualitative methods can shape analysis of this object of study.

2 Race, Ethnicity, Gender, and Sexuality

"You speak English so well!? How long have you lived in the United States?" Many Asian Americans have encountered these remarks, even those born and raised in the United States. This is a daily example of how Asian Americans experience race, as presumed non-Americans. This chapter explains this experience, along with ethnicity, gender, and sexuality, which future chapters then elaborate upon. The chapter first overviews key sociological approaches to understanding these social dimensions. It then defines key terms and reviews the dominant Asian-American stereotypes: the "model minority" and "yellow peril" (including the post-9/11 "terrorist"); the geisha and dragon lady; and the effeminate gay and the nonexistent lesbian. It borrows heavily from racial formation theory in order to understand Asian Americans' racial experiences. More than reviewing stereotypes, the chapter explains how they operate within the constructs of the nation, patriarchy, capitalism, and imperialism. Attention also is paid to how assimilation theory, which anticipates little if any racism against upwardly mobile minorities, makes sense of Asian-American race relations. Substantive issues that demonstrate these hierarchies include immigration laws, hate crimes, and racial profiling.

Defining race, ethnicity, gender, and sexuality

One of the most commonly used terms in sociology is "social construction." Sociologists refer to popular notions that appear as biologically based or as simply common sense and "natural" as actually the result of social construction. This means that they are created by a society and are not "real" in a predetermined way. Race, ethnicity, gender, and sexuality are all social constructions. We will discuss and define each one. We then will concentrate on how Asian Americans experience race and how and why race is socially constructed in the United States.

Race as a social construction

In the United States, when we see someone, we generally think we can identify that person's "race." Race is such a significant way of organizing and categorizing people in American society that we are often confounded when we encounter a person whose "race" we cannot immediately make sense of. People typically "look" Asian or Native American or black or white or Latino.[1] People have distinguishable skin tones, hair textures, facial features, eye contours. These are biologically based. So, how is race a social construction? While people have genetic distinctions, it is not the case that people classified as the same "race" have more in common genetically with one another than with those of different races.[2] There is no single gene particular to one race. The physical differences apparent between races, such as skin color, have no bearing on other characteristics, such as intelligence, facial characteristics, and so on. These physical differences stem from the geographic regions of origin of one's ancestors. Yet, in American society, these physical differences have been used to differentiate people into separate groups such as white, black, or Asian, both on an everyday level and at the level of government classification. Moreover, these categorizations are ordered in hierarchical ways, which has resulted in people being treated unequally.

Race developed as a way of distinguishing people from colonial times (Feagin 2009; Prashad 2000). Colonizers used phenotype as a way to differentiate themselves from the colonized and rationalize the exploitation of people considered morally different. Race developed as a concept in order to justify the slavery of Africans in the United States. In other words, race and racism did not lead to slavery as much as slavery led to racial formations and racism. Race similarly was used to define Native Americans, Latinos, and Asian Americans as in some way deviant and threatening to white Europeans in order to secure greater resources (e.g. land, jobs, higher wages, better work conditions, and so on).

Racial classifications have changed historically, further indicating that racial categories are a political and social invention rather than biologically based. For instance, Irish Americans always have been phenotypically white but were not always considered "racially" white (Ignatiev 1995). In the mid-1800s, Irish Americans were considered more akin to African Americans than to free whites. African Americans were even referred to as "smoked Irish." Only after Irish Americans took jobs that distinguished them from African Americans, endorsed slavery (despite Irish leaders' condemnation of the practice), and joined the dominant white voting blocs did they become accepted as "whites." Chinese Americans in Mississippi in the late 1800s also shifted their racial classification from black to white (Loewen 1971). They became small-business owners and gradually associated more with whites rather than blacks. More recently, in the 1970s, Indian Americans petitioned to have their race changed in the US Census from white to Asian American (Das Gupta 2006). They believed that their racialized experiences best resembled other Asian Americans, and there were economic and political gains in being designated a racial minority, such as more attractive small-business loans.

If we take a comparative perspective and examine how racial categories are assigned in countries beyond the United States, it becomes even clearer how race is socially constructed. People who may appear to share the same phenotypic features and might be categorized in a similar way in the United States (say, as "black") in a country like Brazil may actually be divided into different categories (Telles 2004).

Race is a politically created concept. Racial categories are externally imposed, and groups must navigate within and between them. Groups with greater power over social discourse, media, and the economy assign the racial categories of a society, and minorities attempt to jockey for position within those options. Members of the same race may have nothing in common except for a shared phenotype (and, even then, those phenotypes are not actually identical). This process of being externally assigned a racial group is an example of racial formation.

Durability of race

Even as race is a social construction, unfortunately it is not going away. Once categorized as a distinct racial category, people begin to believe it. Race is hard to eradicate at the subjective level, partly because both the majority and minorities start to feel strong bonds to members of their socially constructed race. It is continually reinforced "as a fundamental principle of social organization and identity formation" (Winant 2000: 184). Being part of a group creates comfort. Cultural norms start to develop over time. Without a racial group, one could have a harder time feeling attached to others. Just as importantly, moreover, racialization has become embedded in many social institutions. Racial categorization was (and continues to be) codified in the law. The US Constitution is a case in point. In the United States' founding document, African Americans were defined as "three-fifths" a person.

Another challenge in eradicating race as a concept is our cognitive dependence on it, even as that dependence misguides us. The brain classifies people in terms of social categories, including race, in order to simplify our reading of people. The brain tends to put people, objects, or ideas into groups and give them labels, so that we can then act on them in a predetermined way without having to consider the item's (whether person, object, or idea) individual characteristics. This makes daily interactions much easier. For example, we have a mental image of what a chair looks like: it has a level seat, four legs, and a back. When we see an object that fits that description, we perceive it to be a "chair" and so we know how to act on it: we sit on it. This makes daily life much easier than inspecting each chair we encounter. Once we have seen lots of chairs, we can allow objects that do not exactly meet that description to still be chairs (e.g. chairs with only three legs).

This is a useful cognitive device that, when applied to people, can have negative consequences. We are quick to classify people based on a little information. Skin tone and hair style are easy means of classifying people into what we call "race." But as explained above, those characteristics do not tell us anything meaningful about people, like intelligence, morals, social skills, and so on. Still, these criteria persist partly because of their significance socially and partly because they are stark visual cues. For instance, we could classify people based on eye color or height. But these are more difficult to either discern or to categorize differently. What this suggests is that the criteria (i.e. skin tone, hair texture, etc.) we have used are relatively random. And the term we have used for these random categories that ultimately serve as cognitive tricks is "race." For all of these historical, political, economic, emotional, and cognitive reasons, race is a social construction but one that does not go away.

Ethnicity

Race is analytically distinct from ethnicity, although they have similarities. Ethnicity refers to a typically self-proclaimed sense of group membership based on a presumed (not necessarily actual) common ancestry, history, and way of life (Cornell and Hartmann 2007). Because it is self-proclaimed, individuals often take pride in their ethnic background. In the United States, ethnicities generally overlap with national homelands (or countries of origin) but are not limited to them. Individuals from a national homeland become an ethnic group. For example, German American,

Brazilian American, Nigerian American, and Korean American are all ethnic groups. Outsiders may overlook distinctions within those ethnicities or national origin groups. For instance, Gujaratis, Punjabis, Bengalis, and so on are meaningful groups within India and Indian America. In the United States, such sub-ethnicities are rarely recognized and so people are simply referred to as Indian.

Ethnicity versus race

Ethnicity and race overlap at times, and the difference can be more analytical than observable. When someone is treated differently based on their physical appearance, then race is active. Race involves power inequalities and a sense of being acted upon. For this reason, race is a problematic concept, and race-based thinking should be eradicated. For example, being treated as black is unavoidable for most African Americans, even for multiracial persons who "look black." President Barack Obama's characterization as America's first "black" president is a case in point. He is, in fact, multiracial, but is treated by virtue of his phenotype as "black." Similarly, when outsiders refer to a Korean American as "Korean" or "Asian" based on physical appearance, it is a racial interaction. When that African American or Korean American himself or herself adopts that label and feels connected to others similarly identified because of a shared history or upbringing, then ethnicity is at work. So, the difference between race and ethnicity in these cases is only analytical. Most of the time, both ethnicity and race are at play. Individuals are assigned an ethnic or racial group and often adopt that group as meaningful to their lives. The difference matters because, as researchers, we want to know how to make sense of how individuals inhabit social categories and the origins of the categories. In later chapters, we will discuss how individuals who are categorized as "Asian" occasionally come to adopt that identity for themselves and come together as Asian Americans, or what is called pan-ethnic identity.

Gender as social construction

Gender is also a social construction. Like race, this too seems dubious at first since there are clearly people who are men and people who are women. Yet genetic differences between men and women are not *gender* differences but *sex* differences. People have distinct sexes. In fact, rather than simply two sexes, male and female, some persons are born with unclearly defined external genitalia or with both ovaries and testicles (Newman 2006). Similarly, some persons born with one sex live their lives mostly accepted as people of the other sex, even if their biological sex is known. If gender was so inherent, people would not be able to cross or blur the boundaries so easily.

Notions of strict differences between the sexes, as between races, develop from power inequalities. Patriarchy reinforces male privilege by prescribing bounded roles for women, often in domestic-related duties. This frees men from competition with women in the workplace and creates more time for them in work, leisure, and other facets of life (Kimmel 1996). Men also compete with other men for gender prestige. Men sideline other men, such as immigrants, minorities, and gays, so as to affirm their masculinity. In other words, gender plays a key role in the quest for power.

Like race, gender and gender differences are maintained for political, economic, emotional, and cognitive reasons. Movements towards gender equality by feminists have led to major victories but also to both a backlash and, ironically, a sense of complacency among some women, who increasingly question the utility of the word "feminist." In addition, feminist attempts to introduce legislation to address different forms of gender inequality have been met with fierce opposition, often from conservative political forces. At the same time, some women question feminism because they believe that to be feminist is to reject motherhood as well as other female experiences and identities.

How one experiences gender depends on one's race and vice versa, which again highlights its socially constructed nature. While we speak of "racial stereotypes," these stereotypes differ by gender, as do their effects. For instance, white men are, on average, paid more than white women who have had the same education, while white women are paid more than black women with the same education (Marlene Kim 2009). Income inequality between these different sets of people is linked to racialized and gender stereotypes, leading to a white woman, earning less than her white male counterpart but being paid more than a black woman. Even within a single group, depictions can vary by class, occupation, or geography. Collins (2000) delineates different media depictions of black women. As black women navigate out of one socioeconomic status and into another (for example from working-class/blue-collar to middle-class/professional), they are still framed as needing to be monitored by white men, white women, and/or black men, while how they may be monitored will differ.

Doing gender

When sex differences are given meaning by the wider society, then they become gender differences passed onto the next generation. As we become socialized into gender roles, gender becomes natural and taken for granted. Children when born have a sex but no gender. They must learn to "do" their gender (West and Zimmerman 1987). For instance, girls often cross their legs when sitting, unlike boys. These are learned behaviors. Teachers respond differently to similar behaviors by boys and girls, thereby creating gender differences for children (Martin 1998). The association of sex with expected behaviors is mostly false. There may be men who are more nurturing than other men and even more nurturing than some women. Even when expected differences do exist, it need not lead to clearly defined roles. For instance, on average men may be more aggressive and women more nurturing. If so, this can mean women are well suited to careers as psychologists, political leaders, and the like, rather than confined within the domestic sphere (Bem 1993).

Sexuality as social construction

Sexuality, similarly, is a social construction. Evidence that sexual preferences are influenced, not predetermined, by genetic dispositions (DeCecco and Elia 1993) can be seen as a breakthrough in the advancement of civil rights for lesbians and gays, for we should not discriminate against people based on genetic differences. That said, how is sexuality a social construction? While sexual preference is not entirely socially constructed, it still stems significantly from societal influence (see our discussion of sexuality and heteronormativity in the following section). Regardless of whether people are biologically predisposed to certain sexual orientations, the media and society at large give different meanings to homosexuals than to heterosexuals. The differences are framed not merely in terms of sexual partner preferences but in terms of entire lifestyles. Typically, the media and society at large depict homosexuals and their lifestyles as deviant and in a generally negative light, while heterosexuals and their lifestyles are considered normal, positive, and ultimately desirable. Yet the prospect that we have a single sexuality is dubious, even if we are predisposed to one versus another. Queer theorists maintain that we have multiple sexualities, that we can move in between sexual acts with one sex and then the other based on circumstances (Stein 1997). We can be attracted to different sexes at different times.

Sexuality and heteronormativity

Heteronormativity is the idea that male–female attraction and relationships are inevitable. This idea becomes so normative that same-sex attraction becomes difficult to imagine for individuals and society at large. Hence, even if someone might be biologically predisposed to be attracted to a member of the same sex, societal influences may prevent that individual from even thinking that it is possible. In order to gain acceptance for their sexual preferences, gays and lesbians have targeted large-scale institutions that promote traditional-gendered roles: the military and marriage. A debate within queer circles has developed as to whether gays should pursue marriage as a civil rights issue (Brandzel 2005). While few supporters of gay rights would question the legitimacy of gay marriage, some question the pursuit of traditional institutions that have long prescribed strict sexual as well as gender roles. To the extent that the state becomes more open to same-sex couples, it does so in a manner that preserves the ideal of the nuclear family (i.e. two married parents and their children) and of strict sexual and gender boundaries. Queer relations and flexible or non-normative sexualities are criticized (indeed, even non-married heterosexual couples or divorced parents are still subject to societal disdain), but same-sex marriage or civil unions mimicking the nuclear family model may be tolerated. Heteronormative assumptions continue to define how other social institutions operate, such as workplace and government policies on what kinds of relationships can qualify for "family leave." Such policies determine if a non-married domestic partner (straight or gay) can apply for "family leave" to take care of their ill partner or whether this is something that only married partners (straight or gay) may do.

Sexuality and intersections of race and gender

Sexuality is a political issue, even outside of issues related to homosexuality. It is politicized in that it is tied to resources. Sex serves not simply as an act of attraction or love but has been tied to conquest and power, and intersects with gender and race simultaneously (Nagel 2003). For instance, the colonization of Native Americans by European Americans did not take place simply in the name of land acquisition. Native American men and women were framed as sexually deviant and needing to be tamed. British colonizers and US slave owners framed African men as hypersexual and with many wives – that is, of perverse sexuality – that must be saved or at least segregated. Asian men were framed as effeminate and unable to control their women, which made them inept at constructing a proper civilization and attending to their land (Okihiro 1994). Colonization was an act of benevolence from this perspective. Though colonial encounters were ostensibly motivated by an interest in spreading Christian heteronormative morals to "savages," they were at times also motivated by homosexual interests (Aldrich 2002). Colonial expeditions sometimes involved homosexual encounters between colonialists and "natives."

Beyond colonization and slavery, race relations in the United States have been legislated along sexual lines. At the macro level, antimiscegenation laws prohibited unions between whites and nonwhites as a means of "preserving" whiteness, and ultimately family and nation, from the sexual threat of minorities (Collins 2000). Historically and still today, minorities' bodies have become commodified as sexual oddities, as either of heightened allure or of disgust, thereby reinforcing racial subjugation. At the everyday level, if a woman is afraid of a black man when walking alone in a dark corridor, she is often not responding to race alone but to the stereotype of black men as sexually aggressive. And beyond legislation on homosexual relationships, policies and informal rules around the "proper family" assume white heteronormative, middle-class nuclear family norms that do not always fit immigrant groups (Shah 2001). How race is experienced, then, is often through sexual dynamics. With this in mind, it becomes clear that race, gender, and sexuality (along with class, discussed in chapter 4) do not operate separately from one another but instead intersect. In order to understand how these social categories work, we have to consider how they inform one another.

From social constructions to stereotypes, prejudice, and discrimination

As people "define situations as real, they are real in their consequences," so goes the famous quote by sociologists W. I. Thomas and Dorothy Swaine Thomas. Regardless of whether race, ethnicity, gender, and sexual orientation are socially constructed, people believe them to be real and act accordingly, leading to real effects. Stereotypes, prejudice, and discrimination are the results of the presumed real nature of these social categories. Stereotypes are blanket generalizations about an ethnic or racial group that reduce its heterogeneity to a few characteristics, which become difficult to refute despite evidence to the contrary (Marger 1995). They originate from the media, statements, and practices from family members and others, and everyday observations filtered through preformed notions of group distinctiveness. Prejudice refers to "an arbitrary belief or feeling toward an ethnic group or its individual members" (Marger 1995: 71). Prejudice exists in one's head. It is impossible to know of someone's prejudice until that person expresses it.

Stereotypes and prejudice are practically meaningless unless they are acted upon, that is, unless they lead to discrimination. Discrimination refers to behaviors, including verbal, that attempt to limit a group's resources in favor of one's own group. The most commonly cited form of discrimination is interpersonal, wherein one person prevents another from attaining a goal because of hatred towards that person's race, gender, or sexuality. Hate crimes (discussed more below) are extreme examples of discriminatory behavior. Yet possibly more of a problem is institutional discrimination.

Institutional discrimination refers to the unequal treatment of groups based on the normal functioning of institutionalized practices. For example, until 1967 it was illegal in many US states for a judge to marry an Asian American to a white person. An individual judge may have been quite sympathetic to such marriages, but, because antimiscegenation laws forbade such marriages, s/he rarely performed them. In this way, even nonprejudiced persons discriminate. Antimiscegenation laws are an example of direct institutional discrimination, of institutionalized practices designed to treat groups unfairly.

Much institutional discrimination is indirect, the product of unintended practices. This can be the hardest type of discrimination to overcome. For example, women typically have or choose to take charge of the "second shift," that is, the domestic work of cooking, child care, and cleaning (Hochschild 1989). This limits their ability to be promoted in the workplace. Many businesses value "face time," that is, measuring an employee's contribution to the office by how often s/he is present. Because mothers rarely put in as much "face time" as fathers and depend on flexible hours, they can miss out on many promotions (Weeden 2005). This is indirect institutional discrimination. "Face time" is not premised on a sexist notion in the same way antimiscegenation laws are premised on racialized and sexist thinking, but the effect is discriminatory towards women as a group because it fails to recognize that women take on the work of child care in families disproportionately more than do men. As another example of indirect institutional racism, individuals convicted of felonies have trouble voting in many states, even after being released from prison and while on parole. This race-neutral law disenfranchises black men to a disproportionate degree, for within the current police, court, and prison industrial complex, they are arrested and convicted of such crimes at a higher rate than others (Alexander 2010). In these cases, people can discriminate without knowing or even being prejudiced.

Ideologies and oppression

Discriminatory practices and prejudice are upheld by oppressive ideologies. An ideology is a "set of principles and views that embodies the basic interests of a particular social group" (Feagin 2009). In the context of race, ethnicity, gender, and sexuality, ideologies rationalize social inequalities as "just" and "fair." Some oppressive ideologies are explicitly hostile to groups, painting them as morally or intellectually inferior, based on religious or scientific standards, and so deserving of unequal treatment. These explicit beliefs are on the wane. Replacing them are ideologies that appear benign or even progressive but still reinforce racial (and other social) hierarchies. For instance, the dominant, American liberal ideology of self-sufficiency and the bootstrap mentality (i.e. "pull yourself up by your bootstraps") which asserts that any group can rise up if it tries hard enough, has strong racial implications (Bonilla-Silva 2003). This set of beliefs is premised on the notion of an open, meritocratic economic system that allows individuals to succeed if they work hard and are deserving. Individuals' rights matter more than groups' rights. If individuals fail, it is their own fault. So, policies that assist people as members of groups, such as affirmative action, are critiqued.

This ideology has been proven false, for there are many challenges to rising up economically for minorities and women, including inadequate access to quality education, closed-job networks, recessions and other macro-economic trends, and more (Fischer et al. 1996). And the ideology covers up many of the atrocities perpetrated on minorities, such as genocide, slavery, forced labor, loss of land, internment, and more. Still, this popular ideology blames minorities for their lack of upward mobility. Another popular ideology is "color-blindness," discussed in chapter 1. This ideology is purportedly anti-racist in its calls to ignore race and treat people as individuals, with the assumption that racism has already gone or will go away. Yet, this represents wishful thinking rather than a realistic appraisal of racial dynamics. As explained above, institutional discrimination persists even for color-blind individuals.

The combination of belief in American meritocracy along with the post-civil rights push to be color blind has led most recently to a "laissez-faire racist ideology." This ideology accepts institutionalized discrimination as the natural order of social relations. As sociologist Lawrence Bobo writes, "laissezfaire racism involves persistent negative stereotyping of African Americans, a tendency to blame blacks themselves for the black/white gap in socioeconomic standing, and resistance to meaningful policy efforts to ameliorate US racist social conditions and institutions" (2006: 17). Because the economic system in the United States, in particular in the South, no longer depends on a caste-like system of highly exploited labor serving white elites in a few capacities, the ideology of race has changed. The new ideology no longer needs groups to be so marginalized along all conditions of social life, and so legislated racism (e.g. Jim Crow segregation laws) and racist anti-immigration laws have faded. Yet this does not mean that the dominant group wants frequent association with minorities and immigrants. It only means that the current economic system does not require extreme discrimination.

Within this framework, the economic system continues to de-privilege minorities but concern over persisting racial inequalities are few. Minorities are blamed for their own conditions, partly because the ideology of color blindness, promulgated most forcefully by white elites, affirms the racial status-quo (Bonilla-Silva 2003). A belief in American liberalism – that individual freedoms and responsibilities are paramount to American identity and upward mobility – supports this ideology. Policies that promote interactions across groups, such as affirmative action, receive tenuous support at best. Regarding Asian Americans, many may become "honorary whites," that is, accepted as akin to whites and separate from blacks, but not equal to whites (ibid.). But, laissez-faire racism makes people ignore problems, such as overcrowded neighborhoods in Chinatowns, garment workers in sweatshops, anti-Asian quotas in higher-education admissions, and other forms of institutionalized discrimination discussed throughout this book.

Privilege

The flipside of discrimination is privilege. Privilege refers to the benefits of being in the dominant group, namely white, male, heterosexual, and middle class and above. Numerous examples of privilege exist in daily life where the dominant race, gender, sexuality, or class considered "normal" is supported in the media, political discourse, and daily interactions. Rather than only focusing on the disadvantages facing sub-ordinate groups, it is necessary to account for the benefits that the dominant group receives. Some are seemingly trivial, such as finding "flesh"-color Band-Aids in any convenience store that actually match one's skin color (McIntosh 1988). Some are of deep consequence, such as being able to rent an apartment of one's choice and price range while others are kept out due to their perceived race or sexual orientation (Lipsitz 1998).

This is not to suggest that white middle-class men do not face their own hard-ships. Wages have not risen at the same pace as expenses. Families are working harder in order to afford the same quality of life as the earlier generation. Cities and states have less money to invest in infrastructure, such as bridges and roads, which all people depend on. We consider macro-economic changes while focusing on the marginalization and opportunities for immigrants and minorities.

These racial, gender, and sexual inequalities and supportive ideologies create chal-lenges for minorities. Yet it is an open question as to how much active discrimination continues to occur. As noted, explicitly racist ideologies are no longer accepted pub-licly. Much discrimination stems from institutional practices rather than by intent. Minorities have attained impressive positions of authority. As explained in chapter 1, some theories of adaptation argue that minorities can overcome what little discrimi-nation still exist.

Asian Americans as racial, ethnic, gender, and sexual minorities

How do Asian Americans experience the intersection of race, ethnicity, gender and sexuality? What do Asian Americans tell us about how and how much these hier-archies work? The book takes up these questions in different arenas, such as how Asian-American women and men experience the labor market, intermarriage pat-terns, and more. Here we elaborate on what these group categories mean for Asian Americans more broadly. Again, we focus on race and attend to how other social categories shape the construction of race.

Black–white binary

We typically think of race within the black–white binary. This means that the minority is defined in the United States as being black, and to be black means to be the oppo-site of white. We measure racial disparities by assessing trends among whites and the differences, typically negative, among minorities. For instance, prison incarceration rates are lower for whites than blacks or Latinos.[3] This is a clear example of racial dis-parities tied to institutionally discriminatory conditions. Differences in stereotypes and media images are similarly assessed. Common stereotypes of blacks are as lazy (in contrast to industrious whites), as criminal (in contrast to upstanding whites), and as sexually aggressive (in contrast to puritanical whites). This is the black–white binary. Minorities are assessed as either like blacks, and so victims of racism, or like whites and so free from racism.

This binary offers a useful means of conceiving of race in the United States, but it is limited. If one is not perceived to be the opposite of white, then one does not clearly suffer from racism. But groups can experience race and racism in ways different to blacks or whites. Historian Gary Okihiro (1994) asks, rhetorically, if "yellow" [i.e. Asian] is "black or white." The answer, of course, is neither. Yet, due to the power of the black–white binary, Asian Americans are framed as either like whites or like blacks. For example, historically, Asian Americans have been defined legally as non-white. In addition, Asian Americans have been stereotyped as morally deviant and explicitly compared to African Americans. For instance, Chinese were depicted in newspaper cartoons in the 1800s as like blacks (Newman 2006). At other times, Asian Americans appear like whites, even "out-whiting whites" in their educational attainment or household incomes. Similarly, they are residentially integrated with whites for the most part, unlike African Americans.

Yet even as they are compared to whites and blacks, they fit neither category completely. Claire Kim (1999) moves beyond the black–white binary without losing its applicability to Asian Americans. According to Kim's notion of racial triangulation, Asian Americans experience racism along two dimensions: degree of cultural and social valorization and degree of civic inclusion into the nation as full citizens. These two dimensions operate separately but are interdependent. Asian Americans can be highly valorized, akin to whites, or lowly so, akin to blacks. Yet, even when Asian Americans are respected relative to African Americans, they can be excluded from the nation. Asian Americans are often considered "forever foreign," despite how long their families may have been settled in the United States. Moreover, Asian Americans' exclusion becomes stricter during times of economic, political, or military threat from Asia.

The "yellow peril"

The main stereotypes impacting Asian Americans – the "yellow peril" and the "model minority" – demonstrate this dual racialization. The "yellow peril" casts Asians and Asian Americans as economic, political, and sexual threats to the West, wanting to take it over. When the "yellow peril" stereotype is active, Asian Americans are not only foreigners but low on the valorization scale. The stereotype is based in Orientalist framing of Asians (broadly defined) and extended to Asian Americans as the opposite of the ideal westerner (Said 1978). As the westerner is rational, kind, and sexually decent, the Oriental is irrational, conniving, and sexually deviant. The West needs to depict the Orient in this light in order to construct itself in its desired image. Critics of this analysis argue that European and American imaginings of the Middle East and Asia were more heterogeneous and complicated than Said suggests (Macfie 2000). Still, Orientalism proved to be a compelling discourse incorporated into much of the West's imaginings of Asia. The threat from Asia was military, economic, sexual, and cultural.

Controlling "Asian threats"

As an extension of Orientalism, in the last century and a half, the American *citizen* has been defined over and against the Asian *immigrant*, legally, economically, and culturally. These definitions have cast Asian immigrants, both as persons and populations, to be integrated into the national political sphere, and as the contradictory, confusing, unintelligible elements to be marginalized and returned to their alien origins. "Asia" has always been a complex site upon which the manifold anxieties of the United States nation-state have been figured: such anxieties have represented both Asian countries as exotic, barbaric, and alien, and Asian laborers immigrating to the United States from the nineteenth century onward as a "yellow peril" threatening to displace white European immigrants.

The "yellow peril" stereotype is not always at play but arises when there is a "crisis of capital," meaning when capitalist interests are not clearly dominant either domestically or globally due to competition and rising costs (Ong, Bonacich, and Cheng 1994). During such times, an external agent, such as the "yellow peril," unites "real Americans." Asia and Asian Americans come to represent the morally suspicious threat to the virtuous and benevolent United States. Orientalist racializations of Asians as physically and intellectually different from whites predominated, especially in periods of intense anti-Asian labor movements, culminating in institutionalized discrimination, such as immigration exclusion acts and laws against the naturalization of Chinese in 1882, Indians in 1917, Japanese and Koreans in 1924, and Filipinos in 1934.

Gender and sexual constructions of the "yellow peril"

The "yellow peril" also poses a sexual threat. Asian-American men, much like black men, seek to "take" white women, either by seducing them with their mysterious powers or by raping them (Nguyen 2002). In either case, the purity of white women is in danger. Nor are Asian-American women considered more benign. In film and on stage, Asian-American women are often portrayed as conniving prostitutes, "dragon ladies," or other temptresses whose true motivations are disguised as they try to seduce white men (Espiritu 2007; Shimizu 2007). In contrast, white women appear attractive but responsible. White men and women benefit from these sexualized stereotypes popular in media and everyday consciousness.

The aberrant sexuality of Asian Americans can cause the "yellow peril" to become a terrorist. Recent terrorizing episodes have been caused by "Orientals," ranging from 9/11 Arab hijackers to the Korean-American murderer at Virginia Tech, Seung-hui Cho. These men have been framed as sexually repressed (Brandzel and Desai 2008). As befitting the "yellow peril" (or "brown" peril in the case of Arabs), their sexual frustration and deviance fuels their already unassimilable nature which explodes in acts of violence. As Brandzel and Desai write of Cho,

> This inability to achieve proper masculinity and heterosexuality may lead to danger-
> ous excess, one that can threaten the object of its desire – namely, white women.
> Hence, the charges of stalking that were associated with Cho characterize him not
> only as deviant and inadequate but also as threatening. In this case, Asian American
> men can also be framed through a sexualized narrative of deviance, evoking the
> historical threat of the "yellow peril" ready to harm white femininity with contami-
> nation and miscegenation by the uncontrolled nonnormative sexuality of the Asian
> American men. (2008: 72)

In other words, Asian Americans threaten the security, economy, and morality of other Americans due to their foreign, untrustworthy, and morally inferior nature. This racial formation does not make them synonymous with blacks but instead as anti-American, in contrast to the prototypical Americans, who are presumably white. So, Asian-American racial inequality becomes framed as Asian American versus white, but does not map onto black–white relations directly.

The "model minority"

The opposite of the "yellow peril" threat is the "model minority," the other dominant stereotype of Asian Americans. When not seen as threatening to the nation, Asian Americans are upheld as "out-whiting whites" with their high scholastic achievements, low incarceration rates, residential integration, entrepreneurship, and emphasis on family unity.

This seemingly positive portrayal has more going on than a representation of imagined social trends. This stereotype has gained currency because, like all stereotypes, it fits various preconceptions and racialized ideologies. First, it works to denigrate Asian Americans, even as it purports to praise them. The "model minority" is cast as subservient and obedient. While the "model minority" appears highly valorized, s/he remains a foreigner. According to the stereotype, their Asian, often Confucian, upbringing enables their success, rather than other sociological factors often cited for influencing children's mobility, such as parents' education level, networks of support, and so on (Park 2005). For this reason, Asian Americans can be successful but not considered assimilated enough to be seen as everyday citizens, much less civic or corporate leaders.

Stereotypes and racialized ideologies of the "model minority"

The "model minority" myth works not only to limit Asian Americans but also to uphold dominant ideologies of the United States race relations discussed above. The fact that a minority can achieve in the United States supports the American liberal notion of an open, meritocratic society that does not discriminate against minorities. The United States instead is enlightened and color-blind. The stereotype also contributes to a laissez-faire racism, whereby groups have strong cultural proclivities that, rather than structural conditions, shape their place in the racial and economic hierarchies (Bobo and Smith 1998). Within this logic, the fact that Asian Americans as a minority can achieve means that any group can, even African Americans. The "model minority" stereotype gives the credit for a group's success or failure to its culture, not to its structural conditions (e.g. family income level, degree of forced segregation, historical disfranchisement, etc.). So, African Americans and most Latinos deserve blame for their relative lack of mobility. A quote from a December 1966 issue of US News and World Report illustrates this point, "At a time when Americans are awash in worry over the plight of racial minorities, one such minority is winning wealth and respect by dint of its own hard work . . . not a welfare check" (1966: 6). It is not a coincidence that the "model minority" stereotype became popular during the civil rights movement of the 1950s and 1960s. At a time when African Americans called out the United States as a racist nation, a counter-discourse of the United States as supportive of minorities was marshaled. The "model minority" demonstrated to the nation and the world that the United States was not racist. The stereotype, in effect, divides minorities, pitting one "good" group against another "bad" group.

Gender and sexual constructions of the "model minority"

The "model minority" stereotype is also popular because it promotes gendered and sexual assumptions. If the "yellow-peril" man threatens to rape women, the "model minority" man is so asexual as to be considered effeminate. Such depictions stem partly from the occupations to which Asian-American men were relegated due to race in the late nineteenth and early twentieth centuries, such as workers in laundries and houseboys, and living in bachelor societies. This depiction continues today, despite Asian Americans' broader occupational representation (Espiritu 2007). Gay Asian-American men similarly play the role of the passive "femme" relative to the dominant white male (Manalansan 2003). Lesbian Asian Americans are presumed not to exist, for that would be too disruptive to the "proper" family (Gopinath 2005). If not characterized as a dragon lady within the "yellow peril" framework, Asian-American women are lotus blossoms ready to cater to men's needs. This subservient, exotic framing, fueled by gendered and sexual assumptions, limits Asian Americans' advancements in the workplace while supporting white men. It also shapes romantic relations with other groups and with other Asian Americans.

"Yellow peril" and "model minority" stereotypes in tandem

The "yellow peril" and "model minority" stereotypes appear as conflicting accounts of Asian Americans but in fact work together (Okihiro 1994). In both cases, there is an underlying supposition of Asian Americans as foreigners to the nation. The "yellow peril" is a foreigner bent on taking over the world. The "model minority" is a foreigner who is helpful to the United States. As long as Asian Americans "stay in their place" as models for how minorities are to behave, they are accepted, even praised. But, as they gain too many resources (in university admissions, in the labor market, etc.) and unlink the "natural" association between whiteness, the nation, and privilege, they become the "yellow peril" and threaten society. Other Americans can unite in opposition to the "yellow peril," thereby helping with the racial imaginary of a white nation that in reality relies upon immigrant labor. So the "yellow peril" and "model minority" go hand-in-hand as complementary stereotypes. As fitting racial formation theory discussed above, a group's characterization is not consistent but changes to fit the needs of political and economic elites.

The "yellow peril" and "model minority" stereotypes also stem from United States' transnational relations within global capitalism (Lowe 1998). The United States has gone to war with Asian and Middle Eastern countries throughout much of the twentieth and twenty-first centuries with imperial ambitions. These countries are often framed as threats to US physical and economic security. Immigration laws have reflected this framing, with Asian Americans being barred from immigrating in the early part of the twentieth century and thereafter only being let in bit by bit under heavy regulation. The immigration laws have changed to allow entry of Asian Americans, mostly in response to the economic needs and ambitions of the United States, creating in turn the "model minority" population.

Reality versus stereotypes

Lost within these dichotomous stereotypes are the many Asian Americans who experience economic insecurity, poverty, discrimination, segregation, underfunded schools, and the like (as seen in future chapters). Asian Americans are not monolithic. Even ethnic groups considered overwhelmingly successful experience real social problems. But it becomes harder to recognize and address these problems, given the dominance of these stereotypes that diverts serious attention.

With this critique in mind, it is important not to forget that many Asian Americans have entered the middle class or even above. They have integrated in many ways, as fitting assimilation theory. Still, the notion of the "model minority" can still be a myth. The reason is that the stereotype is based on the faulty argument that somehow Asian culture drives all of their success, that the United States has no racial hierarchies, and that other minorities carry the blame for their continued challenges. The myth reinforces the notion that Asian Americans' successes are due to the opportunities in the United States, opportunities supposedly available to all. Instead, the successes stem in large part from the educational credentials immigrants often arrived with, the family help they relied on, and a labor market in need of these immigrants' skills and less expensive salary expectations. Those mythical points are embedded within the "model minority." One can recognize Asian Americans' accomplishments without advocating for the "model minority" stereotype or its threatening "yellow peril" cousin.

Towards that goal, assimilation scholars attempt to demonstrate Asian Americans' successful integration as a minority without contributing to racist connotations. According to this perspective, Asian Americans may be seen culturally as threats or as foreigners, but this is minor compared to their overall acceptance as assimilating Americans. So, the significance of these stereotypes are downplayed. Furthermore, this perspective maintains that there is nothing inherently wrong, much less racist, with crediting their success partly to their culture if evidence supports that (Alba and Nee 2003; Zhou and Bankston 1998). And, the stereotype of the passive Asian American may have merit, especially when applied to recent immigrants with limited English abilities. In other words, the assimilation perspective sees the "model minority" stereotype as not malicious but instead as possibly accurate. Such scholars attend to the noncultural factors that define a group, such as income, residential integration, and the like, and they try to avoid racist implications for other minorities. This book will attend to multiple perspectives in analyzing Asian-American social trends.

Real impact of social constructions

While there is debate on the racist basis to, and accuracy of, certain stereotypes, Asian Americans continue to encounter racism. Because Asian Americans exist partly as foreigners, much of the racism they encounter is in the form of nativism. In fact, it may not seem like racism at all and so not appear to assimilation theorists as problematic. Calls for immigrants to "go home" or critiques of bilingual education may stem from an extreme patriotism, from xenophobia, from concern over the use of tax dollars, and/or other motivations. It is not clearly racist, especially when race is understood within a black–white binary. But such calls can carry a racist assumption that certain immigrants, in particular those from less-developed nations, would corrupt the nation with their way of life (Brimelow 1998). The notion of the United States as a cohesive and moral nation is affirmed by framing Asian Americans as outside of the nation, as not full members. Whites become the embodiment of the nation, as Asian Americans are contrasted to them. This occurs in many ways. Only three types are discussed here: immigration laws, racial profiling, and hate crimes. Other consequences of framing Asian Americans as foreigners are discussed in later chapters.

Immigration law

Immigration laws appear, on the surface, removed from race. They deal with national security, borders, sovereignty, and citizenship. Yet, concerns about national interests often contain assumptions about race, in particular regarding Asian Americans and Latinos (Lowe 1998; Hing 2000; Ngai 2004). One way of securing who can belong to the nation is by outlawing certain groups from immigrating. Such laws represent direct, institutional discrimination against would-be immigrants and against those already in the country seeking reunification with relatives. In arguing the passage of the Chinese Exclusion Act, the Asiatic "barred zone," and other restrictive laws (discussed in chapter 3), proponents framed Asian Americans as the economically and morally threatening "yellow peril" (Ancheta 1998).

Comparisons are rarely made between such immigration laws and Jim Crow legislation that undermined African Americans' freedoms and benefited whites. But such comparisons elucidate the racist nature of certain immigration laws. Both sets of laws framed minorities as antithetical to the nation because of their suspect culture and sexuality. And both were based on the economically motivated fears of white workers. Legally speaking, however, there is a difference. According to the Supreme Court, the United States has the right to exclude populations from immigrating, just as it has the right to defend itself against foreign invasions of war (Ancheta 1998). Acting in the name of national sovereignty, the Congress can enact practically any law it wants (Nguyen 2005).

Asians and other immigrant groups also face indirect, institutional discrimination within immigration laws. Such laws are not understood in popular discourse as racially motivated or significant, especially given the popularity of color-blind ideology. But because they often are, immigrants experience racism in ways that are overlooked. For instance, the Immigration and Nationality Act of 1965 seemed racially progressive by eliminating unequal quotas for Asian and other countries. But its preference for relatives of those already residing in the United States reinforced whites' claims on the nation, since they were the ones with the most relatives abroad. Sexual minorities face discrimination within the law as well. It was not until 1990 that open gays and lesbians could immigrate legally to the United States. The 1996 Defense of Marriage Act bans same-sex marriage at the federal level, which precludes sponsorship of same-sex partners abroad for immigration.

Even when a proposed law is popularly understood as racially motivated, it can still pass as race-neutral legislation. For instance, Proposition 187 in California in 1994 aimed to bar undocumented residents (and those suspected of being undocumented) from access to most public institutions (e.g. public schools, social services, and health care) and would have disproportionately impacted Latinos. It was framed by proponents, however, as protective of state resources and as a deterrent to illegal immigration. As another example, the 1996 Personal Responsibility and Work Opportunity Reconciliation Act signed by President Clinton reorganized public assistance (aka welfare). It barred noncitizen, legal immigrants from receiving certain public assistance based partly on stereotypes of immigrant mothers abusing the system (Fujiwara 2008; see chapter 4). One month later, Clinton signed into law the Illegal Immigration Reform and Immigrant Responsibility Act, which called for the deportation of noncitizen, legal immigrants convicted of a felony, even if that felony had no bearing on the political process. Taken together, these laws severely limited the rights of documented immigrants, which disproportionately impacted Latinos and Asian Americans, again without explicitly invoking race whatsoever within the laws. Within the current popular ideology of color blindness, discussed above, it is easier to promote anti-immigrant legislation without being accused of racism since race is downplayed in the public discourse.

Similarly, English-only legislation often stems not simply from the officially stated desire for a simplified mode of communication but also from the belief that other languages, namely Spanish, are associated with inferior lifestyles and people (Chavez 2008). Non-English languages also threaten most white Americans' linguistic privilege and their claim on the national language (even though English is not the official language of the United States) (Ancheta 1998). Partly for these reasons, local residents resist the growth of Asian ethnic enclaves that might not have English store signs but instead signs in the residing immigrant group's language (Fong 1994). Such enclaves threaten to "take over" towns, reminiscent of "yellow peril" fears. These examples of institutional discrimination are embedded within the presumption of Asian Americans (and Latinos) as foreigners to the white nation, even when those "foreigners" live next door.

Racial profiling

Racial profiling refers to the use of an individual's assumed race or ethnicity in creating suspicion about the person otherwise not targeted by an official investigation. Racial profiling has been judged to be ineffective and actually detrimental to crime prevention (Wu 2002).[4] Still, when national security is at stake, as it is when dealing with "foreign" threats that Asians and Asian Americans stereotypically pose, almost any tactic becomes permissible.

A high-profile case of racial profiling has been the mistaken accusations and imprisonment, including solitary confinement, of nuclear physicist Wen Ho Lee. He worked at the Los Alamos National Laboratory. He was accused of sharing secret information regarding nuclear weapons with Chinese authorities. His Taiwanese ethnic background figured in suspicions of him. According to Gotanda, "The spy charges have been maintained, not by evidence, but by constant allegations linking Wen Ho Lee to China. In its reliance upon innuendo rather than facts, the federal government has emphatically played its race card" (2000: 1690). An apology was issued to Lee by the judge for the grave misconduct in the case. Even the *New York Times* offered an apology to its readers for its poor coverage of the affair. As part of a plea bargain, Lee admitted guilt to one charge of mishandling sensitive information. Lee won a civil lawsuit against the government and certain media for their mishandling of his case.[5] Such incidents pale in comparison, of course, to the gross internment of Japanese Americans during World War II, discussed in the next chapter, yet the threat of imprisonment by a feared Asian "enemy" continues.[6]

Some racial profiling is more racially and religiously based, again with the backdrop of Asian Americans as untrustworthy and possible threats. "Operation meth merchant" is the US Drug Enforcement Agency's name given to its crackdown on Indian American run convenience stores in northwest Georgia accused of selling common household items that, when mixed together, can help create methamphetamine (meth). While most stores in that area are white-owned, those targeted were run by Indian immigrants, often with limited English skills.[7] Deportations resulted from this operation.

More wide-ranging, government profiling of South Asian and Arab Americans has risen since 9/11 from its already high rate, with particular emphasis on men from predominantly Muslim countries.[8] Under the "special registration program," male residents in the United States who immigrated from one of twenty-five nations, practically all of which were Middle East and South Asian countries (including Bangladesh and Pakistan), were asked to register with the federal government. A portion of those who did were subsequently deported for having an undocumented status. If one did not report for registration, one could be "charged with 'willful failure to register', damaging their ability to obtain immigration benefits for which they were otherwise eligible" (SAALT congressional testimony, June 2010, p. 13).[9] Deportation has increased significantly among South Asian and Arab American populations. As quoted in congressional testimony in June 2010, "In fact, in the weeks immediately after 9/11, South Asians, Muslims, and Arabs, were apprehended and detained by the FBI and held without charge; eventually, most were deported for minor immigration violations rather than any terrorism-related offenses."[10] Arab Americans and South Asian Americans, in particular Sikhs, can be detained at airports for questioning by security officers without having committed any suspicious activity, based on the color of their skin, their religion, or their dress. Detentions have risen markedly since 9/11 for offenses not tied to terrorism (Shiekh 2011). This is another example of how international relations between the United States and Asian and Middle Eastern countries, often involving US imperial ambitions to shape the outcomes of these nations' political and economic decisions, shape government treatment of US immigrants. In an act of pan-ethnic solidarity, following 9/11, the Japanese American Citizens League came out against the racial profiling of Arab and South Asian Americans.[11]

Hate crimes

Closely associated with racial profiling are hate crimes. The difference between racial profiling and hate crimes is that racial profiling is linked to institutions (like the criminal justice system, for instance) while hate crimes are perpetrated on an individual level without any rational-legal state authority. A hate crime occurs when a victim is attacked in part because of her/his social background (e.g. race, ethnicity, sexuality, gender, religion, disability, etc.). Because Asian Americans are seen as more Asian than American, international relations spur anti-Asian racism.

A vivid example is the murder of Vincent Chin in Detroit in 1982 by two out-of-work autoworkers, Ronald Ebens and Michael Nitz, in the heart of the American auto industry. Chin, a Chinese-American young man, was mistaken for a Japanese American by his killers (Zia 2000). During a brawl in a strip bar, one of the murderers was overheard saying to Chin, "It's because of you little mother fuckers that we're out of work." This was a time of Japanese ascendancy in the US auto market. So, Chin was misread as a Japanese American, who was misread as the Japanese auto industry, which was misread as unfair economic competition. After leaving the bar, Chin was chased by Ebens and Nitz and ultimately beaten to death with a baseball bat. Adding to this tragic story, Ebens and Nitz admitted to murdering Chin but were not sentenced to jail time. Their punishment was three years' probation and a fine of only US$3,000, a startlingly lenient sentence. After an appeal by Chin supporters for violation of his civil rights and another retrial, the case was ultimately dismissed. Vincent Chin was assimilated, having grown up in the United States. Being cultur- ally American was not enough to save his life because physically – that is racially – he remained a "yellow-peril" Asian. This murder shows the limits of assimilation theory.

Hate crimes against Arab and South Asian Americans has increased since the already high rates pre-9/11. At times, the hate crimes are carried out by self- described white supremacists. Even when not directly linked to such extreme racism, hate crimes carry the imprint of a longer history of wars against Asia and the Middle East over decades during which certain countries and their populations are repre- sented as possible threats to US democracy and security. Such hate crimes hark back to the mistreatment of these and other Asian Americans in the late nineteenth and early twentieth centuries. Race riots, racist rhetoric, intolerance of non-Christian reli- gions, misogynist violence, inhumane treatment of workers, forced segregation, and the like described the daily lives of Asian Americans at that time. Today conditions are much better. But hate crimes signal the continued framing of Asian Americans by a segment of the populace as forever foreign, and the heinous nature of their acts demands attention.

Hate crimes against Asian Americans, and any minority group, are not based on race alone. As explained above, race intersects with gender and sexuality to create complicated readings of group members. Vincent Chin was not targeted simply because he was mistaken for a Japanese American. He also posed a sexual and gendered threat to his attackers, for he was an Asian American receiving the atten- tion of female strippers that his male attackers were not (Chang 2000). And while Asian-American women experience hate crimes, it is not necessarily the case that an Asian-American woman would have been seen as stealing white men's jobs. Asian- American women report being targeted by sexual harassment as well as by general attacks based on race.[12] And Asian Americans may be singled out for violent attacks for engaging in homosocial behavior.[13] Hate crimes against South Asian and Arab Americans increased significantly just after 9/11.[14] So hate crimes happen for differ- ent reasons.

How do Asian Americans react to how they are represented and treated along racial, gender, and sexual lines? Much of the book will discuss Asian Americans' reactions to these problems within particular contexts. It is hard to discuss general reactions to these problems since they are experienced in specific ways. People do not simply respond to stereotypes or discrimination generally. They respond to the glass ceiling (i.e. limits to work promotions) through workplace channels. They respond to a media industry and a caricature promulgated at the moment. They respond to hate crimes through political mobilization. And so on. The following chapters elaborate on these trends.

Conclusion

This chapter provided an overview of the key analytic tools that we will use to approach an understanding of Asian Americans with a focus on race while also attending to the ways that race intersects with ethnicity, gender, and sexuality. Drawing from sociological theories of "social construction," this chapter outlined the ways that the ideas of race, ethnicity, gender, and sexuality are in fact social constructions. Though these ideas have biological referents, that is, they draw from differences that can be discerned in the human body, these ideas are, nevertheless "constructed," that is, the meanings assigned to racial, ethnic, gendered, and sexual differences are generally arbitrary and buttressed within systems of power and domination rooted in white supremacy, US imperialism, patriarchy, and heteronormativity. In illustrating the ways that race, gender and sexuality are socially constructed, we have drawn attention to stereotypes and types of discrimination. We also have noted the prevailing ideologies around race that allow racism to go unchecked. We have highlighted various stereotypes to illustrate how race, ethnicity, gender, and sexuality intersect in categorizing Asian Americans. Specifically, we examine how these stereotypes and prevailing ideologies manifest in particular kinds of inequalities for Asian Americans in the areas of immigration law, hate crimes, and racial profiling. How are these concepts experienced at the institutional and individual levels for Asian Americans, with what implications for understanding the United States and globalization? The rest of the book explains this, starting with historical conditions.

Discussion questions

- What are the differences and overlaps between race, ethnicity, and culture? Use a Venn diagram or table to outline the comparisons.
- How are racialization, oppression, and power connected? Create a visual representation to illustrate the connections.
- What does it mean for something to be "socially constructed"? How are race, gender, and sexuality socially constructed? If you are working in groups, each group can address one of these socially constructed categories. Groups can brainstorm and analyze other social constructions, too.

3 Arrival and History

At the heart of a sociological approach to understanding people is being able to understand how all of our lives as individuals and members of different groups require that we situate social life in historical context. Our lives would have been radically different if we had been born in a different time. While a Chinese-American young person today can aspire to having a professional career and living out the "American dream," that same youth, if born in the late nineteenth century, would have been consigned to a low-wage job and would not have been able to have a family life. History matters. A person can be hardworking and very ambitious but only under a certain set of circumstances can that person actualize those ambitions. Any discussion of the contemporary experiences of Asian Americans must include a discussion of immigration from Asia, as well as a review of major historical episodes that have shaped the racialization of Asian Americans. This chapter explains the arrivals and major changes experienced by different Asian ethnic groups over time, including gender differences between them. Moreover, it highlights Asian American experience both as a whole and as part of distinct ethnic/national groups with racism and discrimination.

People in the United States often think of the country as a "nation of immigrants," where individuals and families from around the world decide to move in order to better their lives. Though it is true that many people come to the United States seeking opportunities that they do not have in their home countries, from a socio-logical perspective it is important to examine how the function of social institutions determine immigration. That is, we need to understand that, although individuals make the "choice" to leave their countries of origin to come to the United States, there are forces beyond their immediate control rooted in social institutions like the economy, the political system, and even culture that shape what becomes possible as a "choice."

Indeed, a sociological perspective pays attention to how power and inequality embedded within social institutions form patterns of immigration and settlement. Understanding, for instance, how immigration law has shifted due to the demands of the United States' expanding capitalist economy and its rise as a global superpower becomes important to making sense of Asian immigration.

This chapter aims to fully explore the tensions between the United States' demand for racialized labor from abroad and nativists' (that is, white, generally working-class groups') demand that the United States as a nation be a white one that limits economic and political opportunities to only those who are authentic "Americans." It will explore how gender intersects with race in creating these tensions and there-fore who has been allowed to enter the United States and to ultimately settle into communities in this country. At the same time, it will situate these tensions within the broader context of the United States' emergence as a major world power. Some questions this chapter will explore will include: why did Asians come to the United States in the 1800s and later construct bachelor societies? How were Asian Americans treated legally and how did they contest that, including Japanese-American internment? How did Asian Americans move discursively from a despised to admired minority post-World War II? Why did the United States invade the Philippines, with what impact on Filipino emigration? What were the social protests of the late 1960s? Why did Asians arrive in significant numbers after 1965 and how is their arrival, especially as refugees, tied to US imperialism? And what occurred during the 1992 Los Angeles riots involving Korean Americans, as indicative of inter-minority tensions that can arise from combined immigration and structural discrimination against minorities? In explaining this progression of topics, the chapter argues that Asian Americans have been brought in as labor, as seen within immigration laws, yet at the same time are often constructed as threats to the nation. This is not to say that Asian Americans have not benefited from the process. But, this historical capitalist and racialized dynamic sets the stage for their lack of full citizenship (discussed in chapter 7), and it disrupts the immigrant narrative of the United States having fairly incorporated immigrants who arrive based on their own will.

Sociological approaches to immigration

Sociologist and Asian Americanist, Philip Q. Yang (2010) offers what he calls a "multilevel causation theory" of Asian American immigration that draws from and builds upon general sociological approaches to immigration, which we will use here. According to Yang, immigration from Asia can be explained by looking at three types of interconnected but distinct determinants or causes: (1) inter-country disparities; (2) multilevel connections; and (3) migration policies.

Inter-country disparities

First, although the idea of immigration is something we may take for granted in the United States, given that much of the settlement of this country has taken place through immigration, it can be assumed that most people would not ordinarily consider packing up and leaving the places where they were born to venture to a brand new country if there were adequate opportunities for them to make a living or fulfill their personal aspirations where they were born. Consider how difficult it is for students to leave home to attend college even within the same country. The fact is, major disparities or inequalities have existed (and continue to exist) between many Asian countries and the United States.

Economically, many Asian countries cannot offer their citizens the kind of standard of living that they are able to achieve in the United States. There are crucial wage differentials between Asian countries and the United States. A person can earn more by working in the United States (sometimes even in a job that is of lower status) than in one's home country. But, this does not mean that only the poor emigrate (i.e. leave their country of origin). Indeed, it is not often the poorest of the poor that migrate. It is often people with some kind of means who are able to secure the resources necessary to cross borders. As we discuss the history of the rise of the United States as an advanced capitalist country and global superpower, we will review why these differentials exist between the United States and Asia later (and, in fact, how the United States' economic development is tied to underdevelopment of different countries of Asia), but our point here is to highlight the importance of economic institutions (among other social institutions) in shaping the motivations for migration.

Politically, just as economically, disparities exist between many Asian countries and the United States. People often seek to live their lives abroad to flee political instability in their homeland. For example, late nineteenth-century Chinese migration was due in part to the Taiping Rebellion while post-1970s immigration from the Philippines was caused by the rise of the dictator Ferdinand Marcos. It is often difficult to disentangle the political reasons for people's immigration from the economic ones since they are both quite linked. Finally, among the social reasons why people might leave their countries, and this appears to be true for many Asian immigrants who arrived in the United States after 1965, are the opportunities to pursue an education, particularly higher education. In the United States, there are multiple means by which people can get a college or advanced degree (i.e. by directly getting admitted to four-year college and university courses or more indirectly through community college) that are not often available to people in many Asian countries.

Multilevel connections

After economic, political, and social disparities, a second major factor in shaping immigration according to Yang is multilevel connections. Yang argues that disparities between countries may shape people's motivations for immigration, but "[T]here must be forces that initiate migration and forces that sustain it" (Yang 2010: 18). Multilevel connections between countries can be either macro or micro. On the macro level, connections between the United States and Asian countries can be economic, political, or cultural. Economically, trade and investment ties between the United States and Asian countries create connections between them that can be significant for immigration. According to Yang, "US economic involvement displaces people from traditional economies and creates an emigrant pool; it heightens potential migrants' awareness of the disparities between the United States and their own country; and it consolidates the objective and ideological linkages with the receiving country" (Yang 2010: 19).

Politically, the United States has had deep, often coercive, connections with different Asian countries that initiated and sustained migration. For example, the United States' colonization of the Philippines in 1898 created a tie between these countries that endures to this day. It is no wonder, then, that the Philippines continues to be a major immigrant-sending country for the United States. Cold War military interventions (that is, military interventions tied to the United States' conflict with the former communist bloc, the Soviet Union) in the region, moreover, created connections between the United States and countries like Vietnam during the late 1960s and early 1970s. Though earlier waves of Vietnamese (especially those who left during the Vietnam War) are not considered "immigrants" officially, since they were fleeing a regime with which the United States was in direct conflict, the political connection between the United States and Vietnam would have enduring impacts on

Vietnamese immigration. Finally, the influence of American popular culture globally shapes people's imaginations and how they envision their futures.

These macro-level connections set the stage for the micro, interpersonal connections that motivate people to immigrate. For example, the United States' military presence in a particular country can lead to marriages between US servicemen and local Asian women. Another example of micro-level connections is the stories that immigrants pass on to their relatives in the homeland that, along with US global popular culture, influence how people think about America. Indeed, people's desire to reunite with family members who have settled abroad is an important micro-level connection that facilitates immigration. As another example, trade paths between countries create opportunities for employment for individuals and new businesses to generate more trade.

Migration policies

The third factor in explaining migration, for Yang, is migration policies. Disparities between countries may make people consider migrating, and connections between countries create direct ties between a sending and a destination country. Yet people cannot cross borders legally unless they comply with immigration laws. US immigration policy (more than the sending countries' emigration policies, though they too are important) are crucial. In the next section, we will map out some of the most significant immigration policies for Asian immigration to the United States.

In sum, Yang's framework for analyzing Asian-American immigration, which draws from and builds upon a rich body of sociological scholarship on immigration to the United States, illustrates how individual "choice" alone is not sufficient for understanding why and how immigration occurs in the way it does. A sociological approach to immigration attempts to understand individual "choices" as being made within a broader context. Yang encourages us to see how disparities and multilevel connections between Asian countries and the United States, as well as US immigration law, fashion individual and large-scale migratory processes. Following these ideas, this chapter proceeds thematically to explain Asian immigration.

Race, labor, empire, and immigration

Several key historical periods, tied to the United States' gradual rise to become the world's superpower, have been important in dictating immigrant flows from Asia. Min (2006) organizes Asian immigration history into three key periods: (1) the "old immigration period"; (2) the "intermediate period 1943–1964"; and (3) the "post-1965 immigration period." These three periods roughly correspond to the United States' development as a capitalist country and its emergence as a global superpower (Min 2006). Indeed, to organize our understanding of Asian immigration in this way is to recognize the vital role that the labor of Asian immigrants has played in the United States' economy. The "old immigration" period was the time of the industrial revolution and the United States' first foray as an imperial power in the late nineteenth and early twentieth century. The "intermediate period" covers the United States' triumph as a victor of World War II and its rivalry with the Soviet Union in the Cold War. The "post-1965 period" was the United States' transformation from an industrialized to a postindustrial economy and then its full consolidation as an unrivaled superpower.

To understand US immigration policies and immigrant experiences during these times, it is necessary to appreciate the shifting demands for labor within the United States that shaped immigration policy. Consistent across these labor demands have been a pursuit of less expensive labor and the role of race within that pursuit. As Ong and Liu (2000) argue, "Despite the complexity and uncertainties, it is possible to detect the logic of US immigration policy formation within the larger political economy. US immigration policy objectives have fluctuated because the factors shaping both *racial* and labor issues have changed continuously" (2000: 155). Hence, alongside the development of the US capitalist economy, also important to shaping immigration law was race and its interconnection with labor demand. The United States has long been a country that has depended on racialized labor from the enslavement of Africans at the country's founding to the employment of undocumented Mexican workers today. The presence of Asians in America is, in large part, linked to this structural feature of the US capitalist economy.

Though racialized labor, and relatedly immigrant labor, is a structural feature of the US economy, the United States has, seemingly paradoxically, also restricted or prohibited the immigration of different ethnic/racial groups. Powerful "nativist" interests wanted to stop immigration. Hence, to understand why specific Asian ethnic immigrant groups come at the times that they do, it is important to understand the paradoxical moments of *capitalist* inclusion and *national* exclusion. As Asian American Studies scholar Lisa Lowe states: "The contradiction between the economic need for inexpensive, tractable labor and the political need to constitute a homogeneous nation with a unified culture was 'resolved' through the legislation that 'racialized' Asian immigrants as 'non-whites' even as it consolidated immigrants of diverse European descent as 'white'" (1998: 31). In other words, Asian Americans became the vehicle to fuel capitalism with specialized labor while simultaneously serving as a clearly "foreign" presence that could unite the rest of the country. As racial politics transformed over time, the specific Asian ethnic group that would be the source of racialized labor shifted.

At the same time, the United States' emergence as a superpower has also influenced migration flows. In particular, Cold War military incursions in Southeast Asia, beginning in the 1960s, would displace large populations of people. Many sought refuge in the United States from the upheavals taking place in their own countries. Hence, the Asian population in the United States includes both *immigrants* (people whose immigration to the United States is considered more "voluntary" and due to economic reasons) and *refugees* (people whose immigration to the United States is less voluntary as a consequence of war or repressive political regimes). Indeed, international relations have impacted immigration policies in the United States in other ways. During periods of racialized immigration exclusion from the United States, the US government actually relaxed the exclusions of Asians from countries with which it was allied. For instance, though World War II was a period of racial exclusion in the form of Japanese internment as well as long-standing anti-Asian immigration policies, during that period the United States also opened up limited opportunities for Chinese immigration because China was an ally.

Contradiction and paradox are fundamental features of Asian immigration and settlement in the United States, which this chapter elaborates upon. To understand these dynamics, it is important to distinguish between the state and the nation and, relatedly, between citizenship and belonging, The state refers to governance, including the introduction, passage, implementation, and interpretation of laws. Citizenship is legally defined. The law outlines who is considered a citizen. The nation, on the other hand, refers to the symbolic meanings that are attached to a country. This is where the notion of "belonging" becomes relevant. For instance, despite the fact that enslaved Africans were ultimately emancipated and recognized legally as "citizens" by the state, they were still not treated as full-fledged members of the nation. Similar logics were (and continue to be) at work particularly with racialized immigrant groups, including those racialized as "Asians." Though we discuss the topic of citizenship in more depth in chapter 7, it is important to understand how the United States' racial formation shapes citizenship and notions of belonging and how these in turn have impacted immigration and settlement.

In the following section, we consider how racial politics, alongside capitalist and imperial labor demand, have shaped the ebbs and flows of Asian immigration to the United States during different historical periods. We consider how gender and sexuality have shaped migration patterns. Moreover, we discuss crucial moments that have had a significant impact on the racialization of Asian Americans. We encourage readers to refer to the "timeline" in the appendix as they proceed through the following sections.

The old period of immigration: the industrial revolution and the rise of the US Empire

Before we discuss the major waves of immigration and settlement from Asia to the United States, it is important to note that Asians' presence in the United States long predates the "old period" of immigration that we define in this section. The early presence of Asians in the United States is linked to European colonial legacies in North America. For example, the first documented presence of Filipinos in what is now the United States was in 1587 when Filipino crewmen on a Spanish galleon off of Morro Bay in California were sent on a scouting mission. The Philippines had been colonized by Spain several decades earlier and California was in fact Spanish territory during that same period of time. Indeed, the first major settlement of Filipinos in the United States was Saint Malo, Louisiana in 1763. These "Manilamen" are believed to have been Spanish galleon deserters (Espina 1988).

Chinese immigration

However, in terms of thinking of Asian immigration and settlement as related to the rise of the United States as capitalist economy, most scholars agree that the Chinese were the first major group of Asian immigrants. They had already been present in the United States because many had sought to try their luck in the Gold Rush of California that began in 1848 (Kitano and Daniels 2001). Many of these early Chinese immigrants hailed from Southern China. The region has historically been a crossroads for western countries. Major cities like Hong Kong and Macau (controlled by the British and the Portuguese respectively) were major ports through which both goods and people passed (Chan 1991).

By the late 1860s, the Chinese population had grown tremendously, and after the Civil War it became a new source of cheap labor for what was now a rapidly industrializing United States. With the divisions between the North and the South on the mend and "Manifest Destiny" having extended the borders of the United States from east to west, the country would require an infrastructure that would facilitate the movement of people and goods across state borders. It was at this moment that construction of the transcontinental railroad would begin in earnest, for which Chinese workers were aggressively recruited. Indeed, by 1868, three years after the conclusion of the Civil War, major corporate interests actually lobbied for the Burlingame Treaty with China, which recognized the emigration of China to the United States in exchange for trade privileges for American firms. When the transcontinental railroad was completed in 1869, Chinese immigrants found new forms of employment in agriculture, in the service industries in major different cities in California, as well as in the canning industry in the Pacific Northwest (Friday 1994).

The immigration of the Chinese was gendered: it was predominantly male. This was related in large part to the ways that certain kinds of work were considered most appropriate for men. Moreover, the logic was that unattached males would be a more flexible source of labor to be recruited and expelled as the need arose. Also, families could be an additional expense to employers and the government, which would have to house, clothe, feed, and educate them (Espiritu 2007).

However, just as importantly, immigration policy explicitly excluded Chinese women from immigration. The Page Law of 1875 defined Chinese women coming to the United States to work as prostitutes as a category of immigrants who should be excluded from entering the United States. Though immigration law included family reunification provisions, Chinese immigrant men who wanted to bring their wives over to the United States had a difficult time sponsoring their entry because of the Page Law. Immigration authorities' implementation of the law ended up excluding all Chinese immigrant women, not just those working as prostitutes (Luibhéid 2002). With women unable to immigrate, it became impossible for Chinese families to form, settle, and reproduce in the United States – a clear implication of the Page Law.

Indeed, Chinese immigration would ultimately elicit a backlash from whites. Nativists, including labor unions and political parties such as the Workingmen's Party, constructed Chinese immigrants as a so-called "yellow peril" (Ancheta 1998). As a "yellow peril," the Chinese were figured first as an economic threat who were "taking jobs away" from (white) American citizens by undercutting their wages. Moreover, they were seen as a cultural threat that practiced a strange religion (i.e. were not Christian) and who were prone to abnormal sexual proclivities (because they lived segregated from white society in predominantly male communities or what has been termed "bachelor societies"). Indeed, they were constructed as a threat to white women.

Interestingly, some advocates for Chinese exclusion actually made what might be considered more "benevolent" arguments. These exclusionists argued that the working condition of Chinese immigrants was similar to that of African slaves; hence, if the United States was to fully abolish slavery in all its forms, it needed to end Chinese immigration (Jung 2005). Generally speaking, however, the Chinese suffered from

physical violence as a consequence of the "yellow peril" stereotype, but they also suffered from a series of laws at the local, state, and national levels aimed at making it
difficult for them to live and work.

Eventually, anti-Chinese sentiment would result in the passage of the first explicitly racialized anti-immigration law in the United States: The Chinese Exclusion
Act of 1882. The Act initially suspended the immigration of laborers from China for
ten years while exempting more privileged Chinese immigrants (i.e. merchants,
students, teachers, and diplomats). Ultimately, Chinese exclusion was extended in
1892 and again in 1902. By 1904, Chinese exclusion was indefinite (Chan 1991). With
exclusion in effect in the United States, Chinese migration was rerouted to Canada
and Mexico, but the Chinese would confront exclusionary sentiments in those
countries as well (Lee 2005).

Japanese immigration

Employers would then turn to other Asian countries for labor. The first major source
of labor at this time was Japan. Shortly after the Chinese Exclusion Act was penned in
1882, an agreement was made between US representative, Robert Irwin, negotiated
with the Japanese foreign minister, Kaoru Inoue, for the recruitment and deploy-
ment of Japanese workers to Hawaii's sugar plantations (Chan 1991). Meanwhile,
Japan was suffering difficult economic conditions that would also impel emigration.
Though Japanese immigrated in large numbers to Hawaii, they would ultimately
make their way to the mainland after the United States annexed Hawaii. Like the
Chinese before them, the Japanese worked in agriculture and other dangerous, low-
wage jobs. Like the Chinese, too, the Japanese faced great hostility, which would
culminate in the passage of restrictive immigration legislation in 1907 called the
"Gentlemen's Agreement." The neutral tone of the title of this legislation (it was an
"agreement") as compared with the Chinese Exclusion Act (it is explicitly about
exclusion) reflects Japan's higher status as a country compared with China (Chan
1991). Nevertheless, the outcome was the same: immigrants from yet another Asian
country were prohibited from immigrating to the United States. Unlike Chinese
Americans, Japanese Americans eventually managed to actually lease and own
land. This would in turn spark new forms of anti-Asian sentiment, leading to laws at
the state level like California's Alien Land Law of 1913, which prohibited so-called
"aliens ineligible for citizenship" from being either tenants or small-scale agricultural
proprietors. Later, this law would be expanded to prohibit the US-born children of
immigrants from being able to hold the title of their parents' land (Ancheta 1998).

Notably, the "Gentlemen's Agreement" would allow Japanese immigrant men to
bring their wives to the United States. This would lead to the immigration, between
1908 and 1920, of so-called "picture brides," that is, Japanese women who entered
the United States to marry Japanese immigrant men whom they had only met
through the exchange of letters and photographs (Hune and Nomura 2003). Women
who were single and may have wanted to immigrate to the United States on their
own, however, would not be able to do so under the provisions of this law. However,
when Japanese families came to be seen by nativists as a possible "colonizing" force
in the United States, in part because of their engagement in small-scale agricultural
proprietorship, they too became the target of nativists. Anti-Japanese forces, which

were highly organized like their anti-Chinese predecessors, believed that the rise of imperial Japan meant that Japanese immigrants could be a threat and this ultimately led to this kind of migration being closed off in the United States (Luibhéid 2002). The exclusion of Japanese men and women from the United States would actually fuel migration to other countries in the Americas, such as Peru and Brazil (Sinke 2005).

Filipino immigration

The early movement of Asians into the United States is a consequence of the country's capitalist development, but it is just as importantly linked to its rise as an imperial power. Capitalism cannot flourish within the territorial boundaries of the nation-state alone. By the late 1800s, the United States was poised to become an imperial power. And it did. In addition to annexing Hawaii, the United States colonized Puerto Rico, Cuba, and the Philippines in 1898. When pools of labor from China and then Japan were no longer available due to the anti-Chinese and later anti-Japanese sentiment of nativists, employers turned to America's newest colonial acquisition in Asia – the Philippines – for workers (Chan 1991).

The acquisition of the Philippines was not peaceful. When the United States came to the Philippines, Spain was waning as an empire; in fact, because it was waning, it exploited the Filipino people even more. Yet repression breeds resistance and this would ultimately lead to the 1896 revolution of the Philippines against the Spanish. However, that revolution would go unfulfilled. This had to do with major factions in the revolutionary movement, factions that were divided along class lines. The American colonialists exploited this division and tried to engage with the more elite factions of the revolution, assuring them of assistance against the Spanish. Later, the Americans would turn their guns on the Filipinos though later still they would quite successfully co-opt Filipino elites into the colonial regime.

Having fought against the Spanish and been betrayed by the Americans, Filipinos would continue their struggle against foreign domination. The oft-forgotten Philippine War of Independence claimed many lives on both sides. Historian Luzviminda Francisco actually calls it "the first Vietnam" for the atrocities that took place during the war, as well as for the public debates it elicited in the United States. Filipino revolutionaries were ultimately suppressed (Francisco 1973). With the war's conclusion, the United States immediately set about aggressively implementing its policy of "benevolent assimilation." Though an empire, the United States was (and perhaps still is) a reluctant empire (Ablett 2004). Even as it used violence to conquer the Philippines, it attempted to distance itself from European colonialists like the Spanish or the British by simultaneously introducing "benevolent" institutions like public education and health care that earlier colonial powers did not necessarily develop (Choy 2003). Between massive displacement due to war and then the inculcation of the "American dream" through schooling, Filipinos were primed to leave the Philippines for jobs in the United States when recruiters came to the islands in the early decades of the twentieth century to secure laborers for agricultural employers in Hawaii and California because other sources of labor were becoming unavailable (see Constantino 1970).

It is important to note, however, that while Filipinos constituted the largest number of Asian non-US-born workers after the Chinese and Japanese in the early twentieth century, many scholars are reluctant to consider them an "immigrant" group. This is because Filipinos came to the United States as colonial subjects. For many scholars, to characterize Filipinos' early presence in the United States as a form of "immigration" is to fail to appreciate the United States' imperial history and how the violence of that history is what ultimately led Filipinos to be displaced from the Philippines. Indeed, employers were savvy in having gone to the Philippines for labor to begin with because there was an understanding that the Philippines' status as a colony meant that it was actually "internal" to the United States, not outside of it, and therefore Filipino workers were not actually foreign workers and therefore not subject to immigration restrictions (Campomanes 1997).

Despite their standing as US "nationals" by virtue of being colonial subjects, like the Chinese and Japanese before them, Filipinos would soon experience the wrath of anti-Asian forces in the form of white vigilante mobs and legislation aimed at regulating their lives (Baldoz 2011). Ultimately, this led to the restriction of their entry into the United States with the passage of the Tydings–McDuffie Act of 1934. Interestingly, the restriction of Filipinos was done through the granting of independence to the Philippines. In other words, restricting Filipinos from seeking employment in the United States required making them "foreign" as a newly independent country.

Indian and Korean immigration

Just prior to Filipinos' recruitment to the United States as workers, immigrants from India and Korea also made their way to US shores. Though constituting fewer numbers of immigrants when compared to the Chinese and Japanese before them, their early migration histories are worth noting, especially since they became much more sizeable populations in the United States after 1965. These early ties between the United States and India and Korea respectively have arguably had an impact on more recent flows of immigration from both countries. In the first decade of the twentieth century, several thousand Koreans were recruited for work in Hawaii's plantations (Kitano and Daniels 2001). Around the same time, immigrants from India would also make their way to the United States to work as agricultural laborers, but mainly in California (LaBrack and Leonard 1984). Many Indians from the state of Punjab came to Washington and Oregon from Canada. They settled more in California in the early 1900s as they escaped anti-Indian riots in the more northern states (Melendy 1977; Takaki 1989). A smaller number of Indians from Bengal came as traders or jumped from British ships in New York City (Bald 2013). They lived along the east coast, New Orleans, and a few other cities.

Towards the end of the 1910s, the United States introduced an Immigration Act in 1917. Though the act targeted Indian immigrants, it would effectively ban all immigration from Asia (Cafferty 1983). This act created the so-called "Asiatic barred zone" to define the geographical scope, through latitude and longitude, of Asian immigrant exclusion. This zone of exclusion stretched from South Asia and Arabia to Southeast Asia and islands in the Indian and Pacific Oceans (Hu-De Hart 1999). Indeed, the 1917 act was a culmination of various initiatives, commenced in 1911, by nativist groups to halt migration from India (Melendy 1977).

The Immigration Act of 1924

By 1924, yet another Immigration Act was passed, the Johnson–Reed Act, also known as the Asian Exclusion Act. The act introduced nation-origins quotas, that is, it allocated specific numbers of immigrants to different countries proportional to the origins of the population present in the United States. Ultimately, the act would favor greater numbers of immigrants from Western and Northern Europe to the exclusion of others, since immigrants from Western and Northern Europe far outnumbered immigrants from other regions of the world. Indeed, the logic behind the national-origins quotas was a racializing one as southern and eastern Europeans were targeted for increased access, based on their racialization as not-quite-white "others."

At the same time, the act bolstered the exclusion of Asian immigrants because it contained a provision that prohibited the immigration of aliens ineligible for citizenship. It is important to point out how these restrictions not only spelled who could not come into the United States, but, ultimately, who could and could not be considered "American" – these restrictions turned on ideas of what the nation should be racially. Such restrictions on immigration were aimed ultimately at preserving the United States as a "white" nation (Ngai 1999; Ancheta 1998). Moreover, one gendered impact of this law was that it would bar the entry of the wives of US-born Asian Americans (Espiritu 2007).

Asians as "forever foreign"

Alongside immigration exclusion was exclusion from citizenship. That is, the United States not only limited Asians' entry into the country through immigration exclusions or restrictions, it also precluded those Asians who were already living and working in the United States from being eligible for full membership in the United States as citizens. Even before major influxes of Asians took place in the United States, the US Congress in the Nationality Act of 1790 had already defined naturalization (i.e. the process of becoming a citizen if one was not born in the United States) as a privilege only to be enjoyed by whites. By 1878, a landmark court decision, referred to as *In re Ah Yup*, determined that the Chinese could not be US citizens despite a post-civil war 1870 amendment to the Nationality Act of 1790 which allowed "aliens of African nativity and persons of African descent" to be naturalized (Ancheta 1998).

Indeed, Asian immigrants often engaged the judiciary system to secure citizenship in spite of these exclusions. However, by 1922, in *Ozawa v. the United States*, the Supreme Court had defined Asian immigrants as ineligible for citizenship. Not long after this case, in 1923, the Supreme Court would make another ruling, this time turning down Bhagat Singh Thind's claim that he was actually eligible for citizenship because he was Caucasian (Ancheta 1998). Asian Americans' definition as "aliens ineligible for citizenship" feeds into the notion that Asian Americans are "forever foreign" (Tuan 1998) – in other words, Asian Americans, regardless of their US citizenship, are considered "outsiders." Being "forever foreign" suggests that Asian Americans do not belong to the American nation, something which has shaped the experiences of successive generations of Asian Americans, whether they were born in the United States or naturalized as citizens.

The "Intermediate Period," 1943–1965

World War II and the subsequent Cold War with the Soviet Union (i.e. the USSR) would have an impact on immigration from Asia, as well as on the Asian communities that had developed from earlier flows of immigration. While labor demand on one hand and racial politics on the other would continue to impact immigration flows into the United States, just as importantly, US geopolitics would impact the extent to which specific Asian immigrant groups were excluded from or embraced by the United States (Wu 2012). Immigrants (and their descendants) from countries which were allied to the United States during World War II and the Cold War were treated more favorably compared with immigrants whose countries of origin were the United States' adversaries.

World War II and the differential inclusion and exclusion of Asian groups

In terms of impacting Asian immigration, World War II would lead to the relaxing of earlier exclusions. In 1943, for instance, after decades of Chinese exclusion, new quotas of immigration from China were allowed into the United States. China was an important ally of the United States during World War II, and the United States affirmed ties between China and itself through immigration law. China had first been occupied by the Japanese in 1931 and suffered from subsequent attacks. It was, therefore, a natural ally to the United States.

In 1946, the Luce–Celler Act allowed a quota of immigration to enter the United States from India, reversing the exclusions defined in the Immigration Act of 1917. Indians immigrated in the late 1940s and 1950s (Dhingra 2012). For instance, Gujaratis immigrated to work in the hotel and motel business in San Francisco in the 1940s. Though the Tydings–McDuffie Act of 1934 had ended Filipino immigration, under the Luce–Celler Act, Filipinos were also extended a quota of immigrants (Melendy 1977). Moreover, the "special" (neocolonial) relationship between the United States and the Philippines, perpetuated by the US military after the United States granted the Philippines formal independence, provided another mechanism by which Filipinos would immigrate. Filipinos were recruited to work mainly in low-wage and low-status jobs for the US military and in return they could be eligible to remain and become citizens of the United States (Espiritu 2007). If Chinese and Indians, for example, were now allowed to come into the United States, albeit in small numbers, those already in the United States were given the opportunity to become naturalized US citizens.

The impacts of World War II on Asian communities in the United States were uneven. World War II was devastating for Japanese Americans, both for immigrants and for those born in the United States, who were rounded up and placed in internment upon the signing of Executive Order 9066 in 1942 by President Franklin D. Roosevelt in the immediate wake of the bombing of Pearl Harbor in Hawaii on December 7, 1941. In addition to being forcibly displaced from their homes, many Japanese-American community leaders were arrested on often-false suspicions of being national security risks. While German and Italian immigrants were also considered suspicious, they did not experience the mass incarceration that the Japanese community did (Ng 2002). The different experiences of Asian Americans during

World War II illustrate how racialization in the United States is often linked to US geopolitics. Domestic minority groups are figured more positively if their "home" countries are allies, whereas they are figured negatively if those countries are the United States' foes.

The Cold War and new forms of migration

With the end of World War II, the United States now engaged in a Cold War with the Soviet Union. The Cold War was a contest between the systems of capitalism (represented by the United States) and communism (represented by the Soviet Union, also referred to as the Union of Soviet Socialist Republics or USSR). To protect the "American way of life," the United States engaged in military conflicts throughout Asia as different countries became the battlegrounds for the Cold War. These military conflicts were part of the United States' strategy of "containment," that is, to contain or isolate the spread of communism. Asia was a vital region during the Cold War because of its proximity to the Soviet Union, as well as because of the establishment of the communist People's Republic of China under the leadership of Mao Zedong. Though the Cold War was never fought in either the United States or the USSR, it was fought, and rather violently, in other countries around the world. In Asia, the key battlegrounds for the Cold War were first the Korean War, which led to the division of Korea into North and South, and then the Vietnam War.

The Korean and Vietnam Wars would produce influxes of Asians to the United States. The United States' bid to compete with the Soviet Union for global ascendancy, an extension of the imperialist project begun in 1898, has dramatically transformed the societies impacted by it, providing the context for particular kinds of migration flows from Asia to the United States. While war had similar consequences for Koreans and Vietnamese, which would lead to immigration, the outcomes of the wars meant that their mode of entry to the United States would differ. Because South Korea is considered an ally of the United States, people who come to the United States from South Korea are classed as immigrants. However, because the United States was engaged in a conflict with Vietnamese communist forces, early Vietnamese immigrants to the United States were considered refugees, that is, they were thought of as people trying to flee from a hostile government, whereas Koreans were thought of as people who had made a decision to pursue better economic opportunities (Chan 1991; Fujita-Rony 2003).

War, from World War II through to the Cold War, led to distinctively gendered patterns. The 1945 War Brides Act, which expedited the entry of the alien wives and children of US soldiers, gave rise to the immigration of Asian women (with the exception of Japanese women, at least until 1948). Indeed, the presence of US military bases in Asia to this day continues to shape the immigration of Asian women to the United States, as US military men find brides among the women they encounter around US bases (Luibhéid 2002).

Post-1965 and contemporary immigration

The 1965 Immigration Act and the end of racial exclusions

One of the key imperatives of the Cold War was to build up the United States' military capability and ensure that it at least matched, if not exceeded, the capability of the Soviet Union. Hence, the United States invested heavily in what has come to be called the military-industrial complex. This would come to impact labor demand and ultimately immigration policy. According to Ong and Liu:

> For many, the launching of Sputnik in 1957 was a sign of Soviet scientific superiority. The immediate US response was to focus on improving its education system. Immigration clearly had a central role in the long-range effort to catch the Soviets. The contributions of foreign scientists to the construction of the atomic bomb and later to the development of rocketry proved that highly educated immigrants were crucial to building a technological lead in military weapons. (2000: 161)

In 1965, the United States introduced the Hart-Cellar Act or the Immigration and Nationality Act of 1965 which ended all racial exclusions that were contained in past laws. Additionally, the 1965 Immigration Act was characterized by a logic favoring family reunification. First, preference was extended to the relatives of US citizens as well as US permanent residents. Second, the parents of US citizens were allowed quota-free entry to the United States. Third, the law favored the admission of highly skilled professionals in the sciences and health fields to comply with the new demands of the growing military-industrial complex (Park and Park 2005). Most Asians who immigrated just following the Act did so under this third preference, creating the number of highly educated Asian immigrants of the 1960s and 1970s. The Immigration and Naturalization Act of 1965 has fundamentally changed the makeup of the United States. The increase in Asian Americans today, both in numbers and national diversity, relative to the 1950s would not have occurred but for this act.

While "containment" through wars overseas and the shoring of the military industrial complex domestically was one way that the United States attempted to secure its ascendancy over the Soviet Union, it also engaged in an ideological "war" to assert the superiority of US institutions. This ideological war was "fought," in part, through immigration policy. During the 1950s and 1960s, the same period when the United States was embroiled first in the Korean War and then later in the Vietnam War, it was also embroiled in major racial conflicts at home. The civil rights movement pressed the US government to fulfill its promise of genuine equality. By ending the racialized exclusions in US immigration law, the government could address, however nominally, critiques of activists at home, as well as critiques being issued by its enemies abroad. Communist movements around the world pointed to the United States' failure to address racial inequality as evidence that the system of capitalism that it represented was fundamentally flawed.

From "yellow peril" to "model minority"?

It was also during this time that another shift in the racialization of Asian Americans occurred. If the Chinese and the Japanese were at various times figured as a "yellow peril," they would now be characterized as "model minorities." Indeed, just a decade after their internment, Japanese Americans, through groups like the Japanese American Citizens League, were successful in advocating the removal of the racial bar to naturalization through the McCarran-Walter Act of 1952 (Ancheta 1998). Reports by major national media outlets celebrated the Asian American experience as proof of the United States' system of meritocracy. This stereotype had the effect of contradicting and undermining the demands of civil rights activists for different forms of racial redress or perhaps for justifying the forms of redress that were ultimately offered, which arguably were not as far-reaching as the kinds of demands activists were putting forward.

The birth of "Asian America"

However, Asian Americans actively countered this stereotype by mobilizing around the collective identity "Asian American." During the civil rights movement, and later with the rise of what is popularly known as the "Black Power Movement," African Americans articulated claims for the rights and privileges of citizenship that were being denied to them. Asian Americans were similarly inspired to identify the ways they too, as a racialized group, had been denied the full entitlements of American citizenship. The Black Power Movement "promoted positive views of their communities, looking for the roots of minority issues in sociohistorical contexts, not in the communities' inherent failings" (Liu, Geron, and Lai 2008: 43). Similarly, Asians of different ethnic backgrounds began to recognize their shared histories of immigration and racialization and to forge pan-ethnic identities (i.e. a collective identity that bridges people across ethnic divides).

What emerged during the late 1960s and early 1970s was an "Asian-American Movement" in which Asian Americans, like African Americans and often together with African Americans and other minority groups, participated in mass mobilizations to issue their demands for equality and social justice. These mobilizations were especially focused on higher education, labor, and housing (particularly in urban centers). Despite popular depictions of Asian Americans as a "model minority," they continued to be denied full representation in colleges and universities, exploited as low-wage laborers and relegated to poor and tenuous conditions of housing.

Indeed, if Asian Americans were being represented as highly assimilated and somehow closer to whites, their collective mobilization as Asian Americans, which drew inspiration from African-American social movements, particularly the Black Power Movement, was the moment when they rejected being allied with whites in the United States' racial order. The black–white binary has been a core axis for the ordering of race relations in the United States through which Asians were triangulated (Kim 1999). The "model minority" myth, in fact, is a myth that not only defined what Asian Americans are supposed to be but also what African Americans are not. Asian American Studies historian Daryl Maeda argues, however, that the Asian-American movement drew heavily from the African-American movement, including taking on much of its political cultural style. He states, "performances of blackness . . . constructed a new form of Asian American subjectivity, one organized around racial commonality among Asians" (2009: 92). Some examples of these "performances of blackness" included the adoption of the iconic style and fashion that was associated with the Black Panthers and even the adoption of the "Black Power" slogan of black nationalists by instead claiming "Yellow Power." Indeed, connections between the Asian-American and the African-American struggle ran much deeper, as exemplified in the work of activists like Yuri Kochiyama who was a close comrade of Malcolm X (Fujino 2005).

Asian Americans were not only being inspired by the Black Power Movement, but indeed, by political developments in Asia. Several Asian-American scholars have argued that Asian-American politics cannot be understood merely with respect to Asian Americans' experiences as racialized subjects in the United States but within a broader international, geopolitical context. As Nakanishi states, "by conceptualizing Asian American politics in terms of both domestic and non-domestic dimensions, our research agenda differs from what is usually undertaken under the rubric of minority politics" (Nakanishi 1985).

From the late 1950s into the 1960s, Asian countries were attempting to assert their national sovereignty against their former colonizers, as in the case of Vietnam as well as in the formation of the nonaligned movement in Bandung, Indonesia (Prashad 2007). Indeed, these identifications with Asia (especially anti-US imperialist movements in Asia) might be seen as a rejection of whiteness because it was during the Cold War that the United States attempted to incorporate Asians into its racialized project of global capitalism. In this period, "Asian Americans for the first time faced the possibility (whether fulfilled or not) of being accepted into whiteness" (Maeda 2009: 12). Paradoxically, if the "model minority" myth on one hand and the dismantling of racial exclusions in immigration law on the other were used by the powers that be in the United States as part of its ideological arsenal against communism in Asia, Asian Americans were actually finding inspiration in those very struggles.

Post-1965 immigration

Since the 1965 Immigration Act and the end of the Cold War, Asian Americans have arrived on the shores of the United States in great numbers. First, many Asians have taken advantage of family reunification provisions in the 1965 Immigration Act in order to come to the United States and join their loved ones. Interestingly, when the 1965 Immigration Act was introduced, it was not anticipated that Asians would actually enter in the kind of numbers they did through this provision (Park and Park 2005). It was assumed that more Europeans would immigrate since family reunification had been emphasized in the act, and most US citizens with families abroad were European American. In fact, the law only passed US Congress because of assurances from lawmakers that the racial demographics of the United States would not change as a result of it (Hing 1993). However, Europeans did not immigrate in large numbers. Instead, as noted above, immigrants from Asia took advantage of the third, occupational, preference within the act. Once they arrived and became citizens, they sponsored their families under the preference for family reunification.

Second, linked to Cold War politics, the United States introduced the 1975 Indochina Migration and Refugee Assistance Act, the 1980 Refugee Act and the 1987 Amerasian Homecoming Act, which facilitated the influx to the United States of Vietnamese and other Southeast Asians, including mixed-race people who were the product of unions between Asian women and US military men (Chan 1991). Though the Cold War is now over, the impact of the United States' military interventions in Southeast Asia, particularly Vietnam, continues to shape immigration flows from that country as Vietnamese women engage in marriage migration to non-Asians (Hidalgo and Bankston 2008).

Third, the United States continues to favor highly skilled, professional workers and many Asians are immigrating on these grounds and this is linked to the United States' restructuring from an industrialized to a postindustrialized country. Whereas the United States' economy was once based on manufacturing and many were employed in industrial and factory jobs, manufacturing has increasingly moved abroad. Indeed, the 1990 Immigration Act actually expanded opportunities for employment-based as well as investor migration, which has led to Asian migrants playing a role in contributing to emergent industries like information technology and software development, industries characteristic of a postindustrial economy. The act, however, did not just expand possibilities for immigration (i.e. long-term permanent residence) but, indeed, expanded possibilities for temporary migration with only limited opportunities for settlement (Ong, Bonacich, and Cheng 1994).

Economic fluctuations in the United States continue to impact flows of migration from Asia. Between the passages of the Immigration Acts of 1965 and 1990, different laws and policies were introduced that led to either the curbing or the encouragement of Asian immigration. This is perhaps most evident in the case of health care. For example, in 1976 the Health Professions Act was passed. As a consequence, "[T] o gain admission as medical professionals, alien physicians and surgeons first had to pass the National Board of Medical Examiners' Examination or its equivalent, the Visa Qualifying Exam. They needed also to demonstrate a competency in oral and written English" (Ong and Liu 2000: 165). This law would negatively impact the immigration of healthcare workers trained overseas. Yet, in 1989, Congress passed legislation that would allow 16,000 foreign nurses who were holding only temporary visas to be eligible to qualify as permanent residents. This move would serve to encourage immigration in that field (Ong and Liu 2000).

Though not specifically targeting Asian immigration, the 1986 Immigration Reform and Control Act (IRCA) would impact Asian immigrants. Despite the fact that immigration policies after 1965 offered new opportunities for Asians to enter the United States, provisions like family reunification sometimes did not work fast enough. Many Asian immigrants had to wait for several decades before their family members could join them in the United States. As a consequence, many prospective US immigrants from Asia would enter the United States as tourists but with the intention of overstaying their visas and being rendered "illegal." Through IRCA, many of these undocumented immigrants could and did apply for amnesty, a major feature of that act. At the same time, IRCA imposed tough sanctions against employers of undocumented immigrants. These sanctions led to widespread discrimination against both Asian and Latino immigrants who are often assumed to be "illegal" (Ancheta 1998).

The resurgence of the "yellow peril"

If the 1960s heralded the emergence of the "model minority" myth, it did not necessarily fully eradicate the "yellow peril" stereotype. As in previous periods, Asian immigrants have had to contend with negative stereotypes that figure them as outsiders to the nation, and these stereotypes, as in the past, have sometimes had violent consequences. In the 1980s, with the rise of the Japanese economy, particularly acute competition from the Japanese auto industry, Americans engaged in "Buy American" campaigns that would at times fuel anti-Japanese (or more broadly, anti-Asian) sentiment, including the murder of a Chinese-American, Vincent Chin, who was misrecognized as Japanese. Indeed, also influencing this period were tensions held over from the Vietnam War, resulting in a spate of hate crimes directed specifically at Southeast Asians, particularly the Vietnamese (Ancheta 1998). "Yellow peril" discourses resurfaced in new forms.

These tensions did not just exist between Asians and white Americans, however. In the late 1980s through the 1990s, tensions grew between African Americans and Asian Americans, more specifically Koreans, in different urban centers around the country. Korean immigrant entrepreneurs, often going into business for themselves because they had difficulty in the job market or because (as a consequence of incentives for investors through immigration policy) they already had capital to start their own businesses, were the targets of boycotts and in some cases violence. Owners of small grocery or liquor stores in cities like Los Angeles or New York were accused of mistreating their African-American clientele and/or unfairly crowding out African-American business owners.

Indeed, tensions between African Americans and Korean Americans came to a head in 1992 in the wake of the acquittal of Los Angeles police officers who had been accused of beating Rodney King, an African-American man, after a long car chase but without provocation from King. The acquittal was seen as testament to persistent racism in the criminal justice system against African Americans. The response from African Americans included the targeting of Korean-American businesses. Here, the "model minority" myth, a myth that actually pits African Americans and Asian Americans against one another, took an especially violent turn.

Perhaps the most recent incarnation of the "yellow peril" stereotype has been associated with the post-9/11 period. In the immediate wake of the terrorist attacks on the World Trade Center, the United States launched its "global war on terror" and its domestic counterpart, "homeland security." In ways similar to the reactions to the Japanese after the bombing of Pearl Harbor, which prompted the United States' involvement in World War II, the US government and citizens appraised Muslims (and those they mistakenly racialized as "Muslim," including Indian Sikhs) with fear and suspicion. Though Muslims were not necessarily relocated within the United States *en masse* like the Japanese, they were, like the Japanese, subject to forced removals from their homes. This time, however, forced removal was enacted through detention and deportation (Shiekh 2011). Many Japanese-American community groups have noted these parallels and have been staunch advocates for the end of the stereotyping or racial profiling of Muslims and South Asians as "terrorists."

Conclusion

The aim of this chapter has been to provide an overview of Asian-American community formation in the United States. A sociological perspective on immigration demands that we pay attention to factors beyond individual-level ones to make sense of why people move from countries of birth to settle in a land far away. Dynamics in the United States, in Asia, and between the two situate Asian-American immigration past and present. US immigration laws determine which Asians arrive in the United States and the conditions under which they can work, settle, and reunite with family members abroad. Once in the United States, Asian Americans experience both opportunities and resistance. In response, at times they have come together as Asian Americans, while also asserting ethnic identities and asserting their Americanness. These historical processes created the stage for contemporary Asian America, which the following chapters elaborate on.

Discussion questions

- Interview a peer or a relative who immigrated to the United States. How would you understand their narrative of immigration from a sociological perspective? What social institutions and processes would you consider in explaining their immigration?
- Explore the *New York Times*' Immigration Map: www.nytimes.com/interactive/2009/03/10/us/20090310-immigration-explorer.html

4 Class and Work Lives

How much money you have access to – in your wallet, in your bank account, and in your assets – matters greatly in shaping your lifestyle and life chances. Class shapes one's life outcomes possibly more than any other social category, including race, gender, or sexuality. One's occupation and associated class status impact one's schooling, culture, friends, life partners, health, and more. Class status commonly refers to income and ownership, but it is also more than that. A class is a group of people with comparable wealth, power, and prestige. We will use class and class status interchangeably in this chapter. From a sociological perspective, it is important to consider not only the objective aspects of class but also the meanings attributed to occupying a particular class status. In the United States individuals fall across various class statuses, including the upper, upper-middle, lower-middle, working classes, and the poor.

But class does not act alone. One's experiences at work are informed by one's social background. Class interacts with social inequalities like race, gender, sexuality, and even citizenship to shape life opportunities. Educational attainment is highly influential of one's class status and receives its own attention in chapter 5. To elaborate on the class experiences of Asian Americans, we first describe their general income statuses and poverty rates. We then go beyond statistics to examine their working lives across a variety of occupations. Throughout the discussion of how class and work operate, attention is paid to the intersecting role of race and other social categories, as well as to the role of immigration policy.

Descriptive class status

If people have one impression of Asian Americans, it is that they are economically successful. In truth, Asian Americans have a bipolar economic status. Some ethnic groups have median incomes above the national average and other ethnic groups have median incomes below it. Furthermore, each ethnic group has its share of economically well-off and struggling individuals. Examining Asian Americans' economic status also sheds light on how class status is measured. Depending on which variable one chooses, one creates very different impressions of a group's well-being.

Income and employment

The most common measures of class status are education levels and income levels. Education is discussed in chapter 5. Suffice to say here, education is similar to income for Asian Americans in that there is great variation along the extremes. Based on the

Table 4.1 *Median earnings*

Ethnic Group	Median earnings, men, 2010 (US$)	Median earnings, women, 2010 (US$)
Total population	$46,500	$36,551
All Asian	$52,154	$42,232
Indian	$74,997	$54,918
Japanese	$64,201	$49,490
Chinese	$57,061	$47,224
Korean	$50,108	$40,923
Filipino	$45,331	$43,637
Vietnamese	$39,359	$30,382
Cambodian	$35,460	$30,073
Laotian	$35,659	$30,755
Hmong	$30,763	$26,735
Other Asian	$33,414	$34,635

Source: United States Census Bureau; American Community Survey, 2010 American Community Survey 1-Year Estimates, Table S0201.[1]

2010 American Community Survey, the median earnings of Asian-American men and women vary widely within and across ethnic groups.

As can be seen in Table 4.1, Asian Americans have higher median incomes than the overall population. But this statement alone does not tell a complete story. Men earn substantially more than women in most ethnic groups (and in the nation as a whole). Many Southeast-Asian Americans earn markedly less – at times less than half – than the top-earning ethnic groups, Indian and Japanese Americans. Regarding employment levels in 2010, Asian Americans' rate of participation in the labor force (59.9%) is practically the same as whites (59.4%).[2] Among women, 57.0% of Asian-Americans are in the labor force, below the 58.5% of white women.

Occupations

According to the 2000 US Census (the most recent data for this statistic), most whites and blacks work in sales, operations, and support jobs, followed closely by skilled blue-collar jobs.[3] Together, these make up over half of the jobs held by whites. Not surprisingly, Asian Americans are quite heterogeneous in terms of their occupational distribution. Asian Indians are most represented in computer, scientific, and engineering occupations, followed by sales, operations, and support jobs, accounting for over half of their jobs. Similarly, Chinese Americans are most represented in these two areas, although in reverse, with more holding sales, operations, and support positions than computer, scientific, and engineering jobs. Filipinos and Koreans are like whites in that half of each group is most represented in sales, operations, and support occupations followed by skilled blue-collar jobs. Almost a third of Japanese Americans work in sales, operations, and support, followed next by education, media, and community services. Southeast-Asian Americans (i.e. Vietnamese,

Cambodian, Hmong, and Laotian) were most represented in skilled blue-collar occupations, followed by sales, operations, and support jobs. Of positions in executive and upper-management occupations, whites held an average of 11.2%. Every Asian group except the Japanese (at 14.5%) had a lower rate of such professions than did whites, with Southeast Asians having a lower rate than blacks at 5.5%.

Poverty

With Asian Americans' median income above the national average, one would expect the poverty rate of Asian Americans to be below the national average. But that is not the case. Asian Americans experience poverty at much higher rates than would be expected for a "model minority." The poverty levels of both Asian Americans and whites are the same, 12.5% as of 2010.[4] Yet, adjusting for cost-of-living differences (e.g. the fact that it costs more money to live in San Francisco than in rural Ohio), Asian Americans' poverty rate in 2011 was 16.1%, compared with whites' rate of 10.4%.[5] Asian Americans tend to live in large metropolitan areas (in fact, more so than any other racial group), with New York City, Los Angeles, and San Jose/San Francisco as the three areas with the largest numbers of Asian Americans.[6] Such an urban concentration makes the cost-of-living adjustment on poverty rates important.

Groups typically thought of as economically successful have higher rates of poverty than for the United States as a whole. For instance, Korean Americans have a poverty rate of 15.8% and Chinese Americans of 13.9% (not adjusted for cost of living, which would make them higher), both above the national average of 12.5%.[7] In addition, Southeast Asian Americans also tend to have higher poverty rates than other Asian Americans, with much variation among them as well. In 2008, the poverty rate of Hmong Americans was 37.8%, Cambodian Americans 29.3%, Laotian Americans 18.5%, and Vietnamese Americans 16.6%.[8] Other ethnic groups which receive relatively little academic attention also have extremely high poverty rates. For instance, Bangladeshi Americans have a poverty rate of 24%, double the national average (and not adjusted for cost of living, again suggesting that the real rate is even higher: see Kibria 2011 for more information on Bangladeshi Americans).[9]

Poverty links Asian Americans to other minority groups. According to a report by the National Coalition for Asian Pacific American Community Development, based on the 2010 US Census, "Lower income Asian Americans and Pacific Islanders [AAPIs] in urban areas are more likely to reside in 'communities of color,' i.e., alongside lower income African Americans, Latinos or AAPIs of other nationalities. Hence, the interests and destinies of lower income AAPIs are closely tied to the policies and programs impacting other 'minority' communities."[10] The report also noted that an increasing percentage of Asian Americans in poverty are persons raised in the United States rather than immigrants who arrived in poverty (while immigrants still represent the bulk of the poor), suggesting that poverty will not disappear with more time in the United States.

Analyzing class status

For greater analytical clarity of incomes and labor force participation, it is useful to situate Asian Americans within occupational types. As seen in chapter 3, immigration policy is often devised to fit immigrants into certain occupational sectors. Once immigrants arrive, what are their experiences? What kind of labor market do individuals, in particular immigrant minorities, encounter? Is it an open system in which people move up and down, based on their education and skills, or is it "segmented" into segregated sectors that confine opportunity? Asian Americans elucidate how the labor market works and so advance our understanding of the economy and workers' agency within it.

According to Portes and Rumbaut (2006), people fall into three broad occupational types: professionals, laborers, and entrepreneurs.[11] To this, we add a fourth category: those out of work and/or on public assistance. We will elaborate on the experiences of Asian Americans in the workplace by dividing them along the four occupational divides.

Before explaining Asian Americans' experiences within their occupational types, it helps to first cover the kinds of job markets available to US residents. Immigrants and natives find employment within one of three main markets: the primary, secondary, and ethnic-enclave labor market. The primary labor market refers to stable positions with salaries or consistent wages, which are protected by standard labor regulations. This labor market has two segments. The higher tier consists of professional and managerial jobs. The lower-tier jobs offer limited creative potential but still opportunity for some (if not full) advancement, protection from arbitrary punishments, and job security. Both professional and laborer positions are found within this labor market.

"Dead-end" jobs make up the secondary labor market (Sakamoto and Chen 1991; Waldinger and Lichter 2003). According to Waddoups and Assane, "The secondary segment is composed of unstable jobs accompanied by poor pay and working conditions" (1993: 401). Laborers, not professionals, are found here. The same kind of work can be found in the primary or secondary labor market, depending on its conditions. For instance, unionized manual-labor jobs offer security and support, whereas comparable non-union employment may exploit workers exposed to hazardous conditions. Pay within the secondary labor market similarly varies based on the sector, geography, and labor market. While no jobs in this segment pay high wages, some can lift individuals out of poverty while others, even when worked at full time, cannot.

In addition to the primary and secondary labor markets that all US residents have access to, immigrant communities often form their own job openings within the enclave economy. The ethnic enclave is comprised of stores owned by, worked at, and catering to co-ethnics, often within a geographically enclosed area (Portes and Bach 1985). The businesses typically are independently owned, small, and employ only a handful of paid labor, if any at all. Common examples include restaurants, grocery stores, travel agents, laundromats, small-scale manufacturing, and more.

Asian Americans are employed in jobs across all three of these labor markets. What are their experiences both in finding jobs and on the job? How much does their race, ethnicity, immigrant status, gender, or other social categories impact these experiences? How do their experiences illustrate broader class trends? We analyze each occupational group.

Professionals

Professionals are a key group of analysis for Asian Americans not only because Asian Americans are overrepresented as professionals relative to other racial groups, but moreover because of their theoretical implications. A large number of professionals among a particular minority group presumably indicates the declining significance of race, because if race mattered the minority would not be so successful. In this section we will challenge that assumption. Race can still be active as minorities enter professional occupations.

As coded in US immigration law, "professionals with advanced degrees, or aliens of exceptional ability" are prioritized in receiving visas (Portes and Rumbaut 2006: 24–5). In this way, the US state helps ensure economically and educationally advanced Asian American communities. In other words, a large number of Asian Americans in professional jobs does not result from an inherent Asian culture that values hard work and mobility, as the "model minority" stereotype implies. Instead, these are the immigrants allowed to enter most easily. These professional immigrants include researchers, physicians, nurses, engineers, executives, computer programmers, and the like.

Finding employment

A number of professionals are fluent or proficient enough in English to find work across the United States, not only in ethnic enclaves. Because of their skills and knowledge of the job market, they rely less on networks to find employment than do other immigrants. Instead, they may arrive with a job or place of study already in hand. But, even professionals are not immune to ethnic effects. Richard Ellis and Mark Wright (1999) find that recent immigrants are more likely to work alongside co-ethnics regardless of their education level, suggesting that they do not experience an entirely open job market. "[R]ecent migrants tend to work in the same industries as their resident co-ethnics rather than with workers of equivalent education from other groups. It suggests ethnic resources rather than skills predominate in the sorting of recent arrivals into industrial sectors" (1999: 48). Certain professionals are more likely to congregate with co-ethnics than are others. Those with English fluency, educational degrees recognized by US institutions, enough skills to pass qualifying exams (e.g. to practice medicine), and so on have less need for co-ethnic support.

Because not all professionals are equal in their skills, degree of assimilation, or access to assistance from co-ethnics, some have an easier time finding employment commensurate with their education than do others. For instance, Korean immigrant professionals typically lack English proficiency and recognized professional qualifications, and so congregate with one another for occupational support, or, as we discuss below, may start their own businesses. Filipina and highly-educated Chinese immigrants assimilate into their professions (Ellis and Wright 1999). And, sometimes these experiences vary within the same ethnicity. South Asian immigrants from the 1970s, part of the Asian "brain drain," found employment in their previous line of work. Yet, their co-ethnics from the 1980s and onward who lack English fluency have not been so fortunate. For example, Diditi Mitra (2008) found that 43 percent of her sample of Punjabi taxi drivers has a college education earned abroad. They cannot translate that into other employment because of a lack of English skills, recognition of educational degree, and social capital. That is, without more cultural assimilation or ethnic resources, occupational integration is difficult, even if highly educated. Immigration law also explains why later groups of immigrants came with less overall employable skills. In addition to favoring professional and highly educated people, the law also allowed for family reunification. Once Asian immigrants who were part of the "brain drain" became citizens, they sponsored relatives to join them in the United States. These relatives did not necessarily have to be professionals or highly educated to come.

Asian American professionals encounter challenges not only in entering occupations but also once in their planned line of work. How much those challenges are due to racism, sexism and active discrimination or are due to the standard operation of careers is the subject of much debate. These challenges arise in income compensation and mobility within careers.

Income inequality

Asian American professionals appear not to be burdened with deep economic concerns.[12] Yet, the possibility of income discrepancies has led to charges of racism against this "model minority" who presumably will not protest unfair compensation. The "over-education hypothesis" argues that white men are paid more than Asian American men with the same education level due to racial privilege (Hirschman and Wong 1984). Asian American men are not poorly paid but are not paid as much as they deserve. And, to equal the same pay as white men, they must earn a higher education than white men.

Other scholars critique the notion of racist compensations, such as the over-education hypothesis. It is not in the interest of employers to discriminate, for that would not reward talent and would hurt the quality of worker one can find. In accordance with this assimilation perspective, other surveys find that Asian Americans do not face income inequalities relative to whites, taking into account their education and other background factors (Sakamoto and Xie 2006). And, any income discrepancies facing Asian immigrants results not from racism but from either a lack of assimilation or the natural operations of the job market. For instance, recent immigrants may not have English fluency, enough acculturation to understand the American workplace, the networks to learn of better paying jobs, and the like. Their universities may not be known by employers, also leading to lower pay. Race, per se, may have nothing to do with it. Professionals may even accept lower wages than their white or native-born counterparts, because their frame of reference is a transnational one. For instance, Guevarra (2010) finds that Filipina nurses compare their incomes not to the incomes of the typical nurse in America, but indeed, convert their earnings into Philippine pesos and compare their earnings to that of a nurse in the Philippines. Invariably, the income a Filipina earns as a nurse in the United States is higher than what she would have earned if she had stayed in the Philippines to work. Additionally, Filipina nurses may place greater value on the services provided by their employers to ensure that they become eligible for permanent residency or the offer of flexible schedules for child care and generally do not make demands for higher salaries (see also Chin 2005). So, a lower income for immigrants may not be recognized as a concern.

The longer immigrants reside in the country, the better they often do economically, suggesting that their challenges stem more from a lack of cultural and social assimilation than from a racial discrimination (Tang 1993). In fact, Asian immigrants educated in the United States have incomes on a par with native-born whites, while immigrants educated abroad suffer weaker wages due to the difficulty by US employers to assess university credentials (Zeng and Xie 2004).

To truly test the effects of race on income, one must analyze US-raised Asian Americans relative to whites in comparable circumstances. Here the scholarship is inconclusive and changes over time. Income discrimination appears to have weakened over time. Studies conducted using 1990 census data and earlier found income disparities between whites and Asian Americans, taking into account education levels (Hirschman and Snipp 2001; Hurh and Kim 1989; Zhou and Kamo 1994). More recent findings present a more complicated picture. According to a review essay by Sakamoto, Goyette, and Kim (2009), US-raised Asian Americans have mostly income equality with white peers, controlling for industry, education, age, and other individual-level factors. Yet, given that Asian Americans tend to live in more expensive areas that often carry higher incomes, namely in urban environments and in California, their seemingly equitable incomes may reflect the effect of geography, which means they still face income inequality. The authors state:

> [T]o the extent that region of residence should be considered to be a necessary control variable, then college-educated, native-born Asian American men have yet to reach full wage parity with whites. . . . In sum, region of residence probably entails a higher cost of living for Asian Americans than for whites, but the extent to which this pattern may be interpreted as indicating racial and ethnic discrimination requires further investigation. (2009: 268)

Another complicating layer to understanding income levels is the ethnic variation within the race. Some ethnic groups appear to face little if any income discrimination while others more clearly do. For instance, Filipino Americans' (both men and women) income levels are equal to whites with comparable human capital (Ellis and Wright 1999; Stone, Purkayastha, and Berdahl 2006). Yet, Indian American women earn less than whites, controlling for individual background (Stone, Purkayastha, and Berdahl 2006). Among US-born Southeast Asian Americans, Cambodian, Hmong, and Laotian report low income levels, on a par with African Americans. Vietnamese have higher incomes on a par with whites, controlling for education. And, Asian American women may actually earn more than men for some ethnic groups, in particular second generation Southeast Asian Americans (Sakamoto and Woo 2007).

Projections in the future

While Asian Americans have often higher than national average incomes, with notable exceptions, one should not assume this trend necessarily will continue. Who migrates and what kinds of jobs they find depend on US immigration law. The law changes regularly to privilege some occupations and industries over others. For instance, the number of immigrant medical professionals, such as Filipina immigrants, has fluctuated because allocations for foreign nurses by US immigration authorities has fluctuated. Meanwhile, many Asian men, in particular from China and India, migrate under H1-B visas (which are temporary work visas granted to professionals) to work as computer programmers, accountants, and comparable occupations. H1-B visa holders are thought to be paid less than whites in comparable jobs and locations (Matloff 2003; Varma and Rogers 2004). Restrictions on these visa holders further limit their earning potential. These migrants must leave the country if their work ends, and their spouses (arriving under an H-4 visa) cannot work. The spouse is not seen as a person but as an appendage of the worker. So, both the overall numbers and the family and household incomes of Asian American professionals may go down as immigration law changes.

Glass ceiling

Another type of occupational challenge facing professionals is the glass ceiling, that is the lack of advancement into upper-level management despite qualifications (Friedman and Krackhardt 1997). Asian American professionals often remain in lower-tier positions in the primary labor market despite the credentials for upper-management promotions (Woo 2000). Smith and Elliott (2002) find that Asian American women are much less likely than white women to have authoritative positions. Asian American men, on the other hand, are almost as likely as white men to have positions of authority. Yet, this latter finding does not indicate the irrelevance of race. The authors conclude that, ". . . at least one explanation for [Asian American men's] relative success in the authority attainment process derives from a virtual lock on positions of authority over largely Asian work groups, inside and outside industrial and occupational niches" (2002: 272). Minorities are more likely to have authority at work if they are supervising their own ethnic group, which they refer to as "bottom-up" ethnic matching.[13] Even when Asian Americans are managers, they may not have the same authority and supervise as many employees as do their white peers (Takei and Sakamoto 2008).

The glass ceiling stems from direct and indirect institutional discrimination. As an example of the former, minorities generally are pushed into secondary-level rather than highly influential positions, based often on racial (as well as gender) stereotyping of the candidate and the occupation (Collins 1997). Asian Americans face the "model minority" stereotype that paints them as passive, submissive, technical workers whose foreign nature and lack of acculturation make them unqualified for, and likely even uninterested in, upper management jobs. They may have little trouble getting entrance within their chosen field but find trouble advancing (Leong and Grand 2008). For example, Asian Indian immigrant men in professional occupations in the Bay Area have a lower chance of such promotions compared to white immigrant men, which reflects a racial bias (Fernandez 1998). Indian immigrant women were doubly disadvantaged in receiving promotions and in income equality due to the combination of both gender and race. Even second generation Asian Americans report being stereotyped as passive, as from "backwards" countries, and the like (Dhingra 2007; Kibria 2002). As fitting Blumer's (1958) theory of group prejudice, racism stems from a fear over losing one's resources relative to another group. As Asian Americans and other minorities demonstrate a potential upward mobility, white elites can feel threatened and limit such advancements.

While the siphoning of Asian Americans into lower-level positions within their field represents in part direct racial and gender stereotyping, the inability to move up may represent indirect institutional discrimination. Once in lower-level managerial jobs, it becomes more difficult to make the right connections or learn the necessary skills to move into higher-level management (Shih 2006; Tang 1993). The lack of Asian Americans in key positions becomes self-perpetuating, for those in lower ranks do not have supervisors to nurture them along (Woo 2000). In addition, an "old boys" network continues to isolate minorities and women from key social capital. Without such guidance, Asian Americans may not know how to ask for promotions, how to facilitate positive evaluations from supervisors, how to obtain major assignments, and the like. Being kept out of key social support networks can make it harder to request changes to bureaucratic norms that would suit Asian-American needs, such as extra time for exams or other qualification measures, given language barriers (Woo 2000).

More informal, cultural barriers limit social ties to co-workers as well. Jobs get defined as belonging to a particular group, such as women, and employees construct symbolic boundaries to reinforce this (Epstein 1992). For instance, conversation topics within a niche may be particularly gendered, as might decorations put up in the workplace, all of which communicates what kind of person is most appropriate for the job. Asian Americans may be read as insufficiently assimilated, which can hurt their job performance reviews even when the job tasks are unrelated to degree of acculturation (Leong and Grand 2008). Other cultural dimensions of the workplace can make Asian Americans, among others, uncomfortable. Even the second generation can have trouble connecting with workplace culture. For instance, women claim that their commitments to family are not recognized within the workplace, which puts them in a bind when trying to be both strong employees and dutiful daughters (Dhingra 2007). Others in the second generation cite different leisure preferences to their co-workers (such as whether one plays or watches football). Religious differences, too, can create barriers with co-workers, such as standard celebrations at offices (for instance, at Christmas when not a Christian). This limits one's networks and, by extension, mobility. So, due to intentional or unintentional processes within the workplace, Asian Americans can face a glass ceiling.

Multiple implications of race

Race does not have a single effect for Asian Americans, nor for any other minority. While Asian Americans can face income inequality, a glass ceiling, cultural dislocation, and/or exploitation within particular niches, they can also benefit from their "model minority" status in terms of getting jobs in the first place. Asian Americans often are seen as hardworking, technically skilled, and nonaggressive. These qualities make them appeal to employers and so help them get a foot in the door (Dhingra 2007). In other words, the same qualities that limit them in upper management make them coveted for lower-tier white-collar professions. Contrary to common assumptions, Asian Americans' high employment rates may signify the effect of racial stereotyping rather than demonstrating their integration and a lack of racism. In other words, race can be at work in ways that lead Asian Americans to be on a par with some whites and unequal to others.

Cultural pulls and pushes

The challenges Asian Americans face at work inform how institutional discrimination works. But arguably their lack of mobility also reflects a cultural preference for non-leadership jobs. Just because one has an admirable education level and work experience does not mean one has the skills or desire to be upper management. Personality-wise, Asian Americans, in particular immigrants, can be more passive in the workplace (Woo 2000) and not exhibit the kind of aggressiveness and assertiveness often associated with Americans (whites, but also other native-born minorities). Not being outspoken and prioritizing group conformity rather than individuality are traits not associated with "leaders." Some women, including Asian-American women, are also known to exhibit these tendencies.

The response to this cultural trend – to the extent that it is real for one's workforce – should not be to ignore "passive" persons but instead to develop their leadership potential. Also, workers can have talents overlooked within the standard managerial focus on assertiveness and risk taking. It is easy to assume that an Asian American is passive, given the prominence of the "model minority" stereotype. And the stereotype suggests such a reading, thereby normalizing institutional inequities (Varma 2002). To the extent that the stereotype guides promotions and encourages leaders to overlook the talents of their Asian-American workforce, it hurts both the employees and company goals.

Immigration law and professional employment

An often neglected dimension of job segregation and the glass ceiling is US immigration law. As explained already, the number of immigrants in various occupational fields depends greatly on US immigration law preferences. Since 1991, a major segment of Asian professionals, in particular Indian and Chinese men, have entered under the H-1B visa program. The number of immigrants allowed on H-1B visas has increased from 65,000 in 1998 to 245,442 in 2001 (Park and Park 2005). As explained above, H-1B visa holders are often paid less than white peers, which makes them attractive to employers. Another disadvantage for these workers entails their segregation into technically specific positions with limited upward mobility. Moreover, they have little desire to challenge their employers, given their visa restrictions, creating what has been labeled a "high-tech coolie" labor system facilitated by "body shops" that bring these persons to the United States (Ong 2005). According to Varma, H-1B visa holders,

> are permitted to work mainly in those S&E [science and engineering] roles that are non-competitive with white males. Such occupations grant Asian immigrants a higher social and economic status compared with other minorities. Yet, Asian immigrants face structural barriers in career mobility into positions of authority and power. The general culture in S&E organizations views them as foreigners and holds back their careers. (2002: 338)

Part of the "structural barriers" these professionals face is embedded in the visa program itself. Workers have extreme difficulty leaving their workplace. They are committed to their companies for a specified duration of time, such as two years. If they protest their work conditions, they may be fired. If they are unemployed, they must return back to their homeland. They may not be able to search for new work either in the United States or elsewhere in the diaspora. Employers can ensure compliance by threatening workers with being sent home.[14] In addition, workers can be sued by employers if they break their contract by quitting. Workers live in fear of such lawsuits and displacement. Some employers may keep employees' visas, thereby directly controlling their legal status (Ong 2005). In other words, these visa holders are viewed as commodities rather than people. If they do not excel in their jobs, they can be shipped back, like an object one would buy and then discard when no longer needed. Complicating workers' grievance procedures is a lack of unionization in the high-tech industry generally (Varma and Rogers 2004). Those critical of immigration visa programs point to the challenges posed to native workers, whether in finding a job or in deflated salaries.[15] They argue that qualified resident workers exist for these positions but companies prefer to hire H-1B visa holders because they are paid less and are forced into more docile positions.

Occupational outcomes and national origins

It is not only US immigration law that creates an ethnic niche within an industry. The sending country's own policies set the stage for this in the first place. An example has been Filipina immigrant nurses. There has been a nurse shortage in the United States since the 1940s. US natives did not go into nursing because of its limited pay, despite occupational demand. Wages have stayed low because hospitals collude with set pay rates (Guevarra 2010; Ong and Azores 1994). Historically, nursing, while valuable, has not been paid much. This is partly due to its image as "women's work," which is undervalued. The lack of women going into nursing and the nursing shortage has made hospitals turn to immigrants.

The Philippines in particular have sent many nurses to the United States. Many Filipinos generally migrate to the United States because the Philippines has become very Americanized through colonization, with English as a common language and its educational system modeled on the United States. Regarding nursing, the Philippines trains many more nurses than it can employ. Robyn Rodriguez (2010) argues that the Philippines is actually a "labor brokerage" state that actively mobilizes and facilitates the export of workers, including nurses, because it benefits from the remittances (money sent to the homeland from immigrants when they are working abroad). Nurses often plan on working abroad in the United States, Europe, and the Middle East, where they can earn more money than in the Philippines. The United States in the past has made it easier for immigrant nurses than for those in many other professions to migrate, find work, and become permanent residents (Ong and Azores 1994). While the number of nurses allowed has declined significantly, Filipinas still immigrate and work in the profession. So the state of both the sending and receiving countries has shaped the racial and gender distribution of immigrants across occupational fields.

Responses to occupational challenges

In response to concerns over a glass ceiling and general discomfort at work, Asian Americans often strive to advance themselves without necessarily causing "waves."

Popular responses to workplace barriers rarely challenge the basis of the inequality but instead aim to make the individual concerned more accepted within the confines of workplace norms. These are micro-level responses by Asian American employees. For example, Asian immigrants may be told to alter their outward appearance and behaviors by smiling more often, shaking hands firmly, avoiding Asian attire, and other superficial techniques to demonstrate assimilation and accrue others' favorable opinions. Similarly, other minorities adopt institutionalized workplace norms, such as standard English, that are not practiced in the private sphere (Neckerman, Carter, and Lee 1999).

Yet many Asian Americans seek ways to integrate their cultural preferences in the workplace and to challenge negative assumptions about them. Second-generation Asian Americans create ways to express their culture, such as ethnic language, religious preferences, and respect for elders, in subtle yet still meaningful ways that do not make them appear "foreign" (Dhingra 2007). Other Asian Americans resist the stereotype of passivity by going out of their way to be assertive, which they believe advances their goals (Kibria 2002). And, at times, Asian Americans and other minorities may seek out job assignments tailored to their ethnic group, such as working with co-ethnic clients. The reasoning is that, if one is going to be framed as an ethnic minority, one might as well use that to one's advantage.

Rather than stay within a workplace considered discriminatory, others leave it. One tactic involves using one's networks to "job-hop" out of places considered discriminatory and into places with more hopeful mobility ladders (Shih 2006). Many other Asian Americans leave their jobs to start their own businesses, as explained below. An often-cited reason is a frustration at seeing others with equal or lesser résumés promoted ahead of them.

Overall, an examination of Asian-American professionals' experiences at work elucidates both the white-collar workplace and its relation to racial and other forms of social difference. Asian-American professionals, in particular those raised in the United States and immigrants not on temporary work visas, face few challenges finding work if they have English skills and recognized educational qualifications. The "model minority" stereotype may even help them find work, indicating the continued relevance of race even when minorities are occupationally successful. Yet, under the surface, the intersection of workplace norms and race/ethnicity may limit their advancement and equality. Rarely do problems stem from direct, extreme prejudice. Instead, institutions work in ways that privilege citizens and white men. Asian-American professionals illuminate the inequality embedded within "business as usual" practices, including immigration law. The result is a denial of full occupational options even as they are integral parts of the corporate economy.

Laborers

Laborers refer to employees with limited options for mobility and generally low pay. They work across all three labor markets: primary, secondary, and ethnic. There are a myriad of jobs that one can have within this sector, including taxi driver, nanny, assembly-line worker, construction worker, store clerk, waitress, janitor, and many more. Asian Americans are found within all of these and other types of positions. Even communities thought to be in higher-level positions, such as Filipino, Japanese, and Indian Americans, are represented among laborers.[16] How do they find these jobs, what are their experiences like, and what does that tell us about these class positions?

Finding work

Like professionals, laborers rely on a combination of networks and human capital to find employment. But, while the balance tilts in favor of using human capital for professionals, it moves in favor of using social capital for laborers. Social capital often takes the form of "informal exchanges of information, introductions, and vouching for a person's character" (Sanders, Nee, and Sernau 2002: 282). Through such information and introductions, immigrants learn of opportunities. Family and friends constitute the largest set of immigrants' networks. Connections made within ethnic organizations, such as religious spaces or civic associations, also relay information. Because immigrants use social capital, they frequently end up in the same niches as their co-ethnics. The second generation also relies on social capital to find such work, and their social capital consists of ethnic and non-ethnic networks (Kasinitz et al. 2009).

It is important to note that, while some Asian Americans may have the human capital that should make them eligible to work as professionals, some of the challenges discussed above complicate entry into professions; they may, therefore, work as laborers. In some cases, professionally trained newly arrived Asian immigrants may start off as laborers (because the social capital they possess makes this kind of job more readily available) until they have settled in the United States long enough to be able to apply for and successfully secure professional jobs. Others in labor positions strive to learn professional skills but cannot due to their current employment or other circumstances. As Mitra found for an Indian immigrant taxi driver, "I do want another job. I want to learn computers. I have only worked at a gas station, and now I am driving taxis. I want to get a better job. Every person wants to get a better job. But there is not much time to learn computers while driving taxis" (2008: 312).

Not all immigrants use networks to the same extent, not even all laborers. How much immigrants rely on co-ethnic information depends on several factors. Networks matter especially for those with limited human capital, such as poor English skills, and who are new to an area or job market. Such persons may not know what jobs are available or how to access them. Undocumented migrants in particular rely on networks since they are locked out of many formal job channels and are more comfortable with co-ethnic ties (Ellis and Wright 1999). Oftentimes, women lack as much human capital as men. In turn, they rely on social capital more than men do, and social capital is itself gendered. Sanders, Nee, and Sernau (2002) found this trend among their sample of documented Korean, Taiwanese, and Filipino men and women in Los Angeles.

To some degree, social capital can compensate for a lack of work experience. Yet, networks are not always reliable. The more co-ethnic peers who have already settled in a geographic area and the more established that community, the more social capital a recent immigrant has access to (Ellis and Wright 1999). Yet, when the ratio of recent arrivals to established ethnic population rises, there is more pressure on a community's networks and they become less valuable. When recent arrivals start to outnumber those already settled, they must look outside of established ethnic niches for employment. And, if the community they are entering already lacks many jobs and they are competing with others for scarce resources, it may not be as able or as willing to assist newcomers (Mahler 1995).

Employer preferences

As prospective workers rely on networks to find employment, employers too rely on employees' networks in their hiring (Kasinitz et al. 2009; Waters 1999). Employers prefer to choose new personnel based on the suggestions of valued employees. Having a current employee vouch for a prospective hire gives more support to their candidacy. Employers believe that such a person not only will work hard but also will not cause problems, for doing so would reflect poorly on the employee who vouched for her/him. When ethnic groups lack the connections within a business to hear about openings or to have their applications taken seriously, they become locked out of the niche (Waldinger and Lichter 2003). In this way, certain niches become associated with particular ethnic groups in major cities.

Gendered labor market

While networks guide men and women into particular jobs, the gender segregation of the labor market determines what kinds of jobs are seen as relevant in the first place. It is not a coincidence, in other words, that men and women often occupy different positions. Among immigrant laborers, men more often than women work in construction, as waiters, as cab drivers, and in other positions defined as "masculine."

The women's labor market is even more defined by gender. Women generally do reproductive labor, that is, labor necessary in order for other people to do paid labor. This involves cleaning homes, doing chores, caring for children, caring for elderly, caring for spouses, and the like. Women also work on assembly lines or even as prostitutes (Ehrenreich and Hochschild 2002). Such work is not equally distributed among all women, according to labor organizer Ai-jen Poo in a 2009 essay: "In a recent survey conducted by DataCenter and Domestic Workers United, researchers found that 98% of domestic workers are foreign born and that 59% are the primary income earners for their families. Domestic work remains one of the few professions available to immigrant women in major cities."[17]

Such gendered labor reproduces patriarchy both domestically and transnationally. As women in western nations have advanced feminist goals of equality in the workplace, they have moved into the labor force in larger numbers. Yet the "second shift" of housework has not been picked up by men. Instead, it has been outsourced to restaurants and daycare centers. Or as more relevant here, it has been "insourced" as immigrant women take over the duties inside families' homes (Parreñas 2001). In other words, the achievement of feminist goals by middle-class women in the First World has depended on the labor inequality that leads women from developing countries to leave their families and migrate for gendered work in the United States.

Contrasting experiences in the jobs

A large proportion of Asian-American laborers work within ethnic enclaves. Are these jobs stepping stones to higher-paying work, even to self-employment, or a space of co-ethnic exploitation at the lowest rung of the capitalist ladder? Each extreme depiction finds support. According to Portes and associates (Portes and Bach 1985; Wilson and Portes 1980), enclave jobs pay higher returns on a worker's human capital than does the secondary labor market. Enclave employees do fine if not better than they would outside, where they would be in the secondary labor market (Model 1985, 1992). At least in the enclave they share a common language and norms with their co-workers and employers. A solidarity and sense of trust develops between owner and employees, buffered by the constant oversight that each has on the other outside of the business (Portes and Zhou 1992). Workers outside of the enclave cannot count on such a reciprocal relationship of respect. This perspective on the benefits of working for co-ethnics fits a segmented assimilation theoretical perspective. The ethnic community provides resources that benefit laborers, who otherwise would be fending for themselves. Immigrants adapt more easily into a new society if they have the support of co-ethnics.

The example introduced in chapter 1 illustrates this dynamic. Chin (2005) argues that Chinese American women working for co-ethnic garment manufacturers in New York City accept lower wages than their Latina peers working for non-Chinese manufacturers partly because of the extra benefits of being among co-ethnics. The Chinese-American workers believe they enjoy more flexibility in their work schedule and in balancing their domestic needs (e.g. taking time off to care for their children) (see also Zhou 1992). The workers also can get by without much English and appreciate the solidarity with one another. Even if an opportunity arose to work for non-Chinese employers, it is not clear they would take it. There are no reported cases of exploitation or resentment towards their employer. They are also unionized within garment manufacturers unions. (Some Asian Americans are more likely to be unionized than others. For example, Filipina-American nurses are often unionized through nursing unions; Geron 2010.)

This optimistic portrayal of working for co-ethnics is not without its critics. According to scholars within both the critical labor perspective and straight assimilation perspective, co-ethnic businesses may exploit workers. Immigrants often work long hours without standard breaks or controlled working conditions (Kwong 1995). They put up with this because they need money to repay debts, such as those incurred in immigrating, and because of their ethnic isolation. Workers within small ethnic businesses, which are the norm, rarely have access to unions, for unions mostly have not sought such workers (Geron 2010). Rather than prioritizing solidarity with co-ethnics, the critical labor perspective argues that they stay in these jobs because they lack sufficient proficiency in English to find employment elsewhere, and racist hiring practices may exclude them. The meager pay is only tolerated because of a lack of other options. Furthermore, working with and for co-ethnics makes it harder to agitate for better conditions, for that can jeopardize one's contacts and standing with the employer (Ong 2005). Also, because co-ethnic employers know the home lives of their employees, they can more readily make demands on their home time. For instance, factory workers can be required to take work home. This is especially relevant for undocumented workers, for one's home is less likely to be raided by immigration and customs enforcement officers than a workplace.

The garment industry also provides support for this critical perspective. Garment manufacturers work in unionized spaces as documented by Chin (2005) but also in non-unionized, abusive sweatshops. These sweatshops can even be owned by co-ethnics. A notable case involved Thai women in the El Monte sweatshop (Su and Martorell 2002). Those who ran the factory took advantage of the workers' need for a job and money to pay debts, their lack of familiarity with Los Angeles, and their dependence on the company for their rights. Employees had to work extra hours, buy overpriced food and beverages from the compound, were locked in the building, and suffered other injustices. These sweatshops are part of the garment manufacturing business (Bahar and Carracedo 2007). Major corporate brands hire companies to produce their apparel. These companies then hire other companies to do the actual manufacturing. Corporations at each level make a profit off the level beneath them. So there is immense pressure to cut costs on the lowest levels. The women who actually assemble the garments become the most exploited. Co-ethnic ties between the workers and sweatshop owners do not protect the women from oppression endemic within capitalism. In fact, owners can take advantage of co-ethnics' vulnerability and trust (Kwong 1995).

While not suggesting such severe exploitation, Nee, Sanders, and Sernau (1994) argue that workers fare better in the primary labor market than in the enclave. They argue that workers may start out in enclaves because of their close contacts but gradually seek work in the secondary or primary labor market. Once they move out of the enclave, they do not return if they can gain sufficient English-language skills. The positions they find are in the public sector, such as the post office, and have clear benefits. This trajectory suits assimilation theory because it posits that workers benefit most within the mainstream and outside of their ethnic group. Unclear is how often Asian-American and other minority laborers can move into the primary labor market, given employer preferences and employee reliance on social networks to find jobs.

Because evidence can be found to support competing theoretical perspectives, it is difficult to determine which one best applies to immigrant laborers' work lives. Rather than one perspective inherently being more accurate than another, it is useful to keep in mind the possible relevance of more than one, even within the same industry.

Working for non-co-ethnics

Immigrant and second-generation laborers work for non-co-ethnics as well. While members of the second generation often find their first job through family networks, they rely on peers or college placements for their following jobs and often end up outside of ethnic niches (Kasinitz et al. 2009). Second-generation workers also aspire to higher-status jobs than those held by their laborer parents, especially if they have a higher education.

Yet a number of immigrants work in low wage jobs that do not offer much mobility. A focus on domestic workers illuminates the challenges facing many immigrants, women in particular, working for non-co-ethnics. Women of color experience multiple challenges at work since they are stratified along both gender and race lines (Browne and Misra 2003). The structural conditions of their jobs disenfranchise them. As women typically toil alone in these positions, there is no oversight of their work conditions or employer expectations (Parreñas 2001). Also, they lack co-workers who can validate their grievances and work collectively to challenge the employer, for instance through unions.

Within informal work settings, boundaries between workers and employers blur, which allows employers to alternate between being affectionate surrogate family members and exploitative bosses (Hondagneu-Sotelo 2007). Workers may appreciate being treated as a family member, for that at least brings some respect. Yet, as pseudo-family members, domestic workers can find that the formalities that promote respect and autonomy disappear. The result is a lack of protection for such women. Employers may not feel the need to pay extra for overtime because such work is expected of close relations. Day-to-day life can be constrained as well. They may be told when they can eat, where they should eat, what plates they can use, and so on. As a Filipina domestic worker in Rome, Italy, said to sociologist Rhacel Parreñas, "I want to be treated like a person. Not all employers are good; some are very bad. You can have a high salary but get treated like a slave. I don't care about the high salary as long as I am treated as a person . . ." (2001: 181). And, as is common for women's occupations generally, they must engage in emotional labor, adopting a happy demeanor in order to make those around them feel good (Hochschild 1989). This demeanor masks not only the frustrations of the job but also personal heartbreak. These women are often separated from their families, including their own children, for months or years at a time. Back in their home country or area, other women, such as their siblings, attend to these domestic workers' children and carry out other domestic obligations, creating a "global care chain" (Ehrenreich and Hochschild 2002). These female relatives, in turn, cannot prioritize their own education and work skills, thereby limiting their own mobility.

Even in formal workplaces where immigrant women work for non-co-ethnics, they face exploitation and physical danger. Many women work in manufacturing plants in the United States, often dealing with dangerous chemicals and objects (Pellow and Park 2002). Their racialization as Asian women (and Latinas) contributes to the indifference to their plight. They are considered able, even happy, to take abuse. If nothing else, they are seen as hardworking and unlikely to complain, making them a preferred workforce for these jobs. The combination of employer demand for such women and these women's economic insecurity, lack of human capital, and extended social capital draws them to these positions.

Many Asian-American laborers experience exploitation as they seek workplaces that accommodate their human capital needs, whether linguistic, cultural, family-based, or otherwise. They are preferred workers in various labor markets. Yet this does not lead to full citizenship. As Waldinger and Lichter (2003) argue, the traits which make certain groups desirable workers, such as an extreme work ethic and acceptance of low wages, undermine their fit as residents and full citizens. Class and citizenship intersect in this way. Lacking significant skills for the primary labor market puts these workers at a disadvantage in terms of financial status, power relative to other groups, and social status. The positions they obtain are often restricted to individuals like themselves. Being appreciated as full members of the workforce and society becomes more difficult under these conditions. Further complicating workers' rights is the globalization of labor. The outsourcing of labor limits US workers' options. Linking similar occupational workers across geographic lines becomes a necessary collective action strategy.

Small business owners

Immigrant entrepreneurs tend to own small businesses, defined as having one hundred or fewer employees (depending on the sector of the economy).[18] A few Asian-American groups, most notably Korean Americans, are overrepresented in small-business ownership relative to the national average. Among racial groups, non-Hispanic whites have the highest rates of self-employment in the nation, at 11.8% (between years 2005 and 2007).[19] During that same period, Asian Americans followed at 10.9%, with Latinos at 8.1%, and African Americans at 5.2%. Small-business ownership has been heralded as fundamental not only to the nation's economy but to minority welfare as well. Business ownership has been applauded because it fits a core ideology of US neoliberalism, that is, an ideology of self-sufficiency combined with capitalist goals (Ong 2003). Entrepreneurs are emblematic of neoliberal goals and so more readily have access to full acceptance as Americans. With such political implications, it is important to understand owners' real experiences in small business. What leads to such ownership, what do Asian Americans think of this occupation, and how does it affect their relationships with other groups?

This chapter focuses on the formal economy, that is, recognized legal businesses that pay tax. It is not uncommon, although not highly prevalent, for Asian immigrants and the second generation to be entrepreneurs within the informal or even illegal economy, as DJs, as babysitters, drug dealers, and more (Kasinitz et al. 2009). Such entrepreneurial work of Asian Americans merits more attention.

Motivations for small business ownership

Three key factors promote entrepreneurship among immigrants: limited options in the labor market; personal and group resources; and business opportunities (Yoon 1997). Limited options stem from either discrimination, such as the glass ceiling or a segregated job market, or from a lack of employment/underemployment due to poor English skills, unrecognized educational qualifications, and the like. Immigrant success in entrepreneurship supposedly represents the open nature of the US economy, but ironically their pursuit of small business stems mostly from experiences of blocked mobility. As explained above, most immigrant minorities encounter some kind of hurdle in the labor market. In response, individuals seek employment without externally imposed barriers, which self-employment supposedly offers. So, the turn to entrepreneurship signifies in part a rejection of one's planned line of work rather than an idealized achievement.

Resources for entrepreneurship

Of course, not all minorities who suffer discrimination turn to self-employment. African Americans, for instance, have a lower than average business ownership rate than do Asian Americans. Key to explaining this phenomenon have been the resources that Asian-American groups can access. Again, the Immigration and Naturalization Act of 1965 is crucial here because it drew initial cohorts of Asian Americans who were among the most educated, skilled, and generally most privileged of their respective home countries. Immigrant entrepreneurs can therefore rely on their own education, finances, and experiences in small business abroad or in the United States (Yoon 1997). The more familiarity one has with small-business ownership, in one's homeland or elsewhere in the diaspora, the more likely one is to be able to open up one's own business.

Some immigrants bring over large amounts of financial capital. They also draw from social capital within their ethnic group (Portes and Rumbaut 2006). In contrast to assimilation theory, which argues for abandoning ethnic ties that help economic advance, here reliance on ethnic capital can facilitate mobility. From kin and friends, entrepreneurs borrow money, learn of business opportunities, hear of ways to cut costs, find employees, and more. Many ethnic groups have a cultural tradition of pooling money, which borrowers can then use to start or expand their businesses (Light 1973). In this way, they can get loans despite a lack of experience or collateral that makes affordable bank loans difficult to acquire. Some work in a co-ethnic's store to acquire the skills to run their own.

Owners often hire co-ethnics as employees. Family members – mostly spouses and children – are an invaluable source of labor. Beyond that, the availability of overseas labor interested in immigrating to work in small businesses has spurred business success. This migration results from the severe global economic inequalities impacting Asians in post-colonial and/or war-ravaged countries (Dhingra 2012). Owners prefer such persons because they are easy to find, are assumed to be more trustworthy because of a shared ethnic tie and shared networks, and can be paid less because workers supposedly appreciate a culturally familiar work environment, lack other options, and can learn the business as apprentices (Portes and Zhou 1992). Immigrants also may benefit from government support, which facilitates business ownership.

Asian-American heterogeneity

It is important to note that there are differences across Asian ethnic groups in terms of which groups are most likely to engage in self-employment, how educational backgrounds factor in self-employment, and even the types of businesses that different Asian ethnic groups open. Vietnamese, Japanese, Indian, Chinese, and especially Korean Americans are twice or more as likely to be self-employed than other Southeast Asians and Filipinos.[20] One study finds that entrepreneurship among Korean Americans is higher than among Chinese, Indians, and Vietnamese (Kim, Hurh, and Fernandez 1989). Moreover, among Koreans engaged in self-employment, it is those who completed college in Korea who are most likely to open up their own businesses. This is in contrast to the Chinese, Indians, and Vietnamese. Among these groups, those without a college education are more likely to be entrepreneurs.

Several factors explain these differences. Among them is included the uneven availability of ethnic-based economic and social capital that is, in part, due to cultural differences between Asian ethnics. Koreans, for example, can rely on co-ethnic resources in the form of *kye*, hence, although there may be other opportunities open to them, more Korean college-educated people are engaged in self-employment than other Asian ethnic groups of similar backgrounds. Meanwhile, among other Asian ethnics, it is especially those without a college education who become entrepreneurs. This reflects, perhaps, some of the struggles that non-college educated people are likely to face in the labor market, a struggle that may be especially acute for immigrants without college education.

Asian-American small-business ownership also varies by generation. Rarely do members of the second generation continue in the same business as their parents (Kasinitz et al. 2009; Dae Young Kim 2006; Rangaswamy 2007). Those who do credit the financial and social capital that their parents have built up as motivation for choosing the same industry (Dhingra 2012). The second generation enters self-employment at a lower rate than do immigrants but, when they do, they are more likely to work in professional services (Le 2012).

Opportunities for small-business ownership

Immigrants need more than the motivation and the means to start businesses. The opportunities for a profitable business must present itself. Immigrants tend towards businesses that larger capitalists avoid because they serve niche markets, have low economy of scale, have low startup costs, and/or have unstable customer demand (Aldrich and Waldinger 1990). These constraints also lead immigrant entrepreneurs to choose particular kinds of business: those that serve their own group within an ethnic enclave and those that serve natives ignored by larger corporations due to their marginal status (Zhou 2004). The former are referred to as ethnic enclave owners and the latter as middleman minorities.

Ethnic enclave owners provide services and goods particular to the ethnic group which mainstream stores do not carry. Examples include grocery stores, travel agents, restaurants, beauty salons, tax services, and more. In such stores, owners recreate familiar spaces for customers through the selection of items, ethnic language spoken by employees, understanding of the nuance within a culture, and more (Bonus 2000). The problem this creates for owners, however, is a limited clientele. They become almost exclusively dependent on their ethnic group, especially when in segregated enclaves.

Middleman minorities, on the other hand, cater to natives despite their distinct culture and interests (Cobas 1989; Duany 1989; Zenner 1982). Rather than serving all groups, however, they traditionally serve native minorities abandoned by larger corporations. Middleman minorities connect big capital to these customers, thereby taking the risks that big capital is not willing to take but still giving them considerable profit (Bonacich 1973). Given the small scale of their businesses and the costs associated with doing business in lower-income areas, owners often charge more than larger chains do for similar items. Not all immigrant-owned businesses catering to non-ethnics are middleman minorities (Yoon 1997). Those that are not often rely on transnational links to suppliers in the homeland who can deliver specialized goods at discount rates. Others are engaged in franchised businesses, such as motels, donut shops, sandwich stores, and so on which cater to various clientele, depending on their location.

Tensions and racialized subjugations

Hostility towards middleman-minority owners is not uncommon, in part due to a felt lack of respect from owners and more generally from a frustration with poor living conditions (Min 1996). Much of the focus on immigrant owners' problems has been created by resentful customers, in particular African Americans (as we will discuss in chapter 10). As immigrant owners become framed as "model minorities" in contrast to poor minority customers, tensions can increase (Abelmann and Lie 1995). In response, owners find ways to promote civility with customers. For instance, they will hire employees from the neighborhood (in addition to co-ethnics) to mediate between customers and themselves (Lee 2002). They actively present their stores as non-ethnic in order to avoid hassles from customers or a loss of customers (Dhingra 2012).

Owners encounter a host of other problems besides handling employees and customers. Ethnic entrepreneurship may serve the interests of big capital more than those of the ethnic group (Bonacich 1987). Large corporations often enjoy access to otherwise hard-to-reach customers as immigrants open up businesses in low-revenue spaces. Yet owners engage in self-exploitation, working very long hours in all types of physical and intellectual work. Their public image suffers as well. Those in enclaves can be framed as involved in dirty, unhealthy, underhanded businesses (Shah 2001). Middleman minorities are said to overcharge customers, run businesses that spread social illnesses (like drinking), and not give enough back to the community (Min 1996). According to critics, such businesses should be torn down or given to native minority owners who presumably are locked out of business ownership due to immigrants (Lee 2002). Cultural barriers can also cause problems with suppliers (Min 2008).

Owners also suffer problems within their own community due to intense competition from co-ethnics, since they occupy the same few niches and rely on the same networks (Yoon 1997). Such dilemmas threaten not only the profitability of stores but also the sense of community with co-ethnics, who are one's business competition (Dhingra 2009). Family relations become strained as children have to contribute to the store in lieu of leisure time (Song 1999). It is common for children to assist in the store but they often show little interest in taking it over, due to the long hours and low wages that the work involves (Kasinitz et al. 2009). Wives often complain of a lack of respect for their contributions to the store. Rather than being treated as an equal partner or significant wage earner for the family, their work often becomes read as an extension of their domestic duties (Westwood and Bhachu 1988).

The resulting picture of entrepreneurship belies the neoliberal ideal of family harmony and economic security. While many small businesses fare reasonably well, and families mostly can see their children attain higher education, business life is marked by economic uncertainty, long hours, escalating costs, family sacrifices (e.g. living in one's workplace and use of family labor) and other tensions. In addition, business relations can constrain ethnic community formation. So Asian Americans are not necessarily excluded from economic mobility, but their means of attaining it involves a certain amount of subjugation. This subjugation occurs alongside the mobility that small-business ownership can offer. By relying on ethnic resources (rather than assimilating), available opportunities, and fortunate circumstances, individuals can start their own businesses. This may offer advantages to otherwise struggling families but no financial guarantees.

The poor

An emphasis on the working lives of Asian Americans should not neglect those in poverty, including both the employed and those out of work. As noted above, Asian Americans suffer a higher rate of poverty than whites. The presumption is that poverty is the domain of the unemployed. Yet even employed individuals can be earning below the poverty line. Many Asian Americans find themselves with limited income due to their low educational levels, lack of English skills, reliance on co-ethnic networks for jobs, and other such factors (Ambrose Lee 2010). For instance, ethnic enclave jobs may offer little remuneration. Even if they arrive in the United States with work skills, they may not find employment that uses those skills. Poverty is exacerbated as families send money back home (Sacramento and de la Cruz 2010).

Unemployment

Unemployed Asian Americans suffer economic disparities as well. The causes of unemployment among Asian Americans are those common to other groups: lack of education and job-related skills, lack of transportation to the suburbs where job growth takes place, economic recessions that limit job opportunities, family needs, and so on. Poor English skills and a lack of cultural assimilation into the United States exacerbate these problems. Lacking health insurance makes the unemployed and even the employed vulnerable for greater setbacks. Untreated medical conditions can handicap work abilities. Medical bills can lead to bankruptcy. "Overall, approximately 18 percent of all Asian Americans lack health insurance, compared to 11 percent of non-Hispanic whites" (Blazer and Broder 2010: 520). Many Asian Americans work in jobs that do not offer insurance, including those in the secondary labor market and the self-employed. With that in mind, it is not surprising that almost half of Korean and Southeast-Asian Americans work in positions without insurance (ibid.).

Welfare assistance and lack thereof

Public assistance programs designed to alleviate poverty have become more difficult for Asian Americans to access. The Personal Responsibility Work Opportunity Reconciliation Act (PRWORA), passed by Congress and signed into law in 1996 by President Bill Clinton, reduced welfare opportunities for everyone and was particularly punitive to undocumented immigrants and immigrant women (Fujiwara 2008). Even documented immigrants who had yet to become citizens were denied benefits that were available to citizens. This was part of a broader curtailment of immigrants' rights generally.

A few months later, the Illegal Immigration Reform and Immigrant Responsibility Act was enacted. This made it easier to deport immigrants, again even those with documentation. It also made it even more difficult for immigrants to qualify for public assistance. "Qualified persons" typically refers to, but are not limited to, lawful permanent residents, refugees, and those granted asylum. Qualified persons must wait five years until they can receive benefits (Blazer and Broder 2010).[21] For "qualified aliens" who arrived on or after August 22, 1996, "In general, [they] will not be eligible for any federal means-tested public benefit for a period of five years" (Fragomen 1997: 448). This does not apply to refugees and a few other categories of persons, such as members of the armed forces and their nuclear families. Unfortunately, welfare programs have made it harder for limited English proficiency (LEP) immigrants to find work that will get them out of poverty. They have only 24 months to find jobs, but taking LEP classes is not considered work, even though they are necessary to find work (Sacramento and de la Cruz 2010).

Non-qualified persons, comprised mostly of undocumented immigrants, may receive emergency Medicaid, depending on which state they live in (Blazer and Broder 2010). Overall, the state has drawn stricter lines around who "deserves" basic benefits, with immigrants needing to demonstrate a commitment to the nation. More research should be done on this key section of the population who suffer the brunt of economic inequality.

Conclusion

Asian Americans' class status impacts not only their current economic conditions but also their chances of future mobility, their relationships with co-ethnics and other groups, and how they are seen by individuals and the state. While often depicted either as professionals within science and math-related fields or as small-business owners, in reality Asian Americans encompass a range of professions and economic levels, including being overrepresented below the poverty line. Across each type of occupational category, Asian Americans experience both opportunities and challenges, which vary by gender. Poverty remains a key concern. And much of their class status depends less on any individual effort and more on immigration laws that structure who enters the United States and the communities they join. These findings refute simplistic "model minority" assumptions that individuals can rise within a completely meritocratic America through hard work and by valuing mobility. But the findings do not lead to clear conclusions. Diverse theories of adaptation and their contrasting predictions on mobility find merit. What is consistent is that race and immigration laws continue to shape work lives across all occupational sectors. Because one's class status so sharply influences one's life chances, how Asian Americans experience the workplace and labor markets deserves continued research.

Discussion questions

- What role do social networks play in the occupational outcomes for Asian Americans, and how do they differ across groups?
- Immigrant women often feel optimistic about their class chances compared to opportunities back in the homeland, but at the same time they confront a number of barriers within the United States. How should their class outcomes be understood?
- How is it possible that a racial group with overall high average education levels still has such a large number of people living in poverty?

5 Education

The following quote comes from a newspaper article profiling successful Asian American students, enticingly titled "Are Asian American Kids Smarter than Everyone Else":

> Jackie Chung can feel the pull of Confucius, his scholarly influence embedded in the generations before and manifest now in Jackie's own pursuit of excellence – on this day, seated in a demanding physics class at Strongsville High School. . . . The ancient Chinese teacher's profound philosophies held scholarship as a way to honor self and family. Honor family, avoid shame.[1]

The "model minority's" cultural background presumably enables Asian-American youth, whether 1.5, second, or later generations, to advance in school. Even children whose parents lack a high school diploma have been known to do well relative to other groups in their circumstances. The notion of a suburban Chinese-American student feeling pulled by Confucius is at best a great exaggeration and at worst a damaging stereotype. Regardless of the reason, Asian Americans have been considered as doing well in school.

The key questions this chapter attempts to address are: are aspects of the "model minority" myth actually true? Are 1.5, second-, and later-generation Asian Americans doing as well in school as commonly imagined? If so, how so and, if not, what can be done to assist achievement? Furthermore, looking behind educational progress statistics, what is life actually like for Asian American students?

We find that while the big picture is one of educational integration, with some exceptions (discussed below), the details of scholastic achievement among Asian Americans question the assimilation perspective, both in terms of how they have achieved and how much they have achieved. Instead as predicted by segmented assimilation theory, Asian Americans do well partly because they rely on their own ethnic community rather than fully integrating. In addition, the known success of Asian Americans becomes self-perpetuating: teachers stereotype Asian Americans as doing well at school, which can help performance. The high education and human capital levels, not just community structure, of many immigrant parents is also critical to achievement, which is overlooked by the "model minority" stereotype. Furthermore, despite – or possibly because – of the expectation of success for Asian Americans, Asian-American students encounter a range of problems that go unnoticed. Asian Americans suffer from severe mental health problems and from racism, both among classmates and institutionally. Also, as noted in chapter 4, not all Asian-American groups perform well scholastically. Overall, the Asian-American experience sheds light on educational achievement more broadly and on related issues, such as affirmative action and college admittance.

Asian Americans' educational achievements and struggles

Practically the same number of Asian Americans (immigrant and US-born) as all Americans age 25 and older finish high school. Yet beyond that stage, major differences arise. Half of Asian Americans have a college degree, compared to 28.5% of Americans as a whole.[2] And 20.7% of Asian Americans have completed a graduate (e.g. master's) or professional degree, almost double the 10.6% of Americans generally (ibid.). This general trend and ensuing stereotyping, however, cover up meaningful details that question Asian Americans' perceived achievement. For instance, rather than attending elite private schools, most Asian Americans in higher education are at public universities. And they are distributed evenly across two-year and four-year colleges.[3]

Moreover, educational attainment differs sharply by gender and ethnicity, and such differences belie a simplistic narrative of "model minority" achievement. When considering all Asian Americans (i.e. both immigrants and US-born), there is quite a heterogeneity of scholastic outcomes. As of 2006, an alarming number of Southeast-Asian American adults did not finish high school: 40% of Hmong, 38% of Laotian, and 35% of Cambodian.[4] Based on 2008 American Community Survey data, there exists a wide range of educational outcomes for different Asian-American immigrant ethnic groups (Kao, Vaquera, and Goyette 2013). Asian Indians are at the higher end of the spectrum, with 70% of those aged 25 and older having earned a bachelor's degree while 91% at least complete high school (ibid.). At the lower end of the spectrum, however, are Hmong, Cambodian, and Laotian Americans: among those aged 25 and older, only 12% have graduated with college degrees and about 60–9% have completed high school (ibid.). These figures make them more comparable to Hispanics in terms of educational achievement. Vietnamese Americans are a unique case, in that just over a quarter have not completed high school, compared to 15% of all Americans (ibid.). But a percentage equal to all Americans has finished college (27.7%).

These troubling statistics refer to all Southeast-Asian Americans, that is, first, 1.5, second, and later generations. While Southeast-Asian American children often do not fare as well in school as their Asian-American peers, they still show mobility. For instance, while Hmong parents have very low levels of education, even lower than African Americans, their children have educational attainment on a par with African Americans and are even more likely to have a college degree than are African Americans (Sakamoto and Woo 2007).

Explaining US Asian Americans' educational outcomes

With the general trend of high achievement, it is not surprising that much of the conversation regarding Asian Americans and education has asked why they do well. The reasons why Asian Americans raised in the United States do well are the same as why any student does well: having parents with advanced educations, supportive teachers, schools with resources, supportive peers, community oversight, and a motivation to do well. But Asian Americans have achieved even when they were not in high-resourced schools or even without any of these supportive factors. And within the same school they may perform at a more advanced level than other groups. What is going on, and why do some Asian Americans achieve more than others?

Genetics used to be a common explanation but has long been disputed, even as faulty attempts arise on occasion to further the argument (Fong 2008). Historically, racial disparities between blacks and whites have been attributed to an inferior genetic makeup among African Americans. They supposedly have lower IQs and a higher propensity to commit crime, for instance. This perception of racial difference has been disputed since the 1940s, when evolutionary scientists and anthropologists argued against the notion of genetically definable races.[5]

Cultural explanations and their limits

Today, few people continue to claim that racial disparities are due to genetic differences. Instead, culture has replaced genetics as the key factor explaining racial differences. Culture is a more enlightened approach than a biological determinism, that is, the idea that one's genetic inheritance ultimately shapes an individual's life course, for culture is known to be subject to environmental factors. Still, cultural arguments have traces of outdated racial notions, for in practice culture often is assumed to be static, much like genetics. Inequalities between groups are attributed to deep cultural differences. Indeed, as some sociologists have argued, cultural arguments are just a new form of "color-blind racism" that has emerged in the wake of the civil rights movement in the United States whereby "culture" simply stands in for "race" (Bonilla-Silva 2003). This has the effect of blaming inequality on the disenfranchised group's own cultural deficiencies, rather than on the challenges within its environment.

Also, cultural accounts cannot explain substantial differences between and within Asian groups. If Asians were inherently prone to excel, one would find consistently high levels of accomplishment. The quote at the front of the chapter suggests this. Yet even Asian-American ethnic groups known for their high achievement, such as Chinese Americans, have substantial variation. For instance, almost 45 percent of immigrant adults and one-fourth of US-born adults have only a high-school education or less (Louie 2004). Nor is Asian or Asian American culture static. Chinese Americans were not known for advocating or exhibiting high educational achievement before World War II, when opportunities for Asian Americans became more widespread.

A cultural values explanation for achievement also lacks credence, given that it has been applied to many diverse racial groups. This limits its explanatory significance. As Eric Liu reminds us, "One way to explain the abnormal ambition of a group is to racialize it. Hard work and sacrifice? Deferral of gratification? Devotion to education? Today, anyone will tell you, these are 'Asian values.' But, remember, only a few generations ago these were 'Jewish values.' And once upon a time, of course, they were 'Protestant values'" (1998: 158). And, even if "Asian values" exist, it remains difficult to define what exactly they are. For instance, not all Southeast Asians follow Confucian teachings. Nor do all groups stress an "authoritarian" or "training" parenting style, discussed below.

Another reason why culture does not suffice as an explanation involves the role of noncultural factors. Irrespective of ethnic culture, a supportive family unit, including intact families, facilitates educational success, as does higher socioeconomic achievement (Portes and Rumbaut 2001). A family's socioeconomic status has a durable effect on school performance over other relevant factors, such as class size, school size, or percentage of student attendance (Caldas 1993). In fact, independent of one's own family's income, the higher the family income of one's peer group, the better one performs academically (Caldas and Bankston 1997). English-language skills are another major determinant of educational success (Kao, Vaquera, and Goyette 2013).

This critique of culture does not mean it should be ignored or does not matter. Certain cultures are known for emphasizing education. For instance, in Korea education has very high value since it is one of the only ways to advance economically, and the challenges of gaining admittance to competitive universities leads families to prioritize schoolwork and preparation (Kao, Vaquera, and Goyette 2013).

As we use culture to explain differences in educational outcomes, we must pay attention to the context in which groups operate and to the fact that cultures respond to circumstances. As Vivian Louie (2004) argued for Chinese Americans, their emphasis on authority and educational attainment became most active once they saw the openness of education in the United States and labor-market racism. Parental support, another presumed cultural attribute, is most effective when parents engage with the school, that is, when ethnic values turn into social capital with academic personnel.

Arguably more important than any one kind of cultural background in forming responsible children is having a shared cultural experience between children and parents. Children of immigrants can assimilate very quickly while their parents may not speak English, understand the norms, be able to drive, read their mail, or the like. Children take on adult tasks. When immigrant parents and their children experience such a dissonant acculturation, the educational achievement of the children suffers (Portes and Rumbaut 2001). Within a dissonant acculturation, parents often disagree with their children's choices and parents' authority is diminished.

Parenting styles

In order to better analyze the role of culture, it helps to break it down into discernible parts. Parenting styles are a key type of culture that shapes student outcomes. Much attention has been paid to the supposed "Tiger Mother" style of Asian parenting. Asian and Asian-American parents, in particular East Asian, practice what is commonly perceived to be a Confucian "authoritarian" parenting style, marked by top-down communication, strict orders, and limited opportunities for children's initiative (Gorman 1998). Paradoxically, among the general American population, the authoritarian parenting style has a mixed record in improving student achievement (Cohen and Rice 1997; Dornbusch et al. 1987). This has raised the question of why Asian Americans do well in school under these norms.

The answer may be that Asians are not authoritarian per se but instead utilize a "training" parenting style that, while similar to authoritarianism, involves more contact and involvement of parents with their children (Chao 1994). Also, Asian parents are less authoritarian when it comes to their children's school lives than in general (Leung, Lau, and Lam 1998). In other words, the authoritarian stereotype mischaracterizes a parenting style that sensitively pushes educational attainment. In fact, children of Asian immigrant parents with an overly strict, more clearly authoritarian style fared worse than those with more tolerant parents (ibid.). And, parenting styles for Asian Americans differ across generations, with immigrant parents less permissive than US-born Asian-American parents (Pong, Hao, and Gardner 2005).

More informative than authoritarianism are findings that Asian parents believe education requires a particular focus. Asian Americans tend to push their children to work hard at school and limit distractions that could interfere (e.g. sports, boyfriends, etc.) (Louie 2004). Among Chinese Americans, for instance, this attitude can be traced back to a cultural history of educational success requiring sacrifice and hard work as opposed to being framed as enjoyable or resulting from natural intelligence. This belief makes the work required to do well at school more accepted by students.

Numerous Asian-American youths tell the same anecdotes about always having to study. Even within families that own small businesses, parents often stressed that their children's education came first and store work second (Song 1999). Such youths still faced obstacles balancing their multiple commitments, but few felt that their parents prioritized their stores over education. This was largely the case because parents hoped an advanced education would preempt children from a comparable future of intense labor.

Asian-American parents are also often more involved in their children's education than are other groups, a major boost to student success (Anguiano and Viramontez 2004). While parents rarely discuss the particulars of classes, they stress the importance of college, assist with homework, and discuss the need to do well for the sake of the family (Kao 2004). Such engagement with and encouragement of education contrasts a caricatured authoritarian approach that privileges results over motivation or process.

Not coincidentally, parents without the resources to be highly involved in school or assist in their children's homework, such as those with lower educations, limited time, language ability, or understanding of the school system, cannot assist their children (Park et al. 2007). Southeast-Asian refugees, in particular those from the second wave of immigration, most commonly fit this profile. Cambodian-American youth typically struggle in school. Those who do well do not necessarily have parents who are more involved in schools. Still, their parents give their children moral support (Chhuon et al. 2010). These students also benefited from supportive teachers and a helpful school environment. In addition, such students credited their ethnic culture of "saving face" and not embarrassing the family with encouraging them to aim high in school rather than not try hard (so as to avoid failing and bringing shame on the family). In other words, much of what explains any student's educational outcomes applies to Asian Americans.

Community and structural factors

Supportive structural conditions assist students' educational success beyond family-level variables, as discussed in the above example of Cambodian-American youth. Such conditions may exist in a school, such as helpful teachers, advanced classes, a well-resourced infrastructure, and so on. And they may exist outside of the school in the ethnic community. As fitting segmented assimilation theory, youths do well in school when the lessons of their parents are reinforced by the broader community (Gibson 1988; Waters 1999). Zhou and Bankston (1998) found that Vietnamese youth in New Orleans with smaller extended families or limited community involvement fared worse than their co-ethnic peers with stronger networks. That is, parental and cultural values alone did not sufficiently motivate children to succeed in school (see also Bankston and Zhou 1995). Youths more conversant with their native culture, who were therefore more involved in their community, had higher educational attainment than other co-ethnics. Without community support, the youths approached school in a manner similar to their neighborhood peers, predominantly lower-income minorities who, in this case, did not excel at school (Ogbu 1987a).

Ethnic communities provide not only oversight and encouragement but also resources. For instance, working-class Asian Americans did better in school than their Latino peers living in the same neighborhoods because the Asian Americans had access to ethnic institutions created by middle class Asian Americans, such as after-school classes or language schools (Louie 2012; Zhou 2012). Test-preparation cram schools popular in China, Japan, and Korea have expanded in the United States to reach not only Asian Americans but more and more of the broader American public.[6] Youths without structured after-school activities fare worse scholastically. Without a broader academic and private support system, educational achievement becomes more difficult.

Having said this, class differences continue to impact Asian-American scholastic performance even when community support is available. Louie (2004) studied both working-class and upper-class Chinese Americans in New York City. The upper class Chinese Americans attended the elite Columbia University while working-class Chinese Americans attended the less prestigious Hunter College. Working-class students were more likely to work throughout college and to have older siblings who did not attend college at all.

So, as for other Asian Americans and students generally, Asian Americans' academic success comes from a combination of helpful parents, a motivation to succeed, a supportive academic space, a supportive community, and of course economic resources. Unfortunately, many students whose parents lack educational or cultural resources, such as English proficiency or community organizations, continue to struggle in school, even as parents push them to do well.

Attitudes towards school

While the above factors explain how Asian-American parents convey the importance of education, they do not explain why they value education so much in the first place. The correct question is not why some groups value education, for that implies that other groups do not, which is not true (Warikoo 2011). All groups value education but not all individuals have the same resources and experiences to act on these values or have schools that are trustworthy to offer quality education. Having said that, some groups consider education to be integral to their children's mobility and have the means to actualize it.

Instead of an "Asian culture," much of immigrant parents' emphasis on education is attributable to their "immigrant perspective." Asian immigrants, like immigrants generally, have an "immigrant optimism." They stress education because of a belief in the openness of the American educational system (Kao and Tienda 1995; Portes and Rumbaut 2001). For instance, second-generation Asian Americans have higher educational attainments than either immigrant or third-generation Asian Americans (Yang 2004). First- and second-generation immigrants are more likely to graduate high school and attend college than are the third generation of the same ethnic group, even controlling for class, family background, and other factors. This is especially the case for those who have strong English skills (Kao, Vaquera, and Goyette 2013). An inherent "Asian" culture cannot account for this.

An immigrant optimism in the education system is paralleled by an "immigrant pessimism" in the labor market, which further motivates educational investment (Louie 2004). Parents expect their children to encounter some discrimination in the workplace, which makes strong educational credentials all the more important as a means to combat it. Asian Americans generally lack a political voice. On the one hand, the 'Asian-American Movement' does not have the same visibility as it had in the past to be able to address issues of racism; on the other, Asian Americans are not fully integrated in the electoral process. Hence combating racism may require more individual effort (see chapter 11 for discussion of social movements and politics). A strong education, for some, can help in that regard as it empowers individuals by giving them cultural, social, and economic capital.

Similarly, Ogbu (1987b) argues that voluntary immigrants (in contrast with, say, political refugees or those with histories of forced migration), like most Asian Americans, have a generous attitude towards the school system and the country as a whole because they came of their own volition and do not resent whites from the outset. Nor are the poverty rates or other barriers affecting immigrants *necessarily* the result of racism from whites. Involuntary immigrants, like many African Americans, on the other hand are descended from former colonized or enslaved persons who resent whites for how they were brought here, and in turn do not trust white-dominated institutions, according to Ogbu. Involuntary immigrants do not see the school system as looking out for them. Refugees make an interesting case within Ogbu's highly influential binary system, for they are involuntary migrants but often do well in school over time. Southeast Asians who arrived as refugees have much in common with voluntary immigrants because they know that, in order to succeed, they must adopt a "tourist attitude" to the United States (Ogbu and Simons 1998). This means that they are willing to adopt standardized behaviors and expectations without fear that this will undermine their ethnic cultural commitments.

More than migration history, the length of time spent in under-resourced school districts affects students' perspectives on formal education. MacLeod (1995) found that white youths who grew up in a low-income, under-resourced neighborhood had a more cynical approach to school than a group of black youths who had arrived there more recently. So, as noted earlier, the economic conditions of one's neighborhood and upbringing shape one's approach to school, regardless of ethnicity.

Gendered perspectives on education

Immigrant parents tend either to emphasize educational attainment equally for boys and girls, or to prioritize it for boys. Yet, even when they want girls to receive the same educational opportunities as boys, it may be for gendered reasons. Immigrant parents, in particular those of lower class, believe their daughters need an education so as to take care of themselves and their families if necessary (Louie 2004; Zhou and

Bankston 1998). For this reason, parents invest in both genders' education equally. But girls still must perform disproportionately more domestic chores than boys because being a supportive mother and wife is still expected within dominant heteronormativity. These simultaneous pro-equality and anti-equality gestures create tensions for girls, who feel pulled in different directions by parental expectations.

Overall, the research on academic success and parental ethnic culture affirms the importance of economic and social resources, a supportive community, parental emphasis on high attainment, family involvement with the school system, faith in the school system due to limited historic discrimination, harmonious relations between generations, and recognition of the hard work necessary for achievement. When all of these pieces are in place, as they often are for tight-knit immigrant communities with reasonable resources and an intent to settle in the United States, the result supports a "model minority" outcome. But, as Eric Liu notes, these conditions are not particular to Asian Americans, many of whom do not attain high educational levels.

Children's motivations and struggles

The preceding discussion of Asian-American educational achievement concentrates on parents and ethnic communities, particularly their influence on children's academic achievement. But, of course, it is the academic success of the children that is under discussion here. How do they understand school and what motivates them to do well or not?

In large part, children recognize parental emphasis on education and internalize a motivation to succeed. This motivation has various sources. Youths understand that their parents immigrated to the United States and have made considerable sacrifices so as to provide them with educational opportunities, and so they feel pressured to achieve. For youths whose parents labor in working-class positions, they have accepted the parental belief that school success will enable them to avoid such work. Youths also want to make their families proud, which academic achievement does (Chhuon et al. 2010). For these same reasons, Asian Americans often choose technical fields, leading to well-paid jobs. Race also contributes to children's motivation to succeed. They recognize the parental message that education will best prepare them to deal with possible racial discrimination. Youths hope that good grades, a prestigious university, and a comfortable income – all markers of having "made it" in America – will help them and their families to be recognized as full citizens rather than as foreigners (Park 2005).

This internalized motivation to succeed manifests itself in the tangible effort that high-achieving Asian Americans put into their schoolwork. According to Hune (2002: 16), Asian Americans "spend more hours studying and take more academic courses in high school than other racial and ethnic groups, and this enhances their college eligibility." They are also less likely to skip school than are other racial groups (Wong 1995). Many obey the rules in schools and maintain disciplined behaviors in line with school and parental expectations (Warikoo 2011). Students (of any background) who do not adopt such an adult culture may still value education and want to achieve in school but engage in practices that undermine those efforts, such as fighting (ibid.).

Of course, not all Asian-American youths succeed to the same degree educationally. As noted above, those Asian Americans with more economic resources have an edge. Also, those with greater ties to their ethnic community tend more often to excel, as predicted by segmented assimilation theory. In fact, the longer that children of immigrants have been in the United States, for example being born here rather than recently immigrating, the fewer hours they put into their schoolwork and the less important they consider grades to be (Portes and Rumbaut 2001). Girls in particular demonstrate "significantly higher levels of interest and work effort" in school, for they are often less acculturated into American culture than boys (ibid.: 215).

Mental health challenges within the "model minority"

This motivation to succeed and the "model minority" stereotype, however, also contribute to problems for Asian-American students, not to mention the perceptions of other minority youth. Many of the challenges for Asian Americans involve mental health. For Asian Americans in particular, academic success is a very poor predictor of happiness and mental health. For instance, depression, anxiety, and low self-esteem are more common among Chinese-American youths than for either whites or Chinese peers in China (Zhou et al. 2003). Even more drastic, suicide has become a concern for Asian-American students. Asian-American girls aged 15–24 have higher rates of depression and suicide than peers of other racial groups (Qin, Way, and Mukherjee 2008). Second-generation Filipino Americans, for instance, can experience extreme anxiety and depression due in part to family pressures within transnational lifestyles, which are particularly stressful for females (Wolf 1997). And, more anecdotally, in 2005 Asian Americans at Cornell University constituted 50 percent of those committing suicide but comprised only 17 percent of the student population (Qin, Way, and Mukherjee 2008). Even compared to other minorities, Asian Americans often have the most fragile mental health (Way and Chen 2000).

A most extreme and graphic case of depression has been Seung Hui Cho, a student at Virginia Tech who murdered himself and 32 others on campus on April 16, 2007. It was the deadliest shooting rampage in US history. Counselors, teachers, and peers described Cho as mentally unstable and isolated, fitting the classic profile of such a murderer. His rampage was not necessarily tied to his ethnicity. But his actions illustrate how destructive the outcome of depression can be. While he received counseling before arriving at Virginia Tech (though it is often assumed and there is some evidence indicating that Asian immigrant parents do not always address issues of mental health in their children, this was not the case with Cho) and his teachers at Virginia Tech raised concerns about his mental stability, less extreme cases often go unnoticed.

The causes of such poor mental health include both family and external factors, often tied to the "model minority" stereotype. With parents pushing their children so hard to do well, youth internalize high expectations. Even when they do well in school, and especially when they do not, they can feel inadequate and near-failures. For instance, Chinese-American college students felt worse about their achievements than comparable Dominican-American peers (Louie 2006). They compared themselves to other Chinese Americans, whom they imagined were more successful, while Dominican Americans compared themselves to peers back in the homeland who presumably performed worse. So the "model minority" image becomes the unrealistic measuring stick for Asian Americans.

Parenting styles, peer relations, and self-esteem

Parenting styles also impact the well-being of students. Chinese-American teenagers whose parents preached obedience to authority suffered from greater distress than those whose parents also nurtured respect for elders, an appreciation of education, and developing a sense of self (Qin 2008). The different parenting styles often varied by class status, with middle-class parents having more time to attend to their children and working-class parents unable to do so, which led them to rely on more strict parenting strategies. Tied to parenting styles, children's and parents' degree of shared acculturation affects self-esteem. For instance, youth who are fluent bilinguals, like their parents, have much higher levels of self-esteem than those who cannot speak their native tongue (Portes and Rumbaut 2001). Among a wide sample of Latino, West Indian, and Asian-American youth, girls reported lower self-esteem and higher depression than boys (ibid.). Reasons may include the stricter parental oversight they received, the stress on good grades, and sexist treatment of adolescent girls generally relative to boys.

Factors external to the family also contributed to mental challenges. A study on Chinese-American adolescents found that discrimination from peers contributed to lower self-esteem (Rivas-Drake, Hughes, and Way 2008). Minority peers can be jealous of the positive attention and image that Asian Americans receive from teachers. In addition, those adolescents who believed Chinese Americans had a weaker public image, possibly as nerds or wimps or unattractive, were more likely to report depressive symptoms. Asian Americans have been found to have higher levels of family conflict and social stress than other minorities and especially than whites, but they also lack resources to handle such challenges (Choi, Meininger, and Roberts 2006). Also, the stresses associated with the acculturation process can lower Asian Americans' self-esteem (Rhee, Chang, and Rhee 2003).

As these problems worsen, they often go untreated. Because Asian Americans rarely seek out psychological counseling and because the "model minority" stereotype suggests that the community has no troubles, they do not receive the help they need (Suzuki 2002). Nor may they be offered sufficient academic advice, based on the belief that they are already organized and driven (Hune 2002).

English-language difficulties

Another significant set of challenges facing Asian Americans concerns English-language difficulties. The importance of English skills cannot be overstated. Strong English skills improve school performance, in particular in verbal as opposed to math and science fields, and overall grade point average (Liu et al. 2009). English proficiency among immigrant parents also facilitates youths' school success as well as their mental health. When parents and children speak English in addition to their native tongue, generational relations are much smoother (Liu et al. 2009; Portes and Rumbaut 2001). In fact, it was argued at the Supreme Court that Chinese-American students in San Francisco were not receiving adequate assistance due to their limited English proficiency. The case, *Lau v. Nichols*, established bilingual education as a student right: without it, students are denied a full education (Wang 1983).

Yet, for Asian Americans who arrive after puberty, as is especially common for Southeast Asian refugees, learning English remains a severe challenge (Ima and Rumbaut 1995). Not only do they arrive late in life for fluent English-language development, but their parents typically speak little English and are struggling economically. The bilingual programs in schools are often limited, with children sent to special education programs rather than receiving the direct language support they need (Ima and Rumbaut 1995). As Southeast-Asian American youth get older, they mostly speak in their native tongue with their parents but overall prefer to speak English (Portes and Rumbaut 2001). Nor are these challenges limited to Southeast Asians. For instance, in Seattle approximately 40% of all Asian-American high-school students in the 1986–7 school year scored less than 50% in the state's reading exam, placing them "at risk" academically (Pang 1995). A greater percentage of Chinese, Filipino, Indian, Korean, and Southeast-Asian Americans scored below 50% than did whites.

Struggling to find help

The "model minority" stereotype covers up and limits those struggling academically. As a backlash against the stereotype, those Asian-American students who struggle academically frame their successful peers as "geeks." Rather than emulate them, they instead embrace a countercultural style in order to be seen as "cool" by others (Chiu 2007). Those who struggle may have to repeat grades, attain weaker grades, drink alcohol and smoke, and be suspended from school (Choi 2008).

Those students who struggle utilize few school resources. Instead, they often report feeling isolated or associate with peers who are also struggling (Lew 2006). In college, Asian Americans do not engage faculty for help as frequently as white students, even those whites who perform well. This is partly because Asian Americans are overrepresented in larger universities where faculty–student interactions are fewer, partly because of poor language skills and partly because faculty tend to assume that Asian-American students are academically self-disciplined and do not need assistance (Kim, Chang, and Park 2009). In general, students who interact more often with faculty receive higher grades and enjoy college more, which puts Asian Americans at risk on these measures. In addition, Asian Americans report racial tensions, such as bullying or violence, from peers at school, mostly African Americans and Latinos, as mentioned above (Rivas-Drake, Hughes, and Way 2008; Rosenbloom and Niobe 2004). Such interracial tension takes place within a larger racialized atmosphere. African Americans and Latinos often report racism from their teachers. They are seen as deviants, unruly, lazy, and the like. Asian Americans, on the other hand, are framed within the positive, model-minority stereotype in their teachers' eyes, which makes them a population whose problems may be ignored. This stereotyping, along with possible preferential treatment from teachers, exacerbates tensions with other minorities.

Possible quotas and affirmative action

Asian Americans face academic hurdles not only when they do poorly in school but also when they do well. In response to the increasing number of Asian-American students in higher education, some major universities instituted informal quotas in the 1980s for the number of Asian Americans they would accept (Wang 1995). University of California, Berkeley, University of California, Los Angeles, Stanford University, Massachusetts Institute of Technology, Harvard University, and Yale University were accused of this practice. This was a flashback to the quotas placed at top medical schools on Jewish Americans soon before World War II. Asian-American leaders recognized the possibility of quotas at UC Berkeley as the number of admitted Chinese Americans dropped by 30 percent between 1984 and 1985, despite predictions of their increased enrollment (ibid.). In addition, UCLA admissions officials wrote a memo, not meant for outside publication, indicating concern over the decline of white students due in part to the rise of Asian Americans. In a strange twist on the Supreme Court case, *The Regents of the University of California v. Bakke* of 1978, which supported affirmative action by allowing universities to take race into account when selecting students, race was now being used to assist whites. Asian Americans had become the problem. The "model minority" became the "yellow peril." Asian Americans were heralded when they achieved and then discriminated against when they "overachieved," that is, when they threatened the hegemony, or dominance, of white students in higher education.

In response to accusations of quotas, universities denied institutionalized racial discrimination. They stated that their selection process sought a more diverse student body and moved to criteria that relied less on grades and instead incorporated nonacademic factors, such as extracurricular interests, geographic diversity, and alumni parents. This change in criteria limited Asian Americans. Another rationale by universities in effect blamed Asian Americans for their own lack of admittance. Asian Americans tend to major in business and technical fields so they compete with one another for few slots. But Asian Americans were admitted at lower rates than whites, regardless of their intended major, for instance at Stanford University. Even Asian American applicants in the humanities, where Asian Americans are not overrepresented, saw their admittance rate drop.

Political conservatives who agreed that unfair quotas limited Asian American admittance blamed affirmative action, using the logic that reserving spots for African Americans, Latinos, and Filipinos was taking away opportunities for other Asian Americans (Omi and Takagi 1996).[7] In response, Asian Americans supportive of affirmative action argued that racial diversity was not at odds with meritocracy. It is possible to reserve spots for qualified affirmative action recipients and use a complete meritocratic system for others, in which Asian Americans should not face quotas, the goal being a diverse, strong student body.

These activists blamed anti-Asian bias of the late 1970s and 1980s for the downturn in enrollments (Takagi 1992). Asian Americans were seen to be taking over universities and the US-educated elite, just as they were taking over the iconic US auto industry. Evidence for this racialized analysis was found in the cultural sphere. For instance, Massachusetts Institute of Technology (MIT) had been nicknamed "Made In Taiwan," University of California, Los Angeles (UCLA) as "University of Caucasians Lost among Asians," University of California, Irvine (UCI) as "University of Chinese Immigrants," and so on (Okihiro 1994). Ultimately, Asian-American activists and their allies called for more transparent admittance criteria and for an end to any informal quota system, without a challenge to affirmative action. The basis of their argument remained that race might be a factor in selecting students but must be used with the goal of promoting racial equality and not hurting minorities.

Asian Americans and the affirmative action debate

While many Asian Americans supported affirmative action when defending their own interests, other Asian Americans have critiqued desegregation policies as a barrier to their equality. Most notably, the San Francisco Unified School District held that no single ethnic/racial group could comprise more than 40 percent of the student body, so as to prevent racial segregation. This decision stemmed from a city-wide school desegregation policy pushed by the NAACP in 1983. In federal case *Brian Ho, Patrick Wong, & Hilary Chen v. SFUSD*, Chinese-American parents protested that the policy of the San Francisco United School District violated the US Constitution's Equal Protection Clause by unfairly limiting the number of admitted Chinese Americans and evaluating them using higher criteria than for other students. It was doubly unfair to limit Chinese Americans since they were a racial minority, according to the plaintiffs. In effect, Chinese Americans were protesting desegregation policies and arguing that civil rights should be evaluated at the individual rather than the group level, for if a policy infringes any individual's opportunities, such as attending a desired school, it is unconstitutional, even if it promotes a group's equality, as it might African Americans or Latinos (Robles 2006). Eventually, the lawsuit was settled along the lines that race could be considered but might no longer be a dominant factor in selecting admissions within the San Francisco Unified School District (Wu 2003). As seen here, Asian Americans have been at the center of court decisions on the role of race in education.

While critiquing affirmative action in some spaces, Asian Americans have championed it in others when advantageous to them, such as in police and fire departments (Wu 2003). But Asian Americans cannot have it both ways. They cannot argue against affirmative action programs and then push for programs that promote them as Asian Americans (ibid.). The inconsistency threatens to undermine critiques of the glass ceiling. As discussed in the previous chapter, oftentimes the glass ceiling results not from overt prejudice or discrimination but from the normal workings of business culture and networks. Arguing against such practices on behalf of Asian Americans means that businesses should pay attention to Asian Americans as a racial group. This would ensure that they are not being overlooked within the standard course of promotions. However, such a focus on Asian Americans as a group would contradict the position against any desegregation plans. Even if Asian Americans deserve to be hired in fields in which they are currently underrepresented or to be promoted above the glass ceiling, making that happen often requires direct attention to them, just as direct attention needs to be paid to other minorities within higher education selection. So, Asian Americans will face challenges as they try to work both ends of the "model minority" stereotype, claiming that they are model groups at some points but mistreated minorities at others. As legal scholar Frank Wu (2003) argues, it is in their interests to work with other minorities more consistently. While Asian Americans critique affirmative action, it mostly benefits whites, for whites make up the largest application pool for colleges and most jobs.

Asian American Studies and the Asian-American Movement

It was the children of earlier generations of low-wage Asian-American immigrants who participated in struggles to increase the admission of Asian Americans and other students of color into college beginning in the late 1960s. These educational struggles were part of the broader Asian-American movement that emerged at that time, as discussed in chapter 3. Increased university admission was one of the key demands of the San Francisco State College Strike, led by the interracial coalition of which Asian Americans were part, called the Third World Liberation Front (TWLF), in 1968.

The Third World Liberation Front

The TWLF fought for more opportunities for young people of color to get access to higher education but, just as importantly, the strike called for a radical redefinition of college and university education. Student activists believed that quality higher education (i.e. professional training in fields like medicine, business or law, even liberal arts education) was being reserved for whites. Meanwhile, if they were given access to education beyond high school at all, people of color were being confined to education in the trades. In short, higher education was organized in the United States in such a way that whites were given the skills that would allow them to occupy privileged class positions, as professionals while people of color would be confined to lower-skilled, lower-status jobs (Umemoto 1989).

In addition to fighting for increased numbers of students of color on the San Francisco State University campus, the TWLF demanded a transformation in the very content and purpose of the university's education. They called for ethnic studies courses to be taught by community-based scholars for the purpose of providing students of color with the skills to be able to contribute to the uplift of their communities. The strike at San Francisco would inspire many similar actions at colleges and universities around the country (Liu, Geron, and Lai 2008).

Formation of Asian American Studies

Struggles for increased admittance would ultimately give rise to affirmative action programs in colleges and universities. Moreover, these struggles led to the establishment of ethnic studies programs. At San Francisco State University, the TWLF-led strike brought about the establishment of the College of Ethnic Studies which would also house the Department of Asian American Studies. Other universities across the nation during this period of time followed San Francisco State University's example (Umemoto 1989). By 1979, a critical mass of Asian American scholars had formed the Association for Asian American Studies (AAAS). As a professional association, the AAAS seeks to advance the teaching and research of Asian Americans at institutions of higher learning. Its formation is evidence of the increasing numbers of Asian Americanists joining the professorate and producing knowledge about Asian Americans from a range of disciplinary perspectives.

Student struggles for Asian American Studies, however, have continued well into the present day at universities across the country, especially in places experiencing increases in their Asian-American populations. In the Midwest, for example, students fought for Asian American Studies programs to be established in the late 1980s and throughout the 1990s. Engaging in sit-ins, hunger strikes, demonstrations, petitions and other forms of contentious politics, students were successful in their aims. In 1989, the University of Michigan was the first mid-western university to establish an Asian American Studies program. Other universities in the region followed suit. As Asian American Studies has been successfully institutionalized across the country as a field of study, it has become more legitimized. Students can minor or even major in Asian American Studies through Asian American Studies programs and departments in some institutions, while others may benefit from taking Asian American Studies courses taught in more traditional disciplines like English, history or sociology. Meanwhile, the AAAS continues to provide a space of support for Asian-American scholars and other Asian Americanists as well as an institutionalized presence for the field in the American academy.

An area of the academy needing support is Asian American representation among university administration and for K-12 education as well. Fewer than 1 percent of the nation's college/university presidents is Asian American.[8] A growing number are deans but this is still an area that needs focus. Struggles for Asian American Studies indicate that higher education is not necessarily a site where Asian Americans have been fully integrated. At the K-12 level, Asian American Studies remains relatively absent, in particular outside of California. AAAS has worked with local K-12 teachers to promote that education. Other institutions, such as the Asian Pacific American Center at the Smithsonian Institution, have created curricula for middle schools on particular ethnic groups.

Conclusion

The segmented assimilation theory is supported in the research on Asian Americans' educational attainment, along with other factors generally attributed to student success (regardless of students' ethnic community), such as well-resourced schools and highly educated parents. In the case of Asian Americans, it must be underscored that the 1965 Immigration Act favored highly skilled and educated applicants. The relative privilege that post-1965 immigrants enjoyed in their home countries has had a major impact on their ability to integrate economically into the United States, which in turn has had positive impacts on their children's educational attainment. Community support, engaged parents, a motivation to overcome barriers, and other factors combine with economic and educational resources of parents and schools to explain achievement. But the "model minority" stereotype disguises problems: mental health challenges, a backlash against Asian Americans' achievements, those struggling academically and linguistically, and the fewer administrative positions in higher education that might address and remedy these problems. Why students excel in schools or not will continue to arouse public debate, and Asian Americans will be part of that conversation. Better understanding of the entirety of their scholastic experiences – as students and beyond – informs the social institution of education more broadly.

Discussion questions

- How do the stereotypes of the "model minority" and "yellow peril" inform quotas on admissions of Asians to US colleges and universities?
- How significant is class background relative to cultural or ethnic factors in shaping academic success?
- What accounts for your own academic achievement? What role, if any, did the school, family, and/or community play in your achievements?
- What roles do race and racism play in Asian-American scholastic trajectories?
- To what extent are parental pressures on children to succeed helping or hurting Asian-American and other children?

6 Family and Personal Relations

Asian-American families appear in popular rhetoric in two ways. They can be seen as hyper-assimilated with intermarriage between Asian Americans and whites as well as the adoption by whites of Asian babies seemingly on the rise. Or they are represented as hyper-traditional, distinct from whites, producing well-behaved children but also characterized by domestic abuse and highly conservative gender and intergenerational relations. Within this rhetoric, some assimilation is considered good whereas not enough is thought to have damaging effects.

Among the questions this chapter seeks to address is whether these popular representations are actually valid. Are Asian Americans marrying whites more than co-ethnics or other minorities? What explains the apparent trend in the transnational adoption of Asian babies? Do Asians actually maintain "traditional" families upon immigration and what are the impacts of these family forms on second-generation Asian-American immigrants? Moreover, to the extent that these trends are real, do they mean what they are normally taken to represent? This chapter also asks how Asian-American families are changing due to processes of globalization, as families can no longer be presumed to live under the same roof. In contrast to popular narratives either of significant assimilation among Asian-American families or of the need for more assimilation, this chapter argues that Asian Americans' family formations are influenced by hierarchies of race, gender, sexuality, class, and imperialism.

Family patterns tell us about the boundaries between groups and therefore about how groups are faring relative to one another. Ethnic boundaries are a particularly useful way of conceptualizing intergroup dynamics and hierarchies. Boundaries are illustrated that distinguish one group from another. For example, when a Taiwanese-American man speaks in English to a white American but in Mandarin to a co-ethnic, he is enacting a boundary. Similarly, when a white American gets promoted faster than a Taiwanese-American despite comparable credentials, a group boundary is being enforced, albeit externally. By examining how groups interact, we have more opportunities to see how boundaries are performed and reproduced, intermingled, or overcome (Barth 1969; Nagel 1994).

Sociologists often assess immigrants' adaptation by measuring how they compare with and are connected to whites and other groups along key variables such as income, education, friendship circles, and the like. The closer they are on these measures, the weaker the boundaries are that separate groups. Few measures of group boundaries are as telling as family and intimate relations. How people form such relations signifies the strength and placement of group boundaries. Personal decisions are key indicators: who one decides to spend one's life with, whether one leaves one's birthplace to be with someone in another country, with whom one decides to have children as well as how one raises one's children, and the like. So the family formations of Asian Americans signify much of their connections with other groups or lack thereof.

Families help gauge immigrant adaptation also by serving as a symbol of the nation (Chang 2000; Lee 1999). Within political rhetoric, the "family" is constantly invoked as the most important and sacred institution in the nation, one which must be protected and supported. Note that when speaking of the "nation" as opposed to the state or the government, we are embodying the meaning and symbolism associated with a country. Perceptions of Asian-Americans' family formations impact how much they will be accepted as well as signaling what kinds of family are valued in the United States. Family dynamics also bear on the demographic future of the country. As Asian Americans engage in interracial relationships (between partners but even through adoption), they demonstrate the racial mixing of the nation. It was not until 1967 that the US Supreme Court declared all antimiscegenation laws (laws prohibiting the marriage of white to nonwhites) unconstitutional, an example of family formations being shaped by the state and not just personal desire. To understand family formations and their implications for racial/ethnic hierarchies, it is necessary to first examine the personal relationships that adults form with one another, whether through marriage, life partners, dating, or cohabitation. We then discuss parent–child relations, both domestically and transnationally.

Intermarriage and assimilation theory

Asian Americans have higher intermarriage rates than either blacks or Latinos (Qian and Lichter 2007). In fact, most marriages of US-born Asian Americans are to persons outside of their ethnic group, including high numbers of intermarriage with whites (Min and Kim 2009). As of 2006, the endogamy (i.e. in-marriage) rate of Asian Americans overall was 44.9 percent.

Acculturation

Assimilation theory has been the most widely used theoretical perspective to understand intermarriage patterns, particularly interracial marriage with whites, but it is not without its controversies, as seen below. Within this perspective, intermarriage signifies the weakening of boundaries between groups (Gordon 1964). As fitting assimilation theory, intermarriage between Asian Americans and whites increases as Asian Americans (or any ethnic minority) become more acculturated, that is, speak fluent English and spend more time in the United States (Hwang, Saenz, and Aguirre 1997). Studies of US-born Asian Americans indicates that 55 percent marry non-ethnic partners, with a high rate of intermarriage with whites (Min and Kim 2009). Indeed, this data is not only an indication of native-born immigrant children's acculturation, but it is an assumed indicator of their parents' tolerance for interracial marriage.

Asian Americans also date interracially at high rates, even higher than they marry. As for those who intermarry, more acculturated persons and those with fewer Asian American friendships more likely date whites, even if they have strong ethnic identities (Mok 1999). That is, one need not reject one's ethnicity in order to prefer dating or marrying outside one's ethnic group. White ethnic groups similarly profess ethnic identities even as they out-marry (Alba 1990; Waters 1990).

Shared educational backgrounds

Similarly, higher-educated Asian Americans are more likely to marry whites than are lower-educated ones because those with higher education typically speak English fluently and have more opportunities to meet whites (Qian and Lichter 2007). When Asian Americans do marry whites, they tend to marry those with similar levels of education. Education is the single strongest predictor of marital choice. People generally, including those in interracial relationships, marry those of comparable education levels (Qian, Glick, and Batson 2012). This further supports assimilation theory since education, rather than race or ethnicity, is increasingly important in shaping marital choices.

Intermarriage not only represents an assimilative step by the ethnic partner but furthers assimilation among the next generation (Hidalgo and Bankston 2010). Children of Asian-American and white marriages typically identify as white and marry whites (Qian and Lichter 2007). According to assimilation theory, as structural and cultural integration occurs, intermarriage with whites is practically inevitable. Data suggesting that Asian–white marriages are, moreover, relatively stable and not particularly prone to dissolution (Zhang and Van Hook 2009) and are just as likely to produce children as same-race couples (Fu 2008) seem to further substantiate this notion.

Ethnic differences

Examining intermarriage between the US-born children of post-1965 Asian immigrants and white Americans, however, reveal differences between the various Asian ethnic groups in terms of intermarriage rates (Fu and Hatfield 2008). Japanese Americans and Filipino Americans have higher rates of intermarriage compared with Korean, Indian, and Vietnamese Americans (Min and Kim 2009). For example, Japanese Americans' intermarriage rates are a reflection of the declining numbers of new immigrants from Japan since 1965 and, therefore, of the multigenerational character of the Japanese-American community in the United States. Japanese-Americans, having been more acculturated to the United States as well as having achieved occupational and residential assimilation over time, are more likely to marry whites (ibid.). Min and Kim's analysis of Filipinos' intermarriage rates as linked to the history of US colonialism in the Philippines points to yet another approach to understanding intermarriage, one that emphasizes the United States' role as a military superpower in Asia (ibid.). There are gender differences as well. US-born Chinese-American and Filipino-American women are more likely than their male counterparts to intermarry (Qian, Glick, and Batson 2012).

Intermarriage, ethnicity, pan-ethnicity, and race

Nonwhite interracial marriages

Other research, however, counters assimilation approaches to intermarriage. Interracial marriage and dating are not confined to marriage and dating whites. Asian

Americans also date and marry blacks, Latinos, and other racial minorities, though this area of research is much less developed than the research tracking white–non-white couplings (Wilson, McIntosh, and Insana 2007). The research that does exist indicates that there are differences among Asian Americans in terms of marriage to other racial minorities. In a study comparing Chinese, Korean, Indian, Filipino and Japanese Americans, Filipino and Japanese Americans were found to marry other racial minorities at higher rates, 18 percent and 13 percent respectively (Min and Kim 2009).

Co-ethnic marriages

While interracial marriages attract much attention in popular discourse and amongst academics, they are not the most common type of marriage for Asian Americans. Marriage within one's ethnic group (aka in-marriages) and marriages with other Asian Americans (aka pan-ethnic marriages) make up the majority of Asian-American marriages. When accounting for both the US-born and immigrants, most Asian American marriages were in-marriages in 1990 (Qian, Blair, and Ruf 2001). And in 2000 in-marriages had increased. Qian and Lichter go so far as to say, "Indeed, for Hispanics and Asian Americans, the significant upward trend in intermarriage observed over recent censuses has ended" (2007: 77).

The rise in in-marriages results from a number of factors and serves in part as a critique of assimilationist predictions. The most significant factor has been the increased number of Asian Americans available to marry. Since 1965, Asian immigration has increased dramatically, leading to more adult immigrants, more in the 1.5 generation (i.e. someone who immigrated to the United States as a child) and more in the second and later generations. Studies find that US-born Asians are increasingly marrying foreign-born (immigrant) Asians (Qian and Lichter 2011) and Asian immigrants are more likely to marry their native-born counterparts (this is truest among the college-educated). In fact, of US-born Asian Americans who in-marry, most do not marry another US-born co-ethnic (Min and Kim 2009). Instead, they – in particular men – more often marry an immigrant or 1.5 generation. With increased transnationalism (i.e. roots simultaneously in the United States and in Asia) among Asians in the United States, the second generation is more drawn to its parents' homeland. US-born Asian Americans who speak their native language and practice ethnic boundaries are more likely to seek out co-ethnic marital partners.

This pattern could have a gendered component, as Asian-American men prefer what they consider to be more traditional women. Parents may encourage such unions since they reinforce ethnic commitments. Nor is it simply immigrant parents pushing for a marriage with someone from the homeland. Parents in the homeland often seek a partner living abroad for their children. According to Lessinger (1995), the promise of a green card makes marriage to someone living in the United States very appealing to parents in India. In fact, Indian American parents of daughters in the United States can substitute a green card for a costly dowry to a son's family in India. Indians have highest rate of cross-generational in-marriages among Asian Americans (Min and Kim 2009).

Pan-ethnic marriages

Not only are ethnic in-marriages on the rise, pan-ethnic marriages are not uncommon either, although there is some debate over their popularity. Pan-ethnic marriages declined between 1990 and 2006, accounting for even fewer Asian-American marriages (9%) than with other minorities (11%) (ibid.). Still, there is significant ethnic variation that suggests pan-ethnicity is more meaningful for some groups than others. Among pan-ethnic marriages, most take place among and between East and Southeast Asians, namely Chinese, Japanese, Korean, Filipino, and Vietnamese Americans. At the extremes, US-born Chinese and Japanese Americans have pan-ethnic marriages at a much higher rate (16% and 15%, respectively), while Indian Americans only do so at 2.2%. This trend of pan-ethnicity divided between East and Southeast Asians and South Asians has been found in 1990 marriage figures as well (Qian, Blair, and Ruf 2001) and fits qualitative research on the self-perceptions of Asian Americans (Dhingra 2007). A pan-ethnic identity stems from Asian Americans' shared experiences with racism, from being referred to as "Asian" or "Oriental" due to their appearance and from having similar upbringings within immigrant households (Kibria 2002). Given that many white Americans have trouble distinguishing between types of East and Southeast-Asian Americans, a pan-ethnic identity forms more easily among these groups.

Pan-ethnic identities, cultivated on college campuses among US-born, college-educated Asian Americans or because of attachments to an "Asian" identity due to experiences of racism and discrimination, facilitate inter-ethnic marriages as well (Qian, Glick, and Batson 2012). This trend leads Rosenfeld to state, regarding pan-ethnic identity, "Asian American identity and Hispanic identity are more than abstractions or situational identities that political groups use when interacting with white society; these identities seem to be truly significant in the socially important process of mate selection" (2001: 172). These trends signify the importance of race and ethnicity to Asian Americans with regard to marriage, in contrast to the assimilation perspective.

Marital preferences and structural approaches to marriage

While the actual rate of pan-ethnic marriage may be somewhat low, the numbers alone do not give the entire picture. To gauge marriage patterns and their implications for ethnic identities, it is necessary to account for structural factors, namely group size and residential propinquity (Blau, Blum, and Schwartz 1982). The smaller an ethnic group, the fewer marital partners there are for members. Smaller ethnic groups, therefore, tend to have higher intermarriage rates, unlike large groups. For this reason, actual marriage rates are not a precise indicator of marriage *preferences*. People may want to marry someone of their ethnic or racial group but not find someone, and so turn to a different group. In order to understand true marriage preferences, it is necessary to account for group size. So, while Asian Americans have greater intermarriage rates than Latinos, this is partly due to the fewer number of Asian Americans. Once statistically controlling for group size, Latinos are more likely to intermarry than are Asian Americans (Qian and Lichter 2007). Instead of preferring to out-marry to whites, once group size is taken into account, Asian Americans demonstrate a preference for in-marriages and pan-ethnic marriages (Jacobs and Labov 2002). They are more likely to marry other Asian Americans when their racial group size increases and when they are not residentially or occupationally segregated, as fitting the structural as opposed to assimilation perspective on marriage (Okamoto 2007).

Gendered patterns

Further challenging assimilationist interpretations of intermarriage are gendered differences. Asian-American women intermarry more often than men for most ethnic groups. For all major Asian American groups, except for Indian Americans, women had lower in-marriage rates than did men. The lowest rate of in-marriage was found among Japanese-American women, at 28.5%, while the highest rate was for Indian-American women, at 71.1% (recall that the Asian-American average was 44.9%) (Min and Kim 2009). And when Asian-American women do intermarry, they choose whites at a higher rate than do Asian-American men (ibid.). Yet Asian-American men who intermarry choose other Asian Americans at a higher rate than do Asian-American women who intermarry. The number of immigrant women married to non-Asian American servicemen partly, but not completely, explains this difference (Jacobs and Labov 2002).

The other major explanation for the gender differences has to do with racial and gender stereotypes held by Asian Americans. Asian-American women often worry that Asian-American men, even those US-born, are too patriarchal and unassimilated compared to white American men. Some never marry, partly out of an avoidance of co-ethnic men (Ferguson 2000). Conversely, Asian-American men who marry white women see them as more assertive (Chow 2000). The same trend emerges in dating. When out-dating, Chinese-American and Japanese-American women date whites more than Chinese-American and Japanese-American men do, and the men date other Asian Americans more than the women do (Fujino 1997). Women who believe whites are more attractive and who valued attractiveness out-date more. Men who want powerful, less traditional women out-date to whites more. As Fung and Yung put it in their study of Chinese-American and Japanese-American men and women who intermarry, "if given two acculturated Americans, they will choose the 'real' American who is white over the 'imitation' who is Asian American" (Fung and Yung 2000: 600).

Some of these stereotypes of Asian-American men and women may be true. Yet the image of white men and women representing the most enlightened notions of gender suggests that notions of whiteness have become internalized. White men come to represent the ideals of material security and modernity within a global hierarchy, especially compared to Asian women (Nemoto 2006). Furthermore, the fact that both Asian-American women and men feel assimilated means they could choose one another but instead see their race as too foreign and instead seek out whites. This is, again, an instantiation of having internalized dominant racist ideas about Asian Americans.

Whites' gendered preferences for Asians account for this discrepancy as well. Asian-American men who out-marry tend to be more assimilated than those who in-marry (Okamoto 2007). Asian-American women, on the other hand, need not be as assimilated as men to out-marry. For instance, they do not need to be fluent in English. Instead, their foreignness is read as exotic and submissive. The geisha and other images of Asian American women as exotic and submissive serves as a warning to white women as well, for if they argue too much for full equality, they can be replaced by Asian Americans (Espiritu 2007). Still, highly assimilated Asian-American women tend to out-marry more than men. Even among the highly educated, women out-marry to whites more, signaling a clear gender difference not explained by other factors (Jacobs and Labov 2002).

There is one exception to this gendered pattern: Indian-American men out-marry more than women (Min and Kim 2009). Partly this can stem from the heightened familial control over daughters' sexuality (Das Gupta 1997). Also, with more Indian-American male than female immigrants, such as on H-1B visas, a short-term visa for professionally trained immigrants, there is more opportunity for them to intermarry. Implications for how South Asian men are seen within a racialized masculinity relative to East Asian men needs to be examined.

Intermarriage and war

Just as intermarriage can represent racialization and gendered assumptions more than assimilation, it also can represent the effects of war and American empire building. For instance, Japanese–American intermarriage has been popular since at least 1945, with the passage of the War Brides Act. This permitted the entry of American soldiers' Japanese brides in the wake of World War II. Korean and American intermarriages took place during the Korean War. High Filipino American intermarriage rates also stem from such global, not just family level, factors. Filipino–American intermarriage rates, according to Min and Kim (2009), can be attributed to the Philippines' history as a (neo)colony of the United States. A legacy of imperialism included the rapid loss of the mother tongue among Filipino Americans born in the United States, as well as greater acceptance of American cultural norms.

Multiple interpretations

Asian-American marriage and dating trends allow for multiple interpretations. On the one hand, there are clear assimilation implications. With more intermarriages, even as intermarriage rates decline, and the more multiracial or multi-ethnic children come to be, the more the boundaries between groups dissipate (Lee and Bean 2007). Factoring in issues of racialization and gender, however, it becomes clear that intermarriage does not fully fit an assimilation trajectory. Asian Americans remain a distinct group for which racial and gendered hierarchies can impact their marriage patterns, as fitting racialization and other critical approaches. Moreover, intermarriage may be on the decline. Still, even as intermarriages can indicate the continued significance of race, the result is the weakening of boundaries for those individuals involved. No single interpretation – greater integration or the reinforcement of stereotypes – suffices alone.

The contradictory implications lead Hidalgo and Bankston to conclude that the meaning of race for those intermarried will depend on their surrounding racial context, "Where there are Asians, Whites, and Blacks, Asians will tend to become White.

Where there are only Whites, Asians, including even those of multiracial background, may well continue to be distinguished" (2010: 297). Because the black–white binary remains so entrenched, Asian Americans appear "less racial" (i.e. white) relative to African Americans and "more racial" when simply relative to whites. As seen elsewhere, Asian-Americans' racial position alters, based on the preferences of others with greater discursive power. Race and ethnicity, then, do not go away, even for those who intermarry or for their children, but their meaning is contextual. Gender infuses the meanings as well.

Under-recognized gay/lesbian relationships

Race and gender shape lesbian and gay relationships as well. Within a community known as the "model minority" and believed to have culturally traditional lifestyles, sexuality generally, not simply homosexuality, is often overlooked. Queer (i.e. those who question standard heteronormative relationships) persons' relationships elucidate the adaptation of Asian Americans within broader hierarchies. Yet LGBTQ (lesbian, gay, bisexual, transgender, questioning/queer) Asian Americans face the added challenge of homophobia, both within their ethnic group and in broader society.

Asia and homosexuality

Asian Americans often deny homosexuality within their ethnic group. Some Asian cultures do not have words for gay and lesbian sexual relationships, even though men and women can have close ties within their sex (Islam 1998). Certain proponents of religious faiths contend that homosexuality is not allowed by their teachings. For instance, the Indian movie *Fire*, which depicts a love affair between two women, was severely criticized as anti-Hindu by Hindu extremists in India.[1] The erasure of the concept of lesbian relationships is an extension of the notion that women are asexual generally, and so are incapable of sexual desire (Hahm and Adkins 2009).

While relevant, the view of Asian culture as alone explaining Asian Americans' heteronormativity obscures several points. First, Asian cultures and state policies are quite diverse internally and across nations in this regard, and queers within Asia have been active in arguing for their rights. In the Philippines, Japan, and India, for example, consensual homosexual relations between adults in private are legally protected. Nor is homophobia within Asia simply due to traditional culture. For instance, intolerance of homosexuality in China has been traced back to western influences during the mid-1800s (Hinsch 1990). Immigrants bring with them great pride in their sexuality. Major lesbian, gay, bisexual, and transgender organizations in the United States have been started by immigrants, not just the second generation. Second, many western cultures deny gay/lesbian/bisexual/and queer relationships. For instance, homosexuality is considered a sin by Catholicism. So, considering homophobia to be a product of "Asian cultures" overlooks this reality.

Third, other factors beyond Asian culture contribute to the denial of non-heterosexual relations among Asian Americans. Asian Americans have been framed as passive foreigners within America. In order for Asian Americans to be accepted as "good citizens," they need to uphold a heternormative, nuclear-family domesticity, which puts pressure on them to deny homosocial relations within their communities (Shah 2001). To fight their racialization, Asian-American men have traditionally claimed to be full citizens, that is, culturally assimilated and masculine. Also central to this have been the claims of heterosexuality, in contrast to effeminate imagery of men living in bachelor societies as houseboys, running laundromats, and the like (Leong 1995; Ordona 2003). Similarly, Asian-American women have had to become the idealized wives and mothers so as to affirm the heteronormative family and its fit within the US nation (Puri 2002). Lesbian or bisexual relations have no place in this construct.

Identity choices and constraints

Regardless of the origin, Asian-American communities have been slow to embrace their queer brothers and sisters. Asian Americans have had to choose whether to identify as Asian American or as LGBTQ, for each excludes the other (Zia 2006). Within this context, coming out of the closet can threaten not only one's personal relations but what it means to be Asian (Operario, Han, and Choi 2008). People feel that they must choose between their race and sexuality, a pressing dilemma that divides the self. Queer Asian American youths often claim that activists helped them realize their sexuality as Asian Americans, especially within family and cultural environments that precluded discussion, much less acceptance, of non-heteronormativity (Kumashiro 2003).

To move past this dilemma, it is necessary to recognize queer Asian Americans. The question is how to do so. According to Dana Takagi (1994), we cannot simply add identities one on top of another. That is, being gay is not separate to being Asian American. Instead, how someone experiences her/his sexuality (regardless of type) is influenced by race and gender. By analyzing how Asian Americans experience their sexuality, we learn more about how identities intersect generally.

Gay representations and relationships

Representations of Asian-American lesbians and gays have differed based on gender. In essence, there are multiple references to Asian-American men as gay and an almost complete denial of Asian-American women as possibly lesbian. When not seen as threatening white women, Asian-American men have consistently been portrayed as effeminate, possibly homosexual, or asexual (Lee 1999). The April 2004 issue of the mainstream fashion and lifestyle magazine *Details* had a one-page photo, entitled "Gay or Asian." It pictured an East Asian American young man, accompanied by the text "Whether you're into shrimp balls or shaved balls, entering the dragon requires imperial taste. . . ." The implication that Asian-American men are gay, or at least indistinguishable from gays, reasserts this connection between race, gender, and sexuality.

Not only are Asian-American men always possibly gay, they are a particular kind of gay: passive, subservient, and hoping to please white gay men. Asian gay men are often fetishized by certain white gays who are known as "rice queens," given their exoticized preference for Asian men. This niche has such a large presence that voyeuristic magazines are aimed at white gay Americans, some of whom are sexual tourists in Asia. The magazines depict men in Asia in an Orientalist, servile, sexy fashion (Hagland 1998). In these magazines, Asian men never reject the advances of a white man, no matter his age or appearance. The gay film industry similarly depicts Asian and Asian-American men as serving white men. In these films, Asian men are always penetrated rather than penetrating white men. The white male is the center of the film, the one that the audience is supposed to identify with. The Asian-American man serves him. The *Details* magazine story also invoked stereotypes of Asian men in servile jobs (e.g. houseboys, waiters) for the benefit of gay white men. When a rare Asian gay film star has an active, rather than passive, position relative to a white man, he is depicted as the exception rather than the rule for Asian men generally (Hoang 2004). He is highly assimilated, in contrast to the hapless Asian foreigners surrounding him.

The image of Asian-American gay men as highly effeminate and servile shapes their experiences with white gays. Asian and Asian-American men are highly aware of "rice queens" and the exotification that occurs. Gay bars and clubs are supposedly safe spaces for gays but prove to be contested terrain for Asian men (Ng 2004). Even when in clubs with Asian themes, they are on display for rice queens who seek out those spaces. To fit into gay districts, like West Hollywood in Los Angeles, Asian-American men must either act stereotypically Asian or practically deny their background to resist typification. In either case, they must deal with racist stereotypes that limit their comfort. Other avenues for meeting men also carry this racialization. For instance, personal ads in magazines request submissive Asian men (Ng 2004). Some Asian-American men use the stereotype to their advantage by acting subservient and then confronting their partners unexpectedly (Manalansan 2003). So how Asian-American men experience their sexuality is shaped by their race. Trying to separate their experiences of race and sexuality would be impossible.

Lesbian representations and relationships

While there are representations of Asian-American gay men (however problematic), Asian-American lesbians are practically nonexistent in the public consciousness. They are rarely accepted as legitimate lesbians within white circles. As mentioned above, Asian-American women are seen as asexual or as geisha women, motivated to serve others. Their hyper-feminine image casts doubts upon them as able to challenge sexual norms and actually be lesbian, especially butch lesbians (Lee 1996).

When they are recognized as lesbians within white circles, they are often tokenized as such, made to feel as if their ancestry was all that mattered (Tsui 1996). This one-dimensional image, along with the lack of recognition of lesbians within Asian communities, makes these women feel practically homeless. Even progressive, feminist portrayals of Asian women recognize Asian male homosexuality but not that of women (Gopinath 2005). The image of women as the bedrock of the family and nation is not challenged, even in depictions of women demanding equality to men. The result is that women need to organize and create groups of fellow Asian-American lesbians and allies (Zimmerman 2000). As for men, Asian-American women's race and gender shapes how they experience their sexuality.

Asian American gay/lesbian rights and resistance

The intersection of identities also shapes Asian Americans' approach to sexual rights. Front and center within the gay rights movement is same-sex marriage. This has been pursued most effectively at the city and state level. At the federal level, the 1996 Defense of Marriage Act has narrowly defined marriage as between a man and a woman. Attempts to overturn the federal law seem remote. While Asian Americans have taken advantage of changes in local laws and sought marriage where possible, there is a counter-sentiment that marriage may not only be unimportant to Asian-American gays and lesbians but also problematic. Marriage at the city or state level will not help Asian Americans sponsor their spouses' immigration or citizenship. Only couples considered married at the federal level receive such benefits. If Asian-American gays and lesbians who are undocumented attempt to sponsor their spouses, their legal status may be revealed and they may be deported (Magpantay 2006).

Rather than focus overwhelmingly on same-sex marriage, other issues are arguably more pressing within the Asian American community. LGBTQ Asian Americans face all the same legal challenges as other Asian Americans, and so immigrant rights are a key concern. In this way, Asian-American gays and lesbians have different priorities from their white peers. The white LGBTQ communities, who lead the national agenda on queer issues, need to better account for the needs of their diverse members. For instance, HIV-prevention and care information is rarely translated into non-English languages and so is not distributed to immigrant populations. Additionally, individuals who are HIV positive may not be able to attain green cards or permanent residence (Cheng 2006). Immigrants applying for permanent residence are subjected to mandatory HIV testing. Of course, HIV is not limited to the gay/lesbian community. At the same time, while not an issue for most gays and lesbians, such obstructions to immigration directly impact some Asian Americans and could become more important within mainstream gay activism. Immigration reform bills, such as those that would make legal those residing in the United States without full documents, often do not include lesbians and gays as protected persons.[2] In addition, white gays and lesbians can be just as racist as other whites, keeping Asian Americans and other minorities out of their organizations.

While the mainstream LGBTQ organizations should better account for Asian American and other minorities' needs, all Asian Americans should promote sexual equality. For instance, parallels exist between the movement for interracial marriage, which benefits Asian Americans, and gay marriage. Fighting for same-sex marriage fits within the history of Asian-American activism (Zia 2000).

Overall, LGBTQ Asian Americans deserve more visibility and respect within ethnic and queer communities. Currently, attempts to recognize them in mainstream queer circles have led to exotification. Links between Asian-American gay organizations and other immigrant organizations exist, but they are more tenuous than with white gay organizations (Das Gupta 2006). This is a relatively unsatisfactory dynamic, for not only are Asian Americans rarely accepted as equals in these spaces, but they do not share the same assessment of social justice needs. As LGBTQ Asian Americans organize more and other groups become less homophobic and racist, a broader coalition of interests can come together. As straight Asian-American organizations open up more to their queer co-ethnics, they cannot simply continue with business as usual and adopt gay/lesbian issues on occasion. They must work to dismantle the heterosexual privileges that intersect with being Asian American, such as the priority on marriage.

Finally, although we have dealt at length with people who are partnered, individuals who reject committed relationships are growing in numbers. One study finds that Asian-American women are only second to African-American women when it comes to non-marriage rates (Ferguson 2000). The reasons that Asian-American women (in this study, Chinese- and Japanese-American women) opt out of marriage range from not wanting to replicate their parents' unhappy and conflict-ridden marriages to women's desires to pursue their educational aspirations.

Transnational, transracial adoption

Asian Americans' romantic relationships both cross racial boundaries and reinforce hierarchies between races. Adoption of Asian children by white families has similar implications. Like intermarriage, such adoptions challenge boundaries between whites (most commonly) and Asian Americans, for they coexist within the same family. Yet they do not signal the evaporation of racial boundaries. What role do the racial differences between parents and children play in these families and outside them?

Transnational transracial adoption (TTA) is increasingly common and is the most common type of transracial adoption in the United States, with Asian countries being the most popular sources of children for white parents (Tuan, Rienzi, and Shiao 2010). Asian countries, including Korea and China, have promoted overseas adoption in the past. Indeed, of all countries receiving adoptees, the United States tops the list (Hollinger 2004).

Racialized constructions of TTA

Race plays an important role in shaping adoptive parents' preferences for babies. White parents prefer Asian or Latino immigrant babies over US-born black babies (Quiroz 2007). Asian children are seen as victims who can be "saved" from their circumstances, namely a Third World country (Shiao, Tuan, and Rienzi 2004). African American children, on the other hand, are seen as in need but possibly unable to be saved. Asian-American children are seen as different from whites but not as different as blacks. Asian Americans' positive stereotypes make their minority status less problematic in the eyes of parents (Dorow 2006). This, in turn, makes the white adopting family appear enlightened and cosmopolitan without threatening their white status, for they are not mixing with blacks.

While parents believe Asian Americans are much more akin to whites than are blacks, they still recognize the racial differences within the family (Tan and Nakkula 2005). Yet, rather than dwell on the child's minority status, parents frame the difference as one of culture: because the child is of Asian origin, she should be made aware of her cultural ancestry. Parents rarely discuss race per se with their children; instead, they mostly adopt a color-blind ideology (Shiao, Tuan, and Rienzi 2004). This approach by parents to dealing with difference has led some scholars of TTA to be highly critical of white adoptive parents. Such parents have been framed within a broader US imperialism in Asia (Jodi Kim 2009). Beyond wanting to "save" Asian children, much like the United States hoped to save Asia from communism during the Cold War, the preference for Asian babies affirms parents' motive of rescuing the vulnerable. This motivation fits into a colonial logic that ultimately serves the white parent, according to the critics.

A more nuanced take on white parents' motives for and reactions to TTA recognizes an exotification of the children and a colonial background to their actions but also gives more agency and credibility to the parents as actively working through racial ideologies (Dorow 2006; Louie 2009). Parents challenge themselves to understand race more deeply and confront even family members in ways they would not have before the adoption. Parents who had more familiarity with Asian America were better able to help their children to deal with racism (Johnson et al. 2007).

Adopted children and ethnic identities

How adopted children understand their ethnicity and upbringing has been much less explored in academic literature. While children often face questions regarding their biological and adopted parents, for Asian adoptees the challenge can be much deeper. Their biological parents appear very different, almost incompatible, to their adopted ones (Eng 2003). Also, growing up Asian American within a white family, often with white social networks, can be difficult. It is not uncommon for such children to grow up thinking they are white and being unprepared to handle instances in which they are not seen as white.

Alternatively, such children are expected to know about their homeland because they were born there, even though they have grown up within predominantly white contexts. In response, some resent their parents' exoticized efforts to teach them about their ancestry as an attempt to deny them their "Americanness" (Louie 2009). Others instead try to learn more about the culture. Trips back to the "homeland" are not uncommon. Those who have more exposure to their background through cultural schools and programs, which many adoptive parents seek out for their children, develop stronger ethnic identities (Huh 2007). While the academic literature on adoptees may still be emerging, adoptees themselves have used creative writing as a medium through which to explore the issues they face (see, for example, Bishoff and Rankin 1997).

Like intermarriage and interracial same-sex relationships, TTA further weakens the boundaries between Asian Americans and whites. Yet, for such transformations and boundary blurring to truly occur, the racial, colonial, and gendered constructs that create TTA must be part of the conversation. Ethnic studies scholars highlight the role of these hierarchies in shaping TTA and so read such adoptions as problematic in the context of broader social justice. Such interpretations, however, must be balanced with the daily life experiences of these families. Asian Americans are further integrating, even as surrounding hierarchies define their experiences and prevent their absorption into whiteness. Adoptees often seek out networking and support opportunities with one another, to define for themselves what TTA means (Tuan and Shiao 2011). More research should be conducted on the children themselves as they mature to understand the implications for these families of broader social relations.

Domestic challenges

Domestic challenges facing Asian Americans get read in popular rhetoric as due to families' lack of assimilation. While some cultural tendencies practiced by immigrants deserve critique, a sociological approach to internal problems within families broadens the analysis to immigrants' place in intersecting contexts. Much like how interracial relationships signal more than assimilation, family challenges signal more than a lack of assimilation. Two main problems found within Asian-American (and other) families are intimate partner abuse and tensions across generations.

Intimate partner abuse

The amount of intimate partner abuse (IPA) taking place between Asian-American partners is hard to quantify because of a history of underreporting. Surveys within Asian-American communities suggest significant rates. For instance, 25 percent of South Asian immigrant women surveyed reported domestic violence in their homes (Midlarsky, Venkataramani-Kothari, and Plante 2006). In fact, actual rates are probably higher because some women are probably not reporting their problems. While rates of domestic violence are high within South Asian communities, they are similarly high in other Asian-American communities. Within Los Angeles County, Korean Americans had the highest rate of spouse abuse among all Asian Americans (Rhee 1997). Also within Los Angeles, as many as 80 percent of Chinese Americans reported verbal or physical violence in the past year (Hee Yun Lee 2010). Other forms of IPA within Asian-American communities include "economic control, coercion and threat, intimidation, public derogation, isolation, minimizing and denial, asserting male privilege, and so forth" (Dasgupta 2000: 176). The most common results were emotional abuse, physical abuse, and sexual abuse (Grossman and Lundy 2007). When women seek assistance for their abuse, their most common needs include "personal/emotional support, . . . legal assistance, . . . emergency housing, . . . and housing assistance" (Grossman and Lundy 2007: 1037).

Causes of abuse

Explanations as to why people abuse their partners range from individual circumstances to environmental factors to the macro system. All dimensions play a role. Those who abuse their partners have often witnessed spousal abuse in their own families and have grown up where male privilege is highly valorized (Yoshioka, DiNoia, and Ullah 2001; Dasgupta 2000). Violence that one witnesses need not be domestic. Living in a war-torn country, as many Southeast Asian refugees did, makes violence part of daily consciousness (Bhuyan et al. 2005).

So how one was raised shapes attitudes towards cruelty. But the impetus to abuse depends on other factors. Not everyone who is prone to attack their spouses does so, and those who are do not act on it all of the time. The sociological theory of status inconsistency can help explain when people will abuse their partners (Yick 2001). According to this theory, partner abuse is an attempt by men to reassert their authority in the house (their status relative to their wives) after their privileges are perceived to be weakened or threatened (i.e. inconsistent with their normal state). Immigration can lead to status inconsistency. Upon immigration, men are often underemployed or unemployed, and the respect they enjoyed in their homelands has been replaced by minority status in the United States. This can be particularly challenging for those who did not arrive voluntarily, such as refugees. Even if paid well, they can work in a lower-status job than previously held in the homeland. Women, on the other hand, often enjoy increased status, for they may be working outside of the home for the first time. Husbands in such circumstances are more prone to abuse their wives (Kibria 1993; Nguyen 2004).

Changing gender practices and identities that emerge through the migration process interact with cultural assumptions to impact marital conflicts, including but not limited to spousal abuse. Kyeyoung Park (2000) finds, for example, that Korean immigrant men get frustrated with their wives' new conceptions of gender roles within the context of marriage, attributing this shift to women's potential for economic independence in the United States. One divorcee explained that his marriage's dissolution is due to the fact that "women, like my ex-wife, often think that they can survive without a husband. That's the new idea that they develop in their lives in America" (Kyeyoung Park 2000: 164). So, it is important not to over-emphasize the role of culture in and of itself in causing IPA since other factors contribute directly (Burman, Smailes, and Chantler 2004).

Hiding abuse

Despite the prevalence of abuse, many women do not report it but instead choose to suffer in silence. Various reasons explain this underreporting. In part these are cultural. Certain Asian cultures, such as that of Cambodia, stress camaraderie and harmony (Yoshioka, DiNoia, and Ullah 2001). While such values should temper the abuse in the first place, their real effect is to make women feel guilty for revealing it. Similarly, women feel that abuse should simply be tolerated and that it is part of marriage and so not deserving of special recognition (Bhuyan et al. 2005; Grossman and Lundy 2007). Many Asian cultures look down upon divorce, which often results from openly confronting abuse. By reporting abuse, they effectively bring shame on themselves. Ethnic communities may shun the accuser. In addition, abuse can be seen as appropriate, even under extremely banal circumstances. For instance, while less than half of the Chinese, Vietnamese, and Cambodian adults sampled approved of violence, 25–50 percent thought violence was justified in the case of "a wife's sexual infidelity, her nagging or making fun of her partner, or her refusal to cook or keep the house clean" (Yoshioka, DiNoia, and Ullah 2001: 922). Also, women may not recognize what counts as mistreatment. For example, a group of South Asian women understood what physical abuse was but not sexual abuse (Dasgupta 2000). Instead, they thought husbands had a right to sex whenever they wished. Within this general culture of silence, ethnic variation exists. Studies have found that Southeast-Asian Americans are less likely to discuss violence than are Chinese Americans or South Asian Americans (Grossman and Lundy 2007; Hee Yun Lee 2010).

Other barriers than culture impede the revelation of abuse. Immigrant communities are invested in the "model minority" stereotype, which depends on an image of cohesive, law-abiding families. This racial game makes communities less likely to support women who want to reveal their abuse, for doing so counters the image of well-behaved immigrants (Bhattacharjee 1998). Within this context, ethnic domestic violence organizations become highly politicized, threatening a "model minority" image by drawing attention to a group's problems.

Another reason why abused immigrant women do not report their problems stems from their legal status. Immigrant wives are more likely than their husbands to have visas that depend on their attachment to their spouse. Separating from their husbands can complicate their legal status (Abraham 2000; Dasgupta 2000). In 1986, immigration laws changed to protect such immigrant women, but problems continued. In order to separate from their husbands and not be deported, wives had to prove their marriage was in good faith or be married for at least two years before leaving the husband. This put extra burdens on women. The law was slightly changed in 1990 and 1994 to protect women, but they still had to prove their abuse. And the abused must still work through the court system and hope for competent attorneys to secure their freedom. Given the nuances within immigration law, many women are unaware of their rights (Bhuyan et al. 2005). This, in turn, impedes seeking protection.

Other barriers to reporting abuse can be found in mainstream feminist organizations' approach to it (Yick 2001). A common goal within domestic violence shelters is to remove the woman from her partner, with the long-term prospect of a full separation. Yet many Asian American women want to maintain their marriages and seek equality within them (Ayyub 2000). The desire to stay with one's husband is both cultural and economic. Wives face extreme vulnerability if they leave their husbands. This is particularly so for those whose immigration status does not allow them to work, such as wives of husbands on H-1B visas (Raj and Silverman 2007).

When Asian-American women do seek help for IPA, they most often turn to family and friends (Lee, Pomeroy, and Bohman 2007). By this point, the abuse typically is severe. These networks may lead victims to ethnic-specific violence shelters, which are, fortunately, on the rise (see the discussion of the shelter Manavi in Das Gupta 2006). Mainstream shelters often lack the necessary linguistic services or cultural attributes such as appropriate food and comforts (Dasgupta 2000). In these shelters, women are counseled in ethnically sensitive, feminist ways rather than having their culture blamed for the abuse (Kallivayalil 2007). They also receive assistance in finding shelter and economic means, for by leaving their partners they often become separated from the ethnic community at large (Grossman and Lundy 2007). Because the abused often turn to family and friends within their community, there needs to be more education and support regarding abuse and more outreach by shelters within these ethnic communities (Bhuyan et al. 2005; Rhee 1997).

Intergenerational relations

Another facet of domestic abuse is child abuse. This is also an underreported problem within Asian-American families. Similar to partner abuse within traditional cultures, corporal punishment is rarely seen as abuse, even when performed in a harsh manner (Oda and Yoo 2010). In parts of Asia, corporal punishment is accepted as a legitimate means of disciplining children. For instance, in some areas of Korea, such abuse is referred to as the "whip of love" (Chang, Rhee, and Weaver 2006). Also, like partner abuse, factors other than cultural contribute to it. The strain on parents, in particular fathers, caused by immigration, unemployment or underemployment, and racism exacerbate tensions within the home.

Cultural gaps

Luckily, most intergenerational relations are not defined by abuse. Instead, like many parents and children regardless of ethnicity, intergenerational relations are marked by standard generational differences. Still, immigrant parents with children raised in the United States experience particular kinds of strain. Much of the strain within families stems from different degrees of acculturation between parents and children. If parents do not acculturate much and the children do, this creates dissonant acculturation within the family and can lead to parent–child conflict (Portes and Rumbaut 2001; Tsai-Chae and Nagata 2008). Furthermore, it is in the family where definitions of ethnicity, which often include the perpetuation of and insistence on the norms and values of the parents' homeland, exacerbate dissonance (see chapter 9 for additional information). In these circumstances, children often reject parents' teachings, for parents are not seen as in touch with their environment and the children do not feel connected to them. If parents have weak English skills, children often represent the families to public authorities, read the mail, and the like. Such an imbalance in conventional authority furthers the disconnect across generations and creates stress for family members (Ying and Han 2007).

Girls in particular can resent a double standard from conservative parents regarding their sexuality (Chung 2001). Highly acculturated girls across a variety of Asian ethnic groups, in grades 7–12, are more likely to have had sex than less acculturated girls (Hahm, Lahiff, and Barreto 2006). Children in general resent restrictions on their social lives caused by family obligations (Fuligni, Yip, and Tseng 2002). As dissonant acculturation widens, children can adopt negative behaviors, such as practicing violence, substance abuse, and teenage pregnancy. Gangs can take on a familial role felt to be missing, especially if friends are in one (Tsunokai 2005).

The answer to this problem at the family level, according to Portes and Rumbaut (2001), is not for parents to quickly assimilate as well, in contrast to assimilation theory. Instead, parents and children should both selectively acculturate. This means that each generation should adopt some American norms while still asserting ethnic norms. With selective acculturation, individuals feel well-balanced in their bicultural identities and connected to the other generation (Kiang and Fuligni 2009; Ahn, Kim, and Park 2009). Children can also maintain ties to their ethnic community and so benefit from a sense of community that prioritizes upward mobility (Zhou and Bankston 1998). Indeed, beyond their families, the children of immigrants can get support from community-based organizations which, Zhou finds, "not only enables parents to establish norms and reinforce each other's sanctioning of children but also provides some space where children and youth can express themselves, easing intergenerational conflicts" (Zhou 2000: 323). Selective acculturation helps prevent "downward assimilation" by the second generation, that is, adopting a hostile approach to school and other institutions (Portes and Zhou 1993).

Family pressures of class, race, and sexuality

Factors other than culture also define intergenerational relations. While money cannot buy happiness, it does reduce stress and allows parents more time to spend with their children. It is not a coincidence that the poorest Asian-American populations have the highest rate of teenage pregnancy (Oda and Yoo 2010). While not reducible to class, neither does this trend result simply from having adopted different amounts of cultural teachings. Racism also exacerbates family tensions. Parents who feel discriminated against are more likely to be physically aggressive towards their children, even if they have high incomes (Lau, Takeuchi, and Alegría 2006). Youths who feel discriminated against and let down by mainstream institutions can develop a reactive ethnicity (Portes and Rumbaut 2001). That is, they develop ethnic identities that contrast with dominant expectations which, in turn, valorize possibly self-destructive behaviors (see Hunt, Moloney, and Evans 2011). More research should be done on the effects of race and of class, and their intersection, on parent-child relations.

Yet another issue that can become a source of intergenerational tension between Asian immigrants and their second-generation children involves homosexuality. Homosexual children struggle with "coming out" to their families, but, just as importantly, parents of homosexual children also struggle to try to accept their children's sexual orientations (Hom 2000b). One study comparing LGBTQ Asians with Asian Americans (including those who immigrated to and those who were born in the United States), however, finds that Asian Americans are typically more open with their families about their sexuality. Family tensions, it likely follows, are less prevalent among LGBTQ Asian Americans than their Asian counterparts (Kimmel and Yi 2004), although generalizing across multiple cultures is difficult.

How families deal with intergenerational tensions has not been adequately researched. Much of the existing research documents how US-raised children selectively express and hide their ethnic culture so as to appease their parents and their mainstream peers (Maira 2002; Shih and Pyke 2010). It is easier to handle intra-family tensions surrounding acculturation compared with frustration fueled by sexism and economic and racial inequality, which in turn can manifest itself in abuse, in criminal activity, in teenage pregnancy, and the like. The more inequality and discrepancy between the Asian-American family and the white mainstream, the harder it is for Asian Americans to deal with family conflicts.

Overall, we should not pathologize culture as the cause of IPA and family tensions. While culture plays a role, it interacts with other dynamics, including economic inequality at the local and global levels, racism, patriarchy, war, and other social dysfunctions. We need to place people within a broader framework to appreciate the complex causes of and solutions to tensions within families.

Transnational families

Asian-American families are increasingly transnational as parents and children may not live in the same country. Moreover, Asian Americans may seek partners overseas rather than marrying interracially, inter-ethnically or pan-ethnically in the United States.

Transnational divides

Transnational families experience their own specific tensions but also opportunities. Within the global economy, parents in the developing world must often migrate to the developed world to work, leaving their children and other relatives at home. Jobs in their own country are scarce and low paid. Western wars held in Asian countries contribute to families' displacement and the need to travel abroad. Yet immigrants rarely migrate without their families to become professionals, although this does happen on occasion (Guevarra 2010). Instead, as explained in chapter 4, a gendered division of labor occurs. Men work as manual laborers, computer programmers, or other entry-level positions. Women migrate to work as domestic servants, child-care providers, sex workers, and other lower-paid, low-status positions (Ehrenreich and Hochschild 2002). At times, such work is in luxurious houses where the income disparities between the owners and the workers are immense (Anderson 2001).

For those who must leave their family behind, it is a guilt-ridden process, one that further time away rarely assuages. Rhacel Parreñas (2001) argues that Filipina domestic workers in Italy and the United States deeply miss their children back home. Some describe experiencing psychological disorders. Others care for their hired families' children in a highly committed fashion, displacing the physical and emotional affection that they cannot give to their own children. The remittances (i.e. money that immigrants send their families in their homelands) of overseas Filipinas help sustain between one-third and one-half of those in the Philippines.

As mothers leave their families to provide needed remittances back in their homeland, one might imagine that they would be heralded as martyrs and heroes. The opposite is the case. Political and religious leaders, as well as mainstream media in sending countries like the Philippines, often chastise these mothers for sacrificing their children's well-being and, with it, the notion of the family in their country (Parreñas 2002). These accusations are based in both ideology and reality. It is true that children left behind often report more developmental problems than their peers. As Hochschild (2002: 22) writes, "Compared to their classmates, the children of migrant workers more frequently fell ill; they were more likely to express anger, confusion, and apathy; and they performed more poorly in school. Other studies of this population show a rise in delinquency and child suicide."

Yet part of the difficulties facing these children stems from the gender ideology that sees parenting as women's work. When the children have supportive networks of extended family, can communicate with their parents, and recognize the reasons for emigration, they report far fewer troubles (Parreñas 2002). Fathers' involvement in parenting while mothers are abroad has received little academic attention, surprisingly. What little we know suggests that fathers feel emasculated when their wives have to become the primary wage-earners and leave them in the domestic sphere (Gamburd 2002). Men, of course, also travel abroad and at times leave wives at home or leave the children with others. When fathers travel abroad, children do not report the same sense of parental loss or abandonment as when mothers do. And it should be remembered that women and men also travel as non-parents. The emphasis on mothers and the impact of their migration on families left behind should not mask the experiences of those outside of the heteronormative family (Manalansan 2006).

For instance, many of the women who travel abroad are single, yet their unique experiences are lost within the discourse on families broken up by transnational labor. Similarly, men travel as well but their familial experiences receive little attention (McKay 2007). So the critique of mothers leaving home is not only unfair but indicative of an internalized gender bias.

Another type of transnational family involves children traveling abroad alone. A dominant type is known as "parachute kids." These are children from wealthy families whose parents send them to the United States to attend school and eventually college (Zhou 1998). Among Asian Americans, parachute kids are most commonly Chinese and Korean (Orellana et al. 2001). These children can enjoy significant freedoms and access to material goods. Parents believe this practice will best promote their children's future mobility and status. The flip side of this phenomenon is Asian immigrant parents sending their US-raised children back to the homeland for school and/or marriage. Parents believe that the children will be safer there, learn more appropriate values, and get in touch with their ancestry. This happens more frequently when the youths do not do well in school or show behavior of which parents do not approve.

Transnational marriages

Transnational families also include transnational marriages. Marrying a co-ethnic across national boundaries has been a common practice for generations. Yet, with the rise of advanced technology, finding spouses and communicating has been easier. To some degree, such marriages between US residents and co-ethnics in Asia are devised by immigrant parents for their children in the United States. Yet another source of such marriages are immigrants themselves seeking partners from back home, reminiscent of Japanese and Korean picture brides from the early 1900s. For instance, working-class Vietnamese immigrant men marry much younger women in Vietnam (Thai 2005). Often, these marriages involve significant tensions between a man expecting a compliant wife and the wife anticipating a progressive, "western" husband.

Globalization and transnationalism are resulting in new family formations. Global inequality makes parents and children seek out access to First World institutions, whether they be in the labor market or education. The result can be dysfunction within the families. Yet, as the trend continues, sending countries come to depend on this dynamic. The United States and other First World countries continue their role as the core nations that shape the lives of people far away. Asian Americans are at the intersection of this dynamic. The adaptation of those in transnational families cannot be framed within the existing theories of assimilation or multiculturalism or racialization. They are forming a distinct way of life that involves constant reminders of loved ones across national borders. The nation-state loses some of its relevance, but the material differences across nations matter more than ever. While scholars understand transnationalism as a global force, what is less understood is how families respond to it and its long-term effects across generations (Dreby 2010). Until this is better researched, we will not know the effects of transnationalism on immigrants' adaptation and experiences.

Conclusion

Framing Asian-American families as hyper-assimilated (with intermarriages and adoption) or hyper-traditional (with abusive relations) not only misrepresents the true nature of the families but also misses the surrounding social structure that shapes Asian Americans' personal lives. Immigration laws, racial and gender stereotypes, heteronormativity, colonial legacies, processes of globalization, transnationalism, and other external dimensions combine with cultural traditions (which are, of course, dynamic and ever-changing) to shape Asian Americans' adaptation. Because the family is one of the primary institutions shaping individuals' lives, how it evolves and the tensions that characterize it signal much about the future of Asian Americans. It is clear that no single theory of adaptation suffices. We have seen how some trajectories that seem assimilationist (e.g. intermarriage with whites and adoption by white families) also illustrate a racial formation. And trajectories like transnational families are influenced by the cultural norms, military ventures, and economic privileges of the West. Attention should be paid to how Asian Americans experience various trajectories, the outcome of which may not fit a single outcome for Asian Americans' adaptation and equality.

Discussion questions

- Mainstream anti-domestic violence service providers often attribute intimate partner and family violence in Asian-American communities to "oppressive cultures." This stereotyping of Asian cultures as intrinsically violent pathologizes communities and limits the quality of service given to Asian-American survivors. Rather than using "cultural values" as a means of rationalizing intimate partner and family violence, how can issues related to racism, classism, and patriarchy create a framework in which domestic violence in Asian-American communities can be understood? For example, why do immigrant status and language barriers matter for Asian-American survivors?
- What are some issues affecting queer Asian Americans that are neglected by heteronormative Asian-American communities and mainstream, majority-white LGBTQ groups?

7 Citizenship

Any nation hopes to treat well those it considers its members. One learns more about a nation's priorities, however, by seeing how it treats those who are not obviously its members. In today's increasingly globalized world, how nations treat their immigrants is especially telling of their character. Though the United States boasts that it is a "nation of immigrants," as we have seen in previous chapters, it has welcomed some groups of immigrants more readily than others. What are the priorities of the nation when it comes to whom it lets in and whom it keeps out? What rights and privileges do those in the country have? Immigration and citizenship policies reveal how a nation defines its people and how it wants to relate to other nations (Ngai 2004). Immigration leads to new populations who are likely to settle permanently in a country, hence it is linked to citizenship because citizenship determines who can claim the rights and duties associated with being members of a country. Immigration and citizenship policies therefore impact the extent to which groups can assimilate.

Some argue that the United States does not owe immigrants full citizenship. This belief rests on a few mistaken assumptions, including that immigrants come to the United States just to take advantage of its public services. As seen in previous chapters, immigrants often come because they have a connection with the United States through colonization and war and/or through family. Others are needed as employees. So the United States helps create its immigrants. As noted below, it also helps create its undocumented immigration population through its visa allocation system. It can be argued that this is all the more reason to owe immigrants full citizenship. In addition, the notion that the state does not owe immigrants equality privileges national sovereignty as a concept over the liberal democratic belief in individual equality, presumed essential to the nation. There will always be these challenges as the nation defines itself in narrow ways.

Citizenship in different countries around the world is determined in one of two ways: by descent (*jus sanguinis*) or by birth in a country's territory (*jus solis*). In the United States, citizenship is immediately granted to those who are born on US soil. Citizenship in this country is conceived as a universal status: all citizens supposedly have the same rights and duties as guaranteed by a government (Glenn 2002). Legal citizenship is recognition by the state of a lawful, dedicated member of the nation. While this is the most obvious type of citizenship, sociologists such as T. H. Marshall argue that citizenship should not be limited to whether people are legally recognized as citizens within a specific country, but that it comprises other dimensions, such as civil citizenship, political citizenship, and social citizenship (Marshall 1964). In addition to the dimensions of citizenship identified by Marshall, Glenn (2002) recognizes cultural citizenship (having your culture respected in the public sphere) (see also

Chavez 2008). These various dimensions of citizenship overlap but still remain distinct so that it is possible to have access to one dimension but not to the others.

Access to citizenship

Individuals' access to US citizenship is dictated by their race, gender, class, and other forms of social hierarchy (Bosniak 2006). Citizenship in the United States has historically been the domain of white, heterosexual, land-owning men. Native-born black Americans, as well as many white Americans, have faced a denial of citizenship. This exclusion from citizenship and the outsider status it assigns to minority groups has long been codified in law. From the inception of this country, the only ones who could be considered authentic "Americans"– full members of the United States – were white. The 1790 Naturalization Act reflects this logic as it restricted the opportunity for citizenship acquisition or naturalization to non-US-born white immigrants.

The 1790 Naturalization Act was amended after the Civil War to include blacks. However, full citizenship was (and continues to be) denied to them in many ways. Even once blacks could vote, they were not always able to make it to the polls without encountering physical violence, for example at the height of Jim Crow. White women were granted citizenship but could not vote until the early twentieth century (Glenn 2002).

In particular, Asian immigrants and their descendants have not been able to fully enjoy the rights of US citizenship. As we discussed in previous chapters, Asian Americans have long been racialized as "forever foreign." The Chinese were denied both immigration and naturalization in the late 1800s, becoming the first group explicitly marked as ineligible for citizenship and then excludable from the United States for that very reason. Filipinos came to the United States because of their conquest rather than fitting the narrative of voluntary immigrants looking for a brighter future. The colonization of the Philippines in 1898 made Filipinos US "nationals" even before they got to US shores to work. Though "nationals," they were still colonized subjects and therefore could not fully exercise their citizenship. Meanwhile, US wars in Asia, namely World War II, the Korean War and later the Vietnam War, also created the impetus for much Asian immigration, both voluntary and forced. Because they had often been adversaries of the United States, groups from these countries have not been considered as fully American. Manifestations of this are the internment of Japanese Americans during World War II, including of those who were citizens (Ngai 2004), as well as the suspicions of those assumed to be Muslim since (and even prior to) 9/11.

Citizenship is not immigrants' only concern. Lisa Lowe suggests that the idea of equality through citizenship actually masks other inequalities, particularly on the basis of class, that are endemic in American society. She states, "Insofar as the legal definition and political concept of the citizen enfranchises the subject who inhabits the national public sphere, the concept of the abstract citizen – each formally equivalent, one to the other – is defined by the negation of the material conditions of work and the inequalities of the property system" (Lowe 1996). In other words, though citizenship in the United States defines people as politically equal (i.e. able to participate in the sphere of democratic politics), it downplays other inequalities that should not be ignored. Still, even as citizenship produces and reproduces inequality, the ideal of citizenship has become the basis for claims to rights that have ultimately expanded ideas and practices of citizenship (Glenn 2000).

In the current era, which this chapter focuses on, immigrants have more access to citizenship. In many ways, this is a result of racialized minorities and women demanding that full citizenship guaranteed by law be extended to include them. Today, all citizens, regardless of gender or place of birth, can vote and have access to full public benefits. Permanent residents who are not citizens also have many protections. Nevertheless, according to Ngai, Asian Americans and Latinos are considered "alien citizens: persons who are American citizens by virtue of their birth in the United States but who are presumed to be foreign by the mainstream of American culture and, at times, by the state" (2004: 2). Disparities exist in access to full citizenship based on one's race, culture, and other factors. In some contexts, these disparities are institutionalized in the law and in other contexts stem from action by individuals and local communities (Glenn 2002).

In this chapter, we focus on the legal, social, and cultural citizenships of Asian Americans and immigrant minorities generally. While these distinctions are made for analytical clarity, such types of citizenship are connected to one another. One type of citizenship affects people's access to the others. This chapter will also illustrate how immigrant minorities have advocated for themselves within these constraints. It pays significant attention to how Asian immigrants have fought to expand the terms of American citizenship, especially cultural citizenship, by insistently retaining cultural practices from their homeland, a privilege they were historically denied. We will end the chapter with a discussion of transnational citizenship. With increasing globalization, Asian Americans (both immigrants and their children) are able to retain their claims to citizenship in their countries of origin. In the process, we better understand how citizenship actually works by privileging some groups over others and how residents interact with it in order to assert their equality.

Legal citizenship

To understand how the United States decides who can become a legal citizen, it is first necessary to consider whom it currently lets in and whom it keeps out. As explained in chapter 3, US immigration law technically no longer discriminates based on national origin. Still, contemporary US immigration policy prioritizes which people can enter first, namely family members of citizens and those fitting particular skills and jobs determined in need. Visa policies are continually revisited so as to respond to corporations' needs, which in turn lead to greater numbers of certain immigrant groups.

Limited access to legal citizenship

Given this emphasis on family unification and the United States' labor market needs, lesbians and gays and those with few needed job skills have had more difficulty immigrating. Openly gay immigrants could not immigrate to the United States before 1990, for they were deemed to be of "psychopathic personality or sexual deviation, or moral defect" (Randazzo 2005: 31). Immigrants who are HIV-positive cannot receive legal permanent status except under special conditions (see also Luibhéid

2002). Thus the United States affirms heteronormative family and corporate interests through its immigration policies. Similarly, those who do not have the professional training or experience required by key industries, and who do not have family in the United States, are likely to face challenges in legally immigrating. Though low-skilled, low-wage workers are certainly in great demand in the United States, they are often seen as undesirable residents. Hence, employers continue to hire immigrants to fill America's most difficult and dangerous jobs but are less interested in ensuring that these workers' and their families can enjoy the security of making the United States their home. By extension, those individuals who best fit this version of the family and corporate needs will be most welcomed into the nation-state as citizens.

Refugee status

Distinct from immigrants are refugees, or those who come to the United States fleeing political and other forms of persecution from countries that the United States considers problematic societies or with whom it is engaged in war. For example, in the wake of the Vietnam War, those who fled the communist-controlled regime were considered refugees. Those given refuge in the United States are considered legal permanent residents (LPRs) and, like other immigrants who share the status of LPR, they are eventually eligible to apply for citizenship.

The process of legal citizenship

Even after one overcomes the challenge of immigrating with proper documents, becoming a legal citizen requires passing more economic and cultural hurdles. Legal citizenship, especially for immigrants, means publicly and legally declaring allegiance to one nation over others, thus gaining access to its political community. People born in the United States are automatically conferred legal citizenship without necessarily having to publicly and legally declare allegiance to this country. Documented immigrants with access to permanent residency (i.e. LPRs) qualify for legal citizenship. Permanent residency allows individuals to live and work in the United States. Individuals attain permanent residency, also known as a green card, after arriving lawfully under one of the various kinds of admission or sponsorship, such as through family members, through an employer, as a refugee, as an investor, and the like. A number of Asians arrive as temporary workers (e.g. H-1B visa holders) or foreign students. Provided that these persons possess valid visas, they enjoy many rights but they are not able to apply for citizenship and eventually are required to return to their homelands unless their legal status in the United States changes, oftentimes through employer sponsorship.

   To naturalize, one must be at least 18 years old, have been in the United States for five years (or for three years if married to a US citizen), be of "good moral character" (e.g. not have been convicted of aggravated felony), must demonstrate knowledge of US government and history, and be able to speak, write, and read English, with few exceptions. Here we see the connection between legal citizenship and social and cultural citizenship. Lacking the latter preempts securing the former. The cost of applying for citizenship as of 2012 was US$680.[1] The net effect is to bar from American citizenship those with limited incomes and little acculturation (Ambrose Lee 2010).

Undocumented immigrants

The term "undocumented immigrant" is a misnomer since many such immigrants have documents, such as drivers' licenses, passports, and so on, but not all of those that are necessary for legal permanent residence. Still, the term indicates that the problem is with a person's paperwork, rather than any inherent status, such as "illegal." The concepts of "illegal immigration" and "illegal alien" are historically new ones, dating from the early twentieth century (Ngai 2004). The US government continues to create its own unauthorized immigration to a degree. For instance, it currently allocates family- and employer-sponsored green cards to 25,620 persons per country. Because some countries have so many more applicants than that, such as Mexico, China, the Philippines, and India, it can take decades to be granted the legal right to emigrate from them, while immigrants from other countries can receive quick admittance.[2] So the United States creates its own level of undocumented immigration through its immigration policies.

While "illegal immigration" is associated almost exclusively with Latinos, and in particular Mexican Americans, 13 percent of such immigrants are Asian American (Yang, Junck, and Ling 2010). Many undocumented Asian immigrants arrive in the United States with proper papers but overstay their visas or change their status without first acquiring proper visas. For example, an individual can arrive on a student visa but then leave school to work in a full-time job. If she does not change her visa status first, she is in violation of her visa and becomes an illegal immigrant. In another example, people may come to the United States on tourist visas but overstay their visas to continue living with their relatives. People opt to come to the United States in this way because the family reunification provisions of immigration law can sometimes entail a very long waiting period. Relatives of US citizens can wait several decades before their immigrant visas are approved. Many would rather risk being without proper status in order to rejoin their loved ones in the United States.

Deportations and detentions

Legal citizenship secures full access to public assistance and also protects against deportation. While deportation is most commonly associated with undocumented immigrants, legal immigrants can be deported too. A major tool in the government's increased surveillance of immigrants has been the Illegal Immigration Reform and Immigrant Responsibility Act of 1996. It has jeopardized documented immigrants on the cusp of gaining legal citizenship. This act expanded the types of crimes that became deportable offenses (Fragomen 1997). If one is convicted of a "first-time, minor criminal offense," one can be removed, even if the conviction happened years ago and one has family in the United States (Yang, Junck, and Ling 2010). This means that legal immigrants convicted of practically any crime live in fear of deportation. Many avoid application for citizenship, despite otherwise qualifying, because applying for citizenship might uncover a past offense (Yang, Junck, and Ling 2010). This fear also threatens people's willingness to get married, for that too is a legal contract and might signal their deportable status. While waiting for deportation hearings or to be deported, immigrants are held in detention centers. These are set apart from central locations, impeding immigrants' access to their lawyers or possibly any lawyers

(Yang, Junck, and Ling 2010). This, again, limits both their social citizenship and their legal options.

Deportation also connects to cultural citizenship (which we will discuss in fuller detail later in this chapter). Those immigrants most excluded from cultural citizenship have trouble retaining legal residence in the United States. That is, those immigrants most considered foreign, most considered outside of the nation-state for so-called cultural reasons, find themselves targeted for expulsion from the United States. Since 9/11, there has been more intense surveillance of Muslim and Middle Eastern immigrants. There has been a special registration of male noncitizens (Iyer 2010). This has led to 13,000 persons being deported, even though not one was charged with terrorist-related crimes, the purported reason behind the registration. Individuals can also be detained based simply on unverified and random tips from the public. For example, a year after 9/11, three Muslim men were arrested in Florida after a Georgian woman overheard their conversation at a restaurant and erroneously reported to police their intent to commit an act of terrorism. The claim was completely false and was likely based on misconstruing their comments, coupled with the men's appearance as brown men, at least one having a long beard and wearing a *kufi*. Instead of criticizing overzealous reactions based at least in part on racial profiling, the tipster was praised by government officials.[3] The medical students were on their way to a hospital in Florida to begin internships. The hospital canceled their internships after the incident but later reversed its decision. The burden of proof falls on the accused, rather than the other way around (Iyer 2010).

In these cases, people become suspect based on "national origins," which is code for culture and/or race but not deemed racist. Still, a lack of cultural citizenship can also have legal consequences. Such accusations may actually be encouraged by the government, for as it wages war against Muslim countries overseas, it feeds public distrust of Muslims at home. As a result of such surveillance, Muslim groups have stopped reporting "crimes for fear of being investigated on unrelated issues, such as immigration or links to terrorism" (Iyer 2010: 531). Also, the Immigration and Naturalization Service (INS), which administered immigration policy for many years, has since 9/11 been dissolved. The Department of Homeland Security (DHS) now administers immigration policy, signaling that immigrants are first and foremost considered a potential threat to the nation, rather than a boon to it (Nguyen 2005).

Non-Muslims have also been increasingly swept up in the "war on terror" domestic crackdowns. As immigration officials carry out greater surveillance, immigrants of all types become increasingly profiled and vulnerable. Because US immigration officials rely on imperfect visual cues to racialize people as being "Muslim," authorities are targeting many non-Muslims. According to Irum Shiekh, "Muslims and Muslim-looking individuals who are detained and deported under immigration charges have no connection to terrorism. However, the state's discourse on national security rationalizes these procedures by implying that these individuals have the potential to become terrorists in the future" (2008: 82).

Furthermore, Latinos have been deported as a result of 9/11 responses from the government. For instance, after the 9/11 attacks, the government sought a stronger crackdown on immigrants who had overstayed their visas. Two of the suspected hijackers had overstayed their visas. One result was Operation Tarmac; it involved a sweep of airports. Hundreds of Latinos who had arrived in the United States without full documents and had been working at airports ended up being arrested, even if they had become citizens since their immigration (Nguyen 2005).[4] Relatedly, Filipino immigrant airport workers, some of whom were US citizens, others of whom were legal permanent residents, disproportionately lost their jobs in the San Francisco Bay Area (where they comprised an overwhelming majority of airport workers) because they were seen as ultimately less reliable as airport security screeners as a result of their immigrant backgrounds (Rodriguez and Balce 2004). Of course, undocumented migrants, under conditions of heightened "homeland security," face more exploitation because others know they live in a heightened police state. For instance, landlords in Texas began charging higher rents to Mexican immigrants, in effect demanding bribes (Nguyen 2005). This exploitation and deportation regime takes place in addition to laws passed or argued in Arizona, Mississippi, and other states. These laws in practice rely on racial profiling to stop Latinos and demand residency documents, which the US Supreme Court has ruled constitutional.

A connection between the profiling of Latinos and Middle Easterners should not be surprising. The targeting of Middle Easterners is an extension of both the mistreatment of Latinos within the war on gangs and on drugs and the rising detention of immigrants within immigrant prisons (Maira 2009). All such crackdowns narrow who belongs in the state and punish the most vulnerable. The "border" between the United States and other countries has become increasingly militarized, but after 9/11 it is everywhere, not just along territorial lines with other nations. Airports, train stations, shipping docks, and so on qualify as borderlands. According to the reigning logic and institutions controlling immigration, possible "enemies" are already in the nation and must be controlled and expunged. At the same time, the curbing of Middle Easterners is connected to a longer history of the United States' targeting immigrants and their US-born children with origins in countries which the United States considers its enemies, as in the case of the Japanese during World War II. People of color in particular are targets of these measures. It is important to recall that, during World War II, internment camps were not created for Americans with German heritage, of which there were many.

Social citizenship

Legal citizenship helps ensure basic rights and protection connected to social citizenship. According to the liberal democratic ideals of the United States, all persons have basic social, civil rights, regardless of their legal citizenship. These include rudimentary health and economic assistance (e.g. welfare assistance), legal protection, and the like. Yet, as we have already discussed, rights and protection are not fully available to everyone and can vary depending on individuals' race, class, gender, and sexuality (Glenn 2002). Moreover, rights are increasingly being set aside exclusively for those with citizenship. According to legal theorist Linda Bosniak, "it seems clear that there are certain characteristics of alienage that structurally shape the lives of most noncitizens, usually in disadvantaging forms" (2006: 12). The condition of being a noncitizen, a condition she refers to as "alienage," becomes a source of inequality. Not only does it deny people social citizenship, alienage, especially the status of being undocumented, buoys up employers' profits because the latter can take advantage of immigrant workers' tenuous legal status and pay them wages well below the legal minimum wage.

Limitations of public assistance

A central element of social citizenship is access to public assistance. Laws regarding public assistance have changed in recent decades. Undocumented immigrants face an increasingly hostile environment. For instance, the infamous Proposition 187 passed in 1994 in California, limited access for undocumented immigrants to public education, social services, and health care, thereby reinforcing a permanent underclass (Jacobson 2008). Proposition 187 was declared unconstitutional because the US Constitution does not technically distinguish between citizens and noncitizen residents (regardless of legal status) when it comes to who is deserving of social citizenship, including civil rights. Nevertheless, there continues to be fierce battles in the United States to narrow the basis on which people can claim different kinds of rights and privileges. Proposition 187 may not have been implemented but it has successors, including anti-immigrant policies, that have been passed at the state level. Such regulations have ramifications for documented immigrants. The undocumented are often part of mixed-status families living with documented immigrants and even citizens (Fix and Zimmermann 2001). The boundary between legal and illegal is blurry.

At the federal level, punitive laws continued. In 1996, Congress enacted and President Clinton ceremoniously signed into law the Personal Responsibility and Work Opportunity Act (PRWORA). PRWORA "ended welfare as we know it" by, among other changes, denying public assistance to immigrants deemed "unqualified" and limiting access to those deemed "qualified." Before this act was passed, immigrants were entitled to the same benefits as citizens. Now, legal citizenship defines one's access to the social safety net, that is, to one's social citizenship. Not that social citizenship has ever been fully developed in US political culture. As Fraser and Gordon observe, "Receipt of 'welfare' is usually considered grounds for disrespect, a threat to, rather than a realization of, citizenship. And in the area of social services, the word, *public* is often pejorative" (1998: 91). As we discussed in chapter 4, not having access to social safety nets necessarily impacts one's class status in American society.

PRWORA has been described less as a welfare reform bill and more as an anti immigration bill (Quiambao 2010: 476). Before passage of the act, immigrants made up a significant part of welfare recipients, accounting for US$4 billion by 1994. The act divided immigrants into "qualified" and "unqualified." The unqualified consisted mostly of undocumented immigrants. They became eligible for only the most basic of services, namely treatment in medical emergencies. Qualified immigrants were immigrants with proper documents, refugees, asylum seekers, and a few others (Blazer and Broder 2010). Qualified immigrants who arrived after August 22, 1996 (effectively an arbitrary date, the one on which the bill was passed) had to wait five years before they could claim "federally means-tested public benefits," which include "Medicaid (except for emergency care), SCHIP [State Children's Health Insurance Program], TANF [Temporary Assistance for Needy Families], Food Stamps, and Supplemental Security Income [SSI]" (Blazer and Broder 2010: 521). This time delay was ostensibly due to the fact that half of immigrants in 1994 who received benefits did so within four years of arrival (Quiambao 2010). Immigrants living in the United States before that date did not automatically qualify for public welfare either. They "were barred altogether from the Food Stamps and SSI programs until they became citizens. (States could provide cash assistance under TANF and Medicaid to legal immigrants who were living in the country on August 22, 1996.)" (Cohen 2007).[5]

Of course, undocumented and other immigrants who do not qualify for most public benefits have fared the worst as a result of this welfare reform act. The legislation had a disproportionate effect on women (Fujiwara 2008). Women of color are routinely framed as weighing down the welfare system. And, as primary caregivers, women face more challenges in attaining the training or other resources necessary to find work and stay employed. Under these conditions, lacking legal citizenship has even starker material consequences. Overlooked in this scapegoating of immigrants is the role of the United States in creating them, as Ngai (2004) argues. Rather than seeing these welfare recipients as products of US military action, such as refugees from Southeast Asia, which they most often are, they are represented as greedy and lazy intruders.

Even as "qualified" immigrants have access to benefits, the anti-immigrant discourse surrounding PRWORA has scared off some from taking advantage of their benefits (Blazer and Broder 2010). The effect is a continued denial of their social citizenship, for they are not receiving needed assistance. Many become confused about their eligibility. They also worry about being denied permanent residency if they apply for benefits. Immigrants considered potentially "a public charge" on the state, namely those in need of welfare, can be deported (Blazer and Broder 2010). This has had the direct effect of barring immigrants from their legally owed and needed benefits. While this rule was changed in 1999 to help ensure that qualified immigrants in need were able to receive benefits, uncertainty and distrust remain in the population. Also limiting deserved access to public welfare has been a dearth of bilingual service employees (Blazer and Broder 2010). These restrictions stand despite the fact that immigrants pay federal and state taxes for these benefits. As noted in chapter 4, Southeast-Asian Americans, who often lack proficiency in English, have some of the highest rates of poverty among Asian Americans and these are higher than the national average. Both the need for and barriers to public benefits have been more extreme for them.

Cultural citizenship

The previous discussion involved challenges to social citizenship mostly for those who lack full documents. Citizens, documented residents, and undocumented migrants, especially if they come from racialized minority groups, face obstacles to cultural citizenship because they are often figured as outsiders even when they may be able to legally claim full membership (i.e. citizenship) in the United States. Cultural citizenship refers to having one's culture considered as "American" and therefore laying claim to be a full member of the nation. People's access to (and exclusion from) cultural citizenship shapes the limits and possibilities of their access to legal and social citizenship. Indeed, the children of undocumented immigrants have claimed that they ought to be eligible for legal status and ultimately legal citizenship on the basis of their cultural citizenship, having spent most of their lives in the United States. They have rallied in support of the DREAM (Development, Relief, and Education for Alien Minors) Act which would give them that opportunity.[6]

Given the surveillance that many Asian Americans and other immigrants live under, it may be surprising to learn that so many do not hide their culture but instead seek ways to express it. Rather than intentionally assimilate, they seek cultural citizenship as *ethnic* Americans, to pray, eat, speak, and live as they want while still insisting on being recognized as fully American. Key measures of Asian-American culture include language, religion, customs, and cultural and social events. This represents a shift as earlier waves of immigrants from Asia, Eastern Europe, and Southern Europe had to change their lifestyles dramatically to fit in. We examine the cultural practices and degree of assimilation among Asian-American communities, in particular the second generation. We also analyze how they assert a cultural citizenship as Americans while maintaining their ethnic practices.

Language

Most immigrants speak their native tongue and prefer to do so. This is not surprising. More telling for cultural citizenship is what the second and later generations speak. Portes and Rumbaut (2001) have conducted some of the most thorough research on this topic. They find a diversity of responses based on ethnic group. Overall, second-generation immigrants can often understand and speak their native language but either prefer to speak English as they get older (Portes and Rumbaut 2001) or to be bilingual (Portes, Fernandez-Kelly, and Haller 2005). In addition to certain Latin American and West Indian groups, Portes and colleagues studied Filipino, Chinese, Cambodian, Laotian, Hmong, and Vietnamese Americans. Filipinos were the most likely to speak English with their parents (only 13 percent spoke a language other than English with them). About half of Chinese immigrants spoke a language other than English at home, whereas about 90 percent or higher of Southeast Asians did (Portes and Rumbaut 2001). The more that parents spoke an ethnic language at home and actively assisted their children in speaking it, such as by enrolling them in ethnic cultural schools, the more likely it was that the children, especially daughters, would learn it as well (Portes and Rumbaut 2001).

For the most part, then, children of immigrants are learning and often preferring English, making English-only legislation more punitive than of assistance. Critiques by nativists (those opposed to immigration) that the United States should enact English-only laws are misplaced since the children of immigrants are learning and preferring English all on their own (Chavez 2008). Instead, such laws, if implemented, would threaten the access of immigrants and citizens not fluent in English to their full rights, such as ballots in non-English languages, bilingual education, and the like. Bilingual education continually faces threats because it is seen as encouraging non-English languages with public tax dollars. This concern over the loss of English is part of a larger narrative of the overtaking of the United States by immigrants, particularly Latinos. Within this "threat" narrative, immigrants are altering the "American" way of life (Chavez 2008). In this sense, Spanish is not critiqued, not because it is not English but because it is considered "American."

Religion

Religion traditionally has been a key institution that immigrants use to satisfy multiple interests, including spiritual needs, community, and cultural teaching of the next generation. For contemporary Asian Americans, religion remains a core part of their cultural lives for the same reasons. One key difference to previous immigration waves is the more obvious religious diversity that current immigrants bring, even relative to the diversity within Christianity among European immigrants. These include Buddhists, Muslims, Hindus, Sikhs, Jains, and more. Rather than hide or assimilate their religion, these groups have built temples and formed private associations within which to practice their religion. Immigrants seek ways to connect with co-ethnics, and religion provides that mechanism. These spaces allow parents to teach their ethnic culture to their children as well. The more associated a religion is with a particular ethnicity, the easier it is for religious teachings to reinforce ethnic commitments (Min 2010). And, because religion is respected in the United States, it is an accepted means of coming together. Immigrants are not critiqued for forming religious spaces.

Islam as threat

One obvious counter-example is the building of mosques. Islam remains not only a foreign religion to the United States within popular discourse, but also a perceived threat. Its mistaken association with terrorism has made the building of mosques a political issue, not simply a spiritual or communal one. Islam serves as more than a religion – it is read racially, that is, as deterministic of one's morality and abilities, and subject to discriminatory treatment by the state and individuals (Rana 2011). Politicians weigh in on the subject of building mosques, and Muslims' rights to do so must be defended within the Constitution.

Islam today resembles Buddhism for Japanese Americans during World War II. For instance, on the "loyalty" test given to Japanese Americans in the internment camps, to determine if they were loyal enough to leave them, a question asked respondents which religious groups they were members of. Those who replied Buddhist were considered more likely to be disloyal. Buddhist ministers were framed as akin to Japanese-language instructors and other community leaders as particular threats within the ethnic group. In fact, the Japanese American Citizens League publicly critiqued the rounding up of Arab and Muslim Americans following the 9/11 attacks as in the same vein as the internment of Japanese Americans.[7] Again, this relates to the issue of cultural citizenship. While the United States guarantees religious freedom, there are religious practices that are considered "un-American," and those who engage in these are often represented as non-American, regardless of what their legal citizenship may be, and struggle to assert themselves as genuinely "American" (Mir 2011).

Growing religious presence across generations

As ethnic groups grow, they gather the resources to build more established sites for communal gatherings. For instance, Hindus have formed a variety of organizations, including *satsangs* (local worship groups), *bala vihars* (educational groups for children), public temples, Hindu student organizations, and Hindu political umbrella groups (Kurien 2007). As immigrants recreate their religion abroad, changes often are made to fit within the new religious context (Fenton 1988). In the United States, this has meant adopting a more "congregational" style of worship, one that relies on lay members voluntarily coming together as a community, rather than a strict hierarchy set from above, to contribute to religious and other services to members (Warner and Wittner 1998; Yang and Ebaugh 2001). This is read as a type of organizational assimilation. Another way of thinking about this is that immigrants attempt to practice cultural citizenship in ways that they feel are closer to the mainstream (Christian) ideal. Indeed, among Asian-American Christians, involvement in church groups appears to enhance civic participation, for instance in voting which is often used as an indicator of political assimilation (Cherry 2009), discussed further in chapter 11.

As multiculturalism has grown in the United States, so has religious interest and even nationalism among immigrants (Kurien 2007). For instance, a set of fundamentalist, conservative Hindus in the United States espouse Hinduism as superior to other religions and agitate for India to become a Hindu rather than a secular state. Chen (2008) similarly finds that Taiwanese immigrants make significant life-changing practices as Buddhists or Christians upon immigration, such as becoming vegetarian or adopting evangelicalism. Their sense of displacement following migration must be compensated by an equally powerful sense of salvation. The more that religion asks of its practitioners, the stronger the sense of community it creates for them, which is particularly attractive to immigrants who otherwise lack strong social ties. In other words, immigrant religious practitioners are assimilating with their organizational form but simultaneously affirm distinctiveness through a religious orthodoxy (Yang and Ebaugh 2001).

Because much of the motivation to start religious organizations is to instill religion and ethnic culture within the second generation, how the second generation approaches religion has become of major interest. Much diversity exists. For instance, some Hindus among the second generation have become politicized and argue for a strident devotion to religion (Kurien 2007). Most others, however, confess to shame over not knowing much about their religion (McDermott 2000). They regret not fully understanding the rituals or practices of the religion and so avoid established temples (Dhingra 2008). Still, religion matters to them as a way to connect with their ethnic culture, as a means to be more grounded spiritually, and as a way to combat discriminatory attitudes towards non-Christians and nonwhites.

Christian immigrants similarly form their own places of worship. For immigrants, much of the motivation to start one's own congregation stems from language preferences, for most immigrants are not as comfortable in English as they are in their native tongue. In addition, religious spaces offer far more than the service itself (Min 2010). They serve as community sites that allow immigrants an opportunity to take a break from their busy work lives, socialize with one another, and strategize for leadership opportunities unavailable in mainstream civil society. Furthermore, by affirming their religion within the diaspora, immigrants secure links to their homeland for themselves and their children (Levitt 2009; Yang and Ebaugh 2001). While churches affirm cultural bonds, they also provide opportunities for immigrants to integrate in their locality, such as by learning about employment or immigration law issues. Finally, ethnic churches can help to enhance immigrant, working-class youths' adaptation in the United States because the church, as a kind of surrogate parent, offers the kinds of emotional support that urban, marginalized young people need (Cao 2005).

While it makes sense that immigrants of the same religion maintain ethnic divisions, one could presume that highly assimilated Christians within the second generation would cross ethnic boundaries within religious settings. However, here we still find many churches divided by ethnicity (and generation). This is despite the fact that services are very assimilated and practically identical to those in other churches. For instance, services are entirely in English and lack references to ethnicity in the sermons (Jeung 2004; Kim 2004). Churchgoers often feel a tension between their ethnic segregation and their religious ties to other like-minded Christians, regardless of ethnicity. It is a problem in the minds of many, both Asian Americans and non-Asian Americans on campuses (Kim 2004). In response, Asian Americans argue that it is important to worship in settings that are comfortable. Because of subtle cultural differences to whites, racial distinctions, family ties to the congregation, and different histories within the church, second-generation Asian Americans feel most comfortable congregating with one another. Some within the second generation even argue that their ethnicity shapes their Christianity. For instance, some Korean Americans believe they are better adherents to their religion than are other groups because the values of honoring family, of respect, and the like are affirmed not only in their religion but within their ethnicity (Busto 1996). They may even criticize their parents for not being sufficiently committed to their religion. Min (2010) found among his sample of Korean Americans in the New York/New Jersey area that one-third of the second generation was evangelical Christian, a higher percentage than their parents. In fact, religion was so dominant in their identities that, even though they often practiced within a Korean-American church, they claimed religion as more important to them than ethnicity. As second-generation Asian Americans form their own churches, it is not merely a desire to worship apart from whites or from their parents. As Kim (2010) notes, "Rather, [second-generation Korean Americans] want to carve out a hybrid third space that is uniquely their own, distinct from mainstream Evangelicalism and from Korean Christianity" (Kim 2010: 99). In other words, they are forming a unique and meaningful religious and ethnic identity together.

Pan-ethnic churches

In addition to ethnic-specific churches, a growing number of pan-ethnic churches have arisen, primarily in California, given its history of pan-ethnic alliances. Cultural citizenship is easier to come by as religious groups become more multi-ethnic and multiracial, for they appear less insular. These serve second- and later generation Asian Americans who identify as Asian American because of a shared political identity or common sense of values (Jeung 2004). These are typically Chinese and Japanese Americans. Pan-ethnic churches signal a distinct form of adaptation than that predicted by assimilation theory. Rather than join mainstream churches as they leave their ethnic congregation, members solidify racial boundaries. This does not mean that members necessarily view race and racism as compelling influences on their lives, but that they still see meaningful differences from whites and similarities with one another, despite their full acculturation.

Becoming a pan-ethnic church is not easy, however. As ethnic-specific churches seek to grow, they often try to become pan-ethnic rather than outreach to all types of Christians. This can create tensions within the congregation, whose members have joined originally because of an affinity for co-ethnics in particular (Dhingra 2004). Churches must selectively attend to ethnic versus pan-ethnic interests in order to appeal to both longtime members who enjoy ethnic solidarity and new members seeking a broader, "Asian-American" experience. One way of accomplishing this is by regulating references to a particular ethnicity to the "backstage," that is, to more private settings within the Sunday service, such as Sunday school. More public spaces, such as the main sermon, are purposefully void of ethnic references. In this way, newcomers do not feel put off or less welcome.

Religious practices in daily life

While much of the academic conversation on immigrant religion has centered on how immigrants' religious organizations have adapted to an American context, and therefore how immigrants exercise cultural citizenship, this has left under-explored the religious practices of those removed from formal or informal organizations. For instance, while mosques are increasing in the United States, not all Muslims have access to them, given their geography or work schedules. As an example of the latter, Muslim taxi drivers in New York City struggle to find the time and place to pray during the day (Smith and Bender 2004). They have a map of the mosques which they stop at when possible, especially on Fridays (the most important prayer day). Given the challenges of finding a mosque while on the job, drivers improvise other means of adhering to religious commitments, such as praying in the backseat of their cab or on a sidewalk. Ethnic and racial divisions persist for Muslims as well. Few African Americans worship alongside South Asians and Middle Easterners, and vice versa. Hindus commonly practice their religion in their homes. They visit temples only on special occasions. More research on religious practices in informal, private settings is needed.

Asian religion in western consciousness

The bulk of interest in Asian America and religion involves religiosity. The other side of that coin is other Americans' take on Asian and Asian-American religion. Asian religious figures have long been a site of infatuation for certain sects within liberal America. Swami Vivekananda, Dali Lama, Deepak Chopra, D. T. Suzuki, and others are part of American popular consciousness (Iwamura 2005). Each of these figures is read in the same vein: peaceful, exotic, and all-knowing. Infatuation with such figures comes and goes historically as the United States searches for alternative spiritual or moral paradigms outside of its Christian normativity in order to justify its capitalist and global efforts. In this sense, Asia continues to serve its Orientalist role, as a culture and peoples who primarily uplift westerners. As long as Asian-American religions serve this role, they can be tolerated, even appreciated, within a multicultural United States (Prashad 2000).

Customs

Cultural citizenship comes easier as individuals adhere to American popular culture. Individuals face the challenge of being drawn to American culture and its privileges while also finding meaning in their ethnic heritage. Given the growing multiculturalism within the United States, it is easier for Asian Americans to maintain their ethnic customs without arousing critique as un-American, but ethnic customs can still elicit stereotyping, if not suspicion.

Food is a key part of culture. Asian food has become increasingly popular with all Americans. Not only restaurants but also ethnic grocery stores are popping up outside ethnic enclaves. The United States has a history of embracing ethnic foods and assimilating them into the national palate. Pizza, bagels, bratwurst, kung pao chicken, tacos, and so many other dishes are now considered as American as they are tied to specific ethnic groups. They can be found within practically any shopping mall food court and airport.

Still, culinary acceptance has limits. For instance, a Muslim woman in Maryland was denied a foster-care license in part due to her religion and decision not to serve pork.[8] What constitutes American culture is a politicized question. And an embrace of food does not mean an embrace of the people behind it. Children become read as "smelly" if their food has distinct spices (Gibson 1988). The more unpopular an ethnic group, the more racialized its food becomes and vice versa (Mannur 2010). Chinese exclusion in the late 1800s was argued partly based on a critique of their food, of rice being inferior to bread and beef (Ruiz 2008). And certain cultural delicacies, such as eating dog in some Asian cultures, provoke disgust in most Americans and push the boundaries of accepted multiculturalism (Wu 2003).

There are a variety of other ethnic customs that Asian Americans practice which bring into question their ability to assert a full cultural citizenship. As discussed in chapter 6, gender relations and parenting styles may be more conservative within Asian families. Arranged marriages, common in certain Asian countries, sharply contrast with western notions of romantic love. Living with one's parents as an adult, also common within Asian and other national cultures, becomes ridiculed as a "failure to launch" in the United States. From this cultural perspective, Asians and Asian Americans do not know how to be "proper" adults.

In response, Asian Americans adopt more western styles of relationships by promoting more gender equality, moving out of their parents' homes, and the like. But they also retain elements of their cultural background. For instance, although they may not embrace a traditional arranged marriage, they may still prefer their parents' input in the process (Dhingra 2007). They may move out of their parents' home but live in close enough proximity to still be dutiful children. In other words, they seek out ways to fit American cultural notions of adulthood while honoring ethnic expectations.

Ethnic religion and customs must be defended when seen as "deviant" from popular trends. Asian Americans' educational and economic accomplishments help in this defense. The more accomplished a group, the easier it is to defend their cultural practices as morally suitable. It is not sufficient simply to be wealthy. Groups must be seen as embracing the neoliberal ideals (i.e. notions of self-sufficiency and hard work) of American culture. Aihwa Ong (2003) argues that by adhering to neoliberal notions, rather than relying on the state, immigrants advance their citizenship. Others, however, are not so convinced. According to Park (2005), embracing neo-liberalism is not sufficient for Asian Americans to overcome their "forever foreign" status. Instead, Asian Americans also consume high-status markers, such as fashion and even elite education, in order to signal their families' trajectory of rags to riches and to be full members of the nation. Unfortunately, according to Park, such efforts do not succeed in achieving full citizenship but instead highlight their distinct nature from others. In any case, economically successful Asian Americans can use their achievements to defend their culture from even greater attack, unless of course they become read as "taking over" in the form of the morally deviant "yellow peril."

Like all groups, Asian Americans find worth in their culture and want to sustain aspects of it. This does not mean that individuals accept all of their culture. They readily critique aspects of it. However, they rarely want to fully assimilate. Some in the second generation worry that they are losing their culture. And often the third generation has weak cultural ties (Tuan 1998). What results is an effort to maintain their distinctiveness alongside a gradual loss of ethnic culture as individuals increasingly interact with other groups, whether white, black, Latino, rich, poor, etc.

Being cultural citizens in cultural organizations

The formation of religious and other cultural organizations can have unintended consequences for Asian Americans, namely for their claims on cultural citizenship. How do Asian Americans respond to the challenge of wanting to maintain their culture within ethnic organizations but also to be accepted as full cultural citizens? On the one hand, they recognize that they have ethnic dissimilarities from others. On the other hand, they argue that, far from illustrating a lack of cultural citizenship, their cultural organizations and practices affirm their commitment to the United States by serving as "model" civic organizations.

According to the dominant logic of civil society within the United States, it is important for cultural and social organizations, such as religious ones, to connect members to those they would not normally meet (Putnam 2000). Otherwise, the organizations are accused of contributing to divisions in the country, with each group only interested in itself (Alexander and Smith 1993). So as not to upset the expectations of civil society, Asian American religious and cultural associations describe themselves as open to all groups. They stress that all groups are welcome in their organizations (even if only their group attends), that their organizations do not denigrate others, and that they do not condone activities that cost taxpayers money but benefit only one group (e.g. public street signs in a non-English language). In these ways, organizations affirm neoliberal assumptions embedded within contemporary citizenship, of individualism, autonomy, and egalitarianism (Outlaw 1998). They do not place any expectations or burdens on others and instead are self-sufficient. The organizations also actively support public citizenship, for instance hoisting up the American flag even at ethnic events and contributing to mainstream charities. Furthermore, individuals argue that, because the United States was founded on the principle of personal freedom, they are fulfilling the American creed by expressing their cultural differences in personal ways (Dhingra 2008).

In addition, organizations espouse a benign multiculturalism as a means to remain good cultural citizens (Rudruppa 2004). This means that organizations define their culture in relatively static ways that support middle-class and upper-class lifestyles, rather than attending to the hybrid nature of culture. Group leaders connect their ethnic culture to the "model minority" stereotype, arguing that their ethnicity helps make them full citizens because it contributes to their success (Dhingra 2007; Hintzen 2001). Such rhetoric helps defend their distinctive cultural practices or religious buildings from accusations of creating negative influences in localities. To accomplish a "model minority" image, however, is not necessarily easy. Groups must exclude elements of their community or heritage that undermine that image. For instance, Indian-American leaders in New York City banned South Asian gay and lesbian organizations from publicly participating in its annual Indian day parade. Within a heteronormative America, homosexuality implies deviance. Muslim Americans have faced even more public suspicion. In response, some organizations in New York City have tried to position themselves more as ethnic groups than religious groups (Slyomovics 1995). Among other tactics, they have instituted a Muslim World Day Parade, akin to popular ethnic festivals there. What these "model minority" efforts show is that what constitutes the cultural representation of a group is a constructed rather than a natural process, one that is guided by concerns over approval from the nation.

Overall, then, rather than being conferred cultural citizenship based on their legal residence or even upbringing in the United States, Asian Americans have to struggle to achieve it. This has not meant assimilation in order to appear worthy of belonging. But it has led to particular forms of practicing and defending one's culture condoned by mainstream culture, as well as to a hyper-embrace of high-status symbols. Given their lack of options, Asian Americans have to conform, even while arguing for their cultural distinctiveness.

However, the denial of full belonging encourages individuals to be committed to one another. In other words, groups may be tied to their background even as they try to fit in with their surroundings. To the extent that the United States denies equal citizenship to its residents – legally, socially, culturally, or otherwise – it furthers group divisions rather than encourages assimilation. So, while individuals often acculturate and have weaker claims on their particular ethnicity, they will be motivated to (re) create connections to co-ethnics in ways that allow them full citizenship, keeping in mind that full citizenship does not guarantee economic equality.

Transnational citizenship

Exclusions from citizenship – legal, social, or cultural – may compel those with immigrant backgrounds to (re)activate connections with their erstwhile homelands. Historically, immigrants have either maintained or initiated links with their countries of origin, but in the contemporary period these linkages can be more easily sustained and forged because of advances in technology, both in travel and communications, which allows immigrants the chance to be present (physically and virtually) at "home."

Just as importantly, however, immigrants' "home" governments have also played an important role in reaching out to their (former) citizens to (re)incorporate them into the "homeland." Some scholars have found evidence for a co-ethnic preference among different states across the globe; that is, many countries tend to discriminate between foreigners, often preferring (or extending preferential treatment to) former citizens. Many Asian countries are very active in cultivating connections with former citizens. More and more labor-sending states are active in trying to ensure that their former citizens send remittances back "home" on a regular basis. The Philippines, for instance, has introduced policies aimed at channeling migrants' remittances through formal banking channels (Rodriguez 2010). Moreover, "emigrant states" (Coutin 2007; Fitzgerald 2009) are expanding the capacities and missions of their ministries for foreign affairs and their consular offices overseas in order to sustain their overseas populations' homeland orientations. Indeed, alongside the expansion of consular activities, labor-sending states engage in constructing nationalist discourses to constitute overseas citizens as extensions of the nation-state to, among other aims, encourage migrants' remittance-sending. Popular culture in sending countries increasingly frames emigrants as still part of the nation (Desai 2004). Some labor-sending states also introduce reforms in citizenship law to formally reincorporate migrants who may have become naturalized citizens in their countries of destination, as their emigrants' sustained sense of membership has become vital to these states' interests.

Some countries actually introduce return migration policies. In South Korea, there has been preferential policy for Koreans, especially those who emigrated to the United States or Canada, mainly to incorporate them as investors during a period of economic crisis (1997–8) (Skrentny et al. 2007). Indeed, many Asian immigrants engage in what Aiwha Ong (1999) calls "flexible citizenship" as they use their multiple citizenships to maneuver across borders in order to advance their entrepreneurial interests. As flexible citizenship grows, the role of the nation-state declines, although only to a degree. As seen in the previous sections of this chapter, the nation-state carries continued significance in defining the legal, social, and cultural belonging of residents.

Conclusion

Citizenship, especially for those who are foreign-born or who are racialized minorities like Asian Americans, can become a major source of inequality. Legal, social, and cultural forms of citizenship have been tenuous for Asian Americans over the decades and even more so since 9/11. Nor does full access to one form guarantee full access to the others. Though an individual may possess legal, formal membership in the United States as a citizen and should, in theory, be eligible for all of the rights and privileges that citizenship offers, racialized minorities may be unable to fully claim or assert those rights and privileges. Despite Asian Americans' exclusions from citizenship, they have attempted to assert their citizenship as Americans, paradoxically enough, through the assertion of their cultural difference. They have exercised their rights as members of a self-proclaimed multicultural society by retaining their cultural practices, including the practice of their religions. No nation-state can have unregulated immigration, but what kinds of regulation it has and its policies post-immigration must be fair to all. A fear of difference and of limited resources leads to stricter definitions of who belongs and what America *really* means. Immigrants remind all of us that the United States should live up to its ideals of democracy, justice, and equality.

Discussion questions

- What are different forms of "citizenship"? List, define, and then provide an example of three dimensions of citizenship.
- How is the "border" conceptualized in this chapter? Provide an example of a border and then analyze it in relation to both legal and cultural citizenship.
- What are some examples of Asian Americans claiming cultural citizenship while also maintaining their ethnic cultures? What are some of the challenges faced in these examples?
- How is US multiculturalism related to Asian American cultural citizenship? Provide and analyze some examples of how multiculturalist practices appropriate Asian culture.

8 Media and Popular Culture

Media, broadly defined, are both tools for promoting discourse on minority groups and for contesting such discourse. This chapter explains both ends of this issue. The media, for this purpose, consist of the news (i.e. newspapers, magazines, television news, radio, etc.), film and television series, and new communications technology, particularly the internet. The media are a major source of popular culture at the present moment. The media and popular culture are crucial sites in which representations and stereotypes of racialized groups are produced.

The chapter starts first with an overview of the sociological approaches to understanding the media. Second, we examine how different forms of media (re)produce stereotypes of Asian Americans in the contemporary moment. As we discussed in chapter 2, the dominant stereotypes of Asian Americans include the "yellow peril" and the "model minority." "Yellow peril" is a stereotype that has had a long history in the United States. Though it has manifested in different ways over the years, this stereotype has had durability. The more recent "model minority" stereotype, while much more positive when compared with the "yellow peril," nevertheless has negative consequences for Asian Americans. Though these stereotypes have been applied to Asian Americans as a group, they have manifested in different ways vis-à-vis specific Asian ethnic groups. Moreover, there are particular gendered and sexualized aspects of these stereotypes that have been circulated in different kinds of media. We examine some examples of how different Asian ethnic groups (and genders) have been represented within the broad categories of "yellow peril" or "model minority," and illustrate how these representations have been depicted in the different media outlets that are our focus in this chapter.

We then draw from sociological approaches to the media to examine what kinds of role Asian Americans play in mainstream media. We will look, for instance, at Asian-American involvement in the field of journalism and its impact on news reporting on Asian Americans, as well as to what extent Asian-American actors actually get roles in television series or the movies and what sort of roles those are. Sociological approaches to the media have generally posited that the integration of minority groups in the media industry can impact the kinds of representation that are produced about them. We evaluate to what extent that is actually true.

Finally, we end by looking at the following set of questions: What have Asian Americans' reactions been to those depictions (e.g. protests or appreciation)? What do Asian American performers think of their performances? What images are presented within Asian-Americans' own artistic creations (Feng 2002; Hamamoto and Liu 2000; Lee 1999)? How do Asian Americans use the media to create community? These questions inform the relationship of minorities to the media more broadly. The chapter argues that fuller images of Asian Americans today are due to the increased presence of Asian Americans as a consuming market, but that Asian-American productions offer more nuanced portrayals.

The sociology of media

Sociologists have long taken an interest in understanding the media, that is, mass communications systems that disseminate either information or entertainment (what is also known as "popular culture") in print and electronic form like newspapers and magazines, radio, film, television, and most recently, the internet, and their impacts on society.

Indeed, the impact of the media on our lives is pretty obvious. Taking a close look at our everyday lives, how often do we check our smartphones for e-mail or use them to "Google" information? How much time do we spend watching television and, beyond that, finding out more information about the stars that populate our TV screens? It is likely that all that screen time would add up to a great portion of our days. The emergence of the term "screen time" alone suggests that in today's world we are interfacing with computer or television and movie screens on a fairly regular basis. Indeed, politicians and corporations alike recognize that the media has great potential for impacting our decisions about who to vote for or what to buy. We can hardly avoid advertisements, whether they are political ads or corporate commercials.

Media images and their impacts on how people perceive society, social relations, and even their own selves are of particular interest to sociologists. Gamson et al. argue that "a wide variety of media can act as teachers of values, ideologies, beliefs. . . . [Media images] can provide images of interpreting the world whether or not the designers are conscious of this intent" (1992: 374). Sociologists' interest in the media and race can be divided into three different areas: first, what sort of images are produced through the media and how different racial groups are represented; second, the media as an industry (i.e. who controls the media) and its implications for the production of representations of racial minorities; and third, how minorities respond to the media.

The media and representations of race

The media have the power to disempower and disenfranchise groups through the negative portrayals of (as well as their failure to portray) minority groups. The media have the power to confer status on individuals (or groups). "Fifteen minutes of fame," for instance, means that an individual can capture audience attention and possibly sway ideas and feelings about an issue or circumstance by virtue of being in the media spotlight, however briefly. Given the way that the media can confer status, it becomes important to minority groups that their lives and perspectives are captured in the media so as to validate them as worthwhile members of society, as people who "count." Social theorists such as the Frankfurt School in Germany were among the first scholars to be attentive to the power of the media to reproduce structures of inequality. Writing during Hitler's rise to power, they were concerned about how the media became effective tools of state power, and, in the case of Germany, how the media promoted propaganda legitimizing the annihilation of the Jewish population.

Sociologists have examined the images generated by the media and to what extent those representations justify or legitimize systems of class, gender, and racial and other forms of inequality. In her research on African-American women, Patricia Hill Collins, a noted sociologist, argues that media and other cultural institutions become a means through which "controlling images" work to stigmatize and "brand" specific racialized, gendered, classed, and so on groups and therefore serve to make racism seem commonsensical and "normal" (Collins 2000). As a major socializing institution, the media are able to reproduce structures of power by shaping the ideas that people hold about different social groupings. Indeed, in the absence of face-to-face interactions between different social groupings, the media can have an especially significant role for shaping different groups' expectations about one another and any kind of social interaction that may (or may not) take place between them. Hence a critical analysis of the media is crucial.

The internet, for some observers, is seen as a venue by which inequalities in media ownership (and by implication, the kinds of representation that could be produced) might be redressed, discussed below. Skeptics and other social critics argue however that the promise of equality through the internet is still a dubious prospect. They argue that there is a "digital divide" that exists between those who have the access and know-how to take advantage of the opportunities offered by it and those who do not. Indeed, this "digital divide" maps onto and even exacerbates existing social inequalities (DiMaggio et al. 2001).

Media as an industry

Sociologists have examined the media and their forms of ownership, production, and distribution (Peterson and Anand 2004). Understanding the dynamics of the media industry is important for sociologists because it is believed that those who dominate the industry have more power in shaping the kinds of representation that the media produce. The news media, entertainment, and new communications technology are multibillion dollar industries. Critical scholars argue that the concentration of media ownership poses fundamental challenges to democratic politics. It can result, for example, in incomplete coverage of politics because media owners may see some political issues or perspectives as less lucrative than entertainment (Dunaway 2008). Moreover, as the media are more and more centralized, they can ultimately become instruments of propaganda for powerful entities that use their control of the media to advance their economic or political agendas. This can have consequences for racial minorities. As one critic observes, "With the deregulation of media in the 1980s, 1990s, and 2000s, the unprecedented consolidation of American media has narrowed the ability of minority and nonminority audiences to obtain diverse programming" (Austin 2011: 734). With media ownership becoming more and more concentrated, this critic argues, racialized groups have much less access to programming that may reflect their experiences. Moreover, they do not have opportunities to influence the kinds of representation that are produced about themselves, nor can they counter portrayals of race relations that might legitimize an unequal racial order (Omachonu and Healey 2009).

Beyond simple media ownership, another issue is the degree to which people of color are employed in different media industries. Similar to the thinking with respect to minority ownership and its impact on the representation of racialized groups, it is believed that the employment of blacks, Latinos, or Asian Americans as journalists, actors, news producers, musicians and so on can somehow mitigate negative stereotypes or offer representations of minority experiences that do not already exist. Minority journalists, for instance, can shape story content by focusing on issues specific to racial minorities or by incorporating minority perspectives on more "mainstream" issues. Indeed, the American Society of News Editors actually set a goal for its members to try to achieve a degree of parity for minority journalists because of its belief that the diversity of journalists can positively impact and increase the representation of minority perspectives (Wu and Izard 2008).

Actors, meanwhile, might be able to offer more nuanced interpretations of roles they have taken. The advertising industry is also a powerful player in the media. The role of advertising in influencing journalism is a particular concern for both sociologists and journalists alike (McChesney 2012). As much as film and television (which includes both fictional and "reality" shows, as well as television journalism) produce representations of people, places, and things, so too do advertisers.

The internet, meanwhile, has often been figured as promising opportunities that could rectify or address inequalities in terms of media representations because everyday people are more able to participate in their shaping (DiMaggio et al. 2001). The internet is in many ways considered a "new frontier" through which alternative representations can be produced with ease and immediacy through platforms like YouTube or the practice of blogging.

Responses to the media: media and community formation

Scholars have also looked at how racialized minorities have responded to and countered dominant representations through their own uses of media. Caspi and Elias make a distinction between media *by* and media *for* minorities. This distinction is important because:

> differentiation between these media prototypes constitutes an important theoretical challenge, since it may have numerous implications concerning these media's mediation between the minority and the majority and their differential potential to promote the minority's rights, as well as to raise our sensitivity towards minority media leaders' motivations and interests and their ability to guarantee the minority's self-expression and empowerment. (2011: 63)

In other words, it matters whether the media are produced by or for minority groups. Minorities' ability to produce their own media has implications for whether and how they can address racialized stereotypes and/or the absence of any representation of their distinctive experiences.

Separate from how racialized minorities may respond to and counter mainstream media's representations of them, the media can be a tool for assimilation. They are mechanisms through which immigrants can create, sustain, and become better integrated into a society because they are the means by which that society's norms and values are conveyed. Early in the twentieth century, noted sociologist Robert Park argued that newspapers actually helped immigrants to adjust to their new lives in the United States by enabling them to understand the customs and expectations of their adopted society. Indeed, the media play a role in shaping prospective immigrants' visions of the United States. The US media's global reach facilitates the rapid and continuous dispersal of images of American life that may produce the desire among people outside the United States to come to this country to become part of the "American dream."

The internet, despite what critics have to say about the "digital divide," has been thought of as an especially good tool for new forms of social interaction and can help to facilitate community formation. Via email or platforms like Skype or social media outlets like Facebook, the internet makes communications easier, thereby allowing individuals more opportunities to make and sustain relationships with those whom they feel some kind of affinity or shared identity including ethnic/racial identity. In addition, it can connect people who are spread over great geographic distance. Indeed, the kinds of communities that may be formed on the internet may well be cross-border and global ones, hence they both reflect and provide the potential for new kinds of transnational, collective identities.

Asian Americans as a group are at the forefront of the ownership and use of advanced technology. Studies from the early 2000s found that Asian Americans are 186 percent more likely to own a digital camcorder and 61 percent more likely than the average American to own a digital still camera (Fetto 2002). A more recent study, meanwhile, suggests that Asian Americans not only have access to new digital media technologies, but are indeed quite competent and capable in their use as compared with other racialized minority groups (Hargittai 2010). Examining how cyberspace has been a site through which Asian Americans are crafting identities and communities therefore becomes an important area of study.

While we have overviewed different sociological approaches to studying the media and popular culture, it is notable that, in the field of Asian American Studies, much of the scholarship is done by humanities scholars and less so by sociologists and other social scientists. Our discussion below draws from a range of disciplines.

From "yellow peril" to "model minority": representations of Asian Americans historically

The mass media have been a major instrument in the racialization and stereotyping of Asian Americans historically. As we discussed in previous chapters, representations of Asian Americans have often swung between two extremes. On one hand, they are figured as an insidious threat, a "yellow peril," to the economic, political, and cultural life of the United States. On the other hand, they are figured as "model minorities" and held up as prime examples of the promise of American institutions and ideals.

Stereotypes of Asian Americans have gendered aspects. The Asian male is figured as either an asexual "model minority" or a dangerously lascivious "yellow peril." The Asian female is figured as either an overly sexual provocateur (the "dragon lady") or a vulnerable and lovelorn romantic in need of "saving" (the "lotus blossom"). Sociologist Yen Le Espiritu argues that, "Though connoting two extremes, these stereotypes are interrelated: Both exoticize Asian women as exotic 'others'– sensuous, promiscuous, but untrustworthy" (2007: 93; also see chapter 7 for an analysis of media representations of LGBTQ individuals). Gendered representations of Asians, whether they are violent or benevolent, serve as justifications for different forms of social hierarchy.

Beyond racialized, class, and sexual politics domestically, representations of Asians in the media have also been linked to US imperial expansion. Here, too, representations of Asians can range from the benign to the menacing. Indeed, though the stereotypes of "yellow peril" and "model minority" have been broadly applied to Asian Americans as a whole, at different historical moments, specific kinds of stereotypes emerge of particular Asian ethnic groups, depending on the ways that the United States relates to the Asian countries from which they descend as either friend or foe.

The following section will focus on how different forms of media have racialized and stereotyped Asian Americans historically and in more recent decades. It will examine iterations of the dominant "yellow peril" and "model minority" stereotypes as they have been applied in different forms of media to specific Asian ethnic groups and/or during particular historical moments in US domestic race relations and US geopolitics.

Early Asian immigration and the Chinese "yellow peril"

Recall that employers still reeling from the Civil War and the emancipation of enslaved Africans in the late nineteenth century recruited Chinese workers. Meanwhile, white working-class, nativist movements were on the rise, fearing this "yellow peril" that they believed threatened their jobs. Fears of the "yellow peril" were often depicted in popular representations of the Chinese during the period. Floyd Cheung, for example, offers examples of political cartoons that appeared in different newspapers during that time. In one especially striking one, he describes how the:

> artist imaginatively unveils a Chinese laborer's productivity as resulting from his monstrous possession of extra limbs. Rolled-up sleeves and an assortment of hand-tools mark these limbs as hard-working and perhaps even manly [. . .] In contrast, six Euro-American boys loiter nearby with their sleeves rolled down and their hands unoccupied. One member of their group is being dragged off toward three possible destinations: the San Quentin prison, an unnamed "house of corrections," and an "industrial school." (Cheung 2007: 297)

In this image, Chinese labor is depicted as directly causing the idleness, linked to a lack of employment, of younger generations of whites. Indeed, representations of Chinese immigrants were at times ambivalent because they were also rendered as violently threatening. Cheung attributes these ambivalent characterizations of the Chinese to different class interests. Employer representations of the Chinese were often at odds with those of working-class whites (Cheung 2007).

The United States' "enemies" abroad

Meanwhile, during the Philippine–American War in the early twentieth century, Filipinos were figured as savages; in fact, they were likened to African and Native Americans, who required forceful subjugation. American newspapers were complicit in disseminating war propaganda. According to media sociologist Philip Ablett, "Any journalists who sought to cover the other side were promptly expelled" (2004: 24). Consequently, the news media circulated a completely one-sided perspective, which served to dehumanize Filipinos as savages and thereby rationalize the violent subjugation of the Philippines. Alternative or critical perspectives on the Philippine–American War were completely silenced and that has had long-standing impacts on how the Philippine–American War has been remembered in the United States. The dominant representation of the conflict between the Philippines and the United States is that it was merely an "insurrection" and not an anticolonial struggle. That this representation has prevailed is perhaps the best evidence for the US government's media-aided successful propaganda campaign (Campomanes 1997).

World War II became a key moment in the representation of different Asian-American groups. If the Japanese were vilified first during Japan's imperial rise at the turn of the twentieth century, with World War II they would continue to suffer vilification in the media. Meanwhile, the Chinese and Filipinos, America's allies on the war's Pacific Front, would be recuperated and represented in more positive ways. In a classic film of the period starring the iconic American actor John Wayne, *Bataan* was key in not merely demonizing the Japanese, but doing so through a displacement of white racism onto the Japanese. The film features a mixed group of soldiers (i.e. soldiers hailing from different branches of the military, of different ranks, and from different racial backgrounds) attempting to fight the Japanese in the Philippines. Locke argues that:

> The film's white and black characters ... bond through the common trait of "American," defined by the yellow peril's un-American essence. Adding a new layer of meaning to the yellow-peril stereotype to tailor it to the racial politics of the time, *Bataan* presents the Asian as the true culprit of bigotry, displacing the stigma of American racism from white onto yellow. (Locke 2008: 11)

In the postwar period, representations of the Japanese, now US allies, would become more favorable while representations of the ("red") Chinese, with the rise of the communists, would be more negative. This would be manifested in the 1950s and 1960s in television programs like *The Adventures of Dr. Fu Manchu*, *The Adventures of Falcon*, *I Spy*, and *The Man from U.N.C.L.E.* (Shah 2003).

The beginnings of the "model minority" myth

By the 1960s, at the height of the civil rights movement, representations of Asian Americans, including the Chinese and the Japanese, shifted decidedly in the positive direction. Two articles in prominent news media outlets, the *New York Times* and the *US News and World Report*, characterized Asians as "model minorities" for their seeming advancement from racially oppressed and exploited low-wage workers to an emergent class of professionals. This "advancement" was attributed to their "culture" as Asians. That this shift to a highly positive representation of Asians took place during the civil rights movement was no mere coincidence. Against demands by African Americans for state-supported social programs to redress inequalities rooted in histories of racial discrimination and economic exploitation, these reports offered the perspective that racial minorities could overcome legacies of marginalization on their own; they could, in other words, "pull themselves up by their bootstraps" through the adoption of different kinds of "values" (Osajima 2000). Images of Asian Americans as "model minorities" would continue throughout the 1980s. For instance, on August 31, 1987, a *Time* magazine cover featured an article entitled "Those Asian-American Whiz Kids." The accompanying photograph featured Asian-American students (mainly East Asian Americans), both girls and boys, ranging from elementary to high school, with schoolbooks in hand.

"Color-blindness" and the "model minority" myth

As more overt and explicit racial imagery and language has come to be seen as socially unacceptable in the post-civil rights era, more covert and implicit ways of representing and talking about race have emerged. Representations of Asian Americans in the post-civil rights era, including but not limited to the "model minority" stereotype, must be understood as being linked to the rise of what sociologist Bonilla-Silva (2003) calls, "color-blind racism." In particular, in place of "race," the notion of "culture" is invoked, as we have seen with the "model minority" myth.

In their study of the major network's web sites and prime-time programming, Deo et al. examine the different ways that the media (at least in television) "frame" Asian Americans in this period of "color-blind racism." A "frame" tells "the audience how to think about an issue and encourages the audience to interpret events in terms of a key idea" (Deo et al. 2008: 149). The invisibility of Asian Americans in television programming contributes to "framing" Asian Americans as "forever foreign" and not fully integral to or integrated into the fabric of American life, according to Deo et al. That is, just by not being visible on television is a way that Asian Americans are framed.

Beyond being framed as "forever foreigners," a second frame echoes and reinforces existing stereotypes of Asian Americans, including the "model minority" myth, the sexually undesirable Asian-American man and the sexually available Asian-American woman. For instance, during the television seasons covered by the research, Deo et al. found Asian-American male characters were typically portrayed as single and not in pursuit of intimate relationships. Meanwhile, Asian-American women characters, in contrast, were not only involved in romantic relationships, these were mainly relationships with non-Asian-American men. Deo et al. argue that these representations served to underscore the notion of Asian-American women as sexually available.

The "yellow peril" persists

The notion of the Asian American as the threatening "yellow peril" has not completely gone away, despite the dominance of the "model minority" stereotype. The "yellow peril" stereotype emerges when Asian Americans are seen as threatening in some sort of way. In previous chapters, we have discussed how anti-Japanese sentiment in the 1980s emerged alongside Japan's dominance of the automobile industry. Anti-Japanese sentiment had violent consequences, for instance, the killing of Vincent Chin, a Chinese-American autoworker who was murdered because he was believed to be Japanese. Since 9/11, South Asian Americans have been seen as potential terrorists.

Moreover, the media uses racialized notions of Asian Americans as a "yellow peril" or "forever foreign" to explain the behavior of different individuals. For example, in 2007 the news media focused its attention on Seung-Hui Cho, a student at Virginia

Tech University who killed several dozen students in a dormitory and classroom there before committing suicide. Asian-American media watchdog groups Media Action Network of Asian Americans and the Asian American Journalists Association raised concerns about the fact that the media had focused on his status as a non-US citizen in their coverage of the shootings, though arguably his citizenship status has nothing to do with the violence he committed (see also Chong 2008).[1] The focus on Cho's citizenship status is among the latest instances where Asian-American representation as the "yellow peril," as well as "forever foreign," makes its appearance. As we mentioned in chapter 2, the representation of Cho was also gendered. Similar representations circulated in the wake of a later mass shooting in 2009 in Binghamton, New York. In this case, Jiverly Wong, a Vietnamese American, entered an immigrant-services center, one from which he had previously received services, and killed thirteen people. An additional four were seriously wounded. According to communications scholar Angie Chuang, the Wong case provides further substantiation of the claim that the media continues to reproduce the "yellow peril" and "forever foreign" stereotypes because Wong, unlike Cho, was a US citizen. Despite his legal citizenship, Wong was still represented as a foreigner and therefore a threat (Chuang 2012).

The "technically competent" Asian

Linked to "color-blind racism" and ultimately rooted in the "model minority" stereotype is the rise of the figure of the "technically competent" Asian American. The relatively recent prominence of "reality" television has not necessarily given rise to more "genuine" (i.e. nuanced, non-stereotypical) representations of Asian Americans (or other racialized minorities, for that matter). American Studies scholar Grace Wang argues that, "[r]ather than represent a wide range of 'real people' who reflect the diversity of the nation, reality TV repackages difference into comfortingly familiar stock characters and stereotypes" (2010: 405). In her examination of Asian-American reality television winners, Wang finds that stereotypes of Asian Americans, particularly that of the "model minority", is reaffirmed but in new forms, such as the "technical robot." That is, Asian Americans are figured as highly competent, and yet that competency is figured as deviant and practically inhuman. The "technical robot" conforms to the "model minority" myth by supporting notions of meritocracy and thereby reinscribing the racial hierarchy with Asian Americans as un-American and "forever foreign" for their supposed lack of feeling and passion (a consequence, presumably of their Asian "culture"). According to Wang, Hung Huynh, winner of the popular *Top Chef*, and Chloe Dao, winner of *Project Runway*:

> affirmed both the meritocratic nature of the nation and the continuing salience of the American Dream. At the same time, as exceptional racialized immigrants who managed to transcend their technical nature through the help of the television program, these characters illustrate the very narrow ways that racialized minorities are allowed to integrate into the nation. For the allegation that Asian Americans are technicians who lack creativity is a barrier that not only helps keep Asian Americans from transcending their racialized labor niches but also serves as an explanation, more broadly, for why people of color cannot make it to the top of their professions. (Grace Wang 2010: 406)

For these reality-show contestants, their biggest obstacle to winning their respective contests was the fact that, though they were highly skilled, they lacked creativity and passion. It was only when these contestants publicly embraced the assessment that they were emotionless robots (i.e. they were too Asian) and then attempted to actively embody more feeling (i.e. they became more Americanized) in their work that they were rewarded with top honors.

Advertising is yet another medium through which representations of racialized minorities are produced. With greater numbers of Asian Americans in the United States, advertisers, not surprisingly, have begun to take more interest in them as a niche market. Growing attention to Asian-American consumers constitutes a shift from earlier practices where Asian Americans were scantly represented (in advertising, as well as in other forms of media and popular culture more broadly). In a study that tracked television commercials during prime-time programming across six of the major national networks, it was found that the representations of Asian Americans that did exist were largely of "young, passive adults at work in technology ads" (Mastro and Stern 2003: 645). This representation is similar, yet somewhat different from the "technical robot"/"technically competent" Asian-American stereotype. Like that stereotype, Asian Americans in these ads are situated in technology jobs. Though we may not necessarily be able to ascertain how well they actually perform these jobs, the assumption is that people who work with technology are somehow more intelligent. Also, similar to that stereotype, the Asian Americans in these ads are depicted as passive, comparable to an unfeeling "robot." What the research suggests is that there has been a shift in advertising to represent Asian Americans more, although still in a narrow manner.

Gender and the representation of Asian-American women

As mentioned in above sections, Asian-American women are framed in specific ways that deserve special note. Paek and Shah's study of magazine advertising, including widely circulated magazines like *Time*, found that, as in other kinds of media, Asian Americans are constructed as "model minorities." They are depicted as highly successful entrepreneurs, technologically savvy, and academic achievers. Moreover, in line with the overly generalized "model minority" stereotype, Asian Americans are depicted as being in mixed-race (with white) couples, furthering the idea of Asian Americans as a highly assimilated racial group. Consistent with the representations of Asian-American women in other media forms, for Asian-American women in magazine advertisements, "the image of petite and exotic beauty remains a common visual theme" (Paek and Shah 2003: 236). Indeed, as Kim and Chung find in their research of major global advertising campaigns that attempt to incorporate more minorities, the depiction of Asian-American women in particular needs to be understood as not simply being about Asian-American women but also about the depiction of white men. These representations are related. Kim and Chung argue that "multicultural imagery of specific advertising campaigns, while expanding its campaign to include multi-racial characters, relies on the 'foreign' and 'seductive' appeal of Asian/American women in order to highlight the supremacy and positionality of White men within the global order" (2005: 73).

Representations of Asian Americans on the internet have followed similar patterns to those identified in other forms of media. Despite the claim that the internet is the great "equalizer," in the sense that it is a form of media that ordinary people can more readily access to produce representations of themselves through web sites or social media platforms like Facebook that are more nuanced and better reflect their experiences, studies find that the internet is not as liberatory as it is often touted to be. Gonzalez and Rodriguez find, for example, that the term "Filipina" when entered into internet search engines always appears to be associated with web sites related to low-wage labor or sex (Gonzalez and Rodriguez 2003).

Progressive visions in mainstream media?

While much of the scholarship on Asian-American representations in television and film has highlighted the ways in which they reproduce dominant stereotypes, some scholars have also attempted to track representations that offer counter or alternative visions of Asian Americans. Davé (2012) argues, for example, that Indian marriages in particular have been depicted in American television as the antithesis to American cultural notions about marriage. Indian "arranged" marriages, marriages that are represented at times as being "forced" or occurring without the consent of the marrying parties, are counterposed to American (western) romantic marriages which are represented as being the product of free choice. Davé argues, however, that the emergence of new kinds of television programming, including reality TV shows like *The Bachelor* or *The Bachelorette*, depict aspects of the marriage process that point to more convergence between these distinct marriage norms than previously shown. This is especially evident in the show *Miss Match*, a program which centers on a character whose business it is to help facilitate partnerships between two compatible individuals. The show itself illustrates how marriage choice in the United States is not solely about romantic love but also about compatibility and that people are willing to consult a third party to help identify possible partners. The compatibility or convergence of Indian and American marriage practices is made especially explicit in an episode of the show where Miss Match (played by Alicia Silverstone, a white actress) becomes involved in matchmaking for an Indian-American woman. By the end of the show, Miss Match displays openness to Indian marriages and her client ends up participating in a modified version of arranged marriage by marrying the brother of her originally intended (Davé 2012).

Moreover, Deo et al. (2008) find possibilities for what they call a "counterideological" frame that can challenge Asian American exclusion on one hand and stereotypical depictions on the other. In their study (which spanned the years 2004–5), they found that there were notable television shows that featured not only dialogue between characters that highlighted the particular kinds of prejudice or racism Asian Americans might face (for example, non-Asians being unwilling to learn how to pronounce Asian names properly; non-Asians misrecognizing specific Asian ethnicities, i.e. thinking all Asians are Chinese) but also prominent Asian-American characters. They found that the programs *ER*, *Grey's Anatomy*, and *Lost* were all notable for having lead Asian-American characters that were depicted with depth and nuance. These characters' work lives, for instance, were not the sole focus of these shows. Their intimate lives with friends and lovers (who were not always white) were also shown. By depicting Asian Americans in the richness and complexity of their lives, these television programs can both provide more visibility to Asian Americans and challenge the one-dimensional stereotypes that dominate television programming (Deo et al. 2008).

Though the scholarship on this area is still rather new, "Linsanity," that is, the widespread media attention to National Basketball Association (NBA) player Jeremy Lin, has generated much debate in the Asian-American community. For many Asian Americans, Lin's professional trajectory in basketball is testament to the persistence of the "model minority" stereotype – that Asian Americans are naturally academically gifted, but also not naturally athletically inclined – and at the same time an opportunity to undo that stereotype (Hsu 2012; Zirin 2012).

Asian Americans in the media industry

It is often assumed that the more that minority groups own, are hired by, or take leadership roles in key mainstream media outlets, the more they can have a role in reshaping the images of Asian Americans away from more stereotyped representations and/or in offering representations of the Asian-American experience where it has been absent. In this section, we evaluate to what extent Asian-American integration in the media industry accomplishes these ends. Whereas the previous section looked at Asian-American representations in the media, this section is concerned with whether Asian-American integration into mainstream media makes a difference in the representation of Asian Americans or not.

Asian American journalists: making a difference in reporting?

Though Asian Americans (particularly women) appear to be a normal fixture on television news, from one-time co-anchor of the CBS Evening News Connie Chung to the anchors that proliferate on local channels, different studies have assessed to what extent Asian-American journalists are able to increase news reporting on the Asian-American community and thereby heighten its visibility for the public, as well as to what extent Asian-American journalists (and other journalists of color) are able to produce less stereotypical representations of Asian Americans and other racialized groups.

In a study that aimed to assess the influence of Asian-American journalists on Asian-American news content, it was found that the presence of Asian Americans on a newspaper's staff had more impact on whether stories about Asian Americans were covered. It found that if there were more Asian-American staff on a particular newspaper, they could have a significant impact on shaping stories, regardless of the actual population of Asian Americans that the newspapers actually served (Wu and Izard 2008).

The lack of journalistic diversity can bias the reporting of news stories. Research on white journalists has found that they tend to judge members of their own race as ethically superior when they were the subjects of news stories as compared with nonwhite (specifically black) subjects. Coleman set out to determine to what extent minority journalists, including Asian Americans, ethically judged story subjects who shared their racial background as superior to their white counterparts. The author defines "ethical judgment" as how one evaluates another (in this case, the subjects of news stories) as being morally right or wrong in their course of action. High moral judgment, it is argued, reflects non-stereotypical thinking because racial stereotypes often depict people of color as morally suspect. Coleman's study found that minority journalists, unlike white journalists in previous research, tend to have high moral judgment of all people of color (and not simply for their own specific racial group). Moreover, connected with this high moral judgment, minority journalists tend to exhibit more empathy for other minorities and this empathetic feeling is connected to less stereotypical bias (Coleman 2011). What this suggests is that increased numbers of minorities in journalism are likely to result in less negative portrayals of people of color in the news media.

Another study focused specifically on the presence and coverage of people of color on local television news (the source from which most people, at least during the time of the study, derive their information on current events). For the researchers, their interest was in gauging not only whether people of color were present in news stories but also in what ways people of color and race relations were framed in news stories. A news frame is a "central organizing idea for news content that supplies a context and suggests what an issue is through the use of selection, emphasis, exclusion, and elaboration" (Poindexter, Smith, and Heider 2003: 527). Based on research of local television newscasts from twenty-six stations in twelve states, Poindexter et al. found that people of color, as anchors, reporters, subjects and sources, were not represented and thereby "frames" of people of color were practically nonexistent.

Asian-American journalists, however small their numbers may be, have actually organized themselves into professional organizations such as the Asian American Journalists Association (AAJA), which was established in 1981 to help better mentor and train Asian-American journalists to be able to secure leadership positions in order to shape newsroom decision-making processes (Fees 2008). As we discuss in other chapters (chapter 9 and 10), however, the "Asian-American" pan-ethnic identity often privileges the people and experiences of East Asians (Chinese, Japanese, Korean) to the exclusion of other groups of Asians. Hence, other organizations, such as the South Asian Journalists Associations (SAJA), were also formed (Banerji 2004). Many SAJA members are also members of the AAJA, however, reflecting the complex and layered identities of Asian-American journalists and indeed of Asian Americans in general.

Asian-American actors: challenging myths?

Asian Americans are slowly becoming more visible in film and television in a variety of roles. There are few instances, if any, now where white actors are cast to play Asian-American characters (often in highly stereotyped ways), a practice some scholars call "yellow face," drawing from the history of "black face" in the United States. Despite this greater visibility, Deo et al. (2008) find that in 2004 and 2005, fewer than 2 percent of the characters in prime-time television were Asian American, despite the fact that Asian Americans make up 5 percent of the population. Indeed, more troubling for the authors is the fact that many of these shows actually take place in areas were Asian Americans comprise a higher proportion of the population (i.e. Honolulu, Southern California, or San Francisco). Moreover, because Asian Americans are not featured in sitcoms, which are often situated in family settings, a fuller rendering of their lives is not possible. Even where Asian-American characters are given more elaboration in occupation-focused roles (i.e. medical personnel in shows like *ER* or *Grey's Anatomy*) or crime dramas (*CSI*, *Hawaii Five-0*), Asian-American actors generally get much less screen time than their white counterparts (Deo et al. 2008).

Other scholars are less pessimistic about the presence of Asian Americans in Hollywood and have argued not only that there are more roles for Asian-American actors and actresses but that these roles offer more nuanced and complex portrayals (Diffrient 2011). Indeed, Asian-American life has taken center-stage because of the presence of Asian-American actors and actresses. For instance, in the early 1990s, Asian (Korean) American comedian Margaret Cho debuted her television comedy *All-American Girl*, which was based on the material she used in her stand-up comedy. According to Chun, Margaret Cho has been able to use her comedy as a way of critiquing racism though, seemingly paradoxically, she does so through a use of what Chun calls "mock Asian." "Mock Asian" is a manner of speaking or linguistic styling that is often stereotypically associated with Asians. Though some might think that Cho's use of "mock Asian" actually plays to stereotypes, Chun argues instead that,

> [I]n the case of Cho, however, an interpretation of social critique is possible because of factors and ideologies that contextualize her revoicings, including the persona she has constructed as someone who is critical of racism, her overt claim that the texts are racist [. . .], paralinguistic cues that align her against rather than with the text, and an ideology of legitimacy that assumes that an in-group member would have neither the intention nor the power to oppress her own community. (Chun 2004: 286)

What Chun means by this is that what allows Cho to be able to use "mock Asian" critically is because the public personality she has cultivated is anti-racist and she makes that stance explicit, especially in her comedic performances.

Even as Asian Americans have been more visible in mainstream media as actors, and notwithstanding that there have been some new opportunities that allow Asian-American life to be a focus, it has not always been a fully empowering turn, according to some cultural critics. For instance, although the film the *Joy Luck Club* (based on the novel by Asian-American author Amy Tan) was directed by an Asian American and enjoyed mainstream popularity in the early 1990s, it drew on themes of Asian female suffering that are somewhat reminiscent of earlier representations of Asian-American women as "lotus blossoms" (Hagedorn 2000; Yin 2005). In an interesting twist, it is second-generation Asian-American women who are figured as vulnerable and suffering because, it is suggested in the film, they have lost a sense of their Asianness by assimilating to American society. Even though the film (and novel) may offer a critique of assimilationist notions in favor of multiculturalist visions, it does so through the figures of disempowered women. Similarly, though Margaret Cho's *All-American Girl* was the very first prime-time TV show to center on Asian-American life, it failed, according to some critics, to truly counter long-dominant representations of Asian Americans because it was ultimately tailored to mainstream (white) audiences (Wong 1994). Meanwhile, Bobby Lee's comedic career as a main character in the sketch comedy show *MADtv*, while offering the opportunity to overturn Asian-American stereotyping, ultimately becomes a more ambivalent treatment of Asian Americans (that is, it in some ways plays into stereotypes even while attempting to criticize them): "he often resorts to an objectifying form of abjection that merely reproduces well-worn Asian stereotypes" (Diffrient 2011: 48).

Perspectives on the industry from Asian-American actors

Despite some of these more optimistic accounts by media scholars of the ways that Asian-American presence in the media industry impact on representations of Asian Americans, Asian-American actors and actresses in mainstream media productions have themselves come forward at different junctures to discuss their sense of isolation, their struggle to get meaningful roles, and their experiences of discrimination towards the Asian-American community, thereby supporting the idea that increased media representation does not necessarily ameliorate racism (in terms of being hired as actors and actresses or playing other kinds of leading roles in media production). In the late 1990s, actor Steve Park was compelled to write an account of his experiences of discrimination in Hollywood for the national Asian-American periodical *AsianWeek*. He recounts one particular incident where he observed an assistant director conduct himself in the following way in response to an Asian-American colleague of his: "[The] first assistant director, in a short tirade, called an Asian American actor to the set over a walkie-talkie with the words, 'I don't have time for this! Where's Hoshi, Toshi or whatever the f—k his name is – get the Oriental guy'" (Steve Park 2000: 270). More recently, the Hmong-American actor Bee Vang, who played the lead role opposite Clint Eastwood in the film *Gran Torino*, has described how he struggled to portray a more nuanced character in the film, despite what he felt were real barriers to doing so. *Gran Torino,* as officially described in the online film database IMDb, as a film about a "[d]isgruntled Korean War vet Walt Kowalski [who] sets out to reform his neighbor, a young Hmong teenager, who tried to steal Kowalski's prized possession: his 1972 Gran Torino."[2] Vang played the teenager who tried to steal Eastwood's character's car. Vang describes, for example, how "most of the script was not very open to interpretation and it was premised on his not having any dignity. He needs to be clueless and have no self-respect in order for the white elder man to achieve his savior role" (Schein 2010: 4). Indeed, no effort was made on the part of the film crew, including Eastwood himself, to try to train the Hmong-American actors in the film because they were asked to act "natural," yet, given the assumptions made by the screenwriter about Hmong-Americans, acting "natural" was ultimately to play into dominant stereotypes about Asian Americans.

Asian-American filmmakers: limits and possibilities

Asian and Asian-American filmmakers have gained some prominence more recently, for example Ang Lee, director of critically acclaimed films like *Brokeback Mountain* or *Sense and Sensibility*, or M. Night Shyamalan, director of blockbuster films *The Sixth Sense* and *The Last Airbender*. Most of the films produced by the like of these directors, however, have not addressed questions related to race and the Asian-American experience. Indeed, director M. Night Shyamalan was actually the target of protests by fans of the cartoon *Avatar: The Last Airbender* because the film version of the cartoon he was directing (*The Last Airbender*) failed to cast Asian-American actors (Lopez 2012a).

Interestingly, in the case of biracial Asian American filmmaker Eric Byler, his initial interest in becoming a filmmaker was not necessarily to depict Asian-American life. In an interview, Byler recounted that he "believed the primary purpose of film to be a venue for escapism and entertainment, and set out to become a filmmaker who provided both" (Chae 2007). However, when his first film received critical acclaim, his racial background became more widely known and he was immediately embraced by the Asian-American community. In the process, he became much more interested in producing films that addressed issues of racial inequality, and, having become quite politically engaged, "he began to use his artistic skills as a means to mobilize the community whenever he witnessed prejudice and injustice" (Chae 2007).

New media frontiers? Digital media and the internet

Asian Americans, as we mentioned above, not only have significant access to new digital media, they are also quite competent in their use. With respect to the internet, Asian Americans have been found to be the "most wired" racialized group (Roach 2002). Indeed, on the video-sharing platform YouTube, Asian Americans have been on the most subscribed-to lists (Considine 2011). Not only does YouTube offer an opportunity for Asian-American performers to "break through" the mainstream media, Balance argues, it also offers Asian Americans, especially Asian-American youths, who are among the most plugged into YouTube as both producers and consumers, an opportunity to perform and construct Asian-American pan-ethnic identities (Balance 2012).

However, it is not clear-cut whether digital media, especially the internet, offer more possibilities for challenging stereotypes than for reinforcing them. For example, South Korean singer/performer Psy gained international renown for his song/video "Gangnam Style," and managed to break into the mainstream US music industry. In 2013, he was nominated in the Billboard Music Awards' Top New Artist category (Rogers 2013). Yet at least one media critic calls Psy's success an "Asian invasion," recalling the "yellow peril" stereotype. In an October 2012 *Rolling Stone* article, entitled "Psy: The First Wave of the Asian Invasion," author Matt Irwin writes:

> When it comes to pop music, at least, Bill O'Reilly is right: Traditional America is dead. And the guy who killed it off is a pudgy, thirtysomething South Korean rapper who invented a funny dance. The forces that led Psy's "Gangnam Style" to become the first Korean pop song in history to make the Top 40 have been converging for some time now: globalization, YouTube, a fast-growing Asian-American population, a ravenously border-crossing hunger for cheesy dance beats. (Hiatt 2012: 72)

Notably, Irwin refers to right-wing Fox news commentator, Bill O'Reilly, who is notorious for his nativist comments, among other conservative viewpoints.

Indeed, as much as there is a visible presence of Asian Americans on YouTube, both as producers and consumers, it is a venue for circulating anti-Asian sentiment. Another viral video that circulated on YouTube was that of a white student at the University of California, Los Angeles (UCLA), who posted her rant against Asian students on the campus (Lovett 2011). Her video also generated much criticism, notably from Asian American Studies faculty in UCLA's Department of Asian American

Studies (Grasgreen 2011). Though UCLA decided not to discipline her, the student opted to leave the school.[3]

Asian Americans in music

We have focused primarily on visual media (television, film, and digital media). However, other important sites for the production of popular culture include music. In mainstream music, Asian Americans have been present, though that presence has been quite marginal until the last decade. In the mid-2000s, the chart-topping pop group Black Eyed Peas' apl.de.ap, a biracial Filipino American and African American, produced and released music on the group's albums, such as "The APL Song," "Bebot," and "Mare," that speak specifically to the Filipino immigrant experience in the United States or include lyrics in Filipino, the Philippines' national language. The songs have gained popularity among Filipinos in the Philippines and diaspora, if not necessarily among the broader American listening public.[4] In 2004, MC Jin, a Chinese-American son of immigrants from Florida, became the first Asian-American rapper to sign to a major label (Winters 2004); however, he enjoyed more success in Hong Kong than in the United States (Wang 2013). In 2012, the hip-hop group Far East Movement became the first Asian American group to top the Billboard charts, as well as to earn a number one spot on iTunes with their single "Like a G6" (Sun 2010). Both MC Jin and the Far East Movement attempt to incorporate their experiences as Asian Americans in their music.

Among the earliest Asian-American jazz groups to break into the mainstream and achieve commercial success was Hiroshima, which earned both a gold record and a Grammy nomination in the mid-1980s. According to sociologist Oliver Wang, "In their conception, music was the way through which they could explore their identity, using sound to tease out the nuances that went into their concept of Asian America. The main method through which Hiroshima tried to achieve this sound was by using traditional Asian instruments in their fusion band, namely taiko drumming, koto playing, and Asian woodwinds" (2001: 453). Though perhaps considered less "mainstream," musical subgenres, like punk and folk, that might be considered "white" genres, given the dominance of white artists within them, have seen the emergence of Asian-American artists. Mike Park, a punk rocker, has become a notable figure who has become a "model of an Asian American male for a non-Asian American audience" (Castro 2007: 224) in a musical genre that is not only white but where artists embody distinctive forms of masculinity (Castro 2007). Meanwhile, in folk music, Magdalen Hsu-Li, a Chinese-American bisexual female artist, has made important inroads. Both Park and Hsu-Li use their music to express their ethnic identities and their sexualities in ways that undermine racialized and gendered stereotypes of Asian Americans as either effeminate men or "dragon lady" women (Castro 2007).

Responding to mainstream media: (re)presenting Asian-America

Researchers find that limited and narrow representations of Asian Americans in the media impacts Asian Americans' self-perception and identity formation in that they may internalize stereotyped representations of Asian Americans and think of themselves in less than favorable ways (Mastro and Stern 2003). Indeed, the role of the media in perpetuating stereotypes of Asian Americans can lead to deleterious effects if mainstream audiences internalize and act out on them as in the case of anti-Asian violence. Asian Americans have attempted to counter mainstream media representations of themselves through direct action against the mainstream media, as well as through the establishment of independent and autonomous media outlets.

Asian Americans have mobilized to directly contest problematic portrayals of themselves in the mainstream media. "Civil rights organizations such as the Asian American Justice Center and the NAACP, along with grass-roots organizations such as the Media Action Network for Asian Americans and union subcommittees focused on diversity initiatives (within the Screen Actor's Guild and other guilds), actively work to protest and alter the invisibility and misrepresentation of APIAs in popular culture" (Deo et al. 2008: 158).

Ethnic newspapers

Asian Americans have actively engaged in countering stereotypes perpetuated by the mainstream media through the production of their own ethnic newspapers. The ethnic news press has offered Asian Americans a source of news that, written in their own languages, speaks to their experiences in the United States, while also offering news of their countries of origin to which they may still feel attached.

Radical Asian American newspapers, that is, news media that emerged from pan-ethnic Asian American activist organizations beginning in the late 1960s not only offered perspectives that were not covered by both mainstream US (white) and ethnic media, as well as critiques of the perspectives they did cover. It also served to cultivate a pan-ethnic Asian-American identity among its readership. One such example was the newspaper, *Gidra*, self-published by students at the University of California, Los Angeles. According to Lopez, *Gidra* helped to cultivate Asian-American identity through the construction of "external conflict." In particular, the paper highlighted Asian Americans' experiences of racial discrimination both past and present for the purpose of "recast[ing] individual incidents within the framework of collective racial discrimination, bringing community members together to stand alongside each other and support a collective cause" (Lopez 2012b: 242).

Yet at the same time, because *Gidra* was part of broader radical movements that had particular political perspectives with respect to racial politics in the United States, it became a site through which conflicts "internal" to the Asian-American community were also hashed out. Many of *Gidra*'s articles aimed at distinguishing its politics from what it considered to be more assimilationist and integrationist perspectives on race relations. For *Gidra*'s writers (and ostensibly its audience), racial injustices could only be addressed through direct confrontations with institutions of power by social-movement building. Addressing (and in some ways provoking) "internal" conflict within the Asian-American community marks a shift from the ways many ethnic newspapers approach issues. Whereas the mainstream ethnic newspapers often attempt to suppress what they may consider the community's "dirty laundry" for the sake of presenting a unified "voice" as an ethnic community, *Gidra* aimed to sharpen the political lines of division between Asian Americans.

Independent filmmaking

Asian Americans have also tried to tackle visual media, including film and video, to produce alternative and more positive representations of themselves. In the late 1960s and early 1970s, alongside the rise of the Asian-American movement, Asian Americans developed so-called "triangular media," "the three sides of which were: (1) community building; (2) mobilizing people to take action; and (3) telling stories about the Asian experience in America from an Asian perspective" (Shah 2003).

Visual Communications is an example of grassroots, Asian-American attempts at producing alternative films. Formed in the early 1970s by film students in Los Angeles, Visual Communications was not only committed to struggling for social change through its productions, but to practicing forms of collective (as opposed to individual) authorship in filmmaking. Indeed, its social justice orientation perhaps requires a more collective approach as it involves a direct engagement with communities. Also established during the same period, but on the East Coast, in New York City, was the Asian CineVision. Interestingly, even as it may have shared some of the goals of Visual Communications in providing a space for Asian-American visual production, it also departed in some ways from Visual Communications as it ventured into explorations of new filmic forms and aesthetics (Okada 2009). The films produced by Asian Americans, therefore, ranged from documentary films that aimed to capture the lives of everyday Asian Americans to combat invisibility, as well as negative and inaccurate stereotypes, to more experimental films that attempted to explore and define the contours of a distinctively Asian-American aesthetic (Okada 2009; Shah 2003).

Music and movements

The Asian-American Movement produced musicians who directly engaged with its ideology and core issues. Jazz artist Fred Ho and folk group A Grain of Sand came out of the movement. Indeed, their very choice of musical genres complemented their politics. For Ho, jazz represented an African-American musical tradition with which he wanted to ally. Like many of his contemporaries, African-American cultural forms inspired Ho (Ho 1999). A Grain of Sand was a folk band. Folk had long been associated with social justice themes in American music and the group built on this tradition by performing songs that addressed issues of racial inequality (Wang 2001).

Though we have discussed the commercial success of Asian American rap and hip-hop artists, Asian Americans have been producing music in these genres outside of and against the mainstream music industry without always breaking into the mainstream. Indeed, as Asian American Studies scholar Cathy Schlund-Vials argues, "hip hop (which includes break dancing, deejaying, emceeing, and graffiti) was from the outset a multidisciplinary vehicle for youth-driven, political resistance" (2011: 160). Asian-American rappers and hip-hop artists have used their music to speak to questions of racial injustice suffered by Asian Americans in the United States as well as of the ravages of US imperialism in Asia (Schlund-Vials 2011). Many artists incorporate musical and cultural elements from their parents' countries of origin to express their ethnic identities (Maira 1998). Others use the music to signal connections with African-American communities (in active resistance to dominant white culture), as well as with the broader diasporas of which they are also part (Sharma 2010).

Competing perspectives on Asian-American culture

Though Asian-American cultural producers have been engaged in trying to counter mainstream representations ostensibly for the benefit of the Asian-American community, they sometimes face challenges from the very community that they are committed to uplifting and collaborating with. Duong and Pelaud discuss how their attempts to offer up alternative representations of Vietnamese Americans have sometimes been met with hostility from the Vietnamese-American community. Duong curated an art exhibit in 2009 entitled *F.O.B. II: Art Speaks* in Southern California which was met by hundreds of Vietnamese-American protestors who took issue with the exhibit's incorporation of communist symbols. Duong and Pelaud state that "we must also negotiate with Vietnamese American anticommunist activists who misinterpret our intentions and denigrate what we do" (2012: 242). Duong and Pelaud describe how the protests seem to have been spurred, in part, by a *Los Angeles Times* article that mischaracterized the exhibit as focusing mainly on communist/anticommunist debates in the community when in fact the exhibit was about "sexuality, identity, refugee histories, and contemporary political issues like Obama's presidency and Proposition 8 in California" (2012: 244). Ultimately, the exhibit was forced to close down. The controversy around the exhibit illustrates how Asian Americans cannot be so easily categorized and represented. Theirs is a wide range of histories and identities that cannot be captured in a single way, even when Asian Americans are doing the work of trying to represent themselves.

Conclusion

The media in all of its various forms have been and continue to be powerful tools for the dissemination of stereotypes of Asian Americans. From the "yellow peril" to the "model minority," stereotypes of specific Asian-American groups or Asian Americans as a whole enjoy a great degree of durability, even if they appear in slightly different forms, such as "forever foreign" or "technically competent". Though Asian Americans are enjoying new kinds of visibility in the mainstream media as producers of media and as actors and actresses, their success in transforming or undermining these stereotypes is uneven. To counter their invisibility in the mainstream media (or their hyper-visibility, albeit in stereotyped ways), Asian Americans have developed alternative, autonomous media outlets. These outlets not only offer counter-representations, they become a site for the cultivation of Asian American pan-ethnic identities.

Discussion questions

- List the number of media devices you own or have access to (television, radio, computer, smartphone, etc.). How much time do you spend on those devices? What percentage of your day is spent consuming media?
- Discuss representations of Asian Americans you have encountered. What kinds of racial and gendered understanding shape those representations? What kinds of stereotype are being invoked in those representations?

9 Identity

Who am I? What does my ethnic origin(s) mean to me? Do I express my ethnic identity in ways similar to others? Do I feel part of my ethnic group?

Self-identity is a major topic for all people but in particular for college-age students. This chapter is primarily concerned with how the children of immigrants (i.e. the second generation), and to some extent people who immigrated to the United States in their youth (what is called the 1.5 generation), construct and enact their ethnic identities (or not). Immigrant adults are expected to have salient ethnic identities, to varying degrees, but much more uncertainty surrounds their children. How do people develop identities? Why do people choose one identity(ies) over another (e.g. an ethnic over an American identity), how do they express identities, and how do they deal with tensions between identities? These are central issues within social science literature on identity, which Asian America can inform. We move past the commonplace notion of a "cultural conflict" or "marginal man" to also describe those with dual identities and instead argue that individuals often bring together their identities in creative ways within racial, gender, class, sexual, and other constraints. How people construct and perform their identities also has implications for theories of immigrant adaptation. The chapter reviews these topics for the 1.5 and second generation of many ethnic groups, starting with how individuals develop identities.

Identity development

Psychological approaches to identity development

Before turning to the sociological study of identity, it is useful to first review the literature on identity development within psychology. Psychology has a long tradition of theorizing how individuals come to understand themselves. Ethnic identity development has been theorized as taking place in stages that individuals go through over time. Depending on the model of ethnic identity development, there are three, four, or five stages (Atkinson, Morten, and Sue 1989; Cross 1995; Phinney 1993; Seaton, Scottham, and Sellers 2006; Vandiver et al. 2002). Across the models there is much consistency. Generally speaking, in stage one, youths have not thought about their ethnic identity. They may see themselves as akin to whites or be highly involved with their ethnic or racial group. In either case, they have not analyzed their identity. In stage two, there is an event or a series of events that make the person think actively about her or his background. It can be a jarring experience of racism, a gradual sense that one's own values or experiences differ from those around one, or some combination. In stage three, one thinks critically about one's background and relationship to the majority. One may develop anti-white feelings or strongly reaffirm one's commitment to ethnic practices, friends, and organizations. In the final stage, one has a healthy understanding of oneself as part of an ethnic or racial group, while also being able to have close relations with members of the majority.

As one becomes more attached to the ethnic group, one increasingly takes on its meanings and symbols. This process is referred to as "self-stereotyping," for one adopts the characteristics most associated with a group (Brewer and Brown 1998). When that identity is active, one exhibits the characteristics of that group, takes pride in that group, and favors it over others (Tajfel and Turner 1986). For instance, as one becomes more attached to one's ethnicity, one feels more committed to speaking the ethnic language, wearing the clothes, listening to the music, or the like when the ethnic identity is active.

This general model, based on the experiences of African Americans, was first developed during the civil rights movement. Since then, it has been applied to second (and later) generation Asian Americans, Latinos, and whites. For Asian Americans, the assumption is that youth are very white-identified during the first stage and become highly invested in learning about their Asian ancestry (as opposed to shared Asian-American experiences) during the third stage. Adolescents commonly feel ashamed of their ethnic and racial differences and struggle with conflicting expectations between ethnic and American lifestyles. Youths gradually come to terms with their biracialism (i.e. having parents who are two different races) and/or biculturalism (i.e. living with American culture norms and practices while simultaneously living with cultural norms and practices from their parents' home country) during the last stage (Kim 2001; Uba 1994; Tse 1999). More recently, scholars recognize the need for greater attention to multi-ethnic/multiracial individuals' identity development (Gonzales-Backen 2013).

Psychological models are powerful heuristics, or learning tools, for a complicated and multifaceted understanding of the identity development process. They are highly generalized and so can speak to a wide set of people, which explains these models' durability over the years. At the same time, the generalizable nature means that the models do not allow for more detailed accounts of how identity development occurs within various contexts. Nor do the models explain how people use their identities or how ethnic identities intersect with other identities. These are spaces where sociology adds to the discussion.

Sociological approaches to identity development

Identity development within sociology takes on a different yet complementary perspective to psychology's, emphasizing the process of development rather than only predicted outcomes. The dominant theory of identity within sociology is identity theory (Stryker 1992). This theory fits within the symbolic interactionist field of sociology, which emphasizes the micro-level ways in which people come to understand their world and themselves. Within symbolic interactionism, identities are meanings assigned to the self. Like psychologists, sociologists are interested in how individuals develop those meanings. Unlike psychologists, sociologists focus less on the stages one goes through (and related psychological conditions like stress, self-esteem, etc.) and more on the process of identity development based on relations with others. According to symbolic interactionism, a person comes to understand herself in a particular way based on her perceptions of how others understand her, as communicated within sustained interactions (Cooley 1902; Mead 1934). In other words, how you perceive others treating you tells you about yourself and shapes your identity. For instance, you may identify as a smart student having been told you are by teachers, parents, and others, after receiving good grades, and the like. This self-identity can change or become more nuanced if, over a period of time, you no longer receive such encouragement or do so only in certain subjects. So there is no natural or given way to identify. Instead, one's identity is the product of one's environment. This means one cannot develop an identity as an athlete, for instance, if never given the chance to physically compete. According to identity theory, the sum of one's multiple identities (as a student, as a boyfriend, as a Filipino American, as a Virginian, etc.) comprises one's overall sense of self.

Individuals learn their identities through interactions with others. But clearly one does not change one's identity after every new encounter. Some people are more important in shaping one's self-identity than are others. They are termed "significant others" (Mead 1934). They consist mainly of authority figures that one encounters frequently and often from an early age. Parents, other relatives, teachers, local religious heads, and the like typically make up this select bunch. Such individuals are part of a small circle of social ties, referred to as one's in-group. During adolescent and later years, peers take on an increasingly important role in the self-identity process.

Beyond significant others, one's community also shapes one's self-identity. The collection of acquaintances, peers, and organizations to whom one is casually attached comprise the "generalized other." Messages from the media and popular discourse are also relevant. Typically, one's self-identity is in line with the generalized other but may contrast with it if sufficiently supported by one's significant others. For instance, one can take great pride in being a Muslim, given family and community support, even if the surrounding environment criticizes the religion.

Racial/ethnic identity

This process of identity development refers to identities broadly. However, there are different types of identity. A single person can identify as gay, liberal, Canadian, basketball player, and so on. Of concern here are ethnic/racial identities. A racial/ethnic identity is a group identity that refers to one's self-conception as part of a (racial or ethnic) group. While there is some overlap between group and individual identities, they are qualitatively different. Individual identities, such as "daughter" or a "friend," are very general and do not have a social group as a clear reference. For instance, there is no community known as "friends" who have agreed-upon leaders, a distinctive history, or cultural affiliations. On the other hand, an ethnic group has an agreed-upon definition within a family or organization or community. This agreed-upon definition is referred to as the social identity or group identity of the ethnic or racial group (Hogg, Terry, and White 1995; Snow and Anderson 1987).

How group identities are defined – and so how people's personal identities are shaped – becomes a central question. Disagreement within a community over the definition of a social identity is common. This can become a politicized debate within a community as different groups battle over whose version of history to prioritize. For example, those who come from particular regions (Kerala versus West Bengal) or who practice different religions (Hinduism versus Catholicism) may differ about how they define what it means to be "Indian." Most typically, how family members and friends define their ethnicity or race comes to serve as a fundamental part of how a child comes to do so. One learns the social identity of one's ethnic group through interactions with significant others and the generalized other (that is, people, media portrayals, and social institutions in general). For ethnic and racial identities, the generalized other is comprised of the multitude of messages one receives about one's ethnicity from school, ethnic organizations, the media, and so on. Some of these messages are positive and complement familial practices. Others can be negative or simply foreign to one's upbringing. In such cases, one rarely overturns the meanings established by significant others, but one can add to that definition if felt appropriate.

Identity work

While the process of developing an identity is portrayed within identity theory in a passive manner, that is, people receive messages on how to identify from others, developing an identity actually takes a considerable amount of effort on the part of individuals. "Identity work" refers to individuals' agency in shaping how they identify with a social group. According to Snow and Anderson (1987), identity work consists of the cognitive and physical practices individuals perform to define themselves in line with a social identity (akin to "self-stereotyping" as psychologists would say, noted above). An individual forms an identity as a Chinese American, for instance, by practicing elements of the ethnic group deemed essential by one's significant and generalized others. If speaking an ethnic language is considered a key element of being ethnic, one may take language classes so as to more fully identify as "ethnic." This is one's identity work. Generally speaking, Asian Americans are expected to know about ancestral history or rituals (Min and Kim 1999; Purkayastha 2005). Individuals feel guilty when they do not live up to these expectations, and their identity work entails studying their culture so as to provide answers. If someone can appear to others as "truly ethnic," then those others will treat that person as such. According to identity theory, this will enable the person to confidently self-identify as ethnic.

Individuals are not simply receptacles of others' definitions of ethnicity. People rarely adopt all of the social identity that is communicated to them by significant and generalized others. What elements of the social identity one chooses depend partly on what is most pronounced within the social identity and partly on personal preferences. Regarding the former, some aspects of the social identity are more likely to be emphasized than others by group members, media depictions, and so on. Drawing from the sociology of culture, those aspects of social identity that are most institutionalized (i.e. most embedded within institutions), that are easy to access (e.g. those most well-known by the individual or easy to perform), that have clear expectations of how to act, and that resonate with one's skills or past experiences are most likely to be popular with the individual as she constructs her identity (Schudson 1989). For example, if one has practiced ethnic dances and lives in an area with access to such dance and has been told that dance is a key part of one's ethnicity, then one is most likely to refer to that as a key part of what it means to be ethnic. One might judge others on their knowledge of dance and say to oneself, "I'm more ethnic than my cousin – he doesn't even know our traditional dance!" On the other hand, someone who cannot speak an ethnic language may recognize the importance of language to the ethnicity but not have it comprise much of their particular ethnic identity, for it will not resonate with them. So one picks and chooses aspects of the social identity that best fit with one's other lifestyles and beliefs.

Pan-ethnic identity work

This same process of identity work, of going out of one's way to claim a social identity (or at least aspects of it), applies to the development of a pan-ethnic Asian American identity. Just as one can identify with one's ethnic group, one also can identify as Asian American. Typically, such identities are stronger at the political and organizational levels than at the personal level (Espiritu 1992). Still, individual Asian Americans, notably East Asian Americans, can develop pan-ethnic identities based on a shared sense of culture (e.g. our parents all stress family togetherness and education) and/or a shared sense of racialization (e.g. we all look alike to outsiders) (Kibria 2002; Park 2008; Tuan 1998). Immigrant parents may encourage pan-ethnic identities as well, when they tell their children to marry another Asian American if not someone of their own ethnicity. As part of such identity work, individuals join pan-ethnic student organizations, take classes on Asian America, make Asian-American friends, and consume pan-Asian culture. Some even adopt the "model minority" image as a way of being seen as "Asian," given the mostly positive image of Asian Americans (Dhingra 2007; Ho 2003). We take up the issue of pan-ethnic identity in more depth later in this chapter and in chapters 10 and 11.

Identity salience

So far, we have reviewed theories of identity development. But what explains why some care so much about their background and others care less? According to identity theory, the salience of an identity depends on how many cognitive or emotional commitments an individual has to others based on that identity (McCall and Simmons 1978). For instance, the more co-ethnics one knows and cares about, the more salient an ethnic identity will be. Conversely, if one lacks co-ethnic attachments, then one tends to identify as American (Portes and Rumbaut 2001).

What leads one to have strong attachments or not? The salience of individuals' ethnic/racial identities depends on their exposure to four major factors: culture, institutions, interests, and categorization (Barth 1969; Cornell and Hartmann 2007; Espiritu 1992; Glazer and Moynihan 1970; Jenkins 1994). How individuals experience significant others and the generalized other, as well as the myriad other influences on identity development, can be divided into these four components. By doing so, we better understand the different factors causing identity salience, that is, the factors that shape how much individuals care about their identities and which identities they exhibit the most.

Culture refers to a group's language, religion, traditions, food, values, family norms, and the like. People become more attached to their ethnic or racial group as they learn more about its culture. Institutions refer to organized sets of people who come together for a common purpose. With greater access to ethnic-oriented institutions, such as extended families or religious organizations, the more likely individuals are to develop stronger identities. Shared interests also lead individuals to be committed to an ethnic or racial identity. Members receive economic or political benefits by interacting with in-group members, leading one to identify as belonging to that group. Finally, ethnic identities result from being categorized as belonging to a group by people outside of that group. Without such categorization, group members would conceive of no difference between themselves and others. Not all four factors of identity salience are equally active for each individual. For example, an individual can feel categorized as an Asian American and have shared political interests but not feel culturally or institutionally tied to her or his race. Others can be culturally committed to their background but not feel other types of connections. And as one progresses through one's life, the types and degree of those connections can change.

How salient are Asian Americans' ethnic and pan-ethnic identities? Are they maintaining strong commitments to their ethnic group, or are they assimilating to dominant "American" cultural norms and practices? The more one expresses one's identity, the more one creates an ethnic boundary with other groups. An ethnic boundary refers to a tangible or cognitive activity that separates the self from others. For instance, speaking an ethnic language, having a co-ethnic partner, attending ethnic organizations, and the like represent ethnic boundaries. Individuals who claim an ethnic identity but otherwise act in assimilated ways have a "symbolic ethnicity" (Alba 1990; Gans 1979; Waters 1990). They indicate no "ethnic boundaries" between themselves and others despite their claims. Are Asian Americans moving towards a symbolic ethnicity or affirming strong boundaries with others?

Strong ethnic identities

As for most topics, competing evidence exists on the degree of Asian Americans' ethnic identities. Numerous studies have documented strong ethnic boundaries for the second generation. Portes and Rumbaut (2001) find that over time, children of immigrants identify less as "American" or as hyphenated American and more just with their ethnic group or with their pan-ethnic group. They also become much more likely to claim that their ethnic national identities are very important to them than they are to claim that about their American identities.

Cultural pulls to identities

Cultural ties to one's ethnic group help predict an individual's choice of an ethnic rather than American identity. Cultural ties include speaking in an ethnic tongue, being born abroad, and less acculturation to American norms (Portes and Rumbaut 2001).

With this in mind, it is noteworthy that 80 percent or more of Cambodian, Chinese, Filipino, Hmong, Lao, and Vietnamese Americans can speak their native language (ibid.). Among these, at least 70 percent of Southeast Asians speak in their native tongue to their peers and parents. Individuals also feel culturally tied to their ethnicity because of a sense of shared values. With such strong cultural ties, it is not surprising that so many claim ethnic identities.

Asian Americans also bond over more subtle cultural differences to other

Americans. Common Asian values include respecting elders, following parental authority, downplaying individual preferences in favour of those of the group, and the like. Asian Americans claim that they have a more communal spirit than their white peers. For instance, when in groups they can prefer not to split the check at a restaurant but instead fight over who pays for the whole bill, with men often insisting on paying for women (Thai 1999). They claim to have a more-the-merrier approach to going out with friends: everyone is invited rather than only a select few. While stereotypical, these differences represent cultural ties to co-ethnics.

Indeed, Asian Americans cultivate ethnic identities through social and cultural practices that may not necessarily be associated with Asian cultures past or present. In a study of the youth car-racing subculture, Soo Ah Kwon finds that "The car, a commodity, is the vehicle in which alternative cultural representations and practices among Asian American youth are produced and negotiated" (2004: 3). In Kwon's research, Asian-American youth appropriate what they believe to be symbols of the "Orient" (using Asian script in car decor or even driving cars made in Japan) to assert their Asianness. Asian-American popular culture creates modes of consumption that mark Asian Americans as akin to other Americans but still unique (Lim 2004). This allows Asian Americans to assert salient ethnic identities without feeling completely disengaged from the mainstream. In addition, certain celebrities make identifying as Asian American feel "cool." For instance, the rise of "Linsanity" over NBA star Jeremy Lin increased male pride in identifying as Asian American.

Transnational culture and identity

The second generation can also experience a transnational upbringing, with significant exposure to their parents' country of origin (Fouron and Glick-Schiller 2002; Levitt and Waters 2002). Some youths make visits as a form of identity work in order to learn about their "homeland" and so better understand their parents and ultimately themselves (Hall 1990; Maira 2002). Transnational weddings are increasingly common, with both partners returning to the homeland to marry or a US resident (typically male) marrying a co-ethnic living in the homeland (typically female) (Purkayastha 2005; Thai 2008). The tourism industry within Asia is also reaching out to the diaspora (that is, its overseas population), encouraging the notion of "natural" links.

Transnational cultural ties also consist of popular culture, such as food, film, music, fashion, and the like (Liu and Lin 2009; Purkayastha 2005). Dramas produced in Korea, for example, with their well-known exciting endings, have become quite popular with Korean Americans among others.[1] Increasingly, these cultural products are marketed to the diaspora, who make up a considerable customer base. Asian popular culture appeals to Asian-American youth, for it connects them to their homeland in Asia in a current rather than a traditional manner. Asian popular culture, such as films, may intentionally carry diasporic themes, identifying immigrant communities as part of the homeland despite their emigration (Desai 2004). This further encourages a transnational affinity. These popular culture elements often promote a traditional version of the homeland, popular with immigrants, demonstrating gendered and heteronormative roles. In response, some cultural representations within the diaspora are explicitly anti-conservative to counteract these tendencies (Baumann 1996; Hall 1990; Werbner 2001). Such representations have a more limited audience than mass-produced items.

Cultural institutions

Facilitating cultural ties, and so identities, among the children of immigrants are cultural institutions established both by themselves and their parents. It is not uncommon for Asian Americans to attend ethnic-specific language schools, dance lessons, sports leagues, beauty pageants, and other organized activities for youth (King-O'Riain 2006; Thangaraj 2012). Immigrants often construct religious sites as a way of honoring their culture, attending to spiritual needs, and providing a cultural setting for their children. Christian Asian Americans of the 1.5 and second generation also prefer ethnic religious spaces partly because of the shared culture and extra comfort of being among those who will not question one's legitimacy or Americanness (Ahn 1999; Chai 1998; Chong 1998; Kim 2004). As US-raised Asian Americans get older, they may leave religious settings but return and build their own approach to religion when they have children (Kurien 2007). The second generation also frequents professional and social organizations. These spaces offer members a chance to network with peers, make friends, and start dating (Dhingra 2007). Similarly, colleges have multiple cultural, social, and political organizations for Asian-American students. Professional and social organizations are popular because they serve multiple needs: members make connections to other professionals or classmates while affirming ethnic ties. Social and cultural institutions encourage salient ethnic identities among the second generation.

Officially defined ethnic neighborhoods (e.g. Chinatown, Manilatown, Koreatown, Little Saigon, etc.) where ethnic institutions exist and thrive, are also important in identity construction because "places, rather than merely denoting the presence of groups, are used to create their coherence" (Cheng 2009: 3; see also Bonus 2000 and Meyers 2006). Asian Americans, however, also congregate in spaces that may not technically be ethnic-related. For instance, Southeast-Asian boys in Southern California dominate cybercafes, where they play video games and claim a masculinity denied them in public discourse (Vo and Danico 2004).

Racialized categorization

Asian Americans' ethnic and pan-ethnic identities also become stronger due to racism and other forms of categorization from outsiders. Asian Americans commonly recount stories of feeling "different" from their white peers due to race (Kibria 2002; Park 2008; Tuan 1998). They are called foreigners, told they smell, and to go back where they came from. "Where are you from?," "You speak English well," "I like your ethnic food," and other essentialist comments remind Asian Americans that they are seen as Asian first and American second. Portes and Rumbaut (2001) find that over time adolescents increasingly claim an ethnic or pan-ethnic identity rather than simply an American one, in part due to discrimination and the constant questioning of their background by others. Such incidents combine with messages from the second generation's family to keep ethnic identities salient. Those children of immigrants who feel the most disenfranchised and oppressed, often those of weaker economic standing, can develop a reactive ethnicity, that is, an ethnic identity that is in reaction to specific sets of conditions (ibid.). For them, ethnicity or pan-ethnicity do not simply represent cultural ties but also, as minorities, recognition of inherent inequalities.

Along with their ethnic identities, Asian Americans form racial identities in response to discriminatory treatment. They recognize themselves as racially distinct from others and as minorities within the United States' racial hierarchy. The more racism they experience, the more Asian Americans feel closer to one another and more distant from whites. However, they interpret racism in various ways which influence their identity formation. As second-generation Asian Americans experience stereotyping by whites and dominant institutions (e.g. the media) as foreigners, geeks, exotic women, and so forth, they affirm a commitment to their ethnic group and to fellow Asian Americans (Kibria 2002). Nonetheless, even after such discrimination, they rarely distrust all whites or identify as people of color alongside blacks. Instead, Dhingra (2007) finds that most Korean and Indian Americans interviewed still felt closer to whites than to blacks. They interpreted racist incidents as exceptions to the rule. Given their middle-class or higher economic standing, they socialized more with whites and felt they had more in common with whites than with blacks, whom they often stereotyped as having an inferior culture. Those Korean and Indian Americans who identified more with blacks than with whites had had more interactions with African Americans and recognized shared experiences as nonwhites, as predicted by symbolic interactionism. Overall, racism guides Asian Americans to move closer to their ethnic group and to recognize ties to other Asian Americans, but does not necessarily lead to identification with other people of color.

Shared interests

Feeling culturally connected to co-ethnics and increasingly disconnected from others encourages the second generation to find common interests with one another. Less-privileged Asian Americans come together if they believe doing so will facilitate their economic success (Gibson 1988; Zhou and Bankston 1998). Professionals, too, create ethnic and class-specific organizations in order to network with those whom they respect culturally and intellectually. These organizations offer important economic benefits as well (Chong 1998; Dossani and Kumar 2011). The first generation uses religious and other institutions to obtain useful information on immigration policy, employment opportunities, educational opportunities for their children, and the like (Kurien 2007). The second generation joins ethnic organizations in order to strengthen ties with their homeland while socializing with co-ethnics who are similarly assimilated. This participation frequently takes place in college, at a time when individuals strengthen their ethnic identities. In these organizations, students often put on cultural shows for their community and the general public (Maira 2002). The shows frequently include dance numbers, fashion shows, skits, and possibly social and political statements. The overall intent is to create an "authentic" space for the participants and audience. The more authentic the show, the more participants feel they have affirmed ties to their homeland. Religious and sports ethnic organizations for students are also common. These allow Asian Americans to affirm their ethnic identity while participating in more Americanized activities.

As the individuals experience cultural, institutional, external, and instrumental ties simultaneously, they create salient ethnic identities. Their trips back to the homeland, their participation in ethnic organizations, their befriending of co-ethnics, their reliance on ethnic networks, their speaking another language, and so on all constitute their identity work. The more they perform this work, the stronger their ethnic boundaries become. As explained above, the impetus to develop ethnic identities depends on their significant others, local particularities, and individual preference. Yet what shapes those identities take and their salience depends on individual, their family, and their community access to these four factors of culture, interest, institutions, and categorization. As fitting social psychological models of identity development, much of this identity work takes place when individuals previously downplayed their ethnicity or had not thought actively about it (even if they had practiced elements of it).

Weak ethnic identities

In contrast to this portrait of strong ethnic boundaries, ample evidence also documents the weakening of ethnic boundaries and the assimilation of second-generation Asian Americans. External categorization in the form of benign questions and harmful discrimination will maintain Asian Americans' interest in their background and will keep such identities alive, rather than American identities. But how much of an ethnic *boundary* will there be? That is, how much do Asian Americans actually perform their identities?

Cultural assimilation and weak institutional ties

Evidence challenges the notion of strong ethnic boundaries, in particular for middle-class Asian Americans. Culturally, Asian Americans may know their ethnic language but do not necessarily choose to speak it. For instance, two-thirds or more (typically much more) of Cambodian, Chinese, Filipino, Laotian, and Vietnamese American prefer to speak English generally, conversing in it with their spouses or partners, even if they know their parents' native tongue (Portes and Rumbaut 2001; Zhou and Xiong 2005). As individuals culturally assimilate, they become more like the major group physically around them, such as white middle or working class, black middle or working class, or otherwise.

The second generation may not sustain other cultural elements. For instance, even those who care about their background and socialize with co-ethnics can have trouble articulating ancestral cultural practices, such as rituals or customs (Ahn 1999; Min and Kim 1999). Being ethnic may mean simply feeling "different" from others and being restricted by one's parents. These generic definitions of what it means to be ethnic hardly distinguish someone, even from non-Asians. Also, while Asian Americans express interest in parts of their culture, they may not actually practice it much. For instance, second-generation Hindu Americans may want to maintain their religious upbringing but have little knowledge of its rituals or meanings, which they regret (Dhingra 2008). Rather than attend a local temple to learn more, their identity work consists of seeking social organizations populated by the second generation or researching the religion on their own. They feel the temple is too "authentic," and so they avoid the cultural space most relevant to their interests.

Transnational practices and assimilation

Researchers similarly have challenged the degree of transnationalism among the second generation. Kasinitz et al. (2002) find that second-generation Chinese Americans rarely visit their homeland, send few remittances back to relatives (compared to Latin American families), and generally have weak ties to their ethnic origins. Rumbaut (2002) similarly argues against a significant transnational perspective among immigrant descendants from Latin America and Asia. Few considered their country of origin as their "home," and visits back to those countries were rare. Hardly any of them move back to their country of origin. And English, rather than their parents' native tongue, dominated conversations between peers and even with parents, weakening transnational ties.

Where some groups have stronger transnational sensibilities than others, this may be due to the availability of transnational institutions, parents' interests, class status, and the point they have reached in their life course (Levitt and Waters 2002). Ironically, those who are otherwise the most assimilated can evince the strongest ties. For instance, immigrant communities with more resources, more education, and who have acquired citizenship travel back home more often and generally keep up long-distance relationships (Guarnizo, Portes, and Haller 2003; Portes 2003). Transnational ties represent some existing degree of integration, rather than a strict orientation towards the homeland. Also, those with relatives in their country of origin are more likely to make such trips (Walton-Roberts 2003). As relatives abroad pass away, individuals' transnational identities wane.

Not only can transnational ties reflect some assimilation among immigrants but also, ironically, can further group integration. Visits to the homeland can make people aware of how Americanized they are relative to their Asian peers, an often unexpected (and unwelcome) recognition (Purkayastha 2005). As transnational ties affirm ethnic identities, individuals may feel more confident in themselves and become more settled in the United States (Louie 2002; Smith 2006). Furthermore, the manner in which the second generation explains its transnational ties can indicate their integration. Second-generation Indian Americans, for instance, frame their participation in ethnic organizations as an "American" practice (Dhingra 2008). The organizations abide by the liberal, individualist doctrine of the US nation-state; that is, they do not seek public funds, criticize other cultures, deny entry to others, and so on. The second generation explicitly relies on these American principles to justify ethnic organizations. The act of belonging to an ethnic organization is seen as supporting and furthering what it means to be an American more broadly.

Weak interests in ethnic boundaries

The second generation may on the other hand have little involvement in ethnic institutions and few compelling interests to associate with co-ethnics. Those Asian Americans who have grown up highly assimilated and have developed leisure pursuits unrelated to their ethnicity have little motivation to join ethnic institutions. Similarly, because so many Asian Americans graduate from high school and college, they can tap into those peers and alumni associations when looking for advice, information, money, and so on. Given their fluency in and preference for English, there are few barriers to joining mainstream associations. In other words, those Asian Americans motivated and able to network with co-ethnics will likely do so, and will affirm their ethnic identities in the process. For instance, the first generation commonly relies on ethnic associations for support. However, the educational accomplishments and acculturation of many in the second generation means they can find support outside of their ethnic group and so have less reason to join ethnic or pan-ethnic organizations. Those without professional networks may rely more on co-ethnic ties, as found within the segmented assimilation literature (Gibson 1988; Zhou and Bankston 1998). Still, as these youths grow up, they will likely search for occupations outside ethnic circles, as immigrants themselves often do (Nee, Sanders, and Sernau 1994). This will weaken ethnic boundaries. If Asian Americans have developed networks outside their ethnic group, they can attain their interests without joining co-ethnics.

Even if the second generation maintains salient ethnic boundaries, their descendants more likely will not. While the third generation may well identify as ethnic American rather than just "American," they still will be highly assimilated. For the third and later generations, English predominates. As Alba (2004) writes, "In the third (and later) generation, the predominant pattern is English monolingualism: that is, children speak only English at home, making it highly unlikely that they will be bilingual as adults. Among Asians, the percentage who speak only English is 92 percent."[2] The third generation also has a weak grasp of ethnic customs, mostly because their parents have not passed them on (Tuan 1998; Kitano 1969). They will also have weak transnational ties and therefore less salient ethnic identities. The loss of ethnic cultural ties is especially likely in the United States since it has not institutionalized multiculturalism at the state level (Steinberg 1981; Taylor 1994). There is little official emphasis placed on cultural diversity.

Racism and other forms of external categorization will prevent full assimilation, as will cultural ties (however weak). As sociologist Mia Tuan (1998) finds, even third-generation Asian Americans who are culturally and socially assimilated with whites still feel treated as foreigners. Vincent Chin was relatively assimilated and was out with his white friend on the night he was killed. So the third generation will maintain ethnic identities, but how much and in what manner they express them is in doubt. At the same time, public images of Asian Americans as geeks, as sexist, as foreigners, and the like limit people's motivation to seek out co-ethnics unless they already know these stereotypes to be false or exaggerated. As seen in chapter 6, negative racial stereotypes of Asian Americans can lead some to avoid dating within their race, and so contribute to the race's integration with other races.

Therefore, competing evidence exists on the salience of the second generation's ethnic identities. In general, practically all individuals claim an ethnic identity. Also, the rise of multiculturalism and its institutionalization on college campuses contributes to people's interest in their ethnicity. The ease of transnational culture makes ethnic boundaries more prevalent. In addition to all of these factors pulling the second generation towards their background, external categorization pushes them towards it. With all these factors in mind, the second and even third generations will assert ethnic identities beyond the purely symbolic level.

Nonetheless, it still takes effort for individuals to maintain such identities. Because so many in the second generation are residentially and occupationally integrated, much of their daily lives do not require them to invoke their ethnicity. They must go out of their way to do so, for it takes motivation to find and attend ethnic organizations, to seek out ethnic music, to speak an ethnic language when English is more natural. Overcoming the overwhelming influence and ease of mainstream culture is particularly challenging for those with limited knowledge of their ethnic backgrounds. So, while assimilation is unlikely, highly developed ethnic boundaries cannot be taken for granted. What results are ethnic identities that are active at some times and not at others. This conclusion raises the question of what makes people decide to act on their ethnic identities. We turn to this after reviewing the literature on pan-ethnic identities.

Pan-ethnic identities

The same factors that motivate ethnic identities – culture, institutions, categorization, and shared interests – also influence pan-ethnic identities. Pan-ethnicity among Asian Americans and other minorities has been studied mostly at the political level (Cornell 1988; Espiritu 1992). For individuals in the second generation, however, there are growing but not commanding pan-ethnic identities. In contrast to the politicized nature of pan-ethnic affiliations by community activists, most lay Asian Americans who have pan-ethnic sympathies refer to cultural ties and a sense of shared racialized experiences (Park 2008). These consist of a shared upbringing within strict Asian families, values of respecting elders and family unity, and stereotyping as foreigners (Tuan 1998). Kibria (2002) found that half of her sample of second-generation Chinese and Korean American college students claimed a pan-ethnic identity based on those cultural factors. Those with stronger pan-ethnic identities are more likely to join pan-ethnic organizations and develop shared interests, such as advocating for civil rights, better media representation, college courses, and the like.

The formation of pan-ethnic identities suggests anti-assimilation among the second generation, for rather than identifying as "American," they are gathering behind a racial category. Yet a pan-ethnic identity also signifies some degree of assimilation. For instance, pan-ethnic ties require speaking English rather than one's native tongue. Marrying outside of one's ethnicity to another Asian American also weakens ethnic boundaries. And, since much of individuals' pan-ethnic identity stems from generic similarities, such as having grown up with strict parents, it signifies an American-based identity rather than a transnational or deeply ethnic one. So becoming Asian American is a means of becoming American (Kibria 2002).

Asian-American ethnic groups vary in their degree of pan-ethnicity. Not surprisingly, East Asian Americans exhibit stronger pan-ethnicity than do South or Southeast-Asian Americans. Partly this is due to a class difference between many East and Southeast Asian Americans. Many in the latter group do not feel enveloped within the "model minority" stereotype that so readily applies to other Asian Americans (Lee 2004). Also, arriving as refugees rather than as voluntary immigrants alters one's relationship with the nation. Furthermore, depending on one's geographic location, intra-racial tensions can limit pan-ethnicity. Ethnic groups compete with each other in the form of businesses, community activists, and so on. At the same time, while many – not all – South Asian Americans share the "model minority" stereotype, they also avoid a pan-ethnic identity (Dhingra 2007; Kibria 1996; Shankar and Srikanth 1998). South Asian Americans have a distinct phenotype, set of stereotypes, religion, dietary preferences, and more from those of most East Asian Americans. They also are not categorized as Asian American by others. The racism most commonly experienced takes the form of accusations of being terrorists, of practicing "pagan" religions, of being passive or exotic, and the like, rather than as "slanty-eyed" (Maira 2009). Post-9/11, the South Asian ethnic divide from other Asian Americans has only increased.

While Asian groups experience a shared Orientalist racism, it, ironically, can weaken pan-ethnicity. Intellectually, these stereotypes might be thought of as applying to other Asian Americans. But they are experienced as ethnic-specific, for often it is one's connection to one's particular homeland that is ridiculed. Slurs such as "chink," "gook," or "camel jockey" are ethnic-specific, even though they stem from a shared set of racialized prejudices. In response to such racism, individuals frequently learn more about their homeland than about Asian America. Racism is most often understood as due to individual ignorance, which educating oneself and others on the "true" nature of one's country of origin can remedy. This is an especially common reaction among middle-class or upper-class Asian Americans who, given their economic privileges, may not worry about structural racism as much as others. Therefore, pan-ethnic boundaries remain situation-specific rather than comprehensive among South and Southeast Asians in particular and among other Asian Americans generally.

Balancing multiple identities

As individuals, we all have multiple identities, including ethnic or pan-ethnic ones. This raises the question of how we handle our multiple identities. How do we choose which identity to perform? What happens when our identities conflict with one another? In other words, how do we live with our identities as we move through daily life?

The question of how we handle our various identities has particular relevance for immigrant communities. Historically, the children of immigrants presumably experienced a "marginal man" scenario. This meant that immigrant communities were pathologized as emotionally unstable because they were torn between a traditional, ethnic lifestyle and the mainstream lifestyle popularized in the media and in school (Stonequist 1937). The former contained such values as respect for elders and the prioritizing of family and community over the individual, and involves ethnic symbols, such as language and dress. The latter celebrates personal independence and individualism, speaking English, and mainstream popular culture. Put another way, the second generation supposedly could not make it to the final developmental stage within psychological identity models of a healthy, reconciled ethnic identity. In one study, Hunt, Moloney, and Evans actually found that Asian-American youths in a dance club/rave scene saw their consumption of drugs as an outgrowth of their identity challenges as Asian Americans. One respondent stated:

> There's a strong . . . definitely a connection between . . . my ethnic background and
> not having community within that and my drug use. . . . I think that really was the
> motivation for me to seek . . . or self-medicate, in a way, to . . . to combat the feelings
> that I was having of confusion or anxiety or . . . feeling alone. (Hunt, Moloney, and
> Evans 2011: 290)

The term "marginal man" not only retains sexist historical assumptions of the universality of the male experience, but in this case it particularly misrepresents the gendered dynamic of identity conflict. Women more often than men cite tensions between their ethnic and American lifestyles, for the former typically carries traditional expectations of serving the family and downplaying personal preferences. While Asian women are often feminists and have helped define the feminist movement globally, the standard definition of American feminism excludes them. So daughters of Asian immigrants more readily experience identity conflict (Das Gupta 1997; Espiritu 2003).

While the "marginal man" conflict remains common, it is not the only way to frame the consequences of multiple identities. It is increasingly common today to hear the 1.5 and second generation refer to having the "best of both worlds" with their dual lifestyles. In fact, being bicultural can improve groups' cognitive abilities because it makes people develop multiple reference points (Portes and Rumbaut 2001).

What is consistent in both the "marginal man" and the "best of both worlds" is individuals' commitment to more than one identity which differ widely from one another. The question becomes: how do people handle their opposing "worlds," be they considered a blessing or a curse? Within the sociological study of identity, this problem is referred to as "role conflict." This means two or more roles have incompatible expectations. Many types of people can experience role conflict, such as mothers with full-time careers, gays who are religiously devout, first-generation students at privileged colleges, and so on. Understanding how Asian Americans handle their conflict informs this sociological dilemma more generally.

There have been two presumed responses to this dilemma. The first is the abandoning of one identity for another. This is a common occurrence, such as when a mother stops her career to take care of her children full-time, a self-identified gay man no longer attends church, a first-generation college student limits relationships with friends from back home, or an Asian American decides to assimilate as much as possible. For Asian Americans, this last choice is common, especially during the first stage of psychological identity development (which may be the only stage for some people) (Chow 2000; Espiritu 2003). Those who choose this typically do not know Asian Americans whom they feel close to. For instance, if one self-defines as a feminist yet feels one's ethnic social identity expects women to be submissive, one may reject the ethnic identity (Dhingra 2007). Those with more knowledge and attachments to the ethnicity tend to overlook those problems. Those with weaker attachments do not.

Rather than abandon one way of life for the other, another common practice is to segregate one's identities. This is especially likely for those who articulate a "best-of-both-worlds" scenario. One chooses one identity when in certain settings or with certain people and acts on the other identity in other settings. According to identity theory, which identity one chooses depends both on the expectations of the setting and the kind of impression one wants to give (Stryker 1992; see also Goffman 1959). Typically, these two factors align so that one wants to fit others' general expectations. For instance, as they come home from school or work, it is not uncommon for immigrant Americans to change into ethnic attire, start speaking an ethnic language, and/or turn on ethnic music (Maira 2002). Some people are even known by different names depending on their environment, such as by an ethnic name when with co-ethnics and by an Americanized name when with others. In these cases, one changes one's identity to fit one's surroundings. Sometimes switching between identities involves deception. Children may mislead their parents as to their activities and whereabouts so as to avoid being seen as too American (ibid.). While lying to one's parents is ubiquitous among teenagers, it takes on a different meaning here. If discovered, youths risk not only being bad children but also bad ethnics, and so losing touch with their ethnic community.

In addition to having to balance symbols and lifestyles, immigrant minorities also switch between types of values. For instance, obeying authority, in particular for women, is privileged within traditionally Asian circles. But individualism and taking initiative are valued in mainstream white spaces. These different expectations can create tensions for Asian Americans (Hong et al. 2007). Such individuals must learn how to move between contrasting value systems as they walk through different spheres in daily life.

This identity segregation is not particular to immigrants. Minorities generally have to balance their lifestyles as they move between the public and private spheres. African-American women in white-collar careers, for instance, can have mostly African American friends outside work but do not refer to those relations with their predominantly white friends at work (Bell 1990). As a result, they often feel that they are moving between parts of themselves every day.

Rather than continuously segregating their identities, people hope to bring them together. Scholars of material culture (e.g. film, food, music) first analyzed immigrant communities' hybrid cultural mixing of their western and eastern lifestyles through cultural creations, like music, fashion, food, and so on (Baumann 1996; Hall 1990). For instance, Maira (2002) documents dance parties and music that combine Indian and western styles in New York City. Even when Asian American DJs were not blending cultural styles, they helped bridge Asian and American identities by performing current American music styles (e.g. hip-hop) in predominantly ethnic-only settings (de Leon 2004). Across the nation, theater organizations, artistic collectives, and the like creatively express Asian Americans' multiple lifestyles and identity conflicts (Kondo 1996; Zia 2000). These efforts affirm community ties both to their homelands and to the United States. Other cultural practices help assert their racial pride as Asian Americans by countering negative stereotyping. For instance, Asian American men in Southern California take part in import car racing which creates a hyper-masculinity that counters the effeminate Asian-American male image (while reinforcing the role of women as subordinate and sexualized objects) (Namkung 2004). Similarly, Asian popular culture consumed by youth, discussed above, also connects them to their heritage but in a manner akin to their enjoyment of mainstream culture.

These cultural practices move past the notion of mutually exclusive identities. Yet, when not listening to hybrid music or the like, the presumption is that individuals go back to segregating their identities. In other words, individuals' daily life stays the same, choosing between identities based on context. The hybrid cultural products and spaces serve as tension-release valves rather than a way of life. Taking from the lessons of cultural studies, Dhingra (2007) argues that ethnic communities bring together their identities within their daily lives rather than only in particular moments. For instance, individuals find ways to express their background while in the workplace, such as by invoking implicit ethnic symbols or speaking about their ethnicity to co-workers, even though the workplace traditionally rewards only a homogenous "American" lifestyle. Similarly, the home sphere often expects a highly ethnic lifestyle, but second-generation Asian Americans also express their Americanized interests there. For instance, they may move out of the parental home or refuse their help in finding a marital partner, as typical of American adults, but still obey other family expectations and seek ethnic partners who will please their parents. In this way, they mimic their Americanized peers' adult lifestyles but in a manner that deviates little from traditionally ethnic outcomes. In these and other ways, ethnic and American lifestyles come together rather than remain segregated, even as individual Asian Americans conceive of their ethnic and American identities as disparate. The same bridging of identities applies to Asian Americans' racial identities as well. The second generation often feels racialized as foreign. Here they bring together their racial and American identities, for instance by arguing that their Asian culture has helped them succeed in their American workplace, akin to the "model minority" stereotype.

This bridging of identities represents a "lived hybridity," that is, the daily ways in which individuals overcome the segregation of identities (Dhingra 2007; Brettell and Nibbs 2009). Through a lived hybridity, individuals can express their multiple identities without being conspicuous and so overcome the "marginal man" scenario. People bridge identities every day in subtle ways, which explains how they handle multiple roles within a racialized and gendered set of external circumstances.

Conclusion

Asian Americans, like people generally, perform identity work in order to develop identities that they are proud of. For ethnic and racial identities, this often means attending to a social identity as defined by their significant others and the generalized other. One's degree of cultural ties, shared institutions, shared interests, and external categorization influence how salient these identities become. For the most part, second generation Asian Americans care deeply about their background and draw boundaries from others. Some even express transnational ties. But significant acculturation takes place concurrently, which draws them closer to those around them. Even as debate continues as to whether the second generation is maintaining highly salient ethnic boundaries or not, many agree that they will maintain some attachments to their ethnic group, if for no other reason than the treatment they receive from outsiders.

Regardless of how strong or weak ethnic and pan-ethnic identities are for Asian Americans, individuals must balance them as they go through daily life. This may involve choosing one identity over the other but typically means finding ways to express multiple identities. Rather than simply ask how much Asian Americans know about their ethnicity or pan-ethnicity, it is more informative for their adaptation to ask how they present themselves to others. How they perform their identities will determine their intergroup relations. The outcome will not be a simple story of increased integration or sustained divisions. Instead, Asian Americans will selectively perform their identities based on what fits their needs and their settings. As their needs or their contexts change over time, so will their performances. We should examine how Asian American identities shift over time and space and the implications for their well-being and intergroup relations.

Discussion questions

- Revisit the exercise from chapter 1 in which you wrote or drew the various institutions, group identities, and oppressions that shape your lives. Revise that activity using new terminology from this chapter to create a more nuanced conceptualization of your identity. Incorporate 2–4 concepts from this chapter in your revision.
- Reflect on this 2011 BBC documentary of an exhibition at the National Portrait Gallery in Washington, DC. In what ways do the artists define who and what is "Asian American"? How is Asian-American identity expressed by individual artists and by the exhibition more broadly? www.bbc.co.uk/news/entertainment-arts-14501196?utm_source=twitterfeed&utm_medium=twitter

10 Inter-Minority Relations

Whereas most of the book has focused on relations between Asian Americans and the (white) majority, this chapter concentrates on inter-ethnic and interracial relations. Inter-ethnic relations, as we define them here, refer to relations between ethnic groups (Vietnamese, Indians, and Chinese, for example) within a broad racialized category (i.e. Asian Americans). Interracial relations refer to relations between different ethnic and/or racialized minority groups (i.e. Koreans and blacks; Filipinos and Mexicans). The first section of this chapter examines the conditions under which Asian Americans come together as a group in the United States and even across national borders. We will also examine, however, the conflicts that exist between Asians of different ethnic backgrounds. We then turn to an examination of interracial conflict. Among other examples used to elaborate on theories of interracial conflict, significant attention is given to reviewing the contested relations between Korean Americans and African Americans. We will also examine how groups try to resolve this particular conflict. The key argument of the chapter is that it is important to understand that solidarities between groups, despite similar experiences or overlapping histories, cannot be readily or easily assumed. One must understand the complex circumstances in which people do or do not come together.

Group formation

(Re)defining terms

In chapter 7, we discussed the process by which people develop a sense of themselves as individuals. Recall that people craft their individual identities through their relations with significant others and generalized others. However, people simultaneously develop a sense of themselves as members of a group. Indeed, we develop a sense of ourselves as members of multiple social groups, including ethnic groups, classes, genders, religions, and the like.

"Asian Americans" as a group are comprised of diverse peoples who descend from countries that have very different cultural traditions, languages, and religions. Indeed, many of these countries may even be in conflict with one another. Despite differences and histories of conflict, "Asian American" has come to be recognized as a group in the United States. According to sociologist Yen Le Espiritu, Asian Americans can be defined as a "pan-ethnic group," that is a "politico-cultural collectivity made up of the peoples of several, hitherto distinct, tribal or national origins" (1992: 2). "Asian American" is a pan-ethnic formation through which people from the countries that constitute the continent of Asia (from China, Korea, and Japan in East Asia, to Vietnam and the Philippines in Southeast Asia, to India and Pakistan in South

Asia) are grouped together by outsiders and/or through elected collective affinity. That is, "[d]espite the distinctive histories and separate identities, these ethnic groups have united to protect and promote their collective interests" (Espiritu 1992: 3).

The construction of pan-ethnic groups

Pan-ethnic groups are different from ethnic groups in several ways. First, pan-ethnic groups are organized on a larger scale of collectivity because they involve multiple ethnic groups. Second, pan-ethnic groups are relatively new as a phenomenon as compared to ethnic groups. Ethnic groups can claim some kind of "origin." Pan-ethnic groups, on the other hand, are forged through the work of interpreting the (emergent) group's history and fate. Ethnic groups are constructed through some imagined "beginning" (often tied to a specific set of historical events within a particular geography). This is not the case for pan-ethnic groups. Furthermore, pan-ethnic groups are distinct from ethnic groups in large part because they do not necessarily share a culture (i.e. language, traditions, etc.), which is often the stuff of ethnic groups. Rather, pan-ethnic groups emerge primarily as a result of externally imposed conditions. The state's categorization and lumping of people from diverse backgrounds into single groups is important to pan-ethnic group formation. According to Espiritu, pan-ethnic groups emerge when "the state uses a unitary pan-ethnic label – rather than numerous national or tribal designations – to allocate political and economic resources, it encourages individuals to broaden their identity to conform to the more inclusive ethnic designation" (1992: 11). Moreover, pan-ethnic groups are formed within the context of intergroup conflict.

Pan-ethnic mistreatment and responses

Pan-ethnicity is a result, in large part, of external categorization rooted in racialized discourses. When this categorization gives rise to hostility or conflict, a pan-ethnic identity may be activated. Indeed, Espiritu suggests that, "[w]hile political benefits certainly promote pan-Asian organization, it is anti-Asian violence that has drawn the largest pan-Asian support" (1992: 134). Part of what explains pan-ethnic identification in situations of group conflict, including anti-Asian violence, is the fact that distinctions across ethnic groups are not made. People suffer from violent attacks for being categorized broadly as "Asian," not because they are Filipino, Japanese, Korean, and so on. This is perhaps most clearly exemplified in the Vincent Chin case, discussed in chapter 2. Chin, a Chinese American, was murdered because his assailants mistakenly categorized him as Japanese. Working and living in Detroit, Michigan, Chin was murdered in 1982 by two unemployed autoworkers. They were white. After a barroom tiff, Chin was stalked by the two men, Ebens and Nitz, and beaten. Chin died several days later from injuries associated with the beating (Wu 2010).

The Asian-American community's response to the Chin murder and aftermath helped further a pan-ethnic identification for the community. When neither man was sentenced to a prison term, the Asian-American community of Detroit formed the American Citizens for Justice (ACJ) to demand prosecution. The ACJ was a pan-ethnic group comprised of a broad range of Asian ethnicities. As one of the ACJ's founders put it, "This case has been about people recognizing across ethnicity and across race that this could have been any one of us, this could have been me, that the danger of racial stereotypes is that real people and real lives are reduced to carica-ture" (Frances Wang 2010: 24). Outside Detroit, the Chin campaign drew attention to and support from groups across the nation (Espiritu 1992; Wu 2010). Indeed, the group initially only focused on the lenient sentence meted out to Chin's murderers, rather than on the racist aspects of the case. It was not until further investigation that it was discovered that one of Chin's attackers accused him of "taking jobs away." Recall, as we discussed in chapter 3, that the 1980s was a period of economic hardship in the United States. Factories were closing down across the country and relocating overseas. Meanwhile, the United States' economic competitors, such as Japan, seemed to be surpassing it. This appeared especially true for the automobile industry (Wu 2010).

When it surfaced that Chin was killed because he had been taken for a Japanese, ACJ decided to press the Justice Department to bring civil rights charges against Ebens and Nitz. Ultimately, only one of the men, Ebens, was convicted of violating Chin's civil rights. The other, Nitz, was acquitted. Later, however, the conviction was overturned on a technicality. The ACJ demanded a retrial but even that did not change the outcome. Neither Ebens nor Nitz were sentenced to prison for Chin's death (Espiritu 1992).

At the conclusion of the campaign for Chin, the ACJ continued to address issues of anti-Asian violence. In addition, however, ethnic organizations also began to develop a pan-ethnic consciousness. Groups like the Organization of Chinese Americans (OCA) took on a pan-ethnic perspective in response to violence perpetrated on other Chinese Americans. They argued, "[i]ronically, most Chinese victims of hate crimes were mistaken for other Asian nationalities. As the wave of Japan bashing propa-gates, all Asian Americans may be vulnerable to racial violence!" (Chen 1992: 13). Hence, the OCA made it its mission to "acquire justice and rights not only for Chinese Americans but also for all Americans" (Chen 1992). Groups like the OCA responded to external categorizations imposed on Asians while also becoming sites for the culti-vation of a pan-Asian consciousness.

Anti-Asian violence has not always resulted in the formation of pan-ethnic iden-tifications. During World War II, for example, when Japanese Americans were being corralled in internment camps, Chinese Americans asserted their Chineseness to avert white antagonism, for instance by wearing buttons to indicate that they were Chinese. This was also the case for Filipino Americans.

Pan-ethnic consciousness has been formed and sustained through new organi-zations (and new orientations in ethnic organizations) responding to anti-Asian violence. It has been as proactive as it has been reactive to anti-Asian violence. Scott Kurashige notes a case in Philadelphia. There, an Asian American was accused of murdering a white person. Local Asian-American organizations responded by reframing the murder as a matter of self-defense and used the case as an opportunity to raise public awareness about longer histories of anti-Asian violence in the area. Rather than simply reacting to anti-Asian violence, this was a proactive assertion of Asian-American pan-ethnicity (Kurashige 2000).

Tensions within "Asian America"

Asian-American pan-ethnicity, even as it has been formed through organizations that have responded to anti-Asian racism and violence and continues to be sustained through pan-Asian organizations, is a tenuous prospect. While Asian Americans have been racialized by the dominant society as a single group through successive immigration laws, for instance, or in everyday interactions between Asian Americans and other racialized groups, what is defined as "Asian American" is unevenly applied to different ethnic Asian groups, because not all Asian Americans share the same physical characteristics (e.g. skin tone). Moreover, Asian presence in the United States derives from very different histories, which in turn shape racialization and therefore the potential for pan-ethnic identification. Other issues that inhibit pan-ethnic group formation are the class, ethnic, and religious differences between Asian ethnic groups.

Racial and historical difference

Many of the groups that comprise "Asian America" are unevenly categorized and racialized. For example, South Asians (those who can trace their origins to India, Pakistan, and other neighboring countries) have arguably always experienced specific forms of racialization by other Asian ethnic groups, due to their distinguishing phenotypic characteristics. They look quite different from other Asian-American groups, such as the Chinese, Japanese or Korean Americans. For instance, as Kibria (1996) argues, South Asians are not black or white, nor are they thought of as "Asian" by other racial groups, or even by other Asian ethnicities. Others who are typically racialized by whites as "Asian" (e.g. Chinese, Japanese, or Koreans) may themselves think of South Asians as falling outside what are defined as "Asian Americans" (Kibria 1996).

The racialized difference of South Asians was perhaps most clearly evidenced in the violence they suffered in the wake of 9/11 when many were mistakenly seen as "Arab" and therefore as terrorists. In the case of Sikh Indians, if they were not necessarily taken for "Arabs," they were presumed to be Muslims (a category that has also been associated with "Arab" and "terrorist") and were subject to hate crimes (Naber 2002; Sheikh 2008). This was not an experience shared by other Asian ethnic groups. The very term "South Asian" is actually its own kind of pan-ethnic identity. It reflects, in many ways, the fact that people from India, Bangladesh, Sri Lanka, Nepal, or Pakistan experience racialization in the United States similarly to each other but differently from other Asian groups. Because racializing processes in the United States depend on skin color, those from South Asia do not experience racialization in the same ways as other Asians.

Indeed, South Asians have been experiencing racialized violence from the (white) majority since before 9/11. In the late 1980s, a group called the "Dotbusters" was formed in New Jersey. It was an anti-Indian group of whites that explicitly attacked Indians, both in the press and physically. According to Misir, "This racialization of Indians into a discrete, identifiable group highlights [. . .] that the paradigm of a pan-Asian American unity does not reflect political and social realities" (2000: 302).

Other scholars raise issues about the extent to which Filipinos or others from

Southeast Asia actually share much in common with East Asians (i.e. Koreans, Japanese, Chinese). Here, similar to South Asians, the issue has to do with whether Southeast Asians do in fact experience racialization similarly to East Asians or not. In the case of Filipinos, scholars suggest that their history of colonial subjugation has led to experiences that are distinct from other Asian ethnic groups. Filipinos were colonial subjects and therefore do not fit the immigrant narrative that may be true for other Asian ethnic groups. Indeed, according to Campomanes (1997), one of the risks of constructing a pan-ethnic identity is that it does not acknowledge the specific history of US colonialism experienced by Filipinos. Southeast Asians, like Filipinos, enter the United States context quite differently to other Asian Americans. Their presence in the United States is due to their refugee status that was the consequence of Cold War imperial interventions in Vietnam and other neighboring countries (Ngo and Lam 2012). Each group, scholars have argued, has a very different orientation to the United States and its experiences of racialization differ from those of other (East) Asian Americans as a consequence. Therefore, they do not necessarily share common cause with other Asian Americans.

Pacific Islanders are often lumped together with Asians under the rubric of "Asian Pacific Islanders." In the case of Pacific Islanders, not only are they dissimilar phenotypically (i.e. their physical traits) from those considered "Asian," neither do they share the history of immigration that characterizes most Asian groups. Indeed, in places like Hawaii, Pacific Islanders and Asians are in a tense relationship because of "settler colonialism." Pacific Islander Vincente Diaz argues that the "condition and status of Indigenity versus Immigrant/Settler Identity" (Diaz 2004: 197) causes major tensions between Asian Americans and Pacific Islanders. Not only do they not share phenotypic characteristics with other people categorized as "Asian American," their experiences, especially their relationship to the state as displaced indigenous people, make pan-ethnic group formation, which is political, a potentially precarious project (Diaz 2004). Indeed, during the incorporation of Hawaii into the United States in the 1950s, the experiences of Asian Americans (specifically Japanese Americans) were used to support statehood, despite the native Hawaiians' mobilization against statehood. In short, the interests of Asian Americans were pitted against the interests of Pacific Islanders (Saranillo 2010).

Class, ethnic, and religious differences

Class, ethnic, and religious differences have and continue to limit pan-ethnic identification. Conflicts between Chinese and Japanese business owners in San Francisco during the 1940s, for example, were linked to home-country tensions as Chinese Americans developed resentment towards their Japanese-American counterparts during the period of Japanese imperial incursions into China. Just as importantly, however, these conflicts were also the consequence of anti-Asian laws that forced Asians to compete with one another (Brooks 2011).

In the present moment, class differences within ethnic groups can limit pan-ethnic identification with "Asian American", especially if this pan-ethnic identification is generally associated with a particular class. Indeed, Espiritu argues that "pan-Asianism has been primarily the ideology of native-born, American-educated, and middle-class Asians" (1992: 50). Yet many Asians are recently arrived immigrants and they may find themselves working as low-wage workers in ethnic enclave economies. Though low-wage Asian immigrant workers work for co-ethnics, the co-ethnic relationship may actually "facilitate the exploitative nature of the relationships between owner and worker" (Ong and Umemoto 2000: 241). Indeed, class differences not only limit pan-ethnic identification but may also make ethnic identification (and therefore solidarity) less tenable. Class differences between Chinese low-wage workers and their Chinese employers, for example, have led to the formation of groups like the Chinese Staff and Workers' Association which has staged collective actions against Chinese restaurant owners in New York's Chinatown on behalf of workers.[1]

In yet another example, Kurien finds that, though some Indians come together with Sri Lankans, Pakistanis, and others around a pan-ethnic identity as "South Asians" which includes but is not exclusively Indian, there are others who come together around an exclusively "Indic" collective identity that is rooted in Hinduism and is generally Indian-centric. These competing group formations have implications for the kind of issues that these groups mobilize around. The differences between the two types of groups were amplified in the wake of the 9/11 attacks on the World Trade Center in New York City and the Pentagon in Washington, DC. South Asian-identified organizations emphasized South Asians' shared racialized experiences as they were targeted for hate crimes, regardless of their ethnic/national (which includes Indians, Bangladeshis, Pakistanis, and Sri Lankans, among others) and religious backgrounds (including Muslims and non-Muslims). Indic groups, meanwhile, were concerned to distinguish Hinduism from Islam and in some cases even allied themselves with right-wing anti-Muslim groups (Kurien 2003).

The different responses from different Indian community groups suggest that the "Dotbusters" violence discussed above did not necessarily lead to a fully consolidated pan-ethnic South Asian, let alone a consolidated Indian, identity. Both class and generational lines split the Indian response to the "Dotbusters" violence. In the first generation, there was a divide between the professionals and the working class. The professionals understood the "Dothead" violence as attributable to class-based animosity from whites because of their own failures to "get ahead," rather than as a racially motivated hate crime. The working class, meanwhile, asserted its ethnic difference and indeed a moral superiority, often speaking in native tongues at rallies in a bid to attain justice for the violence victims. The second generation, unlike their first-generation counterparts, insisted on interpreting the violence as a hate crime and attempted to forge coalitions with other people of color, including other Asian Americans. The sorts of division that emerged among Indian Americans, while not the most significant aspect of the "Dothead" violence, does illustrate how ethnic groups, even when they share a similar set of experiences, may not always come together in unified ways (Misir 2000). At the same time, the responses, particularly of second-generation Indian Americans, illustrate how intergroup conflict can become a source of pan-ethnic group formation.

Transnationalism

If pan-ethnic collective identification, however fraught it may be, is a response to racializing processes, including their most extreme forms as expressed in anti-Asian violence, Asians in the United States may simultaneously, or even as an alternative to pan-ethnic identities, cultivate transnational ethnic/national identities. Many Asian Americans continue to sustain or begin to develop ties with their erstwhile "home-lands," despite long-term residence in the United States or even naturalization as US citizens. Assimilation approaches to understanding how first-generation immigrants become "American" often assume that, over time, immigrants to the United States eventually shed their ethnic/national identities to assume an "American" one. This analysis of ethnicity among immigrants, however, was developed with regard to immigrants from Europe who could ultimately be categorized as "white." Though some European immigrant groups, like the Italians, were not initially categorized as "white" (this was true, for example, during the early twentieth century when the Immigration Act of 1924 was meant to exclude not only racialized groups like Asians from entering the United States but also Southern Europeans, who were seen as "racially" different as well), over time, they were absorbed into the category of "white" and would eventually feel themselves to be "white." Racialized minorities have never been fully absorbed into "whiteness" and, therefore, the prospects of full assimilation are highly unlikely.

In some cases, this experience of racialization and marginalization may lead to pan-ethnic identities, as we suggest above. However, in other cases, it may in fact bolster immigrants' connections to their "home" culture. In the last two decades, many scholars of immigration have questioned and even rejected assimilation approaches and have instead developed a transnational perspective. Scholars of immigrant transnationalism argue that between first-generation immigrants' racialization and marginalization in the United States, on one hand, and new forms of transportation and information technology, on the other, immigrants today can develop more transnational identities (Basch, Glick Schiller, and Szanton Blanc 1994). Because air travel is relatively cheap, they can go home on a more regular basis. Moreover, because they can keep up with current events taking place in their countries of birth, either through television or the internet, they may be more inclined to take an interest in and participate in political processes in their countries of birth. Moreover, immigrants from Asia, as we discussed in earlier chapters, can engage in transnational business, as well as consumption practices (for example, they can readily buy food items or watch television programs from their homelands), which can further develop their transnational identities. Of course, people can experience both (or neither) pan-ethnic and transnational identities since identity is always in flux. Moreover, as with pan-ethnic identities, transnational identities are often born out of experiences of racialization and exclusion and are sustained through institutions and organizations. It is important to note, however, that, even as people form transnational identities, sometimes in response to racialized exclusion, this does not preclude their engagement and investment in US-based politics.

Interestingly, Purkayastha believes that even second-generation Asian Americans develop transnational identities. Though it was the second-generation that was vital in the construction of pan-ethnic Asian-American identity on college campuses in major urban centers, in her study of middle-class, college-educated second-generation South Asian Americans, Purkayastha finds that racializing processes have contributed, rather, to the development of transnational identities (Purkayastha 2005). Similar trends have also been documented among other second-generation Asian Americans (Rodriguez and Balce 2004).

Expanding "Asian America"

Despite some of the difficulties both of building and sustaining a pan-ethnic identity, scholars like Paul Spickard have pointed to new directions for forging pan-ethnic formations. Though, as we discussed above, Pacific Islanders may not share similar experiences of racialization with others who are categorized on a daily basis as Asian American, the fact remains, according to Spickard, that the US government has long included them in its census categorizations. Because the state imposes this categorization on Pacific Islanders and public goods are derived from how the government categorizes groups, it is important to consider Pacific Islanders as part of what it means to be "Asian American." Though Pacific Islanders themselves have hesitated to adopt the pan-ethnic identity of "Asian American," as Diaz points out, non-Pacific Islanders who espoused the pan-ethnic formation not just of "Asian American" but of "Asian Pacific Islander American" did so because "it was thought that lumping the two groups together would increase our political strength" (Lee et al., cited in Spickard 2007). Spickard argues that "Asian Americans and Pacific Islanders have had a great deal of intertwined history and it would be useful as we go forward to explore the intertwining, even as we recognize the Pacific islanders as not a subset of Asian America" (2007: 596).

Beyond Pacific Islanders, Spickard makes the case that Asian-American pan-ethnic identity should also include multiracial Asians and Asian adoptees, and even explore links with Arab and Middle-Eastern Americans. He concludes that, ultimately, a "more flexible vision of what is an Asian American" is called for (Spickard 2007: 603). Chapter 11 will explore in more detail the various ways that Asian Americans have indeed crossed ethnic, class, religious, and other lines of division to assert a pan-ethnic identity for social change on behalf of Asian Americans politically.

Interracial conflict

One's sense of group membership requires being cognizant of what includes someone "in" a group but, simultaneously, of who is defined as outside the group. The "in-group," in this case, is those who are considered members of one's ethnic group; the "out-group" those considered outside that group and, in some cases, those who may even threaten the "in-group." Social groups, particularly racialized groups, are often defined in contrast to (and indeed, in conflict with) one another. For example, whiteness gets defined in relation and often in opposition, to blackness. Groups cannot merely be defined by that which binds them together, but by that which they believe makes them different, sets them apart, and makes them distinct from other groups. Group differences are often a source of conflict. As the classic sociologist Lewis Coser defines it, social conflict is a "struggle over values, or claims to status, power and scarce resources, in which the aims of the conflict groups are not only to gain the desired values, but also to neutralize, injure or eliminate rivals" (Coser 1967: 232). Social conflicts are therefore a response to a sense of deprivation, but engagement in conflict requires group members to mobilize in order to assert or defend their interests (Oberschall 1978).

In the United States, where racial hierarchy is the dominant mode by which society is organized, conflicts between racialized groups have been an issue. Sociologists, however, do not only look at questions of prejudice and discrimination to explain conflict between racial groups, but also at the relationships between groups, what sociologist Herbert Blumer calls, "group position." Blumer explains that his approach "shifts scholarly treatment away from individual lines of experience and focuses interest on the collective process by which a racial group comes to define and redefine another racial group" (Blumer 1958: 3). Sociologists Lawrence Bobo and Vincent Hutchings build on Blumer's theory by examining how "group position" plays out in conflicts between different minority groups. They argue that what becomes important in the formation of group positions and therefore group conflict are feelings of racial alienation. They argue that "[m]embers of a racial group who feel alienated and oppressed are more likely to regard other racial groups as competitive threats to their own group's social position" (Bobo and Hutchings 1996: 956).

Interracial conflict has at times led to violent confrontations. For instance, in the 1960s, during the height of the civil rights movement, many cities across the country were consumed by major race riots – from Watts (in Los Angeles) in 1965 to Detroit in 1967 to Washington, DC in 1968. The conflict between Asian Americans (especially Korean Americans) and African Americans is a useful example for exploring intergroup (interracial) conflict as a social phenomenon.

Urban centers have long been a hub for immigrant newcomers since the country's beginnings. Alongside this international migration and settlement in the cities, post-Civil War, African Americans migrated from the South into the cities of the North and beyond as industrialization in the early twentieth century, then wartime production during World War II, produced labor demand. However, in the 1960s and 1970s, American cities experienced rapid deindustrialization as firms relocated their factories to Third World countries in search of cheaper labor. This led to the contraction of employment opportunities, especially for African Americans. By the 1980s, first with the Reagan administration and continuing through to the Clinton administration in the following decade, social supports were aggressively eliminated. Federal programs that might have eased the burdens of un- and underemployment for African Americans were no longer available in the same way, therefore rendering blacks in places like Detroit, New York, Chicago, and Los Angeles especially marginalized and vulnerable (Barlow 2003).

Meanwhile, like their European predecessors, Asian immigrants post-1965 have settled in America's cities. As we discussed in chapter 3, unlike earlier waves of immigrants, Asians who entered the United States in the immediate wake of the Immigration and Naturalization Act of 1952 tended to come to the United States with more resources and skills because they had been given higher priority by the Immigration Act. Those with economic means engaged in entrepreneurial activities in the city as so-called "middle men" (discussed in chapter 4), in part because business opportunities in the city were relatively easy. The increasing African-American population, as well as the race riots of the late 1960s, accelerated "white flight," the exodus of whites from cities to the suburbs. In Watts, among those whites that fled the city were Jewish business owners, which left it (and many other cities like it) empty of a number of enterprises (Oliver, Johnson, and Farreil 1993). This then created new opportunities for those with sufficient capital to do so to open up shop. Part of the reason that Asians explored entrepreneurial activities was that they sometimes found themselves unable to find employment in their fields because they lacked English-language skills or because employers were biased against the education and training they had received in their home countries (see chapter 4).

Tensions began in the 1970s and heightened in the 1990s between Korean immigrant shop owners and both African-American merchants and customers in many urban centers across the United States. Reports of the tensions began to emerge in the 1980s with African-American merchants fearing that they would be driven out of business by their Korean rivals whom they accused of price-cutting (Rieder 1990). Meanwhile, African-American customers accused Korean merchants of overpricing and of treating them rudely. In New York, the African-American community organized a series of boycotts of Korean businesses (Rieder 1990). In Los Angeles, tensions between Korean merchants and the African-American community flared in 1991, when a Korean merchant killed a 15-year-old African-American girl who allegedly stole orange juice from her store. Nearly a year later, these tensions became a major conflagration in 1992 in Los Angeles in the wake of the trial of police officers accused of beating Rodney King, an African-American man. The acquittal of the police officers triggered an uprising among African Americans in Los Angeles. Though the uprising was primarily in response to the "not guilty" verdict, Korean businesses nevertheless became a target, given the preexisting tensions between the two groups. Indeed, though there was much evidence to the contrary, the uprising was framed by the mainstream media as primarily a black–Korean, inter-minority conflict (Abelmann and Lie 1995).

Drawing from and building on group position theory in her study of the Korean–black conflict, sociologist Jennifer Lee states "conflict is not the result of out-group prejudicial attitudes or realistic group competition. Instead, intergroup conflict surfaces because groups challenge their position in relation to other groups, particularly in a racially and ethnically stratified society" (2006: 905). In other words, according to group position theory, different groupings within a hierarchical society have different ideas and aspirations about how they ought to be positioned and it is in vying for ascendancy that conflict emerges. What is at stake in interracial conflicts are the different *meanings* ascribed to groups in the social order.

Though group position theory tries not to emphasize prejudicial attitudes in explaining group conflict, an unanswered question in these studies is how people craft meanings about their groups in relation to other groups. Scholars like Nadia Kim (2008) attribute Koreans' negative perspectives of African Americans to their exposure to the US military (and indeed, to US media and popular culture more generally) in South Korea. Remember, the United States has had a strong presence in South Korea since the Korean War in the 1950s. According to Kim, Korean ideas about blacks had been formed even prior to coming to the United States. Building on preexisting anti-black perspectives that had been put in place in South Korea during its colonization by the Japanese (who had, in turn, inherited some of their own anti-black attitude from exposure to western ideologies of race), the Americans perpetuated notions of black inferiority. This suggests that racialization is not simply something that happens once immigrants arrive and become acculturated in the United States but that racialization or racial formation processes are transnational, linked in large part to the transnational scope of US economic, political, and military power in the Asian Pacific. Meanwhile, African Americans have been exposed to the "model minority" myth associated with Asian Americans as a group. Indeed, this stereotype is often constructed in contradistinction to African Americans who are represented as a problem. This construction exacerbated tensions between Koreans and blacks (Rieder 1990).

Predating the Korean–black conflict, sociologists documented conflicts between Asian Americans and other minority groups. One case involved conflict between Japanese and Latino (mainly Mexican) communities in the early 1970s. This conflict was quite different in the sense that it was limited in geographic scope as opposed to the Korean–black conflict, which occurred in different urban centers around the country. Moreover, this conflict did not become violent as that in Los Angeles in 1992. Nevertheless, sociologists examined the way that ethnicity played a role in what could be characterized as a class conflict, primarily between employers (Japanese Americans) and workers (Mexicans).

During the early 1970s, Mexican workers in the United Farm Workers (UFW) were engaged in a major struggle with their mainly Japanese-American employers for higher wages and improvements in their working conditions. As discussed in chapter 3, the Japanese had immigrated to the United States immediately following the exclusion of Chinese immigration through the Chinese Exclusion Act in the late nineteenth century. Though initially confined to low-wage labor, some Japanese Americans were able to transition into tenant farmers and then eventually into small landowners. Since the Japanese were able to bring wives into the United States (an exception to the Gentlemen's Agreement, the law excluding Japanese immigration), many could then rely on the family labor of their spouses and eventually of their children. Indeed, the *Issei* (the first generation of Japanese-American immigrants) would secure their family's ownership of the land (especially when that ownership was threatened by laws like the Alien Land Law) for their US-born, second-generation *Nisei* children. By the 1970s, Japanese-American farms were generally in the hands of the *Nisei* (Chan 1991).

Mexicans, meanwhile, were the latest group of racialized workers to be brought into the United States. Following the exclusion of Filipino immigration with the Tydings–McDuffie Act of 1934, the Bracero Progam was initiated at the height of labor shortages during World War II to facilitate the immigration of Mexican workers in agriculture. The UFW, led by labor leader Cesar Chavez, waged a union campaign on Japanese American-owned farms. In the conflict, ethnicity and pan-ethnicity were asserted by different factions of the Japanese-American community as some struggled against the unionization campaign and asserted their Japanese ethnic identities and histories in the process. Others, however, supported the union's efforts and asserted their pan-ethnic identity as Asian Americans in articulating their stance (Fugita and O'Brien 1977).

Members of the Nisei Farmers League (NFL), a group that represented the farm-owners' interests, made public appeals that emphasized their ethnic history in the United States as an oppressed racialized minority. Leaders likened the union campaign to the internment during World War II as if the demands made by the UFW were, similar to internment, an infringement of the rights of Japanese Americans. The president of the NFL commented, "Never again will we suffer the treatment which we went through" (Fugita and O'Brien 1977).

Interracial connections

A classic approach to the mitigation of intergroup conflict, particularly between racialized groups, is the contact hypothesis. That is, tensions between groups derive from a lack of contact between (and therefore the opportunity to build connections to, relationships with, and understanding of) different sets of people. For those who espouse the "contact hypothesis," it is ultimately through sustained contact over time between individuals of different groups that prejudice, and therefore interracial conflict, diminishes. In a study from the late 1960s, sociologist Stuart Cook constructed a social experiment on the "contact hypothesis" to test to what extent contact actually lessens group conflict, as well as to determine what sorts of contact can change people's perceptions of those they consider to be "Others." He found that, in addition to needing to build intimate and sustained relationships with one another (as opposed to brief and distant ones), members of different groups needed to create relationships of mutual dependence (in other words, to develop relationships of trust whereby there is an element of dependency on members of the other group), to be in a situation where they share a similar status, to be in a context that values and normalizes intergroup association, and to possess characteristics that challenge dominant stereotypes (Cook 1969).

Sociologist Ronald Weitzer contends that, at least for the Koreans he studies, contact does not necessarily result in more positive attitudes towards African Americans. Koreans possess negative attitudes born of their positions as "middlemen minorities" in relation to African Americans, which heightens their sense of distance from and feelings of hostility towards them despite the fact that both groups may live and work in close proximity. Indeed, it is because Korean Americans live and work in close proximity to African Americans in a specific way – as business owners – that these negative attitudes are perpetuated. Moreover, as Nadia Kim's work makes clear, Koreans may already have negative attitudes towards blacks that originate in Korea. Weitzer concludes that, by virtue of their daily interactions with African-American customers, "Korean merchants have a relationship with blacks that sets them apart from most other groups" (Weitzer 1997: 602). Weitzer's findings here may confirm Cook's that shared status becomes important to fostering positive relations between groups. Contact by itself, Weitzer suggests, is not sufficient in explaining intergroup dynamics. It is important to understand the specific circumstances and situations under which intergroup contact takes place. If contact between Koreans and blacks is confined to merchant–customer relations and nothing else, then that relation (and the economic disparity it is characterized by) only perpetuates conflict between them.

Even as Weitzer's findings show that Korean Americans and African Americans will not have ameliorated relations just through contact, they can still forge cordial relations in day-to-day interactions. Jennifer Lee suggests that inter-ethnic conflicts between Korean and blacks are overstated and biased. Lee finds that relations between them are in fact characterized by a great degree of civility that is neither depicted in the media nor in scholarly accounts, both of which are biased towards seeing and looking for conflict (Lee 2006).

Miliann Kang, furthermore, finds that Korean-owned nail salons in urban areas present a different picture of Korean–black relations. Though Kang recognizes that the conflict is real in some areas, she believes it is important to locate and explain variations in those relations and the ways that tension may be mediated (Kang 2010: 167). Service-oriented businesses necessitate different relationships between shop-owners and customers. For instance, nail-salon customers spend longer in a nail salon than do shoppers at a corner store and this can foster a more intimate connection.

Kang suggests that "gender identifications that challenge frameworks of racial conflict" (2010: 167) are possible in these kinds of businesses. Indeed, she argues that what is missing in the discussion of Korean–black conflict is an account of gender and the way that gender mediates conflicts between groups. For instance, because Korean nail salons are gendered businesses – that is, they are seen as catering mainly to women – they represent a different kind of institution to corner grocery or liquor stores where the owners (both men and women) may exhibit hypermasculine traits (policing, surveillance, etc.) that people in the community find antagonistic. Interestingly, she finds that blacks do not necessarily always see themselves as the "victim" in Korean–black relations. In her study of nail salons, she found that black customers would sometimes disparage Asian workers for doing labor that they considered beneath them.

Several scholars critique the way that the media and academics have represented the Korean–black conflict. Kyeyoung Park argues that the popular (and scholarly) focus on Korean–black tensions functions as a way of displacing a focus on white–black as well as white–Asian tensions. Park argues, "The African American-Korean American discourse is a triadic relation, not a dyad. It begins with their respective relationships to whites" (Park 1996: 494). For Park, Korean–black conflicts have been "drastically [more] intensified by state intervention than by the actions of blacks or Koreans" (Park 1996: 496). In their study, Nancy Abelmann and John Lie make a similar argument and suggest that representations of African Americans and Koreans were "antipodal," that is, they were constructed in direct opposition and contrast to one another: blacks were figured as the failed underclass, Koreans as the successful entrepreneurs (Abelmann and Lie 1995).

Even if Korean–black tensions have been overstated, there have nevertheless been concerted efforts by the two groups to come together in Los Angeles, such as the formation of the Black–Korean Alliance (BKA) (Diaz-Veizades and Chang 1996). Even the African-American press played a role in trying to shift the discourse around conflict to document cases of cooperation and collaboration between the two groups (Thornton 2011).

Returning to the example of the conflict between the UFW and NFL, in that case, too, different kinds of connections were forged between Japanese Americans and Mexican Americans. For instance, Japanese Americans who were part of the nascent Asian-American Movement and were cultivating a pan-ethnic Asian-American consciousness took a different position on the conflict to that of their counterparts in the NFL. They were vocal supporters of the UFW; many of them actually worked with the union. In the UFW's struggle with the NFL, these Japanese Americans emphasized their pan-ethnic Asian-American identity, not their ethnic identity as Japanese Americans. For them, pan-ethnic Asian-American identity did not simply connect them to other Asian ethnic groups but also to other racialized minorities who experienced histories of labor exploitation. During the Asian-American movement, many who identified as "Asian American" involved with the UFW felt a deep sense of working-class-allied consciousness against the NFL (Fugita and O'Brien 1977). Indeed, many of the members of the UFW were also Asian ethnics (mainly Filipinos) with whom, perhaps, the UFW-supporting Japanese Americans might have also felt connected (Scharlin and Villanueva 2000). The stance of the UFW in supporting Japanese Americans is an example of the complex ways that collective or group identity can work for racialized minorities. At times, group identity is primarily an ethnic identity; at other times, it is a pan-ethnic identity; at yet other times, it can be an identity that connects racialized minorities on a wider scale. What leads one identity to be more active than another are the incentives at stake, external categorizations, and the possible cultural and institutional links between actors.

Conclusion

In this chapter, we examined how "Asian American" has become a pan-ethnic identity, focusing in particular on the way that anti-Asian violence has played a role in its formation. Different Asian ethnic groups, however, experience racialization differently and as a consequence, they can feel less identified as Asian American pan-ethnics. Moreover, the fact is that Asian ethnic groups do have very different histories and are furthermore divided along class, caste, religious, and other lines which makes pan-ethnicity a tenuous project. Though much of this book has examined Asians' conflicts with whites, this chapter has examined interracial conflicts between Asians and other minority groups. It has focused on the Korean–black conflict, in part because it has been a major case study in intergroup conflict in recent years. However, it also called attention to studies of Asian-Hispanic/Latino tensions as well. At the same time, this chapter has illustrated the ways that conflict is mediated and managed. In the next chapter, we look at how Asian Americans proactively pursue collective goals in social movements and through electoral politics and highlight the ways in which cross-racial solidarities are also involved in the process.

Discussion questions

- Examine the debates surrounding the building of an Islamic center near the site of the World Trade Center in New York City. In what ways did different Asian ethnic groups position themselves? To what extent were new group solidarities formed (i.e. between Asian Americans and Arab Americans, perhaps)?
- As more and more Latinos work for Korean American and other Asian-American businesses, how are race relations between those groups faring? Is there similar cordiality and tension as found between Asian-American business owners and African Americans, or is it different?
- How would you assess the impact that participating in pan-ethnic organization or taking a class on Asian Americans has on individuals' degree of pan-ethnic identity?

11 Social Movements and Politics

Social movements and politics share a common objective: to create social change. Regarding social movements, whereas the previous chapter explained how Asian Americans have formed a pan-ethnic identity in part as a result of conflict with other groups, this chapter examines what happens when Asian Americans pursue causes collectively. Specifically, it looks at the ways that different Asian ethnicities come together proactively as "Asian Americans," that is, as pan-ethnics, to pursue collective goals.

Asian Americans have often been depicted as an apolitical group. Linked to the "model minority" stereotype is the idea that Asian Americans are more interested in their economic well-being and have no interest (or need) to engage in politics (Gotanda 2001). Though we have mentioned throughout this book the various ways in which Asian Americans have demanded and asserted their rights, both individually and collectively, this chapter offers an in-depth examination of Asian-American involvement in social movements and politics.

Why and how do people start or join social movements? This is not only a major sociological question but one of direct relevance to Asian American Studies, given its emergence as a field of study through movements for social change. This chapter also asks what major movements Asian Americans have been part of, and what their effect has been. In chapter 3, we discussed the Asian-American movement in detail. Here, we examine other social movements that Asian Americans have been part of, focusing especially on Asian-American involvement in the labor movement, given that their presence in the United States is due historically to the continued US pursuit for cheaper labor. It is perhaps in this section that the "model minority" stereotype of the apolitical Asian American is especially challenged. Whereas it might be thought that Asian Americans do not want to "rock the boat," they actually have a rich history of social movement involvement, including participation in strikes, street protests and the like (Friday 1994; Zia 2000). Through our discussion of Asian-American involvement in the labor movement, we also highlight key theories and concepts in the sociology of social movements. Given the largely immigrant character of contemporary Asian-American communities, it is important to examine political practices beyond traditional indicators (e.g. voting), to understand Asian-American politics (Okamoto and Ebert 2010).

Despite their immigrant character, many Asian Americans can and do participate in electoral politics. Like social movements, electoral politics serves as a means of social change. How involved are Asian Americans in politics as voters, candidates, and elected officials, and what are the main issues they care about? How do Asians and Asian Americans get figured or represented within politics? How effective will politics be as a means to address social inequalities, given the sometimes conflicted relationship of Asian Americans with the state (Lien, Conway, and Wong 2004; Nakanishi and Lai 2003)? These questions are among the key questions asked by political sociologists and political scientists in their studies of immigrant and racialized groups' political incorporation. We also note forms of political involvement that go beyond social movements and electoral politics. Specifically, we look at the emergence of pan-ethnic Asian-American nonprofit, community-based organizations.

Finally, to what extent do Asian Americans engage in transnational politics? Scholars have found that immigrant minorities, though they may be integrated into American political life (as naturalized citizens) and indeed may be very active in their political participation, may simultaneously be involved in social movements and politics in their erstwhile homelands (Portes Escobar, and Arana 2009). The extent to which Asian Americans engage in political transnationalism and what forms that transnational politics takes will also be discussed in this chapter.

Asian Americans in social movements

Structural inequalities and collective identity

The study of social movements is an important topic in sociology. Sociologists define a social movement as "collective efforts by socially and politically subordinated people to challenge the conditions and assumptions of their lives" (Liu, Geron, and Lai 2008: 2). In other words, the rise of different kinds of social movement can be attributed to structural conditions of inequality that people want to change (Walder 2009). At the same time, social movements emerge because the people who participate in them possess a sense of collective identity. Though inequalities in a society may exist, their mere existence is not enough to actually trigger social movement participation. It takes individuals who feel that their experiences are connected with others to actually convince them to mobilize. Sociologists Francesca Polletta and James Jasper offer a rich definition of collective identity as related to social movements:

> collective identity [. . .] is a perception of a shared status or relation, which may be imagined rather than experienced directly, and it is distinct from personal identities, although it may form part of a personal identity. A collective identity may have been first constructed by outsiders (for example, as in the case of "Hispanics" in this country), who may still enforce it, but it depends on some acceptance by those to whom it is applied. (2001: 285)

In chapters 7 and 10, we discussed how the pan-ethnic, collective identity of "Asian Americans" was formed. In chapter 10, we were especially focused on the ways that "Asian American" was constructed by "outsiders," that is, through state categorizations as well as through intergroup conflict. We highlighted in chapter 5 how young people, especially second-generation Asian-American college students, played a role in cultivating "Asian American Studies" as a collective identity. As Espiritu argues, "The Pan-Asian concept, originally imposed by non-Asians, became a symbol of pride and a rallying point for mass mobilization by later generations" (Espiritu 1992: 20). In this chapter, we are especially interested in how Asian Americans have formed social movements as "Asian Americans" to address the inequalities they face.

Political opportunity structures and resources

Structural and personal motivations are not enough for a social movement to form. Social movements emerge under specific sets of conditions including, for example, changing political opportunities or access to resources. In other words, a social movement emerges in part because there may be more political space for it to emerge, such as a more sympathetic government or changing popular attitudes. As mentioned in chapter 3, for example, the Asian-American Movement was founded in the wake of the civil rights movement and alongside the rise of the Black Power Movement. These latter movements opened up a space in public discourse to seriously debate and challenge racial inequalities (Liu, Geron, and Lai 2008). Such favorable political contexts for social movements are what sociologists call "political opportunity structures" (Meyer 2004).

Social movements, moreover, require funds or other institutional resources to organize people collectively, hence sociologists have also examined the resource mobilization of social movements (Jenkins 1983). In the case of the Asian-American Movement, institutions such as colleges and universities became an important resource for its development and growth. College and university students developed their collective identity as pan-ethnic Asian Americans through self-organized courses and study sessions that traced the shared histories of different Asian ethnic groups as racialized laborers (Spickard 2007; Espiritu 1992). College and university campuses would, moreover, meet basic organizational needs like meeting spaces or funding and printing resources for publications (Liu, Geron, and Lai 2008).

Social movements engage in social change activities that distinguish them from more conventional political activities, such as electoral politics where the pursuit of shared goals is achieved through voting or influencing the government. Social movements are often characterized by what are called "contentious politics," that is, they engage in strategies of social change that fall outside the norm of democratic politics (Tilly and Tarrow 2007). Rather than simply registering their concerns through the electoral or legislative process, social movement activists engage in boycotts, strikes, demonstrations, and other forms of direct action to articulate their platforms. Moreover, social movements do not just target governments but can be aimed at employers (in the case of labor movements) or gender relations (as in the case of the women's movement).

There are numerous kinds of social movements (e.g. the environmental justice movement, the immigrant rights movement, etc.). In this section, we will discuss Asian Americans' involvement in the labor movement historically and draw on sociological theories of social movements to analyze that involvement. We will, furthermore, highlight the moments when Asian Americans have asserted themselves as a pan-ethnic group within the broader labor movement. We will also mention some of the other social movements that Asian Americans have participated in, highlighting in particular how they have joined those movements as a pan-ethnic group.

Asian Americans in the labor movement: a case study

Asians often were brought to America to work as low-wage workers. Though employers hoped that they would be a docile and compliant population of laborers, they often were not. Asian Americans have engaged in contentious politics, stood up to their bosses and fought for better wages and working conditions since their arrival on the shores of the United States. Initially, Asian-American involvement in workplace actions was on an ethnic-specific basis. This had to do, in part, with ethnic cleavages among them. However, different groups of Asian workers would occasionally bridge ethnic divides and rally around their shared interests. More recently, Asian Americans have asserted themselves pan-ethnically within the US labor movement to ensure that Asian Americans' specific issues as workers are addressed. Moreover, new Asian-American worker groups have emerged that are explicitly pan-ethnic in orientation.

Early labor struggles: ethnic-specific organizing

Even before they were allowed to join the ranks of trade unions (which, it must be remembered, were among the groups who were behind anti-Asian immigration legislation during the late nineteenth century), different groups of Asian immigrant workers engaged in collective actions against their employers. Historian Sucheng Chan documents the first major strike by Chinese workers taking place on the transcontinental railroad in June 1867, which was participated in by 2,000 men (Chan 1991). Japanese immigrant workers also engaged in labor protests. Their first major strike was organized in Waialua, Hawaii in 1904 (Chan 1991). In 1933, Filipino lettuce-pickers in California staged a one-day walkout. Indeed, not only was the action intended to address wage issues but to earn the recognition of their union by their employer. The mainstream American Federation of Labor refused to organize a union on Filipinos' behalf so they organized outside of the traditional trade union structure (Chan 1991). Throughout the 1930s, Filipinos engaged in a series of labor actions, despite the fact that these often ended in failure. They persisted in organizing, moreover, in the face of both state repression and anti-Filipino vigilantism. By the 1940s, the Filipino Agricultural Laborers Association was successful in several strikes and won wage increases and better working conditions for its members (Melendy 1977).

The beginnings of cross-ethnic organizing

Among the first labor struggles to bring different Asian immigrant groups together was the strike of 1920 that involved Japanese and Filipino plantation workers in Hawaii (Chan 1991; Melendy 1977). A decade later, Japanese, Filipino, and workers of other ethnic and racial backgrounds came together to successfully form a chapter of the International Longshoremen's and Warehouse Union (ILWU) in 1930 (Jung 2003). Meanwhile, on the mainland similar attempts at cross-ethnic labor organizing was also taking place. In California, the Cannery Workers Union Local 18893 attempted to organize not only different Asian ethnic groups but other ethnic and racial groups as well. White radicals took the lead in organizing the union, despite the fact that there was continued resistance to the idea among most white trade unionists. Though the effort to establish a union ultimately failed, it set an important precedent in cross-ethnic (and racial) labor organizing (Friday 1994). From these initial efforts, the Alaska Cannery Workers Union was formed. Notably, this union not only included different Asian ethnic groups and thereby crossed ethnic lines; it also crossed generational lines as US-born Asians joined it. In Washington, the Cannery Workers and Farm Laborers Union would, like the Alaska Cannery Workers Union, be comprised of both Asian immigrants and Asian-American workers of different ethnicities (Friday 1994).

Applying social movement theory to Asian-American labor organizing

Social movement theory can be used to understand how workers were able to come together despite many significant challenges. As just mentioned, many in the labor movement continued to view the inclusion of nonwhite workers with disdain. Moreover, the different workers were racialized in very distinctive ways, and those racialized distinctions undermined the efforts of unionization. Though the labor movement more broadly continued to be characterized by racism, the workers in the Hawaiian ILWU articulated a vision of labor politics that attempted to unite workers across ethnic and racial lines. Meanwhile, political opportunity structures and resources were also vital to the establishment of the ILWU. Whereas plantation owners had been able to depend on the territorial government not interfering during periods of labor strife, in the mid-1930s that began to change with the passage of the Wagner Act on the US mainland. The federal government became much more involved in enforcing labor law in Hawaii as a result of the act, thereby opening up new political opportunities for workers to organize. Moreover, access to highly successful unions on the mainland provided the ILWU in Hawaii with an important source of organizing expertise (Jung 2003).

Asian Americans in the trade union movement

Asian Americans continue to be involved in labor organizing because, as should be clear to readers by now, the notion of all Asian Americans as "model minorities" who are well-paid professionals or business owners is false. There continues to be a large proportion of Asian Americans who work in low-wage, dead-end jobs and, necessarily, there have been people engaged in trying to fight for Asian-American workers' rights, both in the US trade union movement and in more autonomous worker-based organizations.

Asian Americans not only challenged their employers but also their own unions to give them more and better representation. In the late 1970s, they played an important role in transforming the leadership of San Francisco's biggest union, Local 2. Asian-American women were at the forefront of these struggles, alongside their ongoing battles with their employers for higher wages and better working conditions (Liu, Geron, and Lai 2008). In the Midwest during the 1980s, Asian-American labor activists challenged their fellow union members' and union leadership's anti-Asian sentiments which were fueled by the "buy American" campaigns. As we saw in chapters 2 and 10, such sentiments could be fatal, such as when they led to the brutal killing of Vincent Chin (Liu, Geron, and Lai 2008).

An important development in the labor movement was the formation of pan-ethnic labor organizations aimed at bringing Asian-American workers together to collectively address their concerns. The Alliance of Asian Pacific Labor (AAPL), for example, was formed in 1987 to "unite immigrants and American-born women and men" from various Asian backgrounds to provide support for Asian-American trade unionists and to encourage trade unions to recruit and promote more Asian-American unionists in order to grow the unions' ranks (Wong 1994: 345). By 1992, the AAPL would play a crucial role in the formation of the national Asian Pacific American Labor Alliance (APALA) as part of the AFL-CIO (Kent Wong 1994, 2000; Liu, Geron, and Lai 2008). The organization sees itself as a bridge between Asian-American union members and the mainstream labor movement, as well as between the labor movement and the Asian-American community. As of 2013, APALA had thirteen chapters and others in formation, as well as their national headquarters in Washington, DC.

Independent labor organizations

Alongside the development of Asian-American groups working within and in collaboration with the trade union movement, however, more independent and autonomous community-based workers' organizations have also emerged. Despite the kind of work that organizations like APALA have done to advocate for Asian-American workers' issues within the trade union movement, and the strides that trade unions have made in organizing immigrant workers by hiring organizers that can speak workers' languages, for example, or by fighting to promote workers of color to leadership positions, many Asian immigrant workers continue to be and feel excluded (Sullivan and Lee 2008). Indeed, the trade union movement has not only been white and favored US citizens, it has also been very male as it has prioritized unionization efforts in industrial jobs that are more likely to be occupied by men.

Organizations like the Asian Immigrant Women Advocates (AIWA), which was founded in 1983, is one example of an independent worker organization that is autonomous of the traditional trade union movement (Wong 2000). Moreover, it is an example of a pan-ethnic organization focused on women workers. In the 1990s, AIWA was especially intent on organizing Asian immigrant workers in the garment industry (Omatsu 1994).

Though many garment manufacturers have moved abroad for cheaper labor (including to different countries in Asia), many continue to operate in the United States. Workers that are employed by garment manufacturers labor in sweatshop environments. In an effort to save on their costs, garment manufacturers do little to ensure that their employees work in clean and safe conditions. Moreover, they drive workers very hard by imposing difficult production quotas that workers are expected to meet, even if they have to work overtime without extra pay (Sullivan and Lee 2008).

AIWA found that many garment factories in California hired Asian immigrant workers, including many undocumented workers. Employers exploited their workers' lack of legal status to squeeze as much labor from them as possible. AIWA also found that the structural organization of garment production and retail was so complex that, even though the clothing produced by workers would be sold to high-end retailers, those retailers could never be held responsible for workplace injustices. Retailers like Jessica McKlintock, which specializes in gowns and ballroom dresses, subcontracted the manufacture of clothing to smaller proprietors who then did the actual hiring of labor. Though McKlintock earned the bulk of the profits from the arrangement, it could avoid taking full responsibility for the egregious treatment of workers. AIWA, nevertheless, launched a successful struggle that was aimed at publicly shaming McKlintock for profiting at the expense of Asian immigrant women workers. AIWA engaged in street demonstrations and highly effective media campaigns and managed to secure a settlement from the company for workers' back-pay (Anner 1996; Omatsu 1994).

Organizing against co-ethnic employers

Labor issues in the Asian-American community, however, have been complicated by the class divisions between Asian workers and their Asian employers, as also mentioned in chapter 4. Nevertheless, Asian immigrant workers have organized themselves against their Asian employers when those employers have exploited them. In 1995 in El Monte (Southern California), groups like APALA and the Asian Pacific American Legal Center (APALC) mobilized support for the prosecution of the Thai employers of Thai immigrant workers. Indeed, the El Monte case was an especially egregious case of exploitation as workers labored in slave-like conditions (Musikawong and Martorell 2012). Workers hear of jobs through ethnic networks and may prefer to work for a co-ethnic. However, such workers can be abused and face challenges in obtaining justice. Here, pan-ethnic organizations took a lead in organizing (primarily) Thai workers against their Thai employers. Hence, the identity being forged by APALA and APALC is one that is pan-ethnic yet also class-based. Recall the similar situation of the United Farm Workers and Nissei Farmers League conflict discussed in chapter 10. There, too, an Asian-American pan-ethnic identity was a point of mobilization, yet one that was simultaneously rooted in class-based politics.

Beyond labor movements

In chapters 3 and 5, we discussed the Asian-American Movement, which emerged in the late 1960s and early 1970s, and linked to it the movement for Asian American Studies. In this section, we briefly discuss the involvement of Asian Americans in other kinds of social movement activity beyond labor and the university, ranging from housing to US wars of aggression overseas. In particular, we highlight how Asian Americans have mobilized pan-ethnically.

As part of the Asian-American Movement in the late 1960s, labor activists and student activists came together very explicitly in the struggle to save the International Hotel in San Francisco. Racial segregation had confined Asian immigrants to specific areas in urban centers (hence the emergence of "Chinatowns," "Manilatowns," etc.). The International Hotel was one of many residential hotels (or what today might be called single-residency occupancy, or SRO, hotels) where Asian immigrants were allowed to live in San Francisco. By the 1960s, the International Hotel was home to many elderly Filipino *manongs* (a term of respect for older men) who had formerly worked as low-wage workers in agriculture and service-oriented jobs. Mostly single (because immigration restrictions and antimiscegenation laws prevented them from being able to form families), these *manongs* enjoyed the sense of community that the so-called "I-Hotel" and its immediate environs offered.

By the late 1960s, however, the area in which the I-Hotel was located was targeted for major redevelopment. In close proximity to San Francisco's growing central business district, the I-Hotel's location was seen as prime real estate and the city government, in collusion with developers, took steps to close it down. What ensued was a long battle between the city and a wide range of activists, led by Filipino Americans and involving a broad spectrum of Asian-American activists. Indeed, the struggle to save the I-Hotel was one which was central to the overall Asian-American Movement (Habal 2007).

If US imperialism was among the issues that galvanized Asian Americans at the height of the Asian-American Movement, more recently it became yet another issue around which Asian Americans mobilized. Asian Americans not only mobilized pan-ethnically but joined forces with Arab Americans to critique both the "war on terror" that followed the 9/11 attacks on the World Trade Center and its accompanying domestic campaign of "homeland security." Activists worried that Asian Americans and Arab Americans would be targeted as suspicious populations (Rodriguez and Balce 2004). Indeed, if a pan-ethnic identity was being mobilized around the antiwar protests, new connections were also being forged across racial lines between Asian Americans and Arab Americans. In this way, they heeded the call that Spickard makes (discussed in chapter 10) that the pan-ethnic Asian-American coalition should extend itself to include, or at least work alongside, Arab Americans (Spickard 2007).

Asian Americans have also mobilized against gender violence and in support of queer issues. They were involved in the women's rights and queer rights movements that emerged in the 1960s and 1970s and have founded pan-ethnic organizations that specifically address the interconnected issues of race, gender and sexuality for Asian Americans (Hom 2000a). As mentioned above, Asian-American women, like the women of the Asian Immigrant Women Advocates, have organized on a pan-ethnic basis around shared experiences related to workplace exploitation, even as they relate to their shared experiences as women. Additionally, Asian-American women in specific Asian ethnic communities have taken a lead in addressing questions of gender violence and homophobia in their own communities. However, as Das Gupta's research of South Asian communities finds, South Asian women and queer activists organize themselves on an ethnic-specific basis because they are often excluded by mainstream (white) feminist and LGBT movements, which define issues like "domestic violence" or "coming out" in ways that do not align with their experiences (Das Gupta 2006).

Asian Americans have been a major force in the immigrant-rights movement. This movement has been growing in scope and visibility in the last decade in response to ever-increasing immigration enforcement, as well as segregation. This "boundary-marking" strengthens the divides between "immigrants" and "natives". Such processes, along with political opportunity structures and resources, created the conditions for this movement's growth which culminated in massive public demonstrations that took place in several major cities around the country, including New York, Chicago, and Los Angeles on May 1, 2006 (Okamoto and Ebert 2010). Though Latino immigrants garnered the most attention, Asian Americans stood alongside immigrants and immigrant-rights advocates from a range of ethnic/racial backgrounds.

Moreover, Asian Americans have led and participated in movements that have often dismissed or do not centrally address questions of racial inequality, such as the environmental movement. Challenging the movement's focus on natural preservation, Asian Americans, along with other communities of color, engage in "environmental justice" which not only addresses concerns about the natural environment but indeed the unequal impact of environmental degradation on racial minorities. "Environmental justice" as an idea emerged in the United States with activists who called attention to the ways that communities of color disproportionately suffer from exposure to toxic pollution and enjoy far less protection from state authorities. Indeed, polluters undergo much more stringent regulations and penalties in white communities than they do in minority communities (Bullard 1994). Scholarly attention to Asian Americans' participation in the environmental justice movement has increased in the last decade. The issues activists have addressed include exposure to toxins in assembly-line production, such as the computer production industry in Silicon Valley, to fighting for better protections for Asian immigrant groups that are engaged in subsistence fishing (Sze 2004).

Electoral politics

Asian Americans were at one point in history defined as "aliens ineligible for citizenship" and were therefore limited in their ability to participate in electoral politics. This is not to say that they did not try. For example, in 1958, Dalip Saund, who was originally from India, was elected to Congress in California and was in fact a leading force in helping to write the law that would allow immigrants from India to become naturalized US citizens (MacKaye 1958).

Today, Asian Americans, as one of the fastest-growing immigrant populations in the United States, have the potential to become a formidable political force. This section examines how much Asian Americans are participating in the electoral process. Voting is a key measure of political participation and is often used to determine to what extent immigrants are assimilating. We will also examine whether Asian Americans vote as a pan-ethnic grouping or whether they are divided across ethnic and other lines.

It is important to note, however, that Asian-American politics should not be seen in a linear, evolutionary way. That is, we should not mistakenly think that Asian-American politics develops from social movement activism to electoral politics, as if social movement activism becomes irrelevant once the possibilities of more electoral political engagement open up, in part through social movement activism. These two forms of political engagement exist side by side.

Asian Americans in office and voting behavior

As mentioned, Dalip Saund was the very first Asian American to be elected to the US Congress. When Saund came to the United States, he was not even eligible to become a citizen (and therefore run for office) until he paved the way for the naturalization of immigrants from India. George Ariyoshi was the first elected Asian-American governor. He was elected governor in the state of Hawaii and served from 1974 to 1986. In more recent history, the 1990s was an especially important decade because it saw the election of Gary Locke as governor of the state of Washington in 1994. He is the first Asian American to be elected governor outside of the state of Hawaii (Nakanishi and Lai 2003). That same year, the Congressional Asian Pacific American Caucus (CAPAC), which includes Asian-American members of Congress, was formed. By the end of the 1990s, Asian Americans' political presence had become so notable that President Bill Clinton established the White House Initiative on Asian Americans and Pacific Islanders to ensure that the government agencies at the federal level were addressing the communities' distinct needs (Nash 2010).

In terms of Asian Americans' ability to run for and win elected office, several trends have been identified. It should be noted that there is a distinction between politics in Hawaii and that on the US mainland because the demographics in each place are radically different and make for very different political dynamics. Hawaii is what might be termed a "majority minority" state, that is, it is a state where minority groups actually outnumber whites. In Hawaii, Asian Americans have successfully contested political office at all levels of government.

Unlike other minority-elected officials, Asian-American elected officials on the US mainland often come from mainstream (i.e. mainly white) or multiracial districts. Black and Latino candidates, in contrast, have generally won in districts where their populations are highest. Asian-American candidates have to rely on non-Asian votes since the majority of Asian Americans are foreign-born and may not yet be eligible to vote (Wei 1993).

Districts with sizeable Asian-American populations do not necessarily have Asian-American political representation, partly because there may not be sufficient numbers of voters to support an Asian-American candidate. Though there are places where Asian Americans might be geographically concentrated, they are more residentially dispersed in the population compared to other minority groups and may not be concentrated enough to be able to elect an Asian-American candidate, even if they are registered to vote. Nevertheless, when there is an Asian-American candidate and where there are eligible Asian-American voters, these potential voters are more motivated to register and ultimately vote for the Asian-American candidate. What this suggests, then, is that Asian-American success in the electoral field depends not only on pan-ethnic mobilization but also on coalitions with other groups.

Naturalization

Being able to vote (whether for an Asian-American candidate or not) requires US citizenship. Given its predominantly immigrant character, the issue of naturalization is important to Asian-American electoral politics. The length of their residency in the United States determines the rates of naturalization and voter registration for Asian Americans. In other words, the longer one has lived in the United States, the more likely that one will become naturalized and register to vote. Among immigrants, better educated, older, more long-term residents are most likely to go out to actually vote, but voter registration rates for Asian Americans are generally low (Nakanishi and Lai 2003). Among the issues that impact voter turnout are voter registration requirements (i.e. submitting a voter registration application, residency requirements, etc.) (Xu 2005). Groups concerned with increasing Asian-American participation in elections have therefore focused on naturalization campaigns on one hand and, on the other, guaranteed that naturalized Asian Americans are able to fully participate in elections, for instance by assisting Asian Americans with registering to vote and ensuring the availability of bilingual voting material and ballots.

Impact of Asian-American voter turnout

Studies of Asian-American voter turnout in local elections (or their lack thereof) find that low voter turnout negatively impacts Asian Americans' ability to get representation in local governing bodies in the places where they constitute a large share of the population (Hajnal and Trounstine 2005). However, there is evidence that if Asian Americans are directly contacted via telephone or postcard prior to an election, it increases the chances that they will go out to vote (Wong 2005). Moreover, in areas of ethnic/racial population concentration, Asian-American voters perceive the benefits of voting for the broader Asian-American community and accordingly turn out to vote (Jang 2009). Other factors, including Asian Americans' degree of incorporation in traditional political organizations, may also impact their voting practices. One study of Asian-American voters in Chicago, for example, finds that Asian Americans' voter registration rates are high but, paradoxically, voter turnout is low (Pelissero, Krebs, and Jenkins 2000). Pelissero, Krebs, and Jenkins attribute this to local political organization, in the case of Chicago to the persistence of machine-style organizations, that is, party organizations that are controlled by local political "bosses" who have an inordinate amount of power to drive local politics by controlling, for example, what sorts of candidates can be endorsed or how campaigns should be run. They suggest that "Opportunities for greater political incorporation of Asian populations in Chicago may have their best opportunities to take root in the more fertile political ground of independent political organizations and wards in the city" (2000: 766). Hence, in places where political "machines" dominate the political scene, it may make more sense for Asian Americans to form more autonomous organizations where they can exercise more control.

Residential segregation and elections

Yet another issue that impacts the extent to which Asian Americans as a voting bloc can influence the election of Asian-American candidates, as mentioned above, is the fact that they are not as residentially concentrated as their Latino and African-American counterparts. Asian Americans' geographic dispersal means that they are less likely to be able to assert themselves as a bloc in local elections, which are highly dependent on population concentrations in specific places (Cho and Gimpel 2008). One way in which Asian Americans have tried to assert their interests as a voting bloc has been by working in coalition with other minority groups, as mentioned briefly above. Moreover, to guarantee a population concentration in different areas, Asian Americans have collaborated with other minorities on redistricting. This was true in New York City, for instance. Using the 2000 Census data, Asian Americans worked with their allies in an attempt to redistrict electoral districts in their favor (Hum 2002). There have been examples of successful Asian-American mobilization in support of Asian-American candidates in districts without an Asian-American majority. A notable one was the campaign that led to the election of Judy Chu, the first Chinese-American woman to be elected to the US House of Representatives in the San Gabriel Valley of Los Angeles County. Her campaign specifically targeted Asian-American voters, which led to a proportionately higher turnout among them (Lee and Tseng 2010). Organizations, such as the 80–20 Initiative, also work to consolidate the Asian-American vote and other types of electoral participation in targeted directions.

Campaign financing

Beyond being engaged in elections through voting, also important to electoral politics is campaign financing. When they cannot vote for an Asian-American candidate, Asian Americans will contribute financially instead to their campaigns (Lai et al. 2001). Generally, Asian Americans' campaign contributions have been used to support Asian-American candidates who share their particular ethnic backgrounds; these contributions have mainly gone to Democratic candidates (Tam-cho et al. 2003). Indeed, Asian Americans may actually make financial contributions more often than they vote, that is, they may be more inclined to participate politically by donating funds to a campaign, even when they are eligible to vote (Wei 1993). Asian-American political candidates, tend to rely heavily on co-ethnics and/or other Asian Americans. Indeed, "the utilization of ethnic networks to raise money enhances the ability of Asian candidates to mount serious campaigns for public office. Without donations from Asian contributors, it would be much more difficult for Asians to win and hold elective office" (Adams and Ren 2006: 611–12).

Asian-American involvement in campaign financing, however, has been subject to much scrutiny and debate, especially in the late 1990s when Asian-American campaign fundraisers for the Democratic Party were found guilty of having illegally solicited and secured election funds from foreign sources. Though the campaign finance violations were largely technical in nature (i.e. the donations were coming from people who were not US citizens) and were not used to assert undue influence or to bribe recipients, both the media and the Democratic Party's response to the scandal elicited stereotyping of Asian Americans as "forever foreign" and the "yellow peril" and therefore not entitled nor trustworthy to shape the American political process (Gotanda 2001). Moreover, these suspicions represented Asian Americans as having no genuine investment or commitment to politics and as merely interested in influencing politics with their capital. The Democratic Party, for instance, actually went through its list of donors to identify "Chinese-sounding" names to determine their citizenship. This response displays a racializing logic that assumes people with "Chinese-sounding" names are necessarily not American. Nevertheless, as the research discussed above makes clear, Asian Americans participate in politics in a wide range of ways and they responded to the scandal in pan-ethnic ways, that is, they did not see it as something specific to Chinese Americans. The group Asian Americans for Campaign Finance Reform, founded by UC Berkeley Asian American Studies professor Ling-Chi Wang, is an example of this pan-ethnic response (Van Slambrouck 1998).

Political ideologies

The Asian-American community has been, as a whole, Democratic. In 2012, Asian Americans supported the re-election of Barack Obama.[1] There are, however, differences between the various Asian ethnic groups. For example, the Vietnamese who fled communist regimes see the Republican Party as being more anticommunist than the Democratic Party. Political partisanship for this group is also determined by socioeconomic status, political attitudes, and immigration experiences (Phan and Garcia 2009). One study found that ethnic Chinese from Vietnam tended to vote Democratic and that this was primarily due to social and economic discrimination experienced prior to coming to the United States (Lim, Barry-Goodman, and Branham 2006). Indian Americans, on the other hand, were strong Democratic voters for President Obama in both 2008 and 2012, becoming his most reliable group of supporters behind African Americans.[2] Among other Asian immigrants (as compared with their largely Democratic native-born counterparts), party affiliation is much more divided (Cho and Cain 2001).

However, party affiliation is not necessarily a predictor of how Asian Americans will position on different issues. For example, in a study of Asian-American voting behavior on Propositions 187 and 209 in California, laws that were generally believed to be anti-immigrant and anti-affirmative action respectively, party affiliation was not a reliable proxy for determining Asian-American support or opposition. That is, Asian-American Republicans were no more likely to support these propositions than Asian-American Democrats (Cho and Cain 2001). Indeed, Asian-American Republicans exhibit viewpoints that are seemingly contradictory. Though the Republican Party is opposed to affirmative action and often eschews racial identifications among people, in large part because it does not believe racialized inequalities continue to persist, Asian-American Republicans actually take great pride in their Asian-American backgrounds. They speak out against racism, but, like their fellow Republicans, they ultimately oppose affirmative action (Omatsu 1994).

The major political parties, for their part, have been uneven in their outreach to Asian-American voters. The Democratic Party has had a longer history in attempting to bring Asian Americans into its fold. Among the first Democratic presidential candidates to really reach out to Asian Americans was Jimmy Carter during his 1976 presidential campaign. He created the Asian Pacific American Unit for the purpose of connecting to the Asian-American community (Wei 1993). In 1983, the Democratic Party created the Asian Pacific Caucus. The Caucus provided the Party with a platform for Asian-American concerns in the run-up to the 1984 presidential election. Though the Party later disbanded it, other pan-ethnic Asian-American Democratic formations would take its place (Wei 1993). The Republican Party, on the other hand, has more recently begun to reach out to Asian Americans. In a 1991 article for the conservative *National Review*, a prominent Republican made an appeal to the party to take Asian Americans seriously as a potential boon to their base: "Precisely because Asian Americans are making it in their adoptive land, they hold the potential not only to add to Republican rolls but to define a bona-fide language of civil rights" (McGurn 1991: 19).

Given these ideological differences, being able to run "Asian-American" candidates who represent the interests of the Asian-American community becomes difficult because the "Asian-American community" as a unified community is a difficult one to sustain in the face of changing demographics (Nakanishi and Lai 2003). Lien finds, even within ethnic Asian groups like the Chinese, for instance,

> [t]he sharp differences in immigration history, population share, place of settlement, admission classification and occupation status among the three groups of Chinese immigrants who became permanent residents in 2003 give a snapshot of the current sociodemographic divide within Chinese America. This raises the question of whether it makes sense to lump these persons of diverse origins and disparate social standings together under one umbrella (pan-)ethnic label. (Lien 2008: 1383)

Moreover, Asian Americans engage in political practices both domestically and transnationally, as we discuss in more detail below. In fact, Lien finds that Asian Americans' transnational politics can impact Chinese Americans' identities and therefore their politics domestically.

What the research on Asian Americans' political ideologies suggests is that Asian-American pan-ethnic identities can sometimes trump political orientations but at other times ideologies can be more salient. Large ethnic differences exist, too. Moreover, even within specific Asian-American ethnic groups, class differences can impact whether they can sustain ethnically based political outlooks.

Asian-American institutions

Beyond either voting or running (and winning) as political candidates, Asian Americans are also politically engaged in mainstream politics through their connections with nonprofit, Asian-American-serving community-based organizations. Indeed, one study finds that Asian Americans are more likely to vote in places where ethnic organizations are present (Diaz 2012). Nonprofit organizations that are officially registered with the federal government are actually prohibited from engaging in partisan political activities because of their tax-exempt status. Many Asian-American nonprofits are especially concerned with serving relatively recent immigrants from Asia. Despite regulations that limit nonprofits' political participation, sociologist Angie Chung finds that these organizations nevertheless foster ethnic political cultures that range from more subtle forms of politics to more direct-action and militant struggles (Chung 2005). Indeed, what her work indicates is that the lines that often separate our understanding of social movement engagement versus participation in electoral politics are actually quite blurry. Moreover, sociologist Dina Okamoto's national longitudinal study found that many pan-ethnic Asian-American organizations have been formed across the United States in the post-civil rights era into the early twenty first century (Okamoto 2006). Recalling our discussion of pan-ethnic collective identity formation in chapters 9 and 10, these institutions are important sites for the reproduction of pan-ethnic Asian-American identities and therefore in shaping pan-ethnic Asian American politics.

View from "the other side": whites and policies related to race

Sociologists have also taken an interest in public opinion about different political issues, particularly public opinion as it relates to racial policy, that is, policy that attempts to redress racial inequality. There has been interest in tracking whites' attitudes towards policies that benefit racialized minorities by guaranteeing their equal treatment or offering them enhanced opportunities in different arenas, given histories of exclusion and discrimination, for example. Studies have tended to focus on why there is a big discrepancy between those whites who express support for abstract principles of inequality but less support for actual policies that would benefit minority populations. Some scholars find that this discrepancy is linked to whites' sense that the racism of the past (i.e. slavery, segregation, etc.) is intolerable but that racism in the contemporary moment no longer exists in the same way. Therefore, while they support racial equality, they cannot support policies beneficial to minorities. Other scholars, meanwhile, attribute this discrepancy more to nonracial factors (i.e. respondent political party affiliations or ideology) than to racial factors (Krysan 2000).

Transnational politics

Asian-American politics have always been shaped by the broader international context, as developments in their respective "homelands" impacted how immigrants were treated and shaped their collective identities. US relations with countries like China, Japan, Korea, the Philippines, or Vietnam have all had an impact on the racialization of each country's descendants in the United States. Meanwhile, Asian Americans have often drawn inspiration (like during the Vietnam War) from the struggles being waged in Asia.

Homeland politics

Asian Americans, however, have also been actively engaged in the politics of their homelands (or the countries to which they can trace their ancestry). Even though Asian Americans are citizens or eligible for citizenship in the present moment and may be involved in US political efforts, many participate in "homeland" politics. This participation comes in the form of being involved in social movements to oppose undemocratic regimes (as in the case of the anti-Ferdinand Marcos movement among US Filipinos) to offering financial support to political candidates and the like. Just as importantly, migrants' "home" states are playing an increasingly significant role in helping to constitute transnational political communities by officially recognizing their overseas populations and, in some cases, even offering them the chance to vote in homeland elections (Fitzgerald 2009; Goldring 2002; Rodriguez 2010; Smith 2006).

The history of homeland politics

Scholars have found that Asian Americans' homeland political engagement has a long history. Historian Richard Kim documents how Korean immigrants in the United States were actively involved in the anticolonial movement against the Japanese in the 1910s. Part of a diasporic movement that formed the Korean provisional government of the Republic of Korea as an assertion of nationalist self-rule against the Japanese authorities, Kim finds that, "though their population was far smaller than the larger number of Koreans living in Manchuria and Siberia, Koreans in the United States came to hold disproportionate political influence and power within the diaspora" (Richard S. Kim 2006: 51). If Asian Americans have a long history of transnationalism, historical events like the enslavement of "comfort women" by the Japanese imperial army have become a rallying point for more contemporary transnational political engagement, particularly a transnational feminist politics (Thoma 2000).

Indeed, those involved in advocating the "comfort women" inherit a tradition of feminist transnationalism concerned with questions of war and militarism. Asian American involvement in supporting the Vietnamese people against the United States was not confined to protests in American cities. It also involved building individual people-to-people relations and Asian American women were at the forefront of building those relations. In Wu's study, she found that Asian-American activists worked "to name US imperialism and oppose its destructive reach. They also sought an identification and connection with Asia but specifically with revolutionary Asia. In order to critique the perceived corruption of western society, they highlighted the differences between 'radical' Asia and mainstream America. However, instead of denigrating the East, they sought inspiration *from* Asian countries and peoples" (Wu 2007: 579).

Conclusion

Asian Americans as an oppressed and exploited racialized minority have always engaged in different forms of resistance to their conditions of work and life. However, it was only with the forging of a pan-ethnic identity that the beginnings of more collective forms of resistance emerged. It was under conditions of a strengthened collective identity, political opportunity structures and access to resources that the Asian-American movement would come to be between the late 1960s and 1970s. Just as importantly, the Asian-American movement had a role in galvanizing Asian Americans' ability to actually engage in electoral politics. While Asian Americans had been part of the mainstream political process even before the movement, the movement played its role in opening up more space for Asian Americans to be able to run for office or to represent their interests through the electoral process.

Even as Asian Americans assert themselves in American political life, they also engage in the political processes of their erstwhile homelands. Given the nature of globalization, immigrants live transnational lives, either traveling back and forth between the United States and Asia for business or sustaining family members left behind. They therefore may have real investment in the politics of their "homelands." Transnationalism, however, is not necessarily at odds with being politically integrated into American society.

What is the tenability of "Asian American" as a pan-ethnic group? It is not altogether clear. The very emergence of pan-ethnic Asian America was due to demographic shifts in the Asian-American population from an immigrant to a native-born one (Espiritu 1992). As we can see from this chapter, Asian-American immigrants and native-born Asian Americans at times do not see themselves as sharing common goals. Nevertheless, as this and other chapters have argued, Asian Americans have much in common and experience both daily lives and macro-level environments in similar ways. Ultimately, Asian Americans shape the nation and transnational dynamics, and in turn shed light on multiple social processes.

Discussion questions

- Asian American Studies proliferated as a result of radical student activism demanding curriculum changes. What is the role of Asian American Studies within the university? Given that higher education is becoming increasingly inaccessible, (how) can Asian American Studies function as a politicized space of resistance to critique the institutions in which they are located?
- How are different types of political activity in which Asian Americans engage informed by class (i.e. labor organizing versus electoral politics and such)?
- Find web sites of contemporary Asian-American activists and political organizations (such as nonprofits or policy groups) and politicians or community leaders. How do they position themselves as advocates for or representatives of Asian Americans? How are they in conversation with the various manifestations of Asian-American politics discussed in this chapter? What criticism can you make about how they position themselves?

Notes

CHAPTER 1 INTRODUCTION

1 www.census.gov/hhes/socdemo/education/data/cps/2011/tables.html
2 www.census.gov/hhes/www/poverty/data/incpovhlth/2010/highlights.html
3 www.civilrights.org/hatecrimes/fbi/035-hate-crimes-2007.html, accessed August 4, 2013. See also www.civilrights.org/publications/hatecrimes/asian-pacific.html
4 United States Census Bureau; American Community Survey, 2010 American Community Survey 1-Year Estimates, Table S0201; generated by Pawan Dhingra; using American FactFinder
5 www.census.gov/prod/cen2010/briefs/c2010br-11.pdf, p. 22.

CHAPTER 2 RACE, ETHNICITY, GENDER, AND SEXUALITY

1 It should be noted, however, that though "Latino" or "Hispanic" may be used by people on a daily basis in categorizing others, the United States Census does not actually define "Latino" as a racial group. "Hispanic" is used in the Census, but refers to ethnicity and not race. Those who are categorized as "Hispanic" in the US Census must still specify to which racial group they belong: white, black, or Asian.
2 For more information on this, see www.pbs.org/race/000_About/002_04-background-01-x.htm, accessed July 20, 2013.
3 www.sentencingproject.org/doc/publications/rd_stateratesofincbyraceandethnicity.pdf, accessed July 20, 2013.
4 See also www.amnestyusa.org/pdfs/rp_report.pdf, accessed July 15, 2013.
5 www.washingtonpost.com/wp-dyn/content/article/2006/06/02/AR2006060201060.html, accessed July 15, 2013.
6 Because the internment has left a stain on racial profiling in the name of national security, some in support of contemporary profiling of Arab Americans have argued that Japanese American internment was justified (Malkin 2004).
7 www.aclu.org/drug-law-reform/aclu-reveals-proof-racial-targeting-major-meth-investiga-tion, accessed August 4, 2013.
8 SAALT webinar on racial profiling, November 19, 2009.
9 http://saalt.org/wp-content/uploads/2012/09/SAALT-Testimony-to-House-Subcommittee-on-Constitution-Civil-Rights-and-Civil-Liberties-on-Profiling-and-the-South-Asian-Community-June-2010.pdf , accessed July 30, 2013.
10 http://saalt.org/wp-content/uploads/2012/09/SAALT-Testimony-to-House-Subcommittee-on-Constitution-Civil-Rights-and-Civil-Liberties-on-Profiling-and-the-South-Asian-Community-June-2010.pdf, accessed July 30, 2013.
11 www.jacl.org/edu/What%20It%20Means%20To%20Be%20An%20American.pdf, accessed July 23, 2013.
12 www.asianam.org/hate_crimes_2005-2008.htm, accessed July 23, 2013.
13 www.sacbee.com/2007/07/13/270787/beating-death-symbolic-of-local.html,   accessed December 16, 2010.
14 www.advancingequality.org/files/2002_Audit.pdf, accessed December 16, 2010.

CHAPTER 4 CLASS AND WORK LIVES

1 United States Census Bureau; American Community Survey, 2010 American Community Survey 1-Year Estimates, Table S0201; generated by Pawan Dhingra; using American FactFinder, http://factfinder2.census.gov; May 28, 2013.

2 www.dol.gov/_sec/media/reports/asianlaborforce/, accessed July 23, 2013.

3 http://news.newamericamedia.org/news/view_article.html?article_id=aac7a5849d659f7b4ede 46c3c759c9d3, accessed July 23, 2013.

4 United States Census Bureau; American Community Survey, 2010 American Community Survey 1-Year Estimates, Table S0201; generated by Pawan Dhingra; using American FactFinder, accessed July 23, 2013.

5 www.epi.org/publication/impact-geography-asian-american-poverty/, accessed July 23, 2013.

6 www.census.gov/prod/cen2010/briefs/c2010br-11.pdf, accessed July 23, 2013.

7 United States Census Bureau; American Community Survey, 2010 American Community Survey 1-Year Estimates, Table S0201; generated by Pawan Dhingra; using American FactFinder.

8 www.whitehouse.gov/administration/eop/aapi/data/critical-issues, accessed July 23, 2013.

9 United States Census Bureau; American Community Survey, 2010 American Community Survey 1-Year Estimates, Table S0201; generated by Pawan Dhingra; using American FactFinder.

10 www.census.gov/newsroom/releases/pdf/20120502_paf_asian_factsheet.pdf, accessed July 23, 2013.

11 Portes and Rumbaut (2006) include a fourth category when talking about immigrant types, refugees. Because this is not an occupational type and employed refugees enter one of these other three types, it is not included here.

12 www.pewsocialtrends.org/2012/06/19/the-rise-of-asian-americans/, accessed July 23, 2013.

13 The authors refer to this dynamic as a "sticky floor" problem rather than "glass ceiling" problem. By that, they mean that the problems arise due to the lower level at which Asian Americans enter a business, which makes it harder to supervise Asian Americans at a higher level.

14 http://articles.baltimoresun.com/2000-02-21/news/0002210331_1_foreign-workers-visa-hold ers-immigrants/2, accessed July 23, 2013.

15 http://papers.ssrn.com/sol3/papers.cfm?abstract_id=1380343, accessed July 23, 2013.

16 www.drumnation.org/DRUM/Workers_Center.html, accessed September 14, 2010.

17 http://sfonline.barnard.edu/work/poo_02.htm, accessed July 23, 2013.

18 www.sba.gov/content/what-sbas-definition-small-business-concern/, accessed July 23, 2013.

19 Poon, Oiyan A., Linda Tran, and Paul M. Ong, 2009. *The State of Asian American Businesses.* UCLA Asian American Studies Center. www.aasc.ucla.edu/aascpress/nexus9_1_2_full.pdf, accessed August 4, 2013.

20 www.aasc.ucla.edu/aascpress/nexus9_1_2_full.pdf, accessed August 4, 2013.

21 According to the Personal Responsibility and Work Opportunity Act of 1996, immigrants and noncitizens were denied SSI (Social Security Insurance) for the first five years here. After protests, SSI was reinstated in 1997 for those who were receiving benefits in 1996.

CHAPTER 5 EDUCATION

1 Tom Breckenridge, "Are Asian American Kids Smarter than Everyone Else?" Dec. 7, 2003, *Plain Dealer*, Sunday magazine, pp. 12–16.

2 www.census.gov/newsroom/releases/archives/facts_for_features_special_editions/cb13-ff09. html, accessed July 23, 2013.

3 http://professionals.collegeboard.com/profdownload/08-0608-AAPI.pdf, accessed July 23, 2013.

4 www.whitehouse.gov/administration/eop/aapi/data/critical-issues, accessed July 23, 2013.

5 www.understandinggrace.org/history/science/modern_evolutionary.html, accessed July 23, 2013.

6 www.nytimes.com/2013/04/03/nyregion/cram-schools-no-longer-just-an-asian-pursuit. html?pagewanted=all&_r=0, accessed July 23, 2013.

7 In California, Filipinos constitute a separate minority group from Asian Pacific Americans and qualify for affirmative action.

8 www.insidehighered.com/news/2010/10/08/asians and www.nytimes.com/2008/06/10/educ ation/10asians.html, both accessed July 23, 2013.

CHAPTER 6 FAMILY AND PERSONAL RELATIONS

1 Another Indian film about gay men and HIV, *My Brother Nikhil*, did not receive such negative feedback.
2 www.huffingtonpost.com/2013/05/21/immigration-reform-gay-couples_n_3315674.html, accessed July 23, 2013.

CHAPTER 7 CITIZENSHIP

1 www.uscis.gov/portal/site/uscis/menuitem.eb1d4c2a3e5b9ac89243c6a7543f6d1a/?vgnextoid =40a9b2149e7df110VgnVCM1000004718190aRCRD&vgnextchannel=40a9b2149e7df110VgnVC M1000004718190aRCRD, accessed July 23, 2013.
2 www.nytimes.com/2013/01/30/opinion/reforming-immigration-for-good.html, accessed July 23, 2013.
3 www.foxnews.com/story/0,2933,63020,00.html, accessed July 23, 2013.
4 See also http://articles.cnn.com/2002-04-24/travel/airports.sweep_1_operation-tarmac-wash ington-area-airports-immigration-violations?_s=PM:TRAVEL, accessed July 22, 2013.
5 www.cga.ct.gov/2007/rpt/2007-R-0705.htm, accessed July 23, 2013.
6 www.immigrationpolicy.org/issues/DREAM-Act, accessed July 23, 2013.
7 www.jacl.org/news/2010ChicagoJMTEMP033009/documents/2008%20Official%20Transcript% 20EV2.pdf, accessed July 23, 2013.
8 www.huffingtonpost.com/2010/04/15/muslim-woman-denied-foste_n_539723.html, accessed July 23, 2013.

CHAPTER 8 MEDIA AND POPULAR CULTURE

1 www.aaja.org/ and www.manaa.org/, both accessed October 2, 2013.
2 www.imdb.com/, accessed October 2, 2013.
3 www.huffingtonpost.com/2011/03/19/alexandra-wallace-student_n_837925.html, accessed August 1, 2013.
4 http://ph.news.yahoo.com/apl-ap-lines-more-tagalog-tracks-album-065416566.html, accessed July 23, 2013.

CHAPTER 9 IDENTITY

1 www.dailytexanonline.com/life-and-arts/2012/11/08/korean-pop-culture-increasingly-popul ar-in-us, accessed July 23, 2013.
2 http://network.nshp.org/profiles/blogs/bilingualism-is-growing-but, accessed July 23, 2013.

CHAPTER 10 INTER-MINORITY RELATIONS

1 www.cswa.org/www/index.asp, accessed October 2, 2013.

CHAPTER 11 SOCIAL MOVEMENTS AND POLITICS

1 www.voanews.com/content/exit-polls-show-asian-americans-backed-obama-by-wide-margin/1540974.html, accessed July 23, 2013.
2 http://indiaspora.org/blog/the-unusual-political-leanings-of-indian-americans/, accessed July 23, 2013.

References

Abelmann, N., and Lie, J. 1995. *Blue Dreams: Korean Americans and the Los Angeles Riots.* Cambridge: Harvard University Press.

Ablett, Philipp. 2004. "Colonialism in Denial: US Propaganda in the Philippine–American War." *Social Alternatives* 23(3): 22–8.

Abraham, Margaret. 2000. *Speaking the Unspeakable: Marital Violence among South Asian Immigrants in the United States.* New Brunswick, NJ: Rutgers University Press.

Adams, Brian E., and Ren, Ping. 2006. "Asian Americans and Campaign Finance in Municipal Elections." *The Social Science Journal* 43(4): 597–615.

Ahn, Annie J., Kim, Bryan S. K., and Park, Yong S. 2009. "Asian Cultural Values Gap, Cognitive Flexibility, Coping Strategies, and Parent–Child Conflicts among Korean Americans." *Cultural Diversity Ethnic Minority Psychology* 14(4): 353–63.

Ahn, Hue-Sun. 1999. *Juggling Two Worlds: Ethnic Identity of Korean-American College Students.* Unpublished dissertation. University of Pennsylvania.

Alba, Richard D. 1990. *Ethnic Identity: The Transformation of White America.* New Haven: Yale University Press.

Alba, Richard. 2004. "Language Assimilation Today: Bilingualism Persists More Than in the Past, but English Still Dominates." *Working Papers No. 111.* San Diego: Center for Comparative Immigration Studies.

Alba, Richard D., and Nee, Victor. 2003. *Remaking the American Mainstream: Assimilation and Contemporary Immigration.* Cambridge: Harvard University Press.

Aldrich, Howard, and Waldinger, Roger. 1990. "Ethnicity and Entrepreneurship." *Annual Review of Sociology* 16: 111–35.

Aldrich, Robert. 2002. "Homosexuality in the French Colonies." *Journal of Homosexuality* 41(3–4): 201–18. New York: Routledge.

Alexander, Jeffrey, and Smith, Philip. 1993. "The Discourse of American Civil Society: A New Proposal for Cultural Studies." *Theory and Society* 22(2): 151–207.

Alexander, Michelle. 2010. *The New Jim Crow: Mass Incarceration in the Age of Colorblindness.* New York: The New Press.

Ancheta, Angelo N. 1998. *Race, Rights, and the Asian American Experience.* New Brunswick, NJ: Rutgers University Press.

Anderson, Bridget. 2001. "Just Another Job? Paying for Domestic Work." *Gender & Development* 9(1): 25–33.

Anguiano, Ruben, and Viramontez, Patricio. 2004. "Families and Schools: The Effect of Parental Involvement on High School Completion." *Journal of Family* 25(1): 61–85.

Anner, John. 1996. "Sweatshop Workers Win Long Fight with Jessica McClintock." Global Nonviolent Action Database. October 2, 2011. http://nvdatabase.swarthmore.edu/content/asian-immigrant-garment-workers-campaign-economic-justice-san-francisco-usa-1992-1996, accessed July 30, 2013.

Atkinson, Donald R., Morten, George, and Sue, Derald Wing. 1989. "A Minority Identity Development Model," in Donald R. Atkinson, George Morten, Derald Wing Sue (eds), *Counseling American Minorities.* New York: McGraw-Hill, pp. 35–52.

Austin, Caridad. 2011. "Overwhelmed by Big Consolidation: Bringing Back Regulation to Increase

Diversity in Programming that Serves Minority Audiences." *Federal Communications Law Journal* 63(6): 733–63.

Ayyub, Ruksana. 2000. "Domestic Violence in the South Asian Muslim Immigrant Population in the United States." *Journal of Social Distress and the Homeless* 9(3): 237–48.

Bahar, Robert and Carracedo, Almudena. 2007. *Made in L.A.* Independent Television Service (ITVS) (co-production); P.O.V. (co-production); Semilla Verde Productions.

Balance, Christine B. 2012. "How It Feels to Be Viral Me: Affective Labor and Asian American YouTube Performance." *WSQ: Women's Studies Quarterly* 40(1/2): 138–52.

Bald, Vivek. 2013. *Bengali Harlem and the Lost Histories of South Asian America.* Cambridge, MA: Harvard University Press.

Baldoz, Rick. 2011. *The Third Asiatic Invasion: Migration and Empire in Filipino America, 1898–1946.* New York: New York University Press.

Banerji, Shilpa. 2004. "SAJA Works to Raise Profile of South Asia Journalism Profession." *Black Issues in Higher Education* 21(11): 34–5.

Bankston, Carl L., and Zhou, Min. 1995. "Effects of Minority-Language Literacy on the Academic Achievement of Vietnamese Youth in New Orleans." *Sociology of Education* 68(1): 1–17.

Barlow, Andrew L. 2003. *Between Fear and Hope: Globalization and Race in the United States.* Lanham, MD: Rowman & Littlefield Press.

Barth, Fredrick. 1969. *Ethnic Groups and Boundaries.* Boston: Little Brown and Company.

Basch, Linda G., Glick Schiller, Nina, and Szanton Blanc, Cristina. 1994. *Nations Unbound: Transnational Projects, Postcolonial Predicaments, and Deterritorialized Nation-states*: Gordon and Breach Press.

Baumann, Gerd. 1996. *Contesting Culture: Discourses of Identity in Multi-Ethnic London.* Cambridge: Cambridge University Press.

Bell, Ella Louise. 1990. "The Bicultural Life Experience of Career-Oriented Black Women." *Journal of Organizational Behavior* 11(6): 459–77.

Bem, Sandra L. 1993. *The Lenses of Gender: Transforming the Debate on Sexual Inequality.* New Haven: Yale University Press.

Bhattacharjee, Anannya. 1998. "The Habit of Ex-nomination: Nation, Women, and Indian Immigrant Bourgeoisie," in Shamita Dasgupta (ed.), *A Patchwork Shawl: Chronicles of South Asian Women in America.* New Brunswick: Rutgers University Press, pp. 163–85.

Bhuyan, Rupaleem, Mell, Molly, Senturia, Kirsten, Sullivan, Marianne, and Shiu-Thornton, Sharyne. 2005. "'Women Must Endure According to their Karma': Cambodian Immigrant Women Talk About Domestic Violence." *Journal of Interpersonal Violence* 20(8): 902–21.

Bishoff, Tonya, and Rankin, Jo. 1997. *Seeds from a Silent Tree: An Anthology.* Glendale: Pandal.

Blau, Peter M., Blum, Terry C., and Schwartz, Joseph E. 1982. "Heterogeneity and Intermarriage." *American Sociological Review* 47: 45–62.

Blazer, Jonathan, and Broder, Tanya. 2010. "Public Benefits," in Edith Wen-Chu Chen (ed.), *Encyclopedia of Asian American Issues Today*, Vol. 1. Westport, CT: Greenwood Publishing Group, pp. 519–26.

Blumer, Herbert. 1958. "Race Prejudice as a Sense of Group Position." *Pacific Sociological Review* 1(1): 3–7.

Bobo, Lawrence D. 2006. "Inequalities That Endure? Racial Ideology, American Politics, and the Peculiar Role of the Social Sciences," in Maria Krysan and Amanda E. Lewis (eds.), *The Changing Terrain of Race and Ethnicity.* New York: Russell Sage Foundation, pp. 33–42.

Bobo, Lawrence, and Hutchings, Vincent L. 1996. "Perceptions of Intergroup Competition: Extending Blumer's Theory of Group Position to a Multiracial Social Context." *American Sociological Review* 61(6): 951–72.

Bobo, Lawrence, and Smith, Ryan A. 1998. "From Jim Crow Racism to Laissez-faire Racism: The Transformation of Racial Attitudes." *Beyond Pluralism: The Conception of Groups and Group Identities in America.* Champaign: University of Illinois Press.

Bonacich, Edna. 1973. "A Theory of Middleman Minorities." *American Sociological Review* 38: 583–94.

Bonacich, Edna. 1987. "'Making It' in America: A Social Evaluation of the Ethics of Immigrant Entrepreneurship." *Sociological Perspectives* 30(4): 446–66.

Bonilla-Silva, Eduardo. 2003. *Racism without Racists: Color-Blind Racism and the Persistence of Racial Inequality in the United States.* Lanham: Rowman & Littlefield.

Bonus, Rick. 2000. *Locating Filipino Americans.* Philadelphia: Temple University Press.

Bosniak, Linda. 2006. *The Citizen and the Alien: Dilemmas of Contemporary Membership.* Princeton, NJ: Princeton University Press.

Brandzel, Amy L. 2005. "Queering Citizenship? Same Sex Marriage and the State." *GLQ: A Journal of Lesbian and Gay Studies* 11(2): 171–204.

Brandzel, Amy L., and Desai, Jigna. 2008. "Race, Violence, and Terror: The Cultural Defensibility of Heteromasculine Citizenship in the Virginia Tech Massacre and the Don Imus Affair." *The Journal of Asian American Studies* 11(1): 61–85.

Brettell, Caroline B., and Nibbs, Faith. 2009. "Lived Hybridity: Second-Generation Identity Construction through College Festival." *Identities: Global Studies in Culture and Power* 16(6): 678–99.

Brewer, Marilynn, and Brown, Rupert. 1998. "Intergroup Relations," in Daniel T. Gilbert, Susan T. Fiske, and Gardner Lindzey (eds), *The Handbook of Social Psychology.* New York: McGraw-Hill, pp. 554–94.

Brimelow, Peter. 1998. "Immigration and Welfare: A Review of the Evidence," in Peter Duignan and L. H. Gann (eds), *The Debate in the United States over Immigration.* Stanford: Hoover Institution Press.

Brooks, Charlotte. 2011. "The War on Grant Avenue: Business Competition and Ethnic Rivalry in San Francisco's Chinatown, 1937–1942." *Journal of Urban History* 37(3): 311–30.

Browne, Irene, and Misra, Joya. 2003. "The Intersection of Gender and Race in the Labor Market." *Annual Review of Sociology.* Palo Alto: Annual Reviews, pp. 487–513.

Bullard, Robert D. 1994. *Unequal Protection: Environmental Justice and Communities of Color.* San Francisco: Sierra Club.

Burman, Erica, Smailes, Sophie L., and Chantler, Khatidja. 2004. "'Culture' as a Barrier to Service Provision and Delivery: Domestic Violence Services for Minoritized Women." *Critical Social Policy* 24(3): 332–57.

Busto, Rudy V. 1996. "Response: Asian American Religious Identities: Building Spiritual Homes on Gold Mountain," *Amerasia Journal* 22(1): 187–90, esp.189.

Cafferty, Pastora San Juan. 1983. *The Dilemma of American Immigration: Beyond the Golden Door.* New Brunswick: Transaction Books.

Caldas, Stephen. 1993. "Reexamination of Input and Process Factor Effects on Public School Achievement." *The Journal of Educational Research* 86(4): 206–14.

Caldas, Stephen, and Bankston, Carl L. 1997. "Effect of School Population Socioeconomic Status on Individual Academic Achievement." *The Journal of Educational Research* 90(5): 269–77.

Campomanes, Oscar V. 1997. "New Formations of Asian American Studies and the Question of US Imperialism." *Positions* 5(2): 523–50.

Cao, Nanlai. 2005. "The Church as Surrogate Family to Working Class Immigrant Chinese Youth: An Ethnography of Segmented Assimilation." *The Sociology of Religion* 66(2): 183–200.

Caspi, Dan, and Elias, Nellie. 2011. "Don't Patronize Me: Media-by and Media-for Minorities." *Ethnic and Racial Studies* 34(1): 62–82.

Castro, Christi-Anne. 2007. "Voices in the Minority: Race, Gender, Sexuality, and the Asian American in Popular Music." *Journal of Popular Music Studies* 19(3): 221–38.

Chae, Sharon. 2007. "Art, Media, and Social Responsibility for Asian Americans: Profile of Eric Byler, Filmmaker." *Asian American Policy Review* 16: 25–7.

Chai, Karen. 1998. "Competing for the Second Generation: English – Language Ministry at a Korean Protestant Church," in R. Stephen Warner and Judith G. Wittner (eds), *Gatherings in Diaspora.* Philadelphia: Temple University Press, pp. 295–331.

Chan, Sucheng. 1991. *Asian Americans: An Interpretive History.* Boston: Twayne Press.

Chang, Janet, Rhee, Siyon, and Weaver, Dale. 2006. "Characteristics of Child Abuse in Immigrant

Korean Families and Correlates of Placement Decisions." *Child Abuse & Neglect: The International Journal* 30(8): 881–91.

Chang, Robert S. 2000. *Disoriented: Asian Americans, Law, and the Nation-State.* New York: New York University Press.

Chao, Ruth. 1994. "Beyond Parental Control and Authoritarian Parenting Style: Understanding Chinese Parenting through the Cultural Notion of Training." *Child Development* 65(4): 1111–19.

Chavez, Leo R. 2008. *The Latino Threat: Constructing Immigrants, Citizens, and the Nation.* Stanford: Stanford University Press.

Chen, Carolyn. 2008. *Getting Saved in America: Taiwanese Immigration and Religious Experience.* Princeton, NJ: Princeton University Press.

Chen, S. Andrew. 1992. "In Pursuit of Justice against Hate Crime: A Campaign by OCA." *Chinese American Forum* 7(4): 13.

Cheng, Cindy I-Fen. 2009. "Identities and Places: On Writing the History of Filipinotown, Los Angeles." *Journal of Asian American Studies* 12(1): 1–33, esp. 3.

Cheng, Jih-Fei. 2006. "HIV, Immigrant Rights, and Same-Sex Marriage." *Amerasia Journal* 32(1): 97–108.

Cherry, Stephen. 2009. "Engaging a Spirit From the East: Asian American Christians and Civic Life." *Sociological Spectrum* 29(2): 249–72.

Cheung, Floyd. 2007. "Anxious and Ambivalent Representations: Nineteenth-Century Images of Chinese American Men." *The Journal of American Culture* 30(3): 293–309.

Chhuon, Vichet, Hudley, Cynthia, Brenner, Mary E., and Macias, Roseanne. 2010. "The Multiple Worlds of Cambodian American Students." *Urban Education* 45(1): 30–57.

Chin, Margaret. 2005. *Sewing Women: Immigrants and the New York City Garment Industry.* New York: Columbia University Press.

Chiu, Monica. 2007. "Americanization against Academics: Racial Contexts and Lao American Youths in a New Hampshire High School," in Clara Park, Russell Endo, Stacy Lee, and Xue Lan Rong (eds), *Asian American Education: Acculturation, Literacy Development, and Learning.* Charlotte: Information Age Publishing, pp. 1–24.

Cho, Tam, and Gimpel, James G. 2008. "A Political Powerhouse in Search of a Home." *Asian American Policy Review* 17: 91–8.

Cho, Wendy Tam, and Cain, Bruce. 2001. "Asian Americans as the Median Voters: An Exploration of Attitudes and Voting Patterns on Ballot Initiatives," in Gordon H. Chang (ed.), *Asian Americans and Politics: Perspectives, Experiences, Prospects.* Stanford: Stanford University Press, pp. 133–52.

Choi, Heeseung, Meininger, Janet C., and Roberts, Robert E. 2006. "Ethnic Differences in Adolescents' Mental Distress, Social Stress, and Resources." *Adolescence* 41(162): 263–83.

Choi, Yoonsun. 2008. "Diversity Within: Subgroup Differences of Youth Problem Behaviors Among Asian Pacific Islander American Adolescents." *Journal of Community Psychology* 36(3): 352–70.

Chong, Kelly. 1998. "What it Means to be Christian: The Role of Religion in Construction of Ethnic Identity and Boundary Among Second-Generation Korean Americans." *Sociology of Religion* 59(3): 259–86.

Chong, Sylvia Shin Huey. 2008. "'Look, an Asian!' The Politics of Racial Interpellation in the Wake of the Virginia Tech Shootings." *Journal of Asian American Studies* 11(1): 27–60.

Chow, Sue. 2000. "The Significance of Race in the Private Sphere: Asian Americans and Spousal Preferences." *Sociological Inquiry* 70(1): 1–29.

Choy, Catherine Ceniza. 2003. *Empire of Care: Nursing and Migration in Filipino American History.* Durham: Duke University Press.

Chuang, Angie. 2012. "Representations of Foreign versus (Asian) American Identity in a Mass-Shooting Case: Newspaper Coverage of the 2009 Binghamton Massacre." *Journalism & Mass Communication Quarterly* 89(2): 244–60.

Chun, Elaine W. 2004. "Ideologies of Legitimate Mockery: Margaret Cho's Revoicings of Mock Asian." *Pragmatics* 14(2/3): 263–89.

Chung, Angie Y. 2005. "'Politics without the Politics': The Evolving Political Cultures of Ethnic Non-Profits in Koreatown, Los Angeles." *Journal of Ethnic and Migration Studies* 31(5): 911–29.

Chung, Ruth H. 2001. "Gender, Ethnicity, and Acculturation in Intergenerational Conflict of Asian American College Students." *Cultural Diversity and Ethnic Minority Psychology* 7(4): 376–86.

Cobas, Jose. 1989. "Six Problems in the Sociology of the Ethnic Economy." *Sociological Perspectives* 32(2): 201–14.

Cohen, Deborah A., and Rice, Janet. 1997. "Parenting Styles, Adolescent Substance Use, and Academic Achievement." *Journal of Drug Education* 27(2): 199–211.

Cohen, Robin. 2007. PRWORA'S Immigrant Provisions. Available at www.cga.ct.gov/2007/rpt/2007-R-0705.htm, accessed August 5, 2013.

Coleman, Renita. 2011. "The Moral Judgment of Minority Journalists: Evidence from Asian American, Black, and Hispanic Professional Journalists." *Mass Communication and Society* 14(5): 578–99.

Collins, S. 1997. *Black Corporate Executives: The Making and Breaking of a Black Middle Class.* Philadelphia: Temple University Press.

Collins, Patricia Hill. 2000. *Black Feminist Thought: Knowledge, Consciousness, and the Politics of Empowerment.* New York: Routledge.

Considine, Austin. 2011. "For Asian Stars, Many Web Fans." *New York Times*, July 31.

Constantino, Renato. 1970. "The Mis-education of the Filipino." *Journal of Contemporary Asia* 1(1): 20–36.

Cook, Stuart W. 1969. "Motives in a Conceptual Analysis of Attitude Related Behavior," in William J. Arnold, David Levine, and Dalbir Bindra (eds), *Nebraska Symposium on Motivation, 1969.* Lincoln: University of Nebraska Press, pp. 179–231.

Cooley, Charles. 1902. *Human Nature and the Social Order.* New York: Scribner.

Cornell, Stephen. 1988. *The Return of the Native: American Indian Political Resurgence.* New York: Oxford University Press.

Cornell, Stephen Ellicott, and Hartmann, Douglas. 2007. *Ethnicity and Race: Making Identities in a Changing World.* Thousand Oaks, CA: Pine Forge Press.

Coser, Lewis A. 1967. *Continuities in the Study of Social Conflict.* New York: Free Press.

Coutin, Susan Bibler. 2007. *Nations of Emigrants: Shifting Boundaries of Citizenship in El Salvador and the United States.* Ithaca: Cornell University Press.

Cross, William E. Jr 1995. "The Psychology of Nigrescence: Revising the Cross Model," in Joseph G. Ponterotto, J. Manuel Casas, Lisa A. Suzuki, and Charlene M. Alexander (eds), *Handbook of Multicultural Counseling.* Thousand Oaks: Sage Publications, pp. 93–122.

Das Gupta, Monisha. 1997. "What is Indian about You? A Gendered, Transnational Approach to Ethnicity." *Gender & Society* 11(5): 572–96.

Das Gupta, Monisha. 2006. *Unruly Immigrants: Rights, Activism, and Transnational South Asian Politics.* Durham: Duke University Press.

Dasgupta, Shamita Das. 2000. "Charting the Course: An Overview of Domestic Violence in the South Asian Community in the United States." *Journal of Social Distress and the Homeless* 9(3): 173–85.

Davé, Shilpa. 2012. "Matchmakers and Cultural Compatibility: Arranged Marriage, South Asians, and American Television." *South Asian Popular Culture* 10(2): 167–83.

Davé, Shilpa, Nishime, LeiLani, and Oren, Tasha G. 2005. *East Main Street: Asian American Popular Culture.* New York: New York University Press.

de Leon, Lakandiwa M. 2004. "Filipinotown and the DJ Scene: Cultural Expression and Identity Affirmation of Filipino American Youth in Los Angeles," in Jennifer Lee and Min Zhou (eds), *Asian American Youth: Culture, Identity, and Ethnicity.* New York: Routledge, pp. 191–206.

De Cecco, John P., and Elia, John P. 1993. *If You Seduce a Straight Person, Can You Make Them Gay? Issues in Biological Essentialism versus Social Constructionism in Gay and Lesbian Identities.* New York: Haworth Press.

Delgado, Richard, and Stefancic, Jean. 2001. *Critical Race Theory: An Introduction.* New York University Press.

Deo, Meera E., Lee, Jenny J., Chin, Christina B., Milman, Noriko, and Yuen, Nancy Y. 2008. "Missing in Action: 'Framing' Race on Prime-Time Television." *Social Justice* 35(2): 145–62.

Desai, Jigna. 2004. *Beyond Bollywood: The Cultural Politics of South Asian Diasporic Film.* New York: Routledge.

Dhingra, Pawan. 2004. "'We're Not a Korean American Church Anymore': Dilemmas in Constructing a Multi-Racial Church Identity." *Social Compass* 51(3): 367–79.

Dhingra, Pawan. 2007. *Managing Multicultural Lives: Asian American Professionals and the Challenge of Multiple Identities.* Palo Alto: Stanford University Press.

Dhingra, Pawan. 2008. "Committed to Ethnicity, Committed to America: How Second-Generation Indian Americans' Ethnic Boundaries Further their Americanisation." *Journal of Intercultural Studies* 29(1): 41–63.

Dhingra, Pawan. 2009. "The Possibility of Community: How Indian American Motel Owners Negotiate Competition and Solidarity." *Journal of Asian American Studies* 12(3): 321–46.

Dhingra, Pawan. 2012. *Life Behind the Lobby: Indian American Motel Owners and the American Dream.* Stanford University Press.

Diaz, Maria-Elena D. 2012. "Asian Embeddedness and Political Participation: Social Integration and Asian-American Voting Behavior in the 2000 Presidential Election." *Sociological Perspectives* 55(1): 141–66.

Diaz, Vicente M. 2004. "To 'P' or Not to 'P'?": Marking the Territory between Pacific Islander and Asian American Studies." *Journal of Asian American Studies* 7(3): 183–208.

Diaz-Veizades, Jeannette, and Chang, Edward T. 1996. "Building Cross-cultural Coalitions: A Case Study of the Black–Korean Alliance and the Latino-Black Roundtable." *Ethnic and Racial Studies* 19(3): 680–700.

Diffrient, David Scott. 2011. "Beyond Tokenism and Tricksterism: Bobby Lee, *MADtv*, and the De(con)structive Impulse of Korean American Comedy." *The Velvet Light Trap* 67(1): 41–56.

DiMaggio, Paul, Hargittai, Eszter, Neuman, W. Russell, and Robinson, John P. 2001. "Social Implications of the Internet." *Annual Review of Sociology* 27(1): 307–36.

Dornbusch, Sanford M., Ritter, Philip L., Leiderman, P. Herbert, et al. 1987. "The Relation of Parenting Style to Adolescent School Performance." *Child Development* 58(5): 1244–57.

Dorow, Sara. 2006. "Racialized Choices: Chinese Adoption and the White Noise of Blackness." *Critical Sociology* 32(2, 3): 357–79.

Dossani, Rafiq, and Kumar, Ashish. 2011. "Network Associations and Professional Growth among Engineers From India and China in Silicon Valley." *American Behavioral Scientist* 55(7): 941–69.

Dreby, Joanna. 2010. *Divided by Borders: Mexican Migrants and Their Children.* Berkeley: University of California Press.

Duany, Jorge. 1989. "Ethnic Identity and Socioeconomic Adaptation: The Case of Cubans in Puerto Rico." *Journal of Ethnic Studies* 17(1): 109–27.

Dunaway, Johanna. 2008. "Markets, Ownership, and the Quality of Campaign News Coverage." *The Journal of Politics* 70(4): 1193–1202.

Duong, Ian, and Pelaud, Isabelle Thuy. 2012. "Vietnamese American Art and Community Politics: An Engaged Feminist Perspective." *Journal of Asian American Studies* 15(3): 241–69.

Ehrenreich, Barbara, and Hochschild, Arlie Russell (eds). 2002. *Global Woman: Nannies, Maids, and Sex Workers in the New Economy.* New York: Henry Holt and Company.

Ellis, Mark, and Wright, Richard. 1999. "The Industrial Division of Labor among Immigrants and Internal Migrants to the Los Angeles Economy." *International Migration* 33(1): 26–54.

Eng, David L. 2003. "Transnational Adoption and Queer Diasporas." *Social Text* 21(3): 1–37.

Epstein, C. F. 1992. "Tinkerbell and Pinups: The Construction and Reconstruction of Gender Boundaries at Work," in M. Lamont and M. Fournier (eds), *Cultivating Differences.* Chicago: University of Chicago Press.

Espina, Marina E. 1988. *Filipinos in Louisiana.* New Orleans, LA: A. F. Laborde.

Espiritu, Yen Le. 1992. *Asian American Panethnicity: Bridging Institutions and Identities.* Philadelphia: Temple University Press.

Espiritu, Yen Le. 2003. *Home Bound: Filipino American Lives Across Cultures, Communities, and Countries.* Berkeley: University of California Press.

Espiritu, Yen Le. 2007. *Asian American Women and Men: Labor, Laws, and Love,* 2nd edn. Lanham: Rowman & Littlefield.

Feagin, Joe R. 2009. *Racist America: Roots, Current Realities, and Future Reparations.* London: Taylor and Francis.

Fees, Jarre. 2008. "Olympics Put Focus on China." *Television Week* 27(20): 26–30.

Feng, Peter X. 2002. *Identities in Motion: Asian American Film and Video.* Durham, NC: Duke University Press.

Fenton, John. 1988. *Transplanting Religious Traditions: Asian Indians in America.* New York: Praeger.

Ferguson, Susan. 2000. "Challenging Traditional Marriage: Never Married Chinese American and Japanese American Women." *Gender & Society* 14(1): 136–59.

Fernandez, Marilyn. 1998. "Asian Indian Americans in the Bay Area and the Glass Ceiling." *Sociological Perspectives*: 119–49.

Fetto, John. 2002. "Off the Map." *American Demographics* 24(10): 48.

Fischer, Claude S., Hout, Michael, Jankowski, Sanchez, Martin, Lucas, Samuel R., Swidler, Ann, and Voss, Kim. 1996. *Inequality by Design.* Princeton, NJ: Princeton University Press.

Fitzgerald, David. 2009. *A Nation of Emigrants: How Mexico Manages Its Migration.* Berkeley: University of California Press.

Fix, Michael, and Zimmermann, Wendy. 2001. "All Under One Roof: Mixed-Status Families in an Era of Reform." *International Migration Review* 35: 397–419.

Fong, Timothy P. 1994. *The First Suburban Chinatown: The Remaking of Monterey Park, California.* Philadelphia: Temple University Press.

Fong, Timothy P. 2008. *The Contemporary Asian American Experience: Beyond the Model Minority.* Upper Saddle River, NJ: Prentice Hall.

Fouron, Georges, and Glick-Schiller, Nina. 2002. "The Generation of Identity: Redefining the Second Generation within a Transnational Social Field," in Peggy Levitt and Mary C. Waters (eds), *Changing Face of Home.* New York: Russell Sage Foundation, pp. 168–208.

Fragomen Jr, Austin T. 1997. "The Illegal Immigration Reform and Immigrant Responsibility Act of 1996: An Overview," in *International Migration Review* 31(2): 438–60.

Francisco, Luzviminda. 1973. "The First Vietnam: The Philippine–American War of 1899." *Bulletin of Concerned Asian Scholars* 5(4): 2–16.

Fraser, Nancy, and Gordon, Linda. 1998. "Contract versus Charity: Why is there No Social Citizenship in the United States?" in Gershon Shafir (ed.), *The Citizenship Debates: A Reader.* Minneapolis: University of Minnesota, pp. 113–27.

Friday, Chris. 1994. *Organizing Asian American Labor: The Pacific Coast Canned-salmon Industry, 1870–1942.* Philadelphia: Temple University Press.

Friedman, Raymond A., and Krackhardt, David. 1997. "Social Capital and Career Mobility: A Structural Theory of Lower Returns to Education for Asian Employees." *Journal of Applied Behavioral Science* 33(3): 316–34.

Fu, Vincent Kang. 2008. "Interracial–Interethnic Unions and Fertility in the United States." *Journal of Marriage and Family* 70(3): 783–95.

Fu, Xuanning, and Hatfield, Melanie E. 2008. "Intermarriage and Segmented Assimilation: US-born Asians in 2000." *Journal of Asian American Studies* 11(3): 249–77.

Fugita, Stephen S., and O'Brien, David J. 1977. "Economics, Ideology, and Ethnicity: The Struggle between the United Farm Workers Union and the Nisei Farmers League." *Social Problems* 25(2): 146–56.

Fujino, Diane C. 1997. "The Rates, Patterns and Reasons for Forming Heterosexual Interracial Dating Relationships among Asian Americans." *Journal of Social and Personal Relationships* 14(6): 809–28.

Fujino, Diane C. 2005. *Heartbeat of Struggle: The Revolutionary Life of Yuri Kochiyama.* Minneapolis: University of Minnesota Press.

Fujita-Rony, Dorothy B. 2003. *American Workers, Colonial Power: Philippine Seattle and the Transpacific West, 1919–1941.* Berkeley: University of California Press.

Fujiwara, Lynn. 2008. *Mothers without Citizenship: Asian Immigrant Families and the Consequences of Welfare Reform.* Minneapolis: University of Minnesota Press.

Fuligni, Andrew J., Yip, Tiffany, and Tseng, Vivian. 2002. "The Impact of Family Obligation on the Daily Activities and Psychological Well-being of Chinese American Adolescents." *Child Development* 73(1): 302–14.

Fung, Colleen, and Yung, Judy. 2000. "In Search of the Right Spouse: Interracial Marriage among Chinese and Japanese Americans," in Min Zhou and James V. Gatewood (eds), *Contemporary Asian America: A Multidisciplinary Reader*. New York University Press, pp. 589–605.

Gamburd, Michele. 2002. "Breadwinner No More," in Barbara Ehrenreich and Arlie Russell Hochschild (eds), *Global Women*. New York: Henry Holt and Company, pp. 190–206.

Gamson, William A., Croteau, David, Hoynes, William, and Sasson, Theodore. 1992. "Media Images and the Social Construction of Reality." *Annual Review of Sociology* 18(1): 373–93.

Gans, Herbert J. 1979. "Symbolic Ethnicity: The Future of Ethnic Groups and Cultures in America." *Ethnic and Racial Studies* 2(1): 1–20.

Gans, Herbert J. 1992. "Second-generation Decline: Scenarios for the Economic and Ethnic Futures for the Post-1965 American Immigrants." *Ethnic and Racial Studies* 15(2): 173–92.

Geron, Kim. 2010. "Labor Unions." *Encyclopedia of Asian American Issues Today*, Vol. 1: 135.

Gibson, M. 1988. *Accommodation without Assimilation: Sikh Immigrants in an American High School*. Ithaca: Cornell University Press.

Glazer, Nathan, and Moynihan, Daniel Patrick. 1970. *Beyond the Melting Pot*. Cambridge: Massachusetts Institute of Technology Press.

Glenn, Evelyn N. 2000. "Citizenship and Inequality: Historical and Global Perspectives." *Social Problems* 47(1): 1–20.

Glenn, Evelyn N. 2002. *Unequal Freedom: How Race and Gender Shaped American Citizenship and Labor*. Cambridge: Harvard University Press.

Goffman, Erving. 1959. *The Presentation of Self in Everyday Life*. Garden City: Doubleday.

Goldring, Luin. 2002. "The Mexican State and Transmigrant Organizations: Negotiating the Boundaries of Membership and Participation." *Latin American Research Review* 37(3): 55–99.

Gonzalez, Vernadette V., and Rodriguez, Robyn M. 2003. "Filipina.com: Wives, Workers, and Whores on the Cyberfrontier," in Rachel C. Lee and Sau-ling Cynthia Wong (eds), *Asian America.Net: Ethnicity, Nationalism, and Cyberspace*. New York: Routledge, pp. 215–34.

Gonzales-Backen, Melinda. 2013. "An Application of Ecological Theory to Ethnic Identity Formation among Biethnic Adolescents." *Family Relations* 62(1): 92–108.

Gopinath, Gayatri. 2005. *Impossible Desires: Queer Desire and the South Asian Public Culture*. Durham: Duke University Press.

Gordon, Milton. 1964. *Assimilation in American Life*. New York: Oxford University Press.

Gorman, Jean Cheng. 1998. "Parenting Attitudes and Practices of Immigrant Chinese Mothers of Adolescents." *Family Relations* 47: 73–80.

Gotanda, Neil. 2000. "Comparative Racialization: Racial Profiling and the Case of Wen Ho Lee." *UCLA Law Review* 47: 1689–1702.

Gotanda, Neil. 2001. "Citizenship Nullification: The Impossibility of Asian American Politics," in Gordon H. Chang (ed.), *Asian Americans and Politics: Perspectives, Experiences, Prospects*. Washington, DC: Woodrow Wilson Center, pp. 79–101.

Grasgreen, Allie. 2011. "The Mocked Minority," *Inside Higher Education*, March 22. Accessed May 18, 2013 at www.insidehighered.com/news/2011/03/22/ucla_student_s_youtube_video_illustrates_many_asian_racial_stereotypes.

Grossman, Susan F., and Lundy, Marta. 2007. "Domestic Violence Across Race and Ethnicity Implications for Social Work Practice and Policy." *Violence against Women* 13(10): 1029–52.

Guarnizo, Eduardo Luis, Portes, Alejandro, and Haller, William. 2003. "Assimilation and Transnationalism: Determinants of Transnational Political Action among Contemporary Migrants." *American Journal of Sociology* 108(6): 1211–48.

Guevarra, Anna Romina. 2010. *Marketing Dreams, Manufacturing Heroes: The Transnational Labor Brokering of Filipino Workers*. New Brunswick, NJ: Rutgers University Press.

Habal, Estella. 2007. *San Francisco's International Hotel: Mobilizing the Filipino American Community in the Anti-eviction Movement*. Philadelphia: Temple University Press.

Hagedorn, Jessica. 2000. "Asian Women in Film: No Joy, No Luck," in Timothy P. Fong and Larry

Hajime Shinagawa (eds), *Asian Americans: Experiences and Perspectives*. Upper Saddle River, NJ: Prentice Hall, pp. 264–9.

Hagland, Paul. 1998. "Undressing the Oriental Boy: The Gay Asian in the Social Imaginary of the Gay White Male," in Dawn Atkins (ed.), *Looking Queer: Body Image and Identity in Lesbian, Bisexual, Gay, and Transgender Communities*. Binghamton: Haworth Press, pp. 277–94.

Hahm, Hyeouk and Adkins, Chris. 2009. "A Model of Asian and Pacific Islander Sexual Minority Acculturation." *Journal of LGBT Youth* 6(2–3): 155–73.

Hahm, Chris Hyeouk, Lahiff, Maureen, and Barreto, Rose M. 2006. "Asian American Adolescents' First Sexual Intercourse: Gender and Acculturation Differences." *Perspectives on Sexual and Reproductive Health* 38(1): 28–36.

Hajnal, Zoltan, and Trounstine, Jessica. 2005. "Where Turnout Matters: The Consequences of Uneven Turnout in City Politics." *The Journal of Politics* 67(2): 515–35.

Hall, Stuart. 1990. "Cultural Identity and Diaspora," in J. Rutherford (ed.), *Identity: Community, Culture, Difference*. London: Lawrence and Wishart.

Hamamoto, Darrell Y., and Liu, Sandra. 2000. *Countervisions: Asian American Film Criticism*. Philadelphia: Temple University Press.

Hargittai, Eszter. 2010. "Digital Na(t)ives? Variation in Internet Skills and Uses among Members of the 'Net Generation'" *Sociological Inquiry* 80(1): 92–113.

Hiatt, Brian. 2012. "Psy: The First Wave of the Asian Invasion." *Rolling Stone*, December 20.

Hidalgo, Danielle Antoinette, and Bankston, Carl L. 2008. "Military Brides and Refugees: Vietnamese American Wives and Shifting Links to the Military, 1980–2000." *International Migration* 46(2): 167–85.

Hidalgo, Danielle Antoinette, and Bankston, Carl L. 2010. "Blurring Racial and Ethnic Boundaries in Asian American Families: Asian American Family Patterns, 1980–2005." *Journal of Family Issues* 31(3): 280–300.

Hing, Bill Ong. 1993. *Making and Remaking Asian America through Immigration Policy*. Palo Alto, CA: Stanford University Press.

Hing, Bill Ong. 2000. *To Be An American: Cultural Pluralism and the Rhetoric of Assimilation*. New York: New York University Press.

Hinsch, Bret. 1990. *Passions of the Cut Sleeve*. Berkeley: University of California Press.

Hintzen, Percy. 2001. *West Indian in the West: Self-Representations in an Immigrant Community*. New York: New York University Press.

Hirschman, Charles, and Snipp, C. Matthew. 2001. "The State of the American Dream: Race and Ethnic Socioeconomic Inequality in the United States, 1970–1990," in D. B. Grusky (ed.), *Social Stratification*, Boulder, CO: Westview, pp. 623–42.

Hirschman, Charles, and Wong, Morrison G. 1984. "Socioeconomic Gains of Asian Americans, Blacks, and Hispanics: 1960–1976." *American Journal of Sociology* 90(3): 584–607.

Ho, Fred. 1999. "Beyond Asian American Jazz: My Musical and Political Changes in the Asian American Movement." *Leonardo Music Journal* 9(1): 45–51.

Ho, Pensri. 2003. "Performing the 'Oriental': Professionals Who Problematize the Asian Model Minority Myth." *Journal of Asian American Studies* 6(2): 149–75.

Hoang, Nguyen Tan. 2004. "The Resurrection of Brandon Lee: The Making of a Gay Asian American Porn Star," in Linda Williams (ed.), *Porn Studies*. Durham: Duke University Press, pp. 223–70.

Hochschild, Arlie Russell. 1989. *The Second Shift: Working Parents and the Revolution at Home*. New York: Viking.

Hochschild, Arlie Russell. 2002. "Love and Gold," in Barbara Ehrenreich and Arlie Russell Hochschild (eds), *Global Women*. New York: Henry Holt and Company, pp. 15–30.

Hogg, Michael A., Terry, Deborah J., and White, Katherine M. 1995. "A Tale of Two Theories: A Critical Comparison of Identity Theory with Social Identity Theory." *Social Psychology Quarterly* 58(4): 255–69.

Hollinger, Joan H. 2004. "Intercountry Adoption: Forecasts and Forebodings." *Adoption Quarterly* 8(1): 41–60.

Hom, Alice Y. 2000a. "Asian American Women's Organizations: Notes on Issue-Oriented Organizing." *Journal of Asian American Studies* 3(2): 231–6.

Hom, Alice Y. 2000b. "Stories from the Homefront: Perspectives of Asian American Parents with Lesbian Daughters and Gay Sons," in Min Zhou and James V. Gatewood (eds), *Contemporary Asian America: A Multidisciplinary Reader*. New York University Press, pp. 561–71.

Hondagneu-Sotelo, Pierrette. 2007. *Domestica: Immigrant Workers Cleaning and Caring in the Shadows of Affluence*. Berkeley: University of California Press.

Hong, Ying-yi, Wan, Ching, No, Sun, and Chiu, Chi-yue. 2007. "Multicultural Identities," in S. Kitayama and D. Cohen (eds), *Handbook of Cultural Psychology*. New York: Guilford Press, pp. 323–45.

Hsu, Hua. 2012. "Everyone Else's Jeremy Lin." *Amerasia Journal* 38(3): 126–9.

Hu-DeHart, Evelyn. 1999. *Across the Pacific: Asian Americans and Globalization*. New York: Asia Society.

Huh, Nam Soon. 2007. "Korean Adopted Children's Ethnic Identity Formation," in Kathleen Ja Sook Bergquist, M. Elizabeth Vonk, Dong Soo Kim, and Marvin D. Feit (eds), *International Korean Adoption: A Fifty-Year History of Policy and Practice*. Binghamton: Haworth Press, pp. 79–97.

Hum, Tarry. 2002. *Redistricting and the New Demographics*. New York University and Queens College. New York: A/P/A Studies Working Paper.

Hune, Shirley. 2002. "Demographics and Diversity of Asian American College Students," in Marylu K. McEwen, Corinne Maekawa Kodama, Alvin N. Alvarez, Sunny Lee, and Christopher T. H. Liang (eds), *Working with Asian American College Students*. San Francisco: Wiley Periodicals, pp. 11–20.

Hune, Shirley, and Nomura, Gail M. (eds). 2003. *Asian/Pacific Islander American Women: A Historical Anthology*. New York: New York University Press.

Hunt, G., Moloney, M., and Evans, K. 2011. "'How Asian Am I?': Asian American Youth Cultures, Drug Use, and Ethnic Identity Construction." *Youth & Society* 43(1): 274–304.

Hurh, Won Moo, and Kim, Kwang Chung. 1989. "The 'Success' Image of Asian Americans: Its Validity, and its Practical and Theoretical Implications." *Ethnic and Racial Studies* 12(4): 512–38.

Hwang, Sean-Shong, Saenz, Rogelio, and Aguirre, Benigno E. 1997. "Structural and Assimilationist Explanations of Asian American Intermarriage." *Journal of Marriage and Family* 59(3): 758–72.

Ignatiev, Noel. 1995. *How the Irish Became White*. New York: Routledge.

Ima, Kenji, and Rumbaut, Rubén. 1995. "Southeast Asian Refugees in American Schools: A Comparison of Fluent English-proficient and Limited-English Proficient Students," in Don Nakanishi and Tina Yamano Nishida (eds), *The Asian American Educational Experience: A Source Book for Teachers and Students*. New York: Routledge, pp. 180–97.

Islam, Naheed. 1998. "Naming Desire, Shaping Identity: Tracing the Experiences of Indian Lesbians in the United States," in Shamita Das Dasgupta (ed.), *A Patchwork Shawl: Chronicles of South Asian Women in America*. New Brunswick, NJ: Rutgers University Press, pp. 72–96.

Iwamura, Jane Naomi. 2005. "The Oriental Monk in American Popular Culture," in Bruce Forbes and Jeffrey Mahan (eds), *Religion and Popular Culture in America*. Berkeley, CA: University of California Press, pp. 25–43.

Iyer, Deepa. 2010. "South Asians in a Post-9/11th Environment," in Edith Wen-Chu Chen (ed.), *Encyclopedia of Asian American Issues Today*, Vol. 1. Westport, CT: Greenwood Press, pp. 527–34.

Jacobs, Jerry, and Labov, Teresa. 2002. "Gender Differences in Intermarriage Among Sixteen Race and Ethnic Groups." *Sociological Forum* 17: 621–46.

Jacobson, Robin Dale. 2008. *The New Nativism: Proposition 187 and the Debate over Immigration*. Minneapolis: University of Minnesota.

Jang, Seung-Jing. 2009. "Get Out on Behalf of Your Group: Electoral Participation of Latinos and Asian Americans." *Political Behavior* 31: 511–35.

Jenkins, J. Craig. 1983. "Resource Mobilization Theory and the Study of Social Movements." *Annual Review of Sociology* 9(1): 527–53.

Jenkins, Richard. 1994. "Rethinking Ethnicity: Identity, Categorization and Power." *Ethnic and Racial Studies* 17(2): 197–219.

Jeung, Russell. 2004. *Faithful Generations: Race and New Asian American Churches*. New Brunswick, NJ: Rutgers University Press.

Johnson, Kristen E., Swim, Janet K., Saltsman, Brian M., Deater-Deckard, Kirby, and Petrill, Stephen

A. 2007. "Mothers? Racial, Ethnic, and Cultural Socialization of Transracially Adopted Asian Children." *Family Relations* 56(4): 390–402.

Jung, Moon-Ho. 2005. "Outlawing 'Coolies': Race, Nation, and Empire in the Age of Emancipation." *American Quarterly* 57(3): 677–701.

Jung, Moon-Kie. 2003. "Interracialism: The Ideological Transformation of Hawaii's Working Class." *American Sociological Review* 68(3): 373–400.

Kallivayalil, Diya. 2007. "Feminist Therapy." *Women & Therapy* 30(3–4): 109–27.

Kang, Miliann. 2010. *The Managed Hand: Race, Gender, and the Body in Beauty Service Work*. Berkeley: University of California Press.

Kao, Grace. 2004. "Parental Influences on the Educational Outcomes of Immigrant Youth." *International Migration Review* 38(2): 427–49.

Kao, Grace, and Tienda, Marta. 1995. "Optimism and Achievement: The Educational Performance of Immigrant Youth." *Social Science Quarterly* 76: 1–19.

Kao, Grace, Vaquera, Elizabeth, and Goyette, Kimberly. 2013. *Education and Immigration*. Cambridge: Polity Press.

Kasinitz, Philip, Mollenkopf, John H., Waters, Mary C., and Holdaway, Jennifer. 2009. *Inheriting the City: The Children of Immigrants Come of Age*. New York: Russell Sage Foundation Publication.

Kasinitz, Philip, Waters, Mary C., Mollenkopf, John H., and Aniel, Merih. 2002. "Transnationalism and the Children of Immigrants in Contemporary New York," in Peggy Levitt and Mary C. Waters (eds), *The Changing Face of Home: The Transnational Lives of the Second Generation*. New York: Russell Sage Foundation, pp. 96–122.

Kiang, Lisa, and Fuligni, Andrew J. 2009. "Ethnic Identity and Family Processes among Adolescents from Latin American, Asian, and European Backgrounds." *Journal of Youth and Adolescence* 8(2): 228–41.

Kibria, Nazli. 1993. *Family Tightrope: The Changing Lives of Vietnamese Americans*. Princeton University Press.

Kibria, Nazli. 1996. "Not Asian, Black or White? Reflections on South Asian American Racial Identity." *Amerasia Journal* 22(2): 77–86.

Kibria, Nazli. 2002. *Becoming Asian American: Second-Generation Chinese and Korean American Identities*. Baltimore: Johns Hopkins University Press.

Kibria, Nazli. 2011. *Muslims in Motion: Islam and National Identity in the Bangladeshi Diaspora*. New Brunswick, NJ: Rutgers University Press.

Kim, Claire Jean. 1999. "The Racial Triangulation of Asian Americans." *Politics & Society* 27(1): 105–38.

Kim, Dae Young. 2006. "Stepping-Stone to Intergenerational Mobility? The Springboard, Safety Net, or Mobility Trap Functions of Korean Immigrant Entrepreneurship for the Second Generation." *International Migration Review* 40(4): 927–62.

Kim, Jean. 2001. "Asian American Identity Development Theory," in Charmaine L. Wijeyesinghe and Bailey W. Jackson III (eds), *New Perspectives on Racial Identity Development: A Theoretical and Practical Anthology*. New York: New York University Press, pp. 67–90.

Kim, Jodi. 2009. "An 'Orphan' with Two Mothers: Transnational and Transracial Adoption, the Cold War, and Contemporary Asian American Cultural Politics." *American Quarterly* 61(4): 855–80.

Kim, Kwang Chung, Hurh, Won Moo, and Fernandez, Marilyn. 1989. "Intra-group Differences in Business Participation: Three Asian Immigrant Groups." *International Migration Review* 23(1): 73–95.

Kim, Marlene. 2009. "Race and Gender Differences in the Earnings of Black Workers." *Industrial Relations* 48(3): 466–88.

Kim, Nadia Y. 2008. *Imperial Citizens: Koreans and Race from Seoul to LA*. Stanford, CA: Stanford University Press.

Kim, Rebecca Y. 2004. "Second-Generation Korean American Evangelicals: Ethnic, Multiethnic, or White Campus Ministries?" *Sociology of Religion* 65(1): 19–34.

Kim, Richard S. 2006. "Inaugurating the American Century: The 1919 Philadelphia Korean Congress,

Korean Diasporic Nationalism, and American Protestant Missionaries." *Journal of American Ethnic History* 26(1): 50–76.

Kim, Sharon. 2010. "Shifting Boundaries within Second-Generation Korean American Churches." *Sociology of Religion* 71(1): 98–122.

Kim, Minjeong, and Chung, Angie Y. 2005. "Consuming Orientalism: Images of Asian/American Women in Multicultural Advertising." *Qualitative Sociology* 28(1): 67–91.

Kim, Young K., Chang, Mitchell J., and Park, Julie J. 2009. "Engaging with Faculty: Examining Rates, Predictors, and Educational Effects for Asian American Undergraduates." *Journal of Diversity in Higher Education* 2(4): 206–18.

Kimmel, Douglas C., and Yi, Huso. 2004. "Characteristics of Gay, Lesbian, and Bisexual Asians, Asian Americans, and Immigrants from Asia to the USA." *Journal of Homosexuality* 47(2): 143–72.

Kimmel, Michael S. 1996. *Manhood in America: A Cultural History*. New York: Free Press.

King-O'Riain, Rebecca Chiyoko. 2006. *Pure Beauty: Judging Race in Japanese American Beauty Pageants*. Minneapolis: University of Minnesota Press.

Kitano, Harry. 1969. *Japanese Americans: The Evolution of a Subculture*. Englewood Cliffs: Prentice-Hall.

Kitano, Harry H. L., and Daniels, Roger. 2001. *Asian Americans: Emerging Minorities*. Englewood Cliffs, NJ: Prentice Hall.

Kivisto, Peter. 2005. *Incorporating Diversity: Rethinking Assimilation in a Multicultural Age*. Paradigm Publisher.

Kondo, Dorinne. 1996. "The Narrative Production of 'Home,' Community, and Political Identity in Asian American Theater," in Smadar Lavie and Ted Swedenburg (eds), *Displacement, Diaspora, and Geographies of Identity*. Durham: Duke University Press, pp. 97–118.

Krysan, Maria. 2000. "Prejudice, Politics, and Public Opinion: Understanding the Sources of Racial Policy Attitudes." *Annual Review of Sociology* 26(1): 135–68.

Kumashiro, Kevin. 2003. *Restoried Selves: Autobiographies of Queer Asian/Pacific American Activists*. New York: Routledge.

Kurashige, Scott. 2000. "Pan-ethnicity and Community Organizing: Asian Americans United's Campaign against Anti-Asian Violence." *Journal of Asian American Studies* 3(2): 163–90.

Kurien, Prema A. 2003. "To Be or Not to Be South Asian: Contemporary Indian American Politics." *Journal of Asian American Studies* 6(3): 261–88.

Kurien, Prema A. 2007. *A Place at the Multicultural Table: The Development of an American Hinduism*. New Brunswick: Rutgers University Press.

Kwon, Soo Ah. 2004. "Autoexoticizing: Asian American Youth and the Import Car Scene." *Journal of Asian American Studies* 7(1): 1–26.

Kwong, Peter. 1995. "Asian American Studies Needs Class Analysis," in Gary Ohihiro, Marilyn Alquizola, Dorothy Fujita Rony, and Scott K. Wong (eds), *Privileging Positions: The Sites of Asian American Studies*. Pullman: Washington State University Press, pp. 75–81.

LaBrack, Bruce, and Leonard, Karen. 1984. "Conflict and Compatibility in Punjabi–Mexican Immigrant Families in Rural California, 1915–1965." *Journal of Marriage and the Family* 46(3): 527–37.

Lai, James S., Tam Cho, Wendy K., Kim, Thomas P., and Takeda, Okiyoshi. 2001. "Asian Pacific-American Campaigns, Elections, and Elected Officials." *Political Science and Politics* 3: 611–17.

Lau, Anna S., Takeuchi, David T., and Alegría, Margarita. 2006. "Parent-to-Child Aggression among Asian American Parents: Culture, Context, and Vulnerability." *Journal of Marriage and Family* 68(5): 1261–75.

Le, C. N. 2012. "New Dimensions of Self-Employment among Asian Americans in Los Angeles and New York." *AAPI Nexus: Asian Americans & Pacific Islanders Policy, Practice and Community* 10(2): 55–75.

Lee, Ambrose. 2010. "Low Income Workers," in Edith Wen-Chu Chen and Grace J. Yoo (eds), *Encyclopedia of Asian American Issues Today*. Santa Barbara: Greenwood Press, pp. 143–8.

Lee, Erika. 2005. "Orientalisms in the Americas: A Hemispheric Approach to Asian American History." *Journal of Asian American Studies* 8(3): 235–56.

Lee, Hee Yun. 2010. "Family Violence," in Edith Wen-Chu Chen and Grace J. Yoo (eds), *Encyclopedia of Asian American Issues Today*. Santa Barbara: Greenwood Press, pp. 889–900.

Lee, Jee Yeun. 1996. "Why Suzie Wong is not a Lesbian: Asian and Asian American Lesbian and Bisexual Women and Femme/Butch/Gender Identities," in Brett Beemyn and Mickey Eliason (eds), *Queer Studies: A Lesbian, Gay, Bisexual, and Transgender Anthology*. New York: New York University Press, pp. 115–32.

Lee, Jennifer. 2002. *Civility in the City: Blacks, Jews, and Koreans in Urban America*. Cambridge: Harvard University Press.

Lee, Jennifer. 2006. "Constructing Race and Civility in Urban America." *Urban Studies* 43(5–6): 903–17.

Lee, Robert G. 1999. *Orientals: Asian Americans in Popular Culture*. Philadelphia: Temple University Press.

Lee, Stacey. 2004. "Up against Whiteness: Students of Color in our Schools." *Anthropology & Education Quarterly* 35(1): 121–5.

Lee, Clark, and Tseng, Tommy. 2010. "Judy Chu for Congress: A Case Study for Mobilizing Asian Americans and Pacific Islanders for Legislative Campaigns." *Harvard Journal of Asian American Policy Review* 19: 49–58.

Lee, Jennifer, and Bean, Frank. 2007. "Reinventing the Color Line: Immigration and America's New Racial/Ethnic Divide." *Social Forces* 86(2): 561–86.

Lee, Joohee, Pomeroy, Elizabeth C., and Bohman, Tom M. 2007. "Intimate Partner Violence and Psychological Health in a Sample of Asian and Caucasian Women: The Roles of Social Support and Coping." *Journal of Family Violence* 22(8): 709–20.

Leong, Frederick T. L., and Grand, James A. 2008. "Career and Work Implications of the Model Minority Myth and Other Stereotypes for Asian Americans," in Guofang Li and Lihshing Wang (eds), *Model Minority Myth Revisited: An Interdisciplinary Approach to Demystifying Asian American Educational Experiences*. Charlotte, NC: Information Age Publishing, pp. 91–114.

Leong, Russell. 1995. *Asian American Sexualities: Dimensions of the Gay and Lesbian Experience*. New York: Routledge.

Lessinger, J. 1995. *From the Ganges to the Hudson: Indian Immigrants in New York City*. Needham Heights: Allyn & Bacon.

Leung, Kwok, Lau, Sing, and Lam, Wai-Lim. 1998. "Parenting Styles and Academic Achievement: A Cross-cultural Study." *Merrill Palmer Quarterly* 44: 157–72.

Levitt, Peggy. 2009. "Roots and Routes: Understanding the Lives of the Second Generation Transnationally." *Journal of Ethnic and Migration Studies* 35(7): 1225–42.

Levitt, Peggy, and Waters, Mary C. 2002. "The Ties that Change: Relations to the Ancestral Home over the Life Cycle," in Peggy Levitt and Mary C. Waters (eds), *Changing Face of Home: The Transnational Lives of the Second Generation*. New York: Russell Sage Foundation, pp. 123–44.

Lew, Jamie. 2006. *Asian Americans in Class: Charting the Achievement Gap among Korean American Youth*. New York: Teachers College.

Lien, Pei-te. 2008. "Homeland Origins and Political Identities among Chinese in Southern California." *Ethnic and Racial Studies* 31(8): 1381–1403.

Lien, Pei-te, Conway, M. Margaret, and Wong, Janelle. 2004. *The Politics of Asian Americans: Diversity and Community*. New York: Routledge Press.

Light, Ivan. 1973. *Ethnic Enterprise in America: Business and Welfare among Chinese, Japanese and Blacks*. Berkeley, CA: University of California Press.

Lim, P. See, Barry-Goodman, Colleen, and Branham, David 2006. "Discrimination That Travels: How Ethnicity Affects Party Identification for Southeast Asian Immigrants." *Social Science Quarterly* 87(5): 1158–68.

Lim, Shirley Jennifer. 2004. "'Hell's a Poppin': Asian American Women's Youth Consumer Culture," in Jennifer Lee and Min Zhou (eds), *Asian American Youth: Culture, Identity, and Ethnicity*. New York: Routledge, pp. 101–12.

Lipsitz, George. 1998. *The Possessive Investment in Whiteness: How White People Profit from Identity Politics*. Philadelphia: Temple University Press.

Liu, Eric. 1998. *The Accidental Asian: Notes of a Native Speaker.* New York: Random House.

Liu, Haiming, and Lin, Lianlian. 2009. "Food, Culinary Identity, and Transnational Culture: Chinese Restaurant Business in Southern California." *Journal of Asian American Studies* 2(2): 135–62.

Liu, Lisa L., Benner, Aprile D., Lau, Anna S., and Yeong Kim, Su. 2009. "Mother–Adolescent Language Proficiency and Adolescent Academic and Emotional Adjustment among Chinese American Families." *Journal of Youth and Adolescence* 38(4): 572–86.

Liu, Michael, Geron, Kim, and Lai, Tracy 2008. *The Snake Dance of Asian American Activism: Community, Vision, and Power.* Lanham, MD: Lexington Books.

Locke, Brian. 2008. "*Strange Fruit*: White, Black, and Asian in the World War II Combat Film *Bataan*." *Journal of Popular Film and Television* 36(1): 9–20.

Loewen, James W. 1971. *The Mississippi Chinese: Between Black and White.* Cambridge: Harvard University Press.

Lopez, Lori Kido. 2012a. "Fan Activists and the Politics of Race in *The Last Airbender*." *International Journal of Cultural Studies* 15(5): 431–45.

Lopez, Lori Kido. 2012b. "The Yellow Press: Asian American Radicalism and Conflict in Gidra," *Journal of Communication Inquiry* 35(3): 235–51.

Louie, Andrea. 2002. "Creating Histories for the Present: Second-Generation (Re)definitions of Chinese American Culture," in Peggy Levitt and Mary C. Waters (eds), *The Changing Face of Home: The Transnational Lives of the Second Generation.* New York: Russell Sage Foundation, pp. 312–40.

Louie, Andrea. 2009. "'Pandas, Lions, and Dragons, Oh My!': How White Adoptive Parents Construct Chineseness." *Journal of Asian American Studies* 12(3): 285–320.

Louie, Vivian. 2004. *Compelled to Excel: Immigration, Education, and Opportunity among Chinese Americans.* Palo Alto: Stanford University Press.

Louie, Vivian. 2006. "Second-Generation Pessimism and Optimism: How Chinese and Dominicans Understand Education and Mobility through Ethnic and Transnational Orientations." *International Migration Review* 40(3): 537–72.

Louie, Vivian S. 2012. *Keeping the Immigrant Bargain: The Costs and Rewards of Success in America.* New York: Russell Sage Foundation Publications.

Lovett, Ian. 2011. "UCLA Student's Video Rant against Asians Fuels Firestorm." *New York Times,* March 16.

Lowe, Lisa. 1996. *Immigrant Acts: On Asian American Cultural Politics.* Durham: Duke University Press.

Lowe, Lisa. 1998. "The International within the National: American Studies and Asian American Critique." *Cultural Critique* 40: 29–47.

Luibhéid, Eithne. 2002. *Entry Denied: Controlling Sexuality at the Border.* Minneapolis: University of Minnesota Press.

Macfie, Alexander Lyon. 2000. *Orientalism: A Reader.* Edinburgh: Edinburgh University Press.

MacKaye, Milton. 1958. "US Congressman from Asia." *Saturday Evening Post,* 2 August: 25–56.

MacLeod, Jay. 1995. *Ain't No Makin' It: Aspirations and Attainment in a Low-income Neighborhood.* Boulder, CO: Westview Press.

Maeda, Daryl J. 2009. *Chains of Babylon: The Rise of Asian America.* Minneapolis: University of Minnesota Press.

Magpantay, Glenn D. 2006. "The Ambivalence of Queer Asian Pacific Americans Toward Same-Sex Marriage." *Amerasia Journal* 32(1): 109–18.

Mahler, Sarah J. 1995. *American Dreaming: Immigrant Life on the Margins.* Princeton: Princeton University Press.

Maira, Sunaina. 1998. "Desis Reprazent: Bhangra Remix and Hip Hop in New York City." *Postcolonial Studies: Culture, Politics, Economy* 1(3): 357–70.

Maira, Sunaina. 2002. *Desis in the House: Indian American Youth Culture in NYC.* Philadelphia: Temple University Press.

Maira, Sunaina Marr. 2009. *Missing: Youth, Citizenship, and Empire after 9/11.* Durham: Duke University Press Books.

Malkin, Michelle. 2004. *In Defense of Internment: The Case for "Racial Profiling" in World War II and the War on Terror*. Washington, DC: Regnery Publishing.

Manalansan, Martin F. 2003. *Global Divas: Filipino Gay Men in the Diaspora*. Durham: Duke University Press.

Manalansan, Martin F. 2006. "Queer Intersections: Sexuality and Gender in Migration Studies." *International Migration Review* 40(1): 224–49.

Mannur, Anita. 2010. *Culinary Fictions: Food in South Asian Diasporic Culture*. Philadelphia: Temple University Press.

Marger, M. 1995. *Race and Ethnic Relations: American and Global Perspectives*. Belmont: Wadsworth Publishing.

Marshall, T. H. 1964. *Class, Citizenship, and Social Development: Essays*. Garden City: Doubleday.

Martin, Karin A. 1998. "Becoming a Gendered Body: Practices of Preschools." *American Sociological Review* 63(4): 494–511.

Mastro, Dana E., and Stern, Susannah R. 2003. "Representations of Race in Television Commercials: A Content Analysis of Prime Time Television." *Journal of Broadcasting and Electronic Media* 47(4): 638–47.

Matloff, Norman. 2003. "On the Need for Reform of the H1B Nonimmigrant Work Visa in Computer-related Occupations." *University of Michigan Journal of Law Reform* 36(4): 815–914.

McCall, George J., and Simmons, Jerry Laird. 1978. *Identities and Interactions*. New York: Free Press.

McChesney, Robert W. 2012. "Farewell to Journalism." *Journalism Studies* 13(5–6): 682–94.

McDermott, R. 2000. "New Age Hinduism, New Age Orientalism, and the Second Generation South Asian." *Journal of the American Academy of Religion* 68(4): 721–31.

McGurn, William. 1991. "The Silent Minority." *The National Review*, June 24: 19–20.

McIntosh, Peggy. 1988. Working Paper No. 189, Wellesley College Center for Research on Women, Wellesley, MA 02181.

McKay, Steven. 2007. "Filipino Sea Men: Constructing Masculinities in an Ethnic Labour Niche." *Journal of Ethnic and Migration Studies* 33(4): 617–33.

Mead, George Herbert. 1934. *Mind, Self and Society*. Chicago: University of Chicago Press.

Melamed, Jodi. 2006. "The Spirit of Neoliberalism: From Racial Liberalism to Neoliberal Multiculturalism." *Social Text* 24(4 89): 1–25.

Melendy, H. Brett.1977. *Asians in America: Filipinos, Koreans, and East Indians*. Boston: Twayne Press.

Meyer, David S. 2004. "Protest and Political Opportunities." *Annual Review of Sociology* 30(1): 125–45.

Meyers, Jessica. 2006. "Pho and Apple Pie: Eden Center as a Representation of Vietnamese American Ethnic Identity in the Washington, DC Metropolitan Area, 1975-2005." *Journal of Asian American Studies* 9(1): 55–85.

Midlarsky, Elizabeth, Venkataramani-Kothari, Anitha, and Plante, Maura. 2006. "Domestic Violence in the Chinese and South Asian Immigrant Communities." *Annals of the New York Academy of Sciences* 1087(1): 279–300.

Mills, C. Wright. 1959. *The Sociological Imagination*. Oxford: Oxford University Press.

Min, Pyong Gap. 1996. *Caught in the Middle: Korean Communities in New York and Los Angeles*. Berkeley: University of California Press.

Min, Pyong Gap. 2006. *Asian Americans: Contemporary Trends and Issues*, 2nd edn. Thousand Oaks, CA: Pine Forge Press.

Min, Pyong Gap. 2008. *Ethnic Solidarity for Economic Survival: Korean Greengrocers in New York City*. New York: Russell Sage Foundation Publications.

Min, Pyong Gap. 2010. *Preserving Ethnicity through Religion in America: Korean Protestants and Indian Hindus across Generations*. New York: New York University Press.

Min, Pyong Gap, and Kim, Chigon. 2009. "Patterns of Intermarriages and Cross-Generational In-Marriages among Native-Born Asian Americans." *International Migration Review* 43(3): 447–70.

Min, Pyong Gap, and Kim, Rose. 1999. *Struggle for Ethnic Identity: Narratives by Asian American Professionals*. Walnut Creek: AltaMira Press.

Mir, Shabana. 2011. "'Just to Make Sure People Know I Was Born Here': Muslim Women Constructing American Selves." *Discourse: Studies in the Cultural Politics of Education* 32(4): 547–63.

Misir, Deborah N. 2000. "The Murder of Navroze Mody: Race, Violence, and the Search for Order," in Min Zhou and James V. Gatewood (eds), *Contemporary Asian America: A Multidisciplinary Reader*. New York: New York University Press, pp. 501–17.

Mitra, Diditi. 2008. "Punjabi American Taxi Drivers: The New White Working Class?" *Journal of Asian American Studies* 11(3): 303–36.

Model, Suzanne. 1985. "A Comparative Perspective on the Ethnic Enclave: Blacks, Italians, and Jews in New York City." *International Migration Review* 19(1): 64–81.

Model, Suzanne. 1992. "The Ethnic Economy." *The Sociological Quarterly* 33(1): 63–82.

Mok, Teresa A. 1999. "Asian American Dating: Important Factors in Partner Choice." *Cultural Diversity and Ethnic Minority Psychology* 5(2): 103–17.

Musikawong, Sudarat, and Martorell, Chanchanit. 2012. "The Importance of Ethnic Competency: The Thai Case of Labor Trafficking and Temporary Worker Visa Immigration/Migrations." *AAPI Nexus: Asian Americans and Pacific Islanders Policy, Practice and Community* 10(1): 59–74.

Naber, Nadine C. 2002. "'So Our History Doesn't Become Your Future: The Local and Global Politics of Coalition Building Post September 11th.'" *Journal of Asian American Studies* 5(3): 217–42.

Nagel, Joane. 1994. "Constructing Ethnicity: Creating and Recreating Ethnic Identity and Culture." *Social Problems* 41(1): 152–76.

Nagel, Joane. 2003. *Race, Ethnicity, and Sexuality: Intimate Intersections, Forbidden Frontiers*. New York: Oxford University Press.

Nakanishi, Don T. 1985. "Asian American Politics: An Agenda for Research." *Amerasia Journal* 12(20): 1–27.

Nakanishi, Don T., and Lai, James S. (eds). 2003. *Asian American Politics: Law, Participation, and Policy*. Lanham, MD: Rowman & Littlefield Press.

Namkung, Victoria Kerry. 2004. "Reinventing the Wheel: Import Car Racing in Southern California," in Jennifer Lee and Min Zhou (eds), *Asian American Youth: Culture, Identity, and Ethnicity*. New York: Routledge, pp. 159–76.

Nash, Phil T. 2010. "March on Washington: A History of Asian Pacific Americans' Growing Political Power in the Nation's Capital." *Harvard Journal of Asian American Policy Review* 19: 27–37.

Neckerman, Kathryn M., Carter, Prudence, and Lee, Jennifer. 1999. "Segmented Assimilation and Minority Cultures of Mobility." *Ethnic and Racial Studies* 22(6): 945–65.

Nee, Victor, Sanders, Jimy, and Sernau, Scott. 1994. "Job Transitions in an Immigrant Metropolis: Ethnic Boundaries and the Mixed Economy." *American Sociological Review* 59(6): 849–72.

Nemoto, Kumiko. 2006. "Intimacy, Desire, and the Construction of Self in Relationships between Asian American Women and White American Men." *Journal of Asian American Studies* 9(1): 27–54.

Newman, David M. 2006. *Identities and Inequalities: Exploring the Intersections of Race, Class, Gender, and Sexuality*. Boston: McGraw-Hill.

Ng, Mark Tristan. 2004. "Searching for Home: Voices of Gay Asian American Youth in West Hollywood," in Min Zhou and Jennifer Lee (eds), *Asian American Youth: Culture, Identity, and Ethnicity*. New York: Routledge, pp. 269–83.

Ng, Wendy L. 2002. *Japanese American Internment during World War II: A History and Reference Guide*. Westport, CT: Greenwood Press.

Ngai, Mae. 1999. "The Architecture of Race in American Immigration Law: A Reexamination of the Immigration Act of 1924." *The Journal of American History* 86(1): 67–92.

Ngai, Mae M. 2004. *Impossible Subjects: Illegal Aliens and the Making of Modern America*. Princeton: Princeton University Press.

Ngo, Fiona, and Lam, Miriam. 2012. "Southeast Asian/American Studies Special Issue Guest Editors' Introduction," *positions: east asia cultures critique* 20(3): 671–84.

Nguyen, Tram. 2005. *We are All Suspects Now: Untold Stories from Immigrant Communities after 9/11*. Boston: Beacon Press.

Nguyen, Tuyen D. 2004. "Vietnamese Women and Domestic Violence: A Qualitative Examination." *The Qualitative Report* 9(3): 435–48.

Nguyen, Viet Thanh. 2002. *Race and Resistance: Literature & Politics in Asian America.* New York: Oxford University Press.

Oberschall, A. 1978. "Theories of Social Conflict." *Annual Review of Sociology* 4(1): 291–315.

Oda, Alan, and Yoo, Grace. 2010. "Youth, Family, and the Aged," in Edith Wen-Chu Chen and Grace J. Yoo (eds), *Encyclopedia of Asian American Issues Today.* Santa Barbara: Greenwood Press, pp. 841–9.

Ogbu, John U. 1987a. "Variability in Minority School Performance: A Problem in Search of an Explanation." *Anthropology & Education Quarterly* 18(4): 312–34.

Ogbu, John U. 1987b. "Variability in Minority Responses to Schooling: Nonimmigrants vs. Immigrant," in Louise Spindler (ed.), *Interpretive Ethnography of Education at Home and Abroad.* New York: Psychology Press, pp. 255–80.

Ogbu, John and Simons, H. D. 1998. "Voluntary and Involuntary Minorities: A Cultural-Ecological Theory of School Performance with Some Implications for Education." *Anthropology and Education Quarterly* 29(2): 155–88.

Okada, Jun. 2009. "'Noble and Uplifting and Boring as Hell': Asian American Film and Video, 1971–1982." *Cinema Journal* 49(1): 20–40.

Okamoto, Dina G. 2006. "Institutional Panethnicity: Boundary Formation in Asian-American Organizing." *Social Forces* 85(1): 1–25.

Okamoto, Dina. 2007. "Marrying Out: A Boundary Approach to Understanding the Marital Integration of Asian Americans." *Social Science Research* 36(4): 1391–414.

Okamoto, Dina, and Ebert, Kim. 2010. "Beyond the Ballot: Immigrant Collective Action in Gateways and New Destinations in the United States." *Social Problems* 57(4): 529–58.

Okamura, Jonathan Y. 2011. "Barack Obama as the Post-Racial Candidate for a Post-Racial America: Perspectives from Asian America and Hawai'i." *Patterns of Prejudice* 45(1–2): 133–53.

Okihiro, Gary Y. 1994. *Margins and Mainstreams: Asians in American History and Culture.* Seattle: University of Washington Press.

Oliver, Melvin L., Johnson, Jr, James H., and Farreil, Jr, Walter C. 1993. "Anatomy of a Rebellion: A Political–Economic Analysis," in Robert Gooding-Williams (ed.), *Reading Rodney King/Reading Urban Uprising.* New York: Routledge Press, pp. 117–41.

Omachonu, John, and Healey, Kevin. 2009. "Media Concentration and Minority Ownership: The Intersection of Ellul and Habermas." *Journal of Mass Media Ethic* 24(2): 90–109.

Omatsu, Glenn. 1994. "The 'Four Prisons' and the Movements of Liberation: Asian American Activism from the 1960s–1990s", in Karin Aguilar-San Juan (ed.), *The State of Asian America: Activism and Resistance in the 1990s.* Boston, MA: South End Press, pp. 19–69.

Omi, Michael, and Takagi, Dana Y. 1996. "Situating Asian Americans in the Political Discourse on Affirmative Action." *Representations* 55: 155–62.

Omi, Michael, and Winant, Howard. 1994. *Racial Formation in the United States: From the 1960s to the 1990s,* 2nd edn. London and New York: Routledge.

Ong, Aihwa. 1999. *Flexible Citizenship: The Cultural Logics of Transnationality.* Durham: Duke University Press.

Ong, Aihwa. 2003. *Buddha is Hiding: Refugees, Citizenship, and the New America.* Berkeley: University of California Press.

Ong, Aihwa. 2005. "Splintering Cosmopolitanism: Asian Immigrants and Zones of Autonomy in the American West," in Thomas Blom Hansen and Finn Stepputat (eds), *Sovereign Bodies: Citizens, Migrants, and States in the Postcolonial World.* Princeton, NJ: Princeton University Press, pp. 257–75.

Ong, Paul, and Azores, Tania. 1994. "The Migration and Incorporation of Filipino Nurses," in Paul Ong, Edna Bonacich, and Lucie Cheng (eds), *The New Asian Immigration in Los Angeles and Global Restructuring.* Philadelphia: Temple University Press, pp. 164–95.

Ong, Paul, and Liu, John M. 2000. "US Immigration Policies and Asian Migration," in Min Zhou and James V. Gatewood (eds), *Contemporary Asian America: A Multidisciplinary Reader.* New York University Press, pp. 155–74.

Ong, Paul, and Umemoto, Karen. 2000. "Life and Work in the Inner City," in Min Zhou and James V.

Gatewood (eds), *Contemporary Asian America: A Multidisciplinary Reader*. New York University Press.

Ong, Paul, Bonacich, Edna, and Cheng, Lucie. 1994. *The New Asian Immigration in Los Angeles and Global Restructuring*. Philadelphia: Temple University Press.

Operario, Don, Han, Chong-suk, and Kyung-Hee Choi. 2008. "Dual Identity among Gay Asian Pacific Islander Men." *Culture, Health & Sexuality* 10(5): 447–61.

Ordona, Trinity A. 2003. "Asian Lesbians in San Francisco: Struggles to Create a Safe Space, 1970s–1980s," in Shirley Hune and Gail M. Nomura (eds), *Asian/Pacific Islander American Women: A Historical Anthology*. New York University Press, pp. 319–34.

Orellana, Marjorie Faulstich, Thorne, Barrie, Chee, Anna, and Lam, Wan Shun Eva. 2001. "Transnational Childhoods: The Participation of Children in Processes of Family Migration." *Social Problems* 48(4): 572–91.

Osajima, Keith. 2000. "Asian Americans as the Model Minority: An Analysis of the Popular Press Image in the 1960s and 1980s," in Min Zhou and James V. Gatewood (eds), *Contemporary Asian America: A Multidisciplinary Reader*. New York University Press.

Outlaw, Lucius, Jr. 1998. "'Multiculturalism,' Citizenship, Education, and American Liberal Democracy," in Cynthia Willett (ed.), *Theorizing Multiculturalism: A Guide to the Current Debate*. Malden: Blackwell, pp. 382–98.

Paek, Hye Jin, and Shah, Hemant. 2003. "Racial Ideology, Model Minorities, and the 'Not-So-Silent Partner': Stereotyping of Asian Americans in US Magazine Advertising." *Howard Journal of Communications* 14(4): 225–43.

Pang, Valerie. 1995. "Asian American Children: A Diverse Population," in Don Nakanishi and Tina Yamano Nishida (eds), *The Asian American Educational Experience: A Source Book for Teachers and Students*. New York: Routledge, pp. 167–79.

Park, Jerry. 2008. "Second-Generation Asian American Pan-Ethnic Identity: Pluralized Meanings of a Racial Label." *Sociological Perspectives* 51(3): 541–61.

Park, Kyeyoung. 1996. "Use and Abuse of Race and Culture: Black–Korean Tension in America." *American Anthropologist* 98(3): 492–9.

Park, Kyeyoung. 2000. "Sudden and Subtle Challenge: Disparity in Conception of Marriage and Gender in the Korean American Community," in Martin Manalansan (ed.), *Cultural Compass: Ethnographic Explorations of Asian America*. Philadelphia: Temple University Press, pp. 159–74.

Park, Lisa. 2005. *Consuming Citizenship: Children of Asian Immigrant Entrepreneurs*. Palo Alto: Stanford University Press.

Park, Steve. 2000. "What Hollywood Should Know: A Call to Action from an Asian American Actor," in Timothy P. Fong and Larry Hajime Shinagawa (eds), *Asian Americans: Experiences and Perspectives*. Upper Saddle River, NJ: Prentice Hall, pp. 270–2.

Park, Edward J. W., and Park, John S. W. 2005. *Probationary Americans: Contemporary Immigration Policies and the Shaping of Asian American Communities*. New York: Routledge.

Park, Clara, Endo, Russell, Lee, Stacy, and Rong, Xue Lan. 2007. *Asian American Education: Acculturation, Literacy Development, and Learning*. Charlotte: Information Age Publishing.

Parreñas, Rhacel. 2001. *Servants of Globalization: Women, Migration, and Domestic Work*. Palo Alto: Stanford University Press.

Parreñas, Rhacel Salazar. 2002. "The Care Crisis in the Philippines: Children and Transnational Families in the New Global Economy," in Barbara Ehrenreich and Arlie Russell Hochschild (eds), *Global Woman: Nannies, Maids, and Sex Workers in the New Economy*. New York: Henry Holt, pp. 39–54.

Pelissero, John, Krebs, Timothy and Jenkins, Shannon. 2000. "Asian-Americans, Political Organizations, and Participation in Chicago Electoral Precincts." *Urban Affairs Review* 35(6): 750–69.

Pellow, David, and Park, Lisa. 2002. *The Silicon Valley of Dreams: Environmental Injustice, Immigrant Workers, and the High-tech Global Economy*. New York University Press.

Peterson, Richard A., and Anand, N. 2004. "The Production of Culture Perspective." *Annual Review of Sociology* 30(1): 311–34.

Phan, Ngoc, and Garcia, John A. 2009. "Asian-Pacific-American Partisanship: Dynamics of Partisan and Nonpartisan Identities." *Social Science Quarterly* 90(4): 886–910.

Phinney, Jean S. 1993. "A Three-Stage Model of Ethnic Identity Development in Adolescence," in Martha E. Bernal and George P. Knight (eds), *Ethnic Identity: Formation and Transmission Among Hispanics and Other Minorities*. Albany: State University of New York Press, pp. 61-79.

Poindexter, Paula M., Smith, Laura, and Heider, Don. 2003. "Race and Ethnicity in Local Television News: Framing, Story Assignments and Source Selections." *Journal of Broadcasting and Electronic Media* 47(4): 524-36.

Polletta, Francesca, and Jasper, James M. 2001. "Collective Identity and Social Movements." *Annual Review of Sociology* 27(1): 283-305.

Pong, Suet-ling, Hao, Lingxin, and Gardner, Erica. 2005. "The Roles of Parenting Styles and Social Capital in the School Performance of Immigrant Asian and Hispanic Adolescents." *Social Science Quarterly* 86(4): 928-50.

Poo, Ai-jen. 2009. "Domestic Workers' Bill of Rights: A Feminist Approach for a New Economy." S&F Online, available at http://sfonline.barnard.edu/work/poo_01.htm, accessed 30 July 2013.

Portes, Alejandro. 2003. "Conclusion: Theoretical Convergencies and Empirical Evidence in the Study of Immigrant Transnationalism." *International Migration Review* 37(3): 874-92.

Portes, Alejandro, and Bach, Robert. 1985. *Latin Journey: Cuban and Mexican Immigrants in the United States*. Berkeley: University of California Press.

Portes, Alejandro, and Rumbaut, Rubén G. 2001. *Legacies: The Story of the Immigrant Second Generation*. Berkeley: University of California Press.

Portes, Alejandro, and Rumbaut, Rubén G. 2006. *Immigrant America: A Portrait*. Berkeley: University of California Press.

Portes, Alejandro, and Zhou, Min. 1992. "Gaining the Upper Hand: Economic Mobility among Immigrant and Domestic Minorities." *Ethnic and Racial Studies* 15(4): 491–522.

Portes, Alejandro, and Zhou, Min. 1993. "The New Second Generation: Segmented Assimilation and Its Variants." *The Annals of the American Academy of Political and Social Science* Vol. 530: 74-96.

Portes, Alejandro, Escobar, Cristina, and Arana, Renelinda. 2009. "Divided or Convergent Loyalties? The Political Incorporation Process of Latin American Immigrants in the United States." *International Journal of Comparative Sociology* 50(2): 103-36.

Portes, Alejandro, Fernández-Kelly, Patricia, and Haller, William. 2005. "Segmented Assimilation on the Ground: The New Second Generation in Early Adulthood." *Ethnic and Racial Studies. Special Issue: The Second Generation in Early Adulthood* 28(6): 1000–40.

Prashad, Vijay. 2000. *The Karma of Brown Folk*. Minneapolis: University of Minnesota Press.

Prashad, Vijay. 2007. *The Darker Nations: A People's History of the Third World*. New York: New Press.

Puri, Jyoti. 2002. "Nationalism has a Lot to Do with It! Unraveling Questions of Nationalism and Transnationalism in Lesbian/Gay Studies," in Diane Richardson and Steven Seidman (eds), *Handbook of Lesbian and Gay Studies*. London: Sage Publications, pp. 427–42.

Purkayastha, Bandana. 2005. *Negotiating Ethnicity: Second-Generation South Asian Americans Traverse a Transnational World*. New Brunswick, NJ: Rutgers University Press.

Putnam, Robert. 2000. *Bowling Alone: The Collapse and Revival of American Community*. New York: Simon & Schuster.

Qian, Zhenchao, and Lichter, Daniel T. 2007. "Social Boundaries and Marital Assimilation: Interpreting Trends in Racial and Ethnic Intermarriage" *American Sociological Review* 72(1): 68-94.

Qian, Zhenchao, and Lichter, Daniel T. 2011. "Changing Patterns of Interracial Marriage in a Multiracial Society." *Journal of Marriage and Family* 73(5): 1065-84.

Qian, Zhenchao, Blair, Sampson Lee, and Ruf, Stacey D. 2001. "Asian American Interracial and Interethnic Marriages: Differences by Education and Nativity." *International Migration Review* 35(2): 557-86.

Qian, Zhenchao, Glick, Jennifer E., and Batson, Christie D. 2012. "Crossing Boundaries: Nativity, Ethnicity, and Mate Selection." *Demography* 49(2): 651-75.

Qin, Desirée Baolian. 2008. "Doing Well vs. Feeling Well: Understanding Family Dynamics and the

Psychological Adjustment of Chinese Immigrant Adolescents." *Journal of Youth and Adolescence* 37(1): 22–35.

Qin, Desirée Baolian, Way, Niobe, and Mukherjee, Preetika. 2008. "The Other Side of the Model Minority Story." *Youth & Society* 39(4): 480–506.

Quiambao, Rodolfo-Jose Blanco. 2010. "Undocumented Immigrants," in Edith Wen-Chu Chen (ed.), *Encyclopedia of Asian American Issues Today*, Vol. 1. Westport, CT: Greenwood Press, pp. 541–6.

Quiroz, Pamela Anne. 2007. "Latino and Asian Infant Adoption: From Mongrels to 'Honorary White' or White?" *The Journal of Latino-Latin American Studies* 2(3): 46–58.

Raj, Anita, and Silverman, Jay G. 2007. "Domestic Violence Help-Seeking Behaviors of South Asian Battered Women Residing in the United States." *International Review of Victimology* 14(1): 143–70.

Rana, Junaid Akram. 2011. *Terrifying Muslims: Race and Labor in the South Asian Diaspora*. Durham: Duke University Press.

Randazzo, Timothy. 2005. "Social and Legal Barriers: Sexual Orientation and Asylum in the United States," in Eithne Luibhéid and Lionel Cantú (eds), *Queer Migrations: Sexuality, US Citizenship, and Border Crossings*. Minneapolis: University of Minnesota.

Rangaswamy, Padma. 2007. "South Asians in Dunkin' Donuts: Niche Development in the Franchise Industry." *Journal of Ethnic and Migration Studies* 33(4): 671–86.

Rhee, Siyon. 1997. "Domestic Violence in the Korean Immigrant Family." *Journal of Society & Social Welfare* 14(1): 63–77.

Rhee, Siyon, Chang, Janet, and Rhee, Jessica. 2003. "Acculturation, Communication Patterns, and Self-Esteem among Asian and Caucasian American Adolescents." *Adolescence* 38(152): 749–68.

Rieder, Jonathan. 1990. "Trouble in Store." *New Republic* 203(1): 16–22. Web.

Rivas-Drake, Deborah, Hughes, Diane, and Way, Niobe. 2008. "A Closer Look at Peer Discrimination, Ethnic Identity, and Psychological Well-being among Urban Chinese American Sixth Graders." *Journal of Youth and Adolescence* 37(1): 12–21.

Roach, Ronald. 2002. "Survey: Asian Americans are the Most Wired Ethnic Group." *Black Issues in Higher Education* 18(24): 44.

Robles, Rowena A. 2006. *Asian Americans and the Shifting Politics of Race: The Dismantling of Affirmative Action at an Elite Public High School (Studies in Asian Americans)*. New York: Routledge.

Rodriguez, Robyn Magalit. 2010. *Migrants for Export: How the Philippine State Brokers Labor to the World*. Minneapolis: University of Minnesota Press.

Rodriguez, Robyn, and Balce, Nerissa S. 2004. "American Insecurity and Radical Filipino Community Politics." *Peace Review* 16(2): 131–40.

Rogers, Ray. 2013. "PSY Talks 'Gentleman,' Pink & 'Harlem Shake' in Billboard Music Awards Q&A." *Billboard*, May 17, 2013. Accessed May 18, 2013. www.billboard.com/articles/events/bbma-2013/1562711/psy-talks-gentleman-pink-harlem-shake-in-billboard-music-awards-qa.

Rosenbloom, Susan Rakosi, and Way, Niobe. 2004. "Experiences of Discrimination among African American, Asian American, and Latino Adolescents in an Urban High School." *Youth & Society* 35(4): 420–51.

Rosenfeld, Michael. 2001. "The Salience of Pan-national Hispanic and Asian Identities in US Marriage Markets." *Demography* 38(2): 161–75.

Rudruppa, Sharmila. 2004. *Ethnic Routes to Becoming American: Indian Immigrants and the Cultures of Citizenship*. New Brunswick, NJ: Rutgers University Press.

Ruiz, Vicki. 2008. "Citizen Restaurant: American Imaginaries, American Communities." *American Quarterly* 60(1): 1–21.

Rumbaut, Rubén G. 2002. "Severed or Sustained Attachments? Language, Identity, and Imagined Communities in the Post-Immigrant Generation," in Peggy Levitt and Mary C. Waters (eds), *The Changing Face of Home: The Transnational Lives of the Second Generation*. New York: Russell Sage Foundation, pp. 43–95.

Sacramento, Jocyl, and de la Cruz, Aristel. 2010. "Poverty," in Edith Wen-Chu Chen and Grace J. Yoo (eds), *Encyclopedia of Asian American Issues Today*. Santa Barbara: Greenwood Press, pp. 149–56.

Said, Edward W. 1978. *Orientalism*. New York: Pantheon Books.

Sakamoto, Arthur, and Chen, Meichu D. 1991. "Inequality and Attainment in a Dual Labor Market." *American Sociological Review* 56(3): 295–308.

Sakamoto, Arthur, and Woo, Hyeyoung. 2007. "The Socioeconomic Attainments of Second-Generation Cambodian, Hmong, Laotian, and Vietnamese Americans." *Sociological Inquiry* 77(1): 44–75.

Sakamoto, Arthur, and Xie, Yu. 2006. "The Socioeconomic Attainments of Asian Americans," in P. G. Min (ed.), *Asian Americans: Contemporary Trends and Issues*. Thousand Oaks, CA: Pine Forge Press, pp. 54–77.

Sakamoto, Arthur, Goyette, Kimberly A., and Kim, ChangHwan. 2009. "Socioeconomic Attainments of Asian Americans." *Annual Review of Sociology* 35: 255–76.

Salins, P. D. 1997. *Assimilation, American Style*. New York: Basic Books.

Sanders, Jimy, Nee, Victor, and Sernau, Scott. 2002. "Asian Immigrants' Reliance on Social Ties in a Multiethnic Labor Market." *Social Forces* 81(1): 281–314.

Saranillio, Dean Itsuji. 2010. "Colliding Histories: Hawai'i Statehood at the Intersection of Asians 'Ineligible to Citizenship' and Hawaiians 'Unfit for Self-Government.'" *Journal of Asian American Studies* 13(3): 283–309.

Scharlin, Craig, and Villanueva, Lilia V. 2000. *Philip Vera Cruz: A Personal History of Filipino Immigrants and the Farmworkers Movement*. Seattle: University of Washington.

Schein, Louisa. 2010. "Gran Torino's Hmong Lead Bee Vang on Film, Race, and Masculinity." *Hmong Studies Journal* 11: 1–11.

Schlund-Vials, Cathy. 2011. "Hip-Hop Memoirs: An Interview with Khmer American Rapper PraCh." *MELUS* 36(4): 159–73.

Schudson, Michael. 1989. "How Culture Works." *Theory and Society* 18(2): 153–80.

Seaton, Eleanor K., Scottham, Krista Maywalt, and Sellers, Robert M. 2006. "The Status Model of Racial Identity Development in African American Adolescents: Evidence of Structure, Trajectories, and Well-Being." *Child Development* 77(5): 1416–26.

Shah, Hemant. 2003. "'Asian Culture' and Asian American Identities in the Television and Film Industries of the United States." *SIMILE: Studies in Media & Information Literacy Education* 3(3): 1–10.

Shah, Nayan. 2001. *Contagious Divides: Epidemics and Race in San Francisco's Chinatown*. Berkeley: University of California Press.

Shankar, Lavina Dhingra, and Srikanth, Rajini. 1998. *A Part, Yet Apart: South Asians in Asian America*. Philadelphia: Temple University Press.

Sharma, Nitasha Tamar. 2010. *Hip Hop Desis: South Asian Americans, Blackness, and a Global Race Consciousness*. Durham, NC: Duke University Press.

Shiekh, Irum. 2008. "Racializing, Criminalizing, and Silencing 9/11 Deportees," in David C. Brotherton and Philip Kretsedemas (eds), *Keeping Out the Other: A Critical Introduction to Immigration Enforcement Today*. New York: Columbia University Press, pp. 81–107.

Shiekh, Irum. 2011. *Detained without Cause: Muslims' Stories of Detention and Deportation in America after 9/11*. New York City: Palgrave.

Shiao, Jiannbin Lee, Tuan, Mia, and Rienzi, Elizabeth. 2004. "Shifting the Spotlight: Exploring Race and Culture in Korean–White Adoptive Families." *Race and Society* 7(1): 1–16.

Shih, Johanna. 2006. "Circumventing Discrimination Gender and Ethnic Strategies in Silicon Valley." *Gender & Society* 20(2): 177–206.

Shih, Kristy Y., and Pyke, Karen. 2010. "Power, Resistance, and Emotional Economies in Women's Relationships with Mothers-in-Law in Chinese Immigrant Families." *Journal of Family Issues* 31(3): 333–57.

Shimizu, Celine Parreñas. 2007. *The Hypersexuality of Race: Performing Asian American Women on Screen and Scene*. Durham: Duke University Press.

Sinke, S. M. 2005. "Crossing National Borders: Locating the United States in Migration History." *OAH Magazine of History* 19(3): 58–63.

Skrentny, John D., Chan, Stephanie, Fox, Jon, and Kim, Denis. 2007. "Defining Nations in Asia and

Europe: A Comparative Analysis of Ethnic Return Migration Policy." *International Migration Review* 41(4): 793–825.

Slyomovics, Susan. 1995. "New York City's Muslim World Day Parade," in Peter Van Der Veer (ed.), *Nation and Migration: The Politics of Space in the South Asian Diaspora*. Philadelphia: University of Pennsylvania Press, pp. 157–77.

Smith, Elta, and Bender, Courtney. 2004. "The Creation of Urban Niche Religion: South Asian Taxi Drivers in New York City," in Tony Carnes and Fenggang Yang (eds), *Asian American Religions: The Making and Remaking of Borders and Boundaries*. New York University Press.

Smith, Robert C. 2006. *Mexican New York: Transnational Lives of New Immigrants*. Berkeley: University of California Press.

Smith, Ryan A., and Elliott, James R. 2002. "Does Ethnic Concentration Influence Employees' Access to Authority? An Examination of Contemporary Urban Labor Markets." *Social Forces* 81(1): 255–79.

Snow, David A., and Anderson, Leon. 1987. "Identity Work among the Homeless." *American Journal of Sociology* 92(6): 1336–71.

Song, Miri. 1999. *Helping Out: Children's Labor in Ethnic Businesses*. Philadelphia: Temple University Press.

Spickard, Paul. 2007. "Whither the Asian American Coalition?" *Pacific Historical Review* 76(4): 585–604.

Stein, Arlene. 1997. *Sex and Sensibility*. Berkeley: University of California Press.

Steinberg, Stephen. 1981. *The Ethnic Myth: Race, Ethnicity, and Class in America*. Boston: Beacon Press.

Stone, Rosalie A. Torres, Purkayastha, Bandana, and Berdahl, Terceira Ann. 2006. "Beyond Asian American: Examining Conditions and Mechanisms of Earnings Inequality for Filipina and Asian Indian Women." *Sociological Perspectives* 49(2): 261–81.

Stonequist, Everett V. 1937. *The Marginal Man*. New York: Charles Scribner's Sons.

Stryker, Sheldon. 1992. "Symbolic Interactionism: Themes and Variations," in M. Rosenburg and R. Turner (eds), *Social Psychology: Sociological Perspectives*. New Brunswick, NJ: Transaction Publishers, pp. 3–29.

Su, Julie A., and Martorell, Chanchanit. 2002. "Exploitation and Abuse in the Garment Industry," in Marta López-Garza and David R. Diaz (eds), *Asian and Latino Immigrants in a Restructuring Economy: The Metamorphosis of Southern California*. Stanford: Stanford University Press, pp. 21–45.

Sullivan, Richard, and Lee, Kimi. 2008. "Organizing Immigrant Women in America's Sweatshops: Lessons from the Los Angeles Garment Worker Center." *Signs: Journal of Women in Culture and Society* 33(3): 527–32.

Sun, Nicki. 2010. "Rising Sons Far East Movement is Doing Big Things and Staying Fly." *Hyphen Magazine*. Winter. Accessed June 2, 2013. www.hyphenmagazine.com/magazine/issue-22-throwback/rising-sons.

Suzuki, Bob. 2002. "Revisiting the Model Minority Stereotype: Implications for Student Affairs Practice and Higher Education." *New Directions for Student Services*. Vol. 97: 21–32.

Sze, Julie. 2004. "Asian American Activism for Environmental Justice." *Peace Review* 16(2): 149–56.

Tajfel, Henri, and Turner, John C. 1986. "The Social Identity Theory of Intergroup Behavior," in S. Worchel and W. Austin (eds), *Social Psychology of Intergroup Relations*. Chicago: Nelson.

Takagi, Dana Y. 1992. *The Retreat from Race: Asian–American Admissions and Racial Politics*. New Brunswick, NJ: Rutgers University Press.

Takagi, Dana Y. 1994. "Maiden Voyage: Excursion into Sexuality and Identity Politics in Asian America." *Amerasia Journal* 20(1): 1–17.

Takaki, Ronald T. 1989. *Strangers from a Different Shore: A History of Asian Americans*. Boston: Little, Brown.

Takei, Isao, and Sakamoto, Arthur. 2008. "Do College-educated, Native-born Asian Americans Face a Glass Ceiling in Obtaining Managerial Authority?" *Asian American Policy Review* 17: 73–85.

Tam-Cho, Wendy K., Kim, Thomas P., Takeda, Okiyoshi, and Lai, James S. 2003. "Campaigns, Elections, and Elected Officials," in Don T. Nakanishi and James S. Lai (eds), *Asian American Politics: Law, Participation, and Policy*. Lanham, MD: Rowman & Littlefield, pp. 317–30.

Tan, Tony Xing, and Nakkula, Michael J. 2005. "White Parents' Attitudes towards their Adopted Chinese Daughters' Ethnic Identity." *Adoption Quarterly* 7(4): 57–76.

Tang, Joyce. 1993. "The Career Attainment of Caucasian and Asian Engineers." *The Sociological Quarterly* 34(3): 467–96.

Taylor, Charles. 1994. "The Politics of Recognition," in Amy Gutmann and Charles Taylor (eds), *Multiculturalism: Examining the Politics of Recognition*. Princeton University Press, pp. 25–75.

Telles, Edward Eric. 2004. *Race in Another America: The Significance of Skin Color in Brazil*. Princeton: Princeton University Press.

Thai, Hung. 1999. "'Splitting Things in Half is So White!' The Formation of Ethnic Identity among Second Generation Vietnamese Americans." *Amerasia Journal* 25(1): 53–88.

Thai, Hung. 2005. "Clashing Dreams in the Vietnamese Diaspora: Highly Educated Overseas Brides and Low-wage US Husbands," in Nicole Constable (ed.), *Cross-border Marriages: Gender and Mobility in Transnational Asia*. Philadelphia: University of Pennsylvania Press, pp. 145–65.

Thai, Hung. 2008. *For Better or For Worse: Vietnamese International Marriages in the New Global Economy*. New Brunswick, NJ: Rutgers University Press.

Thangaraj, Stanley. 2012. "Playing Through Differences: Black–White Racial Logic and Interrogating South Asian American Identity." *Ethnic and Racial Studies* 35(6): 988–1006.

Thoma, Pamela. 2000. "Cultural Autobiography, Testimonial, and Asian American Transnational Feminist Coalition in the 'Comfort Women of WWII' Conference." *Frontiers: A Journal of Women's Studies* 21(1–2): 29–54.

Thornton, Michael C. 2011. "Meaningful Dialogue? The Los Angeles Sentinel's Depiction of Black and Asian American Relations, 1993–2000." *Journal of Black Studies* 42(8): 1275–98.

Tilly, Charles, and Tarrow, Sidney G. 2000. *Contentious Politics*. Boulder, CO: Paradigm Press.

Tsai-Chae, Amy, and Nagata, Donna K. 2008. "Asian Values and Perceptions of Intergenerational Family Conflict among Asian American Students." *Cultural Diversity and Ethnic Minority Psychology* 14(3): 205.

Tse, Lucy. 1999. "Finding a Place to Be: Ethnic Identity Exploration of Asian Americans." *Adolescence* 34(133): 121–38.

Tsui, Kitty. 1996. "Asian Pacific Lesbian, aka Dead Girl, China Doll, Dragon Lady, or the Invisible Man," in Ginny Vida (ed.), *The New Our Right to Love: A Lesbian Resource Book*. New York: Touchstone, pp. 230–3.

Tsunokai, Glenn T. 2005. "Beyond the Lenses of the "Model" Minority Myth: A Descriptive Portrait of Asian Gang Members." *Journal of Gang Research* 12(4): 37–58.

Tuan, Mia. 1998. *Forever Foreigners or Honorary Whites? The Asian Ethnic Experience Today*. New Brunswick, NJ: Rutgers University Press.

Tuan, Mia, and Shiao, Jiannbin Lee. 2011. *Choosing Ethnicity, Negotiating Race: Korean Adoptees in America*. New York: Russell Sage Foundation.

Tuan, Mia, Rienzi, Elizabeth, and Shiao, Jianbinn. 2010. "Transracial Adoption," in Edith Wen-Chu Chen and Grace J. Yoo (eds), *Encyclopedia of Asian American Issues Today*. Santa Barbara: Greenwood Press, pp. 953–9.

Uba, Laura. 1994. *Asian Americans: Personality Patterns, Identity, and Mental Health*. New York: Guilford Press.

Umemoto, Karen. 1989. "'On Strike!' San Francisco State College Strike." *Amerasia Journal* 15(1): 3–41.

Vandiver, Beverly J., Cross Jr, William E., Worrell, Frank C., and Fhagen-Smith, Peony E. 2002. "Validating the Cross Racial Identity Scale." *Journal of Counseling Psychology* 49(1): 71–85.

Van Slambrouck, Paul. 1998. "Asian Americans Forge Larger Role." *Christian Science Monitor* 24 Feb.: 1.

Varma, Roli. 2002. "High-tech Coolies: Asian Immigrants in the US Science and Engineering Workforce." *Science as Culture* 11(3): 337–61.

Varma, Roli, and Rogers, Everett M. 2004. "Indian Cyber Workers in US." *Economic and Political Weekly* 48(12): 5645–52.

Vo, Linda Trinh, and Danico, Mary Yu. 2004. "The Formation of Post-Suburban Communities:

Koreatown and Little Saigon, Orange County." *International Journal of Sociology and Social Policy* 24(7/8): 15–45.

Waddoups, Jeffrey, and Assane, Djeto. 1993. "Mobility and Gender in Segmented Labor Market: A Closer Look." *American Journal of Economics and Sociology* 52(4): 399–412.

Walder, Andrew G. 2009. "Political Sociology and Social Movements." *Annual Review of Sociology* 35(1): 393–412.

Waldinger, Roger, and Lichter, Michael. 2003. *How the Other Half Works: Immigration and the Social Organization of Labor*. Berkeley: University of California Press.

Walton-Roberts, Margaret. 2003. "Transnational Geographies: Indian Immigration to Canada." *The Canadian Geographer/Le Géographe Canadien* 47(3): 235–50.

Wang, Frances K. 2010. "From a Whisper to a Rally Cry: Commemorating the Vincent Chu Case." *Harvard Journal of Asian American Policy Review* 19: 23–6.

Wang, Grace. 2010. "A Shot at Half-Exposure: Asian Americans in Reality TV Shows." *Television New Media* 11(5): 404–27.

Wang, Hansi Lo. 2013. "Jin, 'The Chinese Kid Who Raps,' Grows Up." *NPR*. Accessed on June 7, 2013 at www.npr.org/2013/01/19/167883591/jin-the-chinese-kid-who-raps-grows-up

Wang, Ling-Chi. 1983. "Lau v. Nichols: History of a Struggle for Equal and Quality Education," in Don Nakanishi and Tina Yamano Nishida (eds), *The Asian American Educational Experience: A Source Book for Teachers and Students*. New York: Routledge, pp. 58–94.

Wang, Ling-Chi. 1995. "Meritocracy and Diversity in Higher Education: Discrimination against Asian Americans in the Post-Bakke Era," in Don Nakanishi and Tina Yamano Nishida (eds), *The Asian American Educational Experience: A Source Book for Teachers and Students*. New York: Routledge, pp. 285–302.

Wang, Oliver. 2001. "Between the Notes: Finding Asian America in Popular Music." *American Music* 19(4): 439–65.

Warikoo, Natasha Kumar. 2011. *Balancing Acts: Youth Culture in the Global City*. Berkeley, CA: University of California Press.

Warner, Stephen and Wittner, Judith. 1998. *Gatherings in Diaspora: Religious Communities and the New Immigration*. Philadelphia: Temple University Press.

Waters, Mary C. 1990. *Ethnic Options: Choosing Ethnic Identities in America*. Berkeley: University of California Press.

Waters, Mary C. 1999. *Black Identities: West Indian Immigrant Dreams and American Realities*. Cambridge, MA: Harvard University Press.

Way, Niobe, and Chen, Lisa. 2000. "Close and General Friendships among African American, Latino, and Asian American Adolescents from Low-income Families." *Journal of Adolescent Research* 15: 274–300.

Weeden, Kim. 2005. "Is There a Flexiglass Ceiling? Flexible Work Arrangements and Wages in the United States." *Social Science Research* 34: 454–82.

Wei, William. 1993. *The Asian American Movement*. Philadelphia: Temple University Press.

Weitzer, Ronald. 1997. "Racial Prejudice among Korean Merchants in African American Neighborhoods." *The Sociological Quarterly* 38(4): 587–606.

Werbner, Pnina. 2001. "The Limits of Cultural Hybridity: On Ritual Monsters, Poetic Licence and Contested Postcolonial Purifications." *Journal of the Royal Anthropological Institute* 7(1): 133–52.

West, Candace and Zimmerman, Don H. 1987. "Doing Gender." *Gender and Society* 1(2): 125–51.

Westwood, Sallie, and Bhachu, Parminder. 1988. "Introduction," in Sallie Westwood and Parminder Bhachu (eds), *Enterprising Women: Ethnicity, Economy, and Gender Relations*. New York: Taylor and Francis.

Wilson, Kenneth L., and Portes, Alejandro. 1980. "Immigrant Enclaves: An Analysis of the Labor Market Experiences of Cubans in Miami." *American Journal of Sociology* 30(1): 295–319.

Winant, Howard. 2000. "Race and Race Theory." *Annual Review of Sociology* 26: 169–85.

Wilson, Shauna B., McIntosh, William D., and Insana, II, Salvatore P. 2007. "Dating Across Race: An Examination of African American Internet Personal Advertisements." *Journal of Black Studies* 37(6): 964–82.

Winters, Rebecca. 2004. "Stereo Playah." *Time*, November 1, 105.

Wolf, Diane. 1997. "Family Secrets: Transnational Struggles among Children of Filipino Immigrants." *Sociological Perspectives* 40(3): 457–82.

Wong, Janelle S. 2005. "Mobilizing Asian American Voters: A Field Experiment." *The ANNALS of the American Academy of Political and Social Science* 601(1): 102–14.

Wong, Kent. 1994. "Building an Asian Pacific Labor Alliance: A New Chapter in Our History," in Karin Aguilar-San Juan (ed.), *The State of Asian America: Activism and Resistance in the 1990s*. Boston, MA: South End Press, pp. 335–50.

Wong, Kent. 2000. "Building an Asian Pacific Labor Movement," in Wei-han Ho and Carolyn Antonio (eds), *Legacy to Liberation: Politics & Culture of Revolutionary Asian Pacific America*. Edinburgh: AK Press, pp. 89–98.

Wong, Morrison. 1995. "The Education of White, Chinese, Filipino, and Japanese Students: A Look at 'High School and Beyond,'" in Don Nakanishi and Tina Yamano Nishida (eds), *The Asian American Educational Experience: A Source Book for Teachers and Students*. New York: Routledge, pp. 221–34.

Woo, Deborah. 2000. *Glass Ceilings and Asian Americans: The New Face of Workplace Barriers*. Lanham: Rowman & Littlefield.

Wu, Denis H., and Izard, Ralph. 2008. "Representing the Total Community: Relationships Between Asian American Staff and Asian American Coverage in Nine US Newspapers." *Journalism & Mass Communication Quarterly* 85(1): 99–112.

Wu, Ellen. 2012. "Introduction to Journal of American Ethnic History Special Issue on Immigration and the Cold War." *Journal of American Ethnic History* 31(4): 7–11.

Wu, Frank H. 2002. "Profiling in the Wake of September 11: The Precedent of the Japanese American Internment." *Criminal Justice* 17(2): 52–60.

Wu, Frank. 2003. *Yellow: Race in America Beyond Black and White*. New York: Basic Books.

Wu, Frank H. 2010. "Embracing Mistaken Identity: How the Vincent Chin Case United Asian Americans." *Harvard Journal of Asian American Policy Review* 19: 17–22.

Wu, Judy Tzu-Chun. 2007. "Journeys for Peace and Liberation: Third World Internationalism and Radical Orientalism during the US War in Vietnam." *Pacific Historical Review* 76(4): 575–84.

Xu, Jun. 2005. "Why Do Minorities Participate Less? The Effects of Immigration, Education, and Electoral Process on Asian American Voter Registration and Turnout." *Social Science Research* 34(4): 682–702.

Yang, Bo Han, Junck, Angie, and Ling, Sin Yin. 2010. "Detention and Deportation," in Edith Wen-Chu Chen and Grace J. Yoo (eds), *Encyclopedia of Asian American Issues Today*, Vol. 1. Santa Barbara: ABCCLIO, pp. 491–502.

Yang, Fenggang, and Ebaugh, Helen Rose. 2001. "Transformations in New Immigrant Religions and Their Global Implications." *American Sociological Review* 66(2): 269–88.

Yang, Philip Q. 2004. "Generational Differences in Educational Attainment among Asian Americans." *Journal of Asian American Studies* 7(1): 51–71.

Yang, Philip Q. 2010. "A Theory of Asian Immigration to the United States." *Journal of Asian American Studies* 13(1): 1–34.

Yick, Alice G. 2001. "Feminist Theory and Status Inconsistency Theory Application to Domestic Violence in Chinese Immigrant Families." *Violence against Women* 7(5): 545–62.

Yin, Jing. 2005. "Constructing the Other: A Critical Reading of *The Joy Luck Club*." *Howard Journal of Communications* 16(3): 149–75.

Ying, Yu-Wen, and Han, Meekyung. 2007. "The Longitudinal Effect of Intergenerational Gap in Acculturation on Conflict and Mental Health in Southeast Asian American Adolescents." *American Journal of Orthopsychiatry* 77(1): 61–6.

Yoon, In-Jin. 1997. *On My Own: Korean Businesses and Race Relations in America*. University of Chicago Press.

Yoshioka, Marianne R., DiNoia, Jennifer, and Ullah, Komal. 2001. "Attitudes Toward Marital Violence: An Examination of Four Asian Communities." *Violence against Women* 7(8): 900–26.

Zeng, Zhen and Xie, Yu. 2004. "Asian-Americans' Earnings Disadvantage Reexamined: The Role of Place of Education." *American Journal of Sociology* 109(5): 1075–108.

Zenner, Walter P. 1982. "Arabic-speaking Immigrants in North America as Middleman Minorities." *Ethnic and Racial Studies* 5(4): 457–77.

Zhang, Yuanting, and Van Hook, Jennifer. 2009. "Marital Dissolution among Interracial Couples." *Journal of Marriage and Family* 71(1): 95–107.

Zhou, Min. 1992. *Chinatown: The Socioeconomic Potential of an Urban Enclave.* Philadelphia: Temple University Press.

Zhou, Min. 1998. "'Parachute Kids' in Southern California: The Educational Experience of Chinese Children in Transnational Families." *Educational Policy* 12(6): 682–704.

Zhou, Min. 2000. "Social Capital in Chinatown: The Role of Community-Based Organizations and Families in the Adaptation of the Younger Generation," in Min Zhou and James V. Gatewood (eds), *Contemporary Asian America: A Multidisciplinary Reader.* New York University Press, pp. 315–35.

Zhou, Min. 2004. "Revisiting Ethnic Entrepreneurship: Convergencies, Controversies, and Conceptual Advancements." *International Migration Review* 38(3): 1040–74.

Zhou, Min. 2012. "The Ethnic System of Supplementary Education: Lessons from Chinatown and Koreatown, Los Angeles," in Ezekiel J. Dixon-Román and Edmund W. Gordon (eds), *Thinking Comprehensively about Education: Spaces of Educative Possibility and Their Implications for Public Policy.* New York: Routledge, pp. 65–81.

Zhou, Min, and Bankston, Carl L. 1998. *Growing Up American: How Vietnamese Children Adapt to Life in the United States.* New York: Russell Sage Foundation.

Zhou, Min, and Kamo, Yoshinori. 1994. "An Analysis of Earnings Patterns for Chinese, Japanese, and Non-Hispanic White Males in the United States." *The Sociological Quarterly* 35(4): 581–602.

Zhou, Min, and Xiong, Yang Sao. 2005. "The Multifaceted American Experiences of the Children of Asian Immigrants: Lessons for Segmented Assimilation." *Ethnic and Racial Studies* 28(6): 1119–52.

Zhou, Z., Peverly, S. T., Xin, T., Huang, A. S. and Wang, W. 2003. "School Adjustment of First-generation Chinese–American Adolescents." *Psychology in Schools* 40(1): 71–84.

Zia, Helen. 2000. *Asian American Dreams.* New York: Farrar, Straus and Giroux.

Zia, Helen. 2006. "Where the Queer Zone Meets the Asian Zone: Marriage Equality and Other Intersections." *Amerasia Journal* 32(1): 1–14.

Zimmerman, Bonnie. 2000. *Lesbian Histories and Cultures: An Encyclopedia.* New York: Garland Publishing.

Zirin, Dave. 2012. "Jeremy Lin: Taking the Weight." *The Nation* (March 19): 24–5.

Index

queer, 23, 103–4, 106–7, 195
quotas, and affirmative action, 90

race, 6, 18
  ethnicity, gender, sexuality and, 18
  ethnicity and culture, 37
  as social construction, 18–20
racial discrimination, 63, 87, 91, 142, 153
racial formation, 23, 31, 43, 116, 183
  perspective, 10, 12
  processes as connected to global dynamics,
    11
  theory, 8–10, 18–19
racial profiling, 34–5
racial triangulation, 28
racialization, 9, 20, 37, 48, 73
  of Asian Americans historically, 38, 43, 50–1
  dual, 28
  gender and, 104–5
  geopolitics and, 202
  intermarriage and, 102
  in the media, 140
  Orientalist, 29
  of Pacific Islanders, 181
  pan-ethnicity, 52, 160, 177
  of South Asians, 177
  of Southeast Asians, 178
  theories of, 115
racism, 8–9, 18–19, 26–8, 32–8, 202
  anti-Asian, 35, 177
  Asian-American Republicans and, 200
  citizenship and, 129
  color-blind, 82, 143, 144
  education and, 80, 83, 86, 96
  identity and, 156, 163–4, 167
  income inequality, 54
  immigrant families and, 108, 112–13, 116
  institutional, 25
  labor movement and, 192
  laissez-faire, 26, 30
  media and, 138, 142, 146, 149–50
  Orientalist, 169
  pan-ethnic identity and, 100
  in prison system, 55
  professional workers and, 62
reactive ethnicity, 113, 164
Reagan, Ronald, 182
refugee, 120
Refugee Act (1980), 53
Regents of the University of California v. Bakke
    (1978), 91
religion, 35–6, 44, 126
  and citizenship, 127–31
  and group formation, 174
  and identity, 158–60, 163, 166, 169
religious organizations, 128, 130, 161

reproductive labor, 70
Republican Party, 200
resistance
  gay/lesbian, 106

same-sex marriage, 4, 23, 33, 106, 108
San Francisco State University, 93
San Francisco Unified School District, 92
Saund, Dalip, 196
second shift, 25, 70
second-generation immigrants, 2, 8, 63–5, 68–9,
    72
  activism, 184, 189
  attitudes toward school, 85–6
  co-ethnic marriage amongst, 99
  cultural assimilation of, 126, 132
  educational achievement of, 81
  identity of, 156–7, 161–72, 180
  intergenerational tensions and, 112–13, 179
  in the media, 149
  mental health challenges amongst, 88
  religious practices of, 128–9
  small-business owners, 74, 76
segmented assimilation, 8, 71, 80, 84, 88, 167
self-employment 71, 74–6
self-esteem, 88–9, 157
self-identity, 8, 156, 158
self-stereotyping, 157, 159
settler colonialism, 178
sexuality
  and heteronormativity, 23
  race, ethnicity, gender and, 18, 23
  as social construction, 22
significant others, 158–60
Sikhs, 35, 55, 127, 177
situational identities, 100
Skype, 140
slavery, 19, 24, 26, 44, 202
small business, 75, 77, 84
  owners, 19, 74
  ownership, 74, 76–7
social capital, 62, 65, 69, 73, 75–6
  in education, 83
social citizenship, 117, 122–5
social discourse, 19
social identity, 158–60, 170, 172
social justice, 4, 52, 106, 108, 154
social movement theory, 189
sociological approaches and theories, 3, 8–9,18,
    38–9, 41
  to/of family, 109
  to/of identity, 156–7, 170
  to/of immigration, 39, 141
  to/of media, 136, 140
  to/of social movements, 190
sociological imagination, 4, 17